ORDINARY LIVES IN THE EARLY CARIBBEAN

Ordinary Lives in the Early Caribbean

Religion, Colonial Competition, and the Politics of Profit

KRISTEN BLOCK

The University of Georgia Press

ATHENS AND LONDON

© 2012 by the University of Georgia Press
Athens, Georgia 30602
www.ugapress.org

Printed digitally in the United States of America

LIBRARY OF CONGRESS CATALOGING-IN-PUBLICATION DATA

Block, Kristen.
 Ordinary lives in the early Caribbean : religion, colonial competition, and the politics of profit / Kristen Block.
    p. cm. — (Early American places)
 Includes bibliographical references and index.
 ISBN-13: 978-0-8203-3867-5 (hardcover : alk. paper)
 ISBN-10: 0-8203-3867-2 (hardcover : alk. paper)
 ISBN-13: 978-0-8203-3868-2 (pbk. : alk. paper)
 ISBN-10: 0-8203-3868-0 (pbk. : alk. paper)
  1. Caribbean Area—Social conditions—17th century. 2. Caribbean Area—Social conditions—18th century. 3. Caribbean Area—History—17th century. 4. Caribbean Area—History—18th century. 5. Caribbean Area—Biography. I. Title.
 F2161.B58 2012
 972.903—DC23

2012001900

British Library Cataloging-in-Publication Data available

Contents

Figures

Acknowledgments

Projects like this often seem interminable, in part because they are collaborations of the largest magnitude. During the long years in which this book moved from concept to reality, I have accumulated many friendships as well as debts of gratitude that I'd like to recognize here. Financial support for research and writing of this project from dissertation to book include fellowships at the John Carter Brown Library supported by the InterAmericas and Ruth and Lincoln Ekstrom trusts, a semester-long fellowship at the Charles Warren Center for Studies in American History at Harvard University, a W. M. Keck Fellowship at the Huntington Library, a Barra Foundation Fellowship for a year of dissertation writing at the McNeil Center for Early American Studies at the University of Pennsylvania, and a semester as a visiting instructor for the Department of History at Beloit College, Wisconsin. Several smaller (but no less vital) travel grants—from the Department of History at Florida Atlantic University, the American Historical Association, Spain's Ministry of Foreign Affairs (*Ministerio de Asuntos Exteriores de España*), Harvard's International Conference for the History of the Atlantic World, and the Graduate School at Rutgers University—helped make my ambitious research agenda possible. Special thanks to the directors and administrators of those funding agencies, especially Bernard Bailyn, Pat Denault, Norman Fiering, Ted Widmar, Valerie Andrews, Bob Hodge, Eula Buchanan, Pilar Lopez Quintela, Heather Pensack, Elizabeth Thomas, Daniel Richter, Amy Baxter-Bellamy, Patricia Kollander, Zella Linn, Susi Krasnoo,

Carolyn Powell, Joyce Chaplin, Larissa Kennedy, and Arthur Patton-Hock. I would also like to thank my academic community in South Florida—especially Ashli White at University of Miami, Jenna Gibbs at Florida International University, and Philip Hough at Florida Atlantic University—for providing venues to meet and discuss my writing with other interested scholars.

Several close friends and colleagues have read and commented on early versions of various chapters, and for that I am eternally grateful. Special thanks to Nadia Celis, Marisa Fuentes, Kate Keller, Anna Lawrence, Jenny Shaw, Margaret Sumner, Kathy Wheeler, and Derrick White for helping me find clarity and confidence in my work. Those whose mentorship and encouragement sparked my journey into the historical profession deserve special recognition: Linda Sturtz and James Robertson; and Phyllis Mack, Christopher Brown, Herman Bennett, Jennifer Morgan, and Jane Landers. During my travel and fellowship stints, I had the privilege of meeting many established scholars whose advice and conversations helped shape the direction of my research and writing: Vincent Brown, Brycchan Carey, Antonio Feros, Sylvia Frey, Amy Froide, Ignacio Gallup-Diaz, Allison Games, April Hatfield, Karen Kupperman, Joseph Miller, Stuart Schwartz, and Enriqueta Vila Vilar. Others who, in ways too numerous to describe in detail, helped enrich or otherwise made it possible to complete this book: Moisés Alverez Marin, Jenny Anderson, Padre Tulio Aristizábal, Allison Bigelow, Carmenza Botero, Asmaa Bouhrass, Martin Bowden, Andrea Campetella, Nana Castello Salvador, Joanne Carter, Lina del Castillo, Carol Cook, Kaja Cook, Christian Crouch, Graciela Cruz Lopez, Stephanie Dodge, Lesley Doig, Marcela Echeverri, Olga Fabiola Cabeza, Lupe Fernandez, Adrian Finucane, Charley Foy, Jorge Gamboa, Diego Garcia Marquez, Katie Gerbner, Carolina Giraldo, Jaime Gomez Borja, Pablo Gomez, Esther Gonzalez, Larry Gragg, Piedad Gutierrez, Karen Graubart, Carina Johnson, Heather Kopelson, Chris Lane, Carla MacDougall, Becka McKay, Javier Mije, Catherine Molineux, Elena Machado, Alfonso Múnera, Karl Offen, Katrina Olds, Alejandra Osorio, Heather Peterson, Amanda Pipkin, Juan Ponce-Vázquez, Joanne Rappaport, Suzanna Reiss, Adriana Maya Restrepo, Esteban Reyes, Linda Rupert, Lucely Salgado, Eric Seeman, Kate Schmidt, Renée Soulodre-La France, Hilit Surowitz, Greg Swedburg, Abby Swingen, Mauricio Tovar, Jennifer Troester, Karin Velez, Karl Watson, David Wheat, and Emily Zuckerman. Finally, I must thank those who reviewed my entire book manuscript for their generous feedback and suggestions for revision. Derek Krissof has been a wonderfully supportive acquisitions editor and a perceptive reader. Thanks also to Tim Roberts, Gary Von Euer, and the entire team working with the Early American Places series for their help with the miraculous transformation into book form. The flaws that remain in this book are entirely my own, but I know that there would have been many more without the time and effort of all those individuals who helped inform my ideas and sustained my spirit.

This book is dedicated to my family—Joseph and Connie Block, and Karl, Jackson, and Caden Block—and to my friends and mentors. Each and every one of you contributed fundamentally to my growth as a thinker, as a scholar, and as a person. I hope each of you will see a small part of the insight and love you provided reflected in this book.

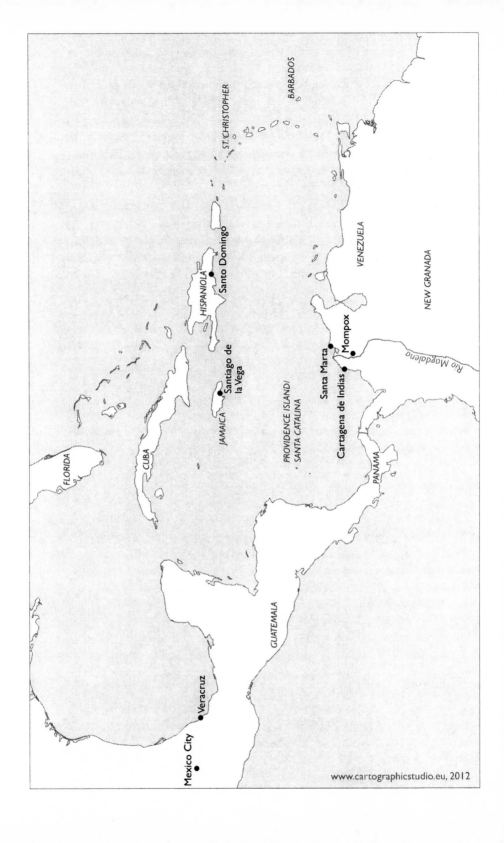

Introduction

This book tells several stories. The first follows Isabel Criolla, a runaway slave who stood before the Spanish governor of Cartagena de Indias and begged him not to return her to her cruel mistress, saying that if she was sent back she would be either driven to suicide or would be beaten to death and die without confession. Isabel warned him that "if her soul was condemned, it would be the fault of the authorities." He heeded her words.

Another story is about Nicolas Burundel, a French Calvinist who served the Spanish governor of Jamaica as a servant-henchman. When the parish priest led a religious procession down Santiago's city streets, Nicolas had to pull off his cap and bow before the Corpus Christi or the image of the Virgin, knowing that many suspected him of being a heretic and would be watching to see how he comported himself.

A third story follows a sailor named Henry Whistler to the Spanish island of Hispaniola, watching with him as a company of rough-and-tumble English soldiers hurled oranges at a statue of the Virgin Mary they discovered in one of the island's abandoned chapels, laughing as they stabbed the statue's darkened face, mocking the Spaniards who must have used it "to enveigle the blacks to worship."

Finally, this book envisions the lives of Yaff and Nell, an enslaved man and woman in the service of a Quaker planter in Barbados named Colonel Lewis Morris, all three of whom struggled to live in a world based on coerced labor without losing their sense of shared humanity. In addition to their regular duties as household servants, Yaff and Nell attended instructional and worship meetings, learned about their master's definition of morality, and perhaps dreamed that this knowledge would lead to a better life for them and their children—a way to lessen the prejudice that assumed they were immoral, unworthy, "natural" slaves.

I tell these stories so as to examine Christianity as a force for social inclusion and exclusion in the early Caribbean, centering on the struggles of ordinary people to survive in this burgeoning capitalistic world. By following enslaved people of African descent and lower-class whites—those at or near the bottom of the socioeconomic ladder—I illustrate how each actively engaged with the rhetoric and rituals of Christianity to create alliances that might help them in their search for justice and opportunity. However, telling the story of their lives together also shows how racial categories began to trump shared religious identities by the end of the seventeenth century, a shift that especially constricted opportunities for economic and social belonging among people of African descent. This change was more marked in the British than in the Spanish colonies, and had as much to do with economics as it did with religion. As the balance of Caribbean power shifted from the elaborate bureaucracies of the Catholic Spanish monarchy to proto-capitalist competitors (many of them Protestant), so too, did the meaning of colonial religious identity.

This book argues that the Caribbean was a central locus for the early modern shift from religion as a primary basis for political and social identity to that of race (or rather, what we would now call race), exploring the years of transition between Iberian and Northern European ascendancy in the Caribbean, from the early seventeenth to the mid-eighteenth centuries.[1] The book begins with the varieties of urban slavery and religious negotiation within the Spanish Caribbean and moves to the emergence of a more uncompromising separation of labor and religious community that developed among the British in their early West Indian plantations. It presents the ways in which European men kept from climbing the ladder of American opportunity could nonetheless access power based on other commonalities: their Christianity, their partisan religious politics, or their whiteness. Throughout, however, the book focuses on the complex and varied interactions between individuals to enact and contest these large-scale shifts on a personal and communal level, showing how imperial contestation between these two global powerhouses structured the options available for negotiation. While my study thus complements decades of rich and important scholarship on the development of merchant capitalism, slave systems, and racial polarization, adding to literature on early modern popular religion and international religious competition, it shifts the focus on how we understand the role of these dramatic shifts in everyday interactions. Through an emphasis on contingency, complexity, and humanity, I tell the stories of how such impersonal forces affected—and were affected by—ordinary people like Isabel, Nicolas, Henry, Yaff, Nell, and Lewis.

Despite their variety, I bring these microhistories together into a single frame, for histories of the Atlantic World demand an integrated approach that moves across empires, beyond simple comparisons, to show what one historian has recently termed the "entangled" histories of European empires in the Caribbean. Few enough scholars attempt to take on this transnational scope in any deep archival work, hampered by the challenges of multiple languages, travel to archives in multiple countries, and the pervasive narrowness of subdisciplinary historiographies.[2] But in our globalized, interconnected world, we cannot afford to view things from one vantage point, admit defeat in cross-cultural communication, or hide behind disciplinary boundaries.

In this serial microhistory, I felt there was a way to capture the realities of how intertwined imperial politics influenced individuals at the lowest socioeconomic levels. For enslaved Africans living in Spanish Cartagena interacted with lower-class foreigners, even shared space with them in the Inquisition's prison; European sailors, soldiers, and drifters often allied with patrons of any nationality if they provided the best opportunities for advancement, learning about different group's religious politics in the process; a few lower-class Northern Europeans were able to rise in the Caribbean world to become planters and merchants (and wives of planters and merchants), and were then forced to negotiate their own moral position in interactions with their free and enslaved laborers. I sought out sources in colonial repositories in Europe, but also went to smaller archives in Barbados and Colombia looking for sources that may have been irrelevant on the imperial level but which offer a closer approximation of the everyday. Exploring official and popular texts in Spanish and English, this book ventures to undertake a comparison of life in the Caribbean from above *and* below, integrating them through a common region and perspective.[3]

The Caribbean during the age of European expansion has often been characterized as especially irreligious, a blanket assumption of scorn for Christian principles. The reasons seem clear enough. From the first days of the region's exploration by Europeans, their presence spelled enslavement and death—first for the island and coastal Amerindians who were nearly exterminated as a result of disease and Spanish slave raiding (which took precedence over the Crown's goal of converting these Indians), and later for West Africans who suffered and perished in the developing plantation systems, a brutal trajectory that broke down human bonds of humanity and empathy at every step. The other standard Caribbean story, that of piracy, is also full of characters who routinely and blithely broke the Christian decree, "Thou shalt not steal" (along with most of the rest of the Ten Commandments). Overall, the enormous profits generated in the Caribbean seemed to have produced rapacious pirates, dissolute colonial masters, and enslaved Africans who understandably rejected the "white man's god," experiencing first-hand the depths of Christian hypocrisy.[4]

Instead of assuming that this rather cynical narrative is all there is to tell, this book explores ways in which Christianity manifested itself in the lives of cruel, greedy, and hypocritical people as well as through the ideals and pious exemplars often associated with the history of religion. Indeed, this book focuses on how the internal tensions within European religious mores and institutions offered unique opportunities for flexibility and protest, allowing the disadvantaged to argue that religious ideals so touted by the colonial elite should be extended to *all* those who shared the same faith. According to Clifford Geertz's seminal explication of "Religion as a Cultural System," religion is not merely a philosophical abstract, a set of doctrines, or even shared "beliefs." Rather, religion can only be defined by the everyday social relationships it creates. Yes, religion serves to naturalize social hierarchies, encouraging its participants to commit to a certain way of looking at the world, thereby codifying extant systems of power, justice, etc. But to make religion work, Geertz argued, everyone has to be willing to *participate* in rituals that fuse together "the world as lived and the world as imagined."[5]

Therefore, the participation of marginalized people in seventeenth-century Caribbean rituals of religious participation—in the Inquisition courtroom or the processions of the Tribunal's *auto de fe*, in battlefield acts of iconoclasm or in petitions claiming the right to live out one's faith in peace and toleration—influenced the ways that Caribbean realities of exploitation, coercion, wealth, and death were interpreted for all strata of society. Through shared rituals and narratives, these everyday acts of participation performatively bound the viewer to the performer. Similarly, people's refusal to participate in ritualized religious performances (even their indifference or irreverence) shaped how Christianity was defined and destabilized. In these acts of participation/nonparticipation, denunciation/acceptance, people engaged with basic questions about suffering, injustice, and the cognitive dissonance between religious ideal and on-the-ground practice. They asked questions that demanded answers: Who should benefit from the magnificent wealth extracted from the Americas? If European nations really came to spread their Gospel, why did their pious intentions end where their pecuniary activities began? Why did the divisions of nation, race, and creed matter so much in a supposedly universal Christian faith? As slaves, servants, sectarians, and sojourners performed Christian identities, they fought for a Caribbean moral ethos that would unite people against the alienating forces of an increasingly competitive economic order. In fact, morality and economics were (and are) intimately linked to ideas of social connection and communal justice. Anthropologist Mary Douglas explained how the ritual of financial transactions relates to religion:

> Money provides a standard for measuring worth; ritual standardizes situations, and so helps to evaluate them. Money makes a link between the present and the future; so does ritual. The more we reflect on the richness of the metaphor, the more it becomes clear that this is no metaphor.[6]

Thus Geertz's definition of ritual as a cooperative process that "creates" religion also applies to the creation of morality in a changing economic landscape. The laborers, the subjugated, were (needless to say) far from equal partners with the colonial elite in defining the region's moral economy—but as subversive elements they served to contest the boundaries of religious orthodoxy and ethical conventions. In everyday tensions and ritualized exchanges between masters and slaves, patrons and clients, religion served as a way to make the excesses of cruelty and exploitation measurable, and to make visible the reality that the Christianity being practiced in this region had become disenchanted by greed. In acknowledging the waning influence of religion to order the world, protestors hoped to rouse a sense of collective consciousness that could counteract the negative effects of religion's diminishing moral force.[7]

To capture these performative, shared experiences, I have drawn on the essential craft of imagination. To engage in speculation is to risk varying degrees of support and scorn among historians, but I agree with those who argue that to "play it safe" may actually do a disservice to our profession.[8] Any study that hopes to take on the perspective of people on the margins must do so with sharp inquisitiveness, for we know that most sources that survive today were written and organized according to the needs and desires of those in positions of authority and dominance. To do justice to the stories of those who did not control their own narratives requires us to recover fragments of disembodied voices and slips of the tongue, and to reassemble them into a new order. We must view our sources with a new awareness, reading against the grain, interpreting what was written between the lines in social interactions, and contemplating what was not written down at all. Many of these silences related to disempowered historical subjects result from what has been called the "politics of the archive"—reflecting the influence of governmental and cultural institutions that preserve and represent the past for a dominant culture at times uncomfortable with the past or anxious about the present.[9] These silences are nonetheless alive with power: they *say something* about who is deemed worthy of recognition, who should remain mute—objects, not subjects. Ignoring the power of silence only serves to replicate the unequal power dynamics of both past and present.

Historians often find the most telling of these silent power plays difficult to access, tied as we are to the vagaries of the written records that have survived three hundred years and more. There are no sermons and religious libraries from a West Indian Cotton Mather; no spiritual biography of a Sor Juana in the convents of Cartagena. The Caribbean poses its own challenges to my project, given the climate, natural disasters, and other forces of disorder that destroyed so many sources necessary to fully understand this place. Inquisitors in Cartagena wrote as early as 1669 to Madrid requesting permission to relocate to Bogotá because the humid climate on the coast rotted their archived papers, and they feared that foreign invaders might destroy much more.[10] The forces of political instability and natural disasters have eliminated many sources potentially useful for a religious study of the Caribbean, whether early parish and notarial records in Spanish Caribbean ports or the well-organized papers usually kept by Barbadian members of the Society of Friends.

But even when conventional sources can be found—like the *relaciones* that Cartagena's inquisitors sent to Madrid, or their painstaking copies of trials requiring further attention—many seemingly inscrutable omissions and silences remain. Many of these silences, I contend, reflect the self-censorship and anxiety of the people who produced those texts. A few examples might better elaborate how silences, uncomfortable and opaque, pertain to the history of religion in the Caribbean. To begin, almost any historical lesson on sixteenth-century colonialism refers to the Spanish Dominican Bartolomé de las Casas, who, in championing the humanity of the indigenous inhabitants of the Caribbean and their right to freedom from enslavement (*Brevíssima relación*), urged the Crown to allow importation of Africans as slaves, whom he asserted would be hardier laborers for the early sugar plantations of Hispaniola.

But far fewer have heard of Las Casas's manuscript treatise *Historia de las Indias*, in which the Dominican friar admitted that "he was soon after repentant . . . because afterwards he saw and confirmed, as will be seen, that the captivity of Negroes was as unjust as that of the Indians." In this unparalleled confession, Las Casas recorded his fear that "his ignorance and good will in this [matter] would [not] excuse him before the bar of Divine Judgment," for he recognized that his countrymen's compulsion for profit would continue to have devastating effects, not least of which was a vicious cycle of enslavement and exploitation.[11] Although Las Casas admitted his guilt on paper, he did not embark on a second public crusade to save the Africans, nor did he openly denounce those who profited from their enslavement. These acts of omission (and the fact that this Las Casas text went unpublished until 1875) effectively silenced his contrition, both for his own generation and for later generations of historians.

Other silent judgments—questions that burdened Christian consciences (even if they failed to shake up colonial practices)—proliferate in the archive. For example, in researching Part II, I struggled to find conclusive evidence to explain the pervasive presence of Northern Europeans sojourning in Spanish territories. Once I stepped back from the sources, however, this silence was not so surprising, given that most foreign collaborations with the Spanish were *illegal*—contraband trade was a never-ending problem that Spanish administrators went to great lengths to hide and thus deny. Nevertheless, it was frustrating to always *assume* that Northern Europeans' frequent recourse to Catholic conversion was an element of their negotiation with the larger Spanish community for mutual benefits.

I could find documents where Spanish investigators *asserted* that local officials were collaborating with foreign interlopers: in one case describing foreigners baptized in Spanish Jamaica, several residents testified that it was common knowledge (*se decía por público*) that one defector from an English privateer had been baptized two or three times already, a grave sin that blasphemed the sacramental nature of baptism. But only one witness exposed the offender's "hidden transcript," recounting how the sailor had bragged to his friends that he knew how to use conversion to survive and thrive: "wherever they caught him he got baptized because they gave him clothes" for the occasion.[12] Here and elsewhere, what was recorded only once turned out to be a key revelation of an open secret. Just as illegal acts were less likely to be written down, attitudes and activities deemed immoral or sinful were also likely to remain under cover of resolute silence. Few wanted to document those things that weighed on their consciences, that might serve to label them as anti-Christian or hypocrites. These silences of shame were nonetheless audible to ordinary people living in the early Caribbean, and can become audible when we take the time to step back from the sources and truly imagine the possibilities of the past. Although Christianity had been used to justify colonial hierarchies of exclusion and exploitation, this book shows that it also became a source for protest when those with power overstepped their morally prescribed bounds to engage in abuse and violence.

To understand the fissures that allowed people like Isabel, Nicolas, Henry, Yaff and Nell to find power in Christian politics requires undertaking an exploration of the world in which they lived. I present here three basic meta-narratives of the Atlantic World and Euro-American settlement as required background for understanding the role of religion as a driving force in the early modern Atlantic world—and especially in the Caribbean. The first presents the role of Christianity in early modern political authority and the second, its impact on related issues of colonial competition, while the third concerns religion's contributions to the Caribbean's economic development.

Peoples throughout the early modern world recognized political authority through the rituals and communal moral compacts that gave religion its structure. In Europe, Christianity had provided monarchs with the theory of divine right, a powerful justification for strict earthly hierarchies. In medieval Western Christendom, monarch and pope stood together at the helm of their kingdoms, and though they did not always agree, church and state supported one another. However, the Protestant Reformation of the sixteenth century produced a cataclysmic break in ideas of authority in Western Christendom, and popular religious enthusiasm among Roman Catholics brought the politics of piety to a sharp focus. As various European monarchs worked to consolidate their power over larger and larger states, they found "confessionalization" (the process of making Protestant or Catholic state religions more uniform and dominant so as to create a unified group ethos) a useful way to help foster their absolutist ambitions.[13] Throughout the sixteenth and seventeenth centuries, the awesome political power that European princes found in

ideologies of divine right helped foment a series of seemingly interminable religious wars between Protestants and Catholics.

These conflicts could not be contained, but rather travelled across
the Atlantic with European explorers and settlers. Therefore, this book
examines two of the most archetypal of these rivals in transatlantic
imperial expansion: first Spain, led by a series of monarchs who claimed
power through the Hapsburg line of the Holy Roman Empire; then England, represented by Queen Elizabeth I's proudly Protestant privateers
Francis Drake, Walter Raleigh, and Henry Hawkins. For both European powers, the impulse to spread Christianity through dominance of
New World trade and territories provided justification for often violent
acts. Spanish colonists gained a reputation as especially cruel and "un-
Christian" by massacring and enslaving Caribbean and mainland Amerindians during their first *conquistas* of the New World, their brutality
made famous by Bartolomé de las Casas. The English, jealous of Spain's
growing political power on the continent (based in no small part on their
economic windfalls from the New World), eagerly latched onto critiques
of Catholic brutality to promote their own expansionist plans as more favored by God. An Indian beckoning the English to "Come over and Save
Us" was not only emblazoned on the seal of the colony of Massachusetts
Bay, but also on the minds of Englishmen hoping to topple the Spanish
for decades to come.

Although Protestants of all stripes—French Huguenots, Dutch free-
booters, and English adventurers—tried to destabilize their Iberian enemies throughout the sixteenth century, no true challenge came from
Northern Europe until the first half of the seventeenth century. English
adventurers managed to get a foothold in various islands and coastal
colonies of the Atlantic littoral; the French largely based their expansion
in the beaver-rich lands of North America; and the Dutch came to excel
at shipping and merchandising commodities produced throughout the
Americas: tobacco, beaver pelts, sugar, indigo, and brazilwood. Spanish
colonists in the Caribbean eagerly traded with the newcomers—a real
problem, since the Iberian monarchs had claimed complete sovereignty
over American lands, excluding any "heretics" from settlement or trade
in the lands designated their by the pope in 1493. But by the middle of
the seventeenth century, the Hapsburg monarchs who ruled Spain (and
Portugal, for a time) saw their power and prestige begin to wane, both
in Europe and the Americas, while their Dutch, English, and French
competitors (mostly Protestants) gained enormous ground. This story of
Spanish decline and Protestant European ascendance was popularized

and exaggerated by historians in the nineteenth and early twentieth century; these scholars regularly extolled the virtues—or decried the failings—of one or another of these great European "empires" and their modern representatives, often portraying the world as progressing from the darkness (metaphorical and phenotypical) of Catholic Iberian, Native American, and African superstition and barbarity to the light of Northern European rationalism and racial ascendance. Along with other recent critics of this narrative, I hope to challenge stereotypes associated with the Black Legend of Spanish cruelty which still exist today.[14]

The Caribbean played a key role in European dynastic struggles, many of them organized around religious difference. It was in the Caribbean that the Spanish treasure fleet gathered resources every year, and there that contrabandists and privateers worked to destabilize Spanish dominance of the region. Tragically, it would also be a place that financed the wealth of European merchants, nobles, and some African rulers and middlemen through the insatiable demand for slave labor. Furthermore, the seventeenth century marked a turning point in the region. As Spanish Caribbean settlements diminished in size and strength, French, English, and Dutch adventurers quickly filled the void. New settlements blossomed from St. Eustatius to St. Christopher, Barbados to Curaçao, with newcomers finding ways to grow cash crops and bring them to European markets, and others attacking Iberian shipping when and where they could. The control of sugar markets moved decisively from Brazil into English and Dutch hands when new technologies and an infusion of capital helped Barbadian planters to turn in their first big crop of sugar in the late 1640s, which helped England gain ground in the region's balance of power. Ten years later, puritan leader Oliver Cromwell made the Caribbean the centerpiece of his ambitions against the Spanish Catholic enemy, authorizing a military expedition that would have lasting effects, including the seizure of Jamaica, before long the jewel in the crown of Britain's West Indian plantations. These two key changes were crucial to the development of the competition between nations in Europe and throughout the Atlantic World, spelling the end of Spain's superpower status in the European economic sphere.

Economic history, by virtue of its calculations and empirical rationalism, has less often dealt with religion as a central subject, although the competition that produced such rapid commercial transformations of the Caribbean and Atlantic worlds was clearly linked to religion and authority. While Spain's fortunes in the region diminished during the seventeenth century, those of Northern European planters and merchants skyrocketed, especially after the first sugar "boom" in Barbados (and subsequent ones in Jamaica, Suriname, Martinique, Guadaloupe, and St. Domingue), the increasing reliability of shipping (much of it led by the Dutch), and the creation of European markets based purely on the promise of future profits. For earlier generations of historians interested in political economy, these changes seemed to confirm a progressive model of Western development—the Dutch and English especially became heroes of modernity, ushering in mercantilism, even "free trade," at a time when absolutist monarchs insisted upon "outdated" monopolies and protectionism. Part of this assumption of Protestant commercial progress must also be attributed to Max Weber's widely read theory about the link between Protestantism and a capitalist work ethic. In fact, much of this theory resonates for the early modern world, as Catholics' anxieties about salvation funneled their riches into churches, charities, and other public manifestations of piety, while good Calvinist Protestants not only went to church but also toiled incessantly, fearful that any private economic failures were portents of divine disapproval.

But in the Caribbean, the bulk of the heavy work fell not to diligent Protestant laborers but to degraded servants and slaves, many of them reviled for their Catholicism (as in the case of Irish servants) or their paganism (a perception of African barbarism has persisted far beyond when Irish Catholics became white). When a generation of West Indian historians who came of age in the mid-twentieth century—just before anticolonial movements for national self-determination—took it upon themselves to critique the triumphant narratives that glorified European economic development, they placed African slavery and the plantation complex front-and-center in the debates over the costs and benefits of modernization. For these scholars, and for subsequent generations, the rise of the West came to be seen not as a triumph of superior political and economic prowess, but rather a deeply troubled process that ushered in exploitative colonialism, modern racism, and a world of economic disparity that continues to impact global relations.[15] The Caribbean, primary way station on the ocean highway from America to Europe and Africa, first produced the economic transformations of the Atlantic World and became a product of the profit-driven culture that pushed peoples into antipathetic relationships.

Nevertheless, the spiritual resonances of captivity, enslavement, coercion, and abuse continued to play a role in early modern European economic expansion. Slavery as an institution had proliferated on both

Christian and Muslim Mediterranean coasts thanks to economic and political competition between Cross and Crescent, but was always portrayed as particularly appalling on the other side of the religious divide. In the Americas, when the deaths and resistance of Amerindian laborers made their enslavement untenable, Africa became the primary source of profits and coerced labor, a move aided by European conceptions of just war and their evangelizing mission to "pagans" throughout the world. But Spanish and English colonists dealt with their perceived religious responsibilities quite differently. Although both groups looked to the Bible for reasons to allow the enslavement of Africans (the Curse of Ham was an especially popular narrative),[16] they dissented on one major issue.

In the Iberian peninsula, church and secular law had codified general ethics on slavery and manumission since the Roman era. The strength of the monarchy and the Catholic Church in Spanish settlements dictated that all enslaved Africans be instructed in the tenets of their faith and receive the same sacramental protections (of baptism, marriage, and confession) as all Christians. Accordingly, slaves appealed to Church leaders and used Christian rhetoric in their efforts to ameliorate their condition, as Isabel's experience in Part I illustrates. However, the first English Caribbean planters who came to rely on African laborers seemed uncertain as to whether to include them and their children in the Christian communities or not—would converts then become free? Slavery and even peonage had disappeared from most parts of Northern Europe, especially England, by the sixteenth century. Despite consistent support from the English Crown for the idea of evangelization and incorporation of enslaved Africans into the Christian community, most merchants and planters responded to such ideas with extreme suspicion and worked to make sure that racial barriers were impermeable in social and even religious terms. Part IV shows how this resistance extended to even the most egalitarian of Protestant denominations (the Quakers) until well into the eighteenth century.

Euro-Caribbean political economy was based on the premise of inequality—on profits flowing to those with pre-existing political or economic power. In the imperial mode, each "national" group looked to corner the market on the Caribbean's lush agricultural potential, to control its commodious ports with access to inland riches. And since religion was, like political economy, a tool of statecraft, the two often overlapped and reinforced one another. However, the region remained a chaotic stew of trade agreements and arrangements, a reality that reflected the Caribbean's unique "moral economy." Strongly influenced by the idea of personal risk that would come to embody capitalism, European adventurers in the Americas promoted among themselves—in the absence of established communal and governmental infrastructures—a moral economy that rewarded their own personal or familial survival and enrichment. Merchants of all nations ignored European trade laws and undercut official monopolies based on royal charters. Local officials might one day accept contraband and the next sequester the ship and imprison its crew for illegal trade. For them, Old World religious and political imperatives might actually threaten their survival, which depended on a blend of ruthlessness and open-mindedness between buyers and sellers who wished to keep the region's astounding profits flowing in their favor. Embedded in nearly every history of the early Caribbean is the prevalence of corruption, deception, greed, and especially violence. The ruthlessness of profit-seeking and competition helped create a culture in which Europeans who survived had to emotionally distance themselves from those who labored, suffered, and died for their profits, labeling them as worthless, inferior, inhuman, soulless "others."

This book thus examines the several ways in which morality was tied to a shift in global economies. Both financially and morally, early modern peoples largely operated on the assumption that resources were finite, and that in times of scarcity, an ethics of cooperation and mutual aid was required to avoid suffering (what is often referred to as a zero-sum game). Perhaps unsurprisingly, those thrust into increasingly competitive New World economies found the resulting depths of suffering and cruelty both unacceptable and immoral. Despite their attempts to craft a new moral economy in the Caribbean, those who prospered could not avoid their Old World religious ethics.[17] The violence and death that permeated the Caribbean forced free and captive migrants to ponder the literal and metaphorical meanings of survival, disease, salvation, and the afterlife. The wealthy were forced to square their economic privilege with a greater spiritual meaning: were their riches simply a temptation of the Devil or a sign that God had rewarded their faithfulness with prosperity?[18] Such uncertainty gave the dispossessed a space in which to stimulate their masters' anxieties, to push against those who would use religion as a tool of domination instead of a force for the common good. Many chose to capitalize on the contradictions between European imperial and economic imperatives for Christianity, tolerance, and community, pushing for a moral contract that made sense of inequality and suffering.[19] These struggles took place on the personal level, through both conflict and conversation.

In an attempt to assemble the fragments of the lives lived by Isabel, Nicolas, Henry, Yaff, Lewis and Nell, this study utilizes methods drawn from social and cultural history, comparative history, and micro-history to blend the personal with a more grounded understanding of the broader world in which they lived.[20] The chapters in Part I are set in Cartagena de Indias (on the Caribbean coast of modern-day Colombia) during the 1620s, and tell the story of Christianized slaves who, like Isabel Criolla, denounced their masters' harsh mistreatment, using their status as baptized Catholics to demand better conditions. Others found that renouncing the Christian god and his institutions could precipitate a blasphemy trial that would remove them from their masters' control. This study draws on records relating to the Jesuit *colegio* in Cartagena de Indias (the center of Spanish efforts to Christianize newly arrived African laborers), trials from Cartagena's Inquisition prosecuting blasphemous slaves, and civil proceedings against masters for cruelty. It emphasizes the pressures on Cartagena's officials to monitor master-slave relations and bolster the implicit social contract with the enslaved, given the threat posed to Spanish Caribbean trade and transportation by escalating maroon and pirate activity in the region.

Part II presents a motley crew of Protestant Northern European contrabandists and sojourners like Nicolas Burundel who lived in the Spanish Caribbean, many converting to Catholicism during their stay. Here I delve deeper into records of Cartagena's Inquisition, established in 1610 to restore order to the devolving frontier spaces of the Spanish Caribbean. When French, English, and Dutch captives, runaways, and contrabandists surfaced in port cities throughout the Spanish Caribbean, they frequently worked with local officials who stood to gain from these foreigners' presence, helping the newcomers to integrate themselves into colonial societies through Catholic conversion. Using Inquisition records and reports and letters sent to Seville's Council of the Indies, I show how Northern European outsiders learned to "perform" Catholic identities that would allow them to switch from "heretics" to "Christians." This section reveals both the continuity of patterns of maritime survival brought from the Mediterranean to the Caribbean, and the ways in which the growing impoverishment of several Spanish Caribbean ports during the first half of the seventeenth century provided new spaces for economic cooperation across the Protestant-Catholic divide.

In Part III, the book's focus shifts to the religious identities and economic ambitions of the English, beginning with Oliver Cromwell's "Western Design" of 1655–1656, a religiously defined Protestant offensive against Spain and its hold on New World wealth. England's seizure of Jamaica has often marked the turning of the tide against Spanish American hegemony, but Henry Whistler recorded how the plan very nearly ended in disaster. Although the commanders Cromwell sent to the Indies adhered to his new puritan order, the troops they commissioned were not so invested in contemporary religious controversies. Troops were happy to exhibit their nationalism in violent attacks against symbols of Spanish Catholicism. However, many balked at submitting to their officers' model of puritan patriarchy, a model that kept "ungodly" men subservient and threatened to lock them out of the Caribbean's promise of wealth and self-sufficiency. I examine new archival finds in Spanish records alongside well-known English sources to show why the lower ranks rebelled against the expedition's leaders as greedy hypocrites who wanted to "enslave" them. This section in particular marks a shift in the politics of religious identity, as the delegitimization of Cromwell's puritan colonial ambitions helped solidify English reliance on racializing tropes to define their politics of profit in the Caribbean.

Part IV explores life on Barbados, where the Society of Friends (Quakers) had gained a substantial following during the second half of the seventeenth century, even among wealthy merchants and planters like Lewis Morris. By the 1670s, George Fox and other English Quaker leaders began to press Barbados Friends to evangelize their enslaved "Ethiopian" laborers—but as Barbados's demography shifted to a slave majority, anxiety about slave uprisings united with old fears about the subversive messages of religious radicals. Exploring literature on West African religious and social structures, this study blends the empirical with the creative, developing a way to give voice to those, like Yaff and Nell, who lack an archival presence. It builds on my earlier prosopographical study of local Quakers—trends and details gained from Barbados census records, wills, and correspondence—to reveal in detail how local Friends compromised their principles of individual conscience, nonviolence, and spiritual egalitarianism and how even slaves who might have sought out spiritual kinship with their masters would have found the process disheartening and unproductive. The failures of the Quakers' evangelization project typify the solidification of racial boundaries throughout the English Atlantic, revealing the limited space that profit-minded Protestants were willing to concede to the enslaved in their construction of a West Indian moral economy.

To conclude, I explain how the explosion of trade and imperial rivalries at the turn of the eighteenth century created new avenues for disenfranchised people to protest against greed and exploitation in religious terms. As Spanish influence continued to wane, English, French, and Dutch economic powers scrambled for control of Caribbean resources, constructing a new Atlantic economy that thrived on extraordinary profits from the African slave trade and poorly policed inter-imperial trade. Using piracy narratives, Inquisition investigations targeting the spread of foreign "heresy," and records of the South Sea Company's *asiento* slave trade, I conclude by re-examining these sources in light of recent scholarship on Spain's religious refuge laws targeted at runaway slaves from circum-Caribbean Protestant colonies, as well as studies of the anticlericalism and "irreligion" of the maritime Atlantic world. The Caribbean's increase in both toleration for international trade and competitive investment in slave-produced goods resulted in the region's further descent into cynicism, hostility, and cruelty—the real reason for its reputation as a particularly irreligious place.

As personal stories have allowed me to emphasize important themes in the early Caribbean, they have also offered me the chance to delve into the complexity of my subjects' experiences. For example, the analysis of Nicolas in Part II in my investigation of Northern Europeans who converted to Catholicism in Spanish Caribbean territories takes into account both his representativeness (an impoverished man with few options, dependent on the patron-client structure of Spanish Caribbean society for survival) and his uniqueness (he stubbornly refused, unlike many others, to give in to the Inquisition's insistence that he repent any real or imposed "heresies"). Thus, by reading Nicolas's story alongside a description and analysis of the larger norms, we can better resist pat summaries or teleological conclusions. Invoking his name helps us remember the humanity and complexity of real lives, full of richness and contradiction. Although this book privileges the voices of resistance in how individuals performed orthodox Christian identities and narrated subversive discourses of Christian morality, I hope readers will not discount the possibility (indeed, the reality) that Christianity could be turned from a tool of the powerful into a theology of liberation, justice, and fulfillment by those who approached it in a different way. If this project is about finding "agency" in the actions and pronouncements of marginalized people in the past, it is also about trying to show them as complex figures, flawed and contradictory in their quest for spiritual and physical survival.[21]

PART I

ISABEL

"If Her Soul Was Condemned, It Would Be the Authorities' Fault"

Warning should be given to those who, in the dominion of masters over their slaves, exercise cruelties neither permitted nor conceivable, for the harm that is done therein demands remedy and punishment. It would be of great service to our Lord and evidence of a well-ordered republic if all those [victims] who, with such just cause and so little power, could find sanctuary from their confinement, rooting out from [our] Christian republic such atrocious acts as these that have already resulted in significant damages: the deaths of many slaves, many apostasies and blasphemies against God our Lord (which the Holy Tribunal of the Inquisition has punished in view of the entire city), as well as the flight of such slaves to untamed hideaways . . .

—LUÍS ZAPATA DE OJEDA,
petition on behalf of Juana Zamba, slave of Catalina Pimienta Pacheco
(Cartagena 1633)

1 / Contesting the Boundaries of Anti-Christian Cruelty in Cartagena de Indias

On the morning of April 4, 1639, a guard unshackled the runaways one by one and brought them from the cell in the public jail before a scribe, where they were made to state for the record their masters' names and the length of time they had been absent from service. Gregorio Álvarez de Zepeda, who as *alcalde* of the Holy Brotherhood of Mompox was in charge of seeking out maroons, further ordered each to give an account of "the cause of their flight." One of the first runaways to have his name recorded was Juan, from the land of the Ararás. Since he was *ladino* (which meant he could communicate in Spanish) and said he was a Christian, they ordered him to swear "by God and Our Lord over a sign of the cross" to tell the truth.[1]

Juan admitted that he had run away to the mountains several times, most recently just after the New Year, when he took advantage of his work as a rower (*boga*) on the Magdalene River to take his freedom. He said he lived in the mountains beside the river, alone, unaffiliated with any *palenque* (the word for maroon community in Spanish territories), nothing more than a "vassal of God (*vassalo con Dios*)." Juan said he left his solitary wanderings when one day he came upon a black woman weeping by the riverside. He approached, "endeavor[ing] to find out what was wrong with her." Juan discovered that the woman's name was Susana, and that "she had fled . . . because her lady doña Eufrasia punished her so much." She told him about how she had received so many lashes to her buttocks that the open wounds never ceased to pain her, and so he promised to take her away to a place where they could be safe. Their escape was short-lived, however—they were soon spotted by Álvarez's slave-catchers. Juan begged Álvarez not to send him back to his former owner but "to order him sold to another master, who he would serve with much good will (*voluntad*), without running away."[2] Susana later made the same plea, citing her own mistress's abuse, then lifted her skirts so that her charges could be verified—Álvarez instructed the scribe to write that her buttocks were covered with "thick white welts, signs of having had old wounds in the said part."[3]

Next he heard from Mariana Mandinga, who testified that she had run away from the same owner as Susana two months earlier and spoke of the severity with which this woman treated her female slaves. Mariana said she was whipped the same as Susana, her wounds so painful "that she couldn't stir or even stand," and so she ran away, begging some Indians in a boat to take her to the other side of the Rio Magdalena. There, she said, "she began to cry, finding herself alone and in so much pain from the whippings, not knowing where she was because she'd never run away before." But then, like an apparition or a guardian angel, "Isabel, a creole Negro, a fellow slave of the said doña Eufrasia," suddenly appeared to help usher Mariana to salvation (long ago, Isabel "had also fled because of the severe punishment . . . of her mistress and because she threatened that she would kill them"). Unfortunately, the safety was short-lived, for both Mariana and Isabel were soon thereafter captured, and Mariana, like Susana, begged Álvarez "for the love of God" not to send her back to doña Eufrasia's house, insisting that "if he did her mistress would kill her with whippings." Álvarez again had the runaway lift her skirt so he could register that they saw "she had signs of whippings" on her buttocks, which he described as "wide mottled welts."[4]

With such vivid descriptions of both physical and emotional anguish, we are convinced of these women's terror at the prospect of being delivered to their mistress and the probability of additional torment. Their gruesome scars and piteous pleading must have caused the *alcalde* Álvarez to recoil in horror—or perhaps not; he might have coldly recorded the testimony and moved on. After all, he was a man of his time, and might even have believed these women deserved such harsh punishments. If the experience of viewing their tears and broken flesh had no effect, the testimony of a third runaway who claimed doña Eufrasia de Camargo's cruelty as the reason for her flight seems to have caught his attention. Instead of lifting her skirts like Susana and Mariana to reveal the physical proof of her maltreatment, Isabel Criolla chose instead to reveal her inner wounds and spiritual pain. She begged Álvarez "for the passion of Our Lord Jesus Christ" to order her sold to anyone but her mistress, or she "would lose her soul." She engaged with him as a fellow Christian, entreating him to listen when she said that she understood

> that her soul and those of all sinners were paid for by the death and Passion of our Lord Jesus Christ, who she asked every day to take her by the hand so as to keep her from falling into any grave sin of desperation, and she would continue to do the same—but *if her soul was condemned* in the future it would be the fault of the justices who didn't remedy the severe punishment that her said mistress doña Eufrasia gives to her slaves . . .

Isabel's final denunciation against her mistress was that "everyone knows that she kills them with whippings, as she has done with four pieces of slaves (*piezas de esclavos*) who died in her house without confession."[5]

Conjuring up both her economic value (*pieces of slaves*) and the rhetoric of Christian damnation (*if her soul was condemned* . . .) to frame the violence and death that haunted her mind, Isabel Criolla tapped into several core ideals and practices that defined Spanish American slavery: commodification, the violence of coercion, and the spiritual core of human rights.[6] The Spanish Crown removed Indians from the class of people considered enslaveable by American colonists with the New Laws of 1542. After the Crown instituted a monopoly slave trading contract with the Portuguese in 1595, Africans were brought over as forced immigrants in ever greater numbers, delivered to one of two mainland Caribbean ports: Veracruz or Cartagena de Indias. The latter was the administrative center closest to Mompox. According to experts on this forced migration, Spanish colonial cities like Cartagena quickly became "slave majority" populations. During the early seventeenth century, three to four thousand slaves worked in Cartagena, a city of only two thousand Spanish *vecinos*; by 1686, a census of the city's population noted 5,700 slaves.[7] Such demographic imbalances fostered an uneasy relationship between masters and slaves. Due to often-violent struggles and the cruelty of masters and mistresses like Camargo, runaways fled Spanish cities to congregate in *palenques* set in rugged or swampy hinterlands beyond the control of urban hubs like Mompox and Cartagena.

Conflict was inherent to the institution of slavery since ancient times, and jurists in different societies had to regulate it for the proper ordering of society. The *Siete Partidas*, a medieval Castilian legal code based on Roman and Muslim precedents, established that "A master has complete authority over his slave to dispose of him as he pleases," and considered the slave an item of property. Moreover, the *Siete Partidas* gave masters the legal right to express their discontent with a slave "by punishing him by reproof, or by blows," leaving little recourse to protest this treatment.[8] However, the same slave code also set out guidelines that moderated the harshness of chattel slavery. Furthermore, Church law stipulated a series of rights and obligations between masters and slaves, requiring that slaves be provided with a Christian education, have time off to attend mass and go to confession at least once a year, and have access to the sacrament of marriage and some protections for conjugal residency. The Koran compares rather well to the *Siete Partidas*, both agreeing that the slave has a right to good treatment, to shelter, food, and clothing, and to secure family ties. They both mandated that masters should behave with moderation towards their slaves (although the guidelines for what constituted "good treatment" and punishments for slaveholders who broke the rules were often less clear).[9]

Laws abridging the power of abusive masters were used to create greater social stability. The matter of severe cruelty was a matter of state concern, even in Roman times: "We also decree that, where a man is so cruel to his slaves as to kill them by starvation, or to wound or injure them so seriously that they cannot endure it, in cases of this kind said slaves can complain to the judge." Such laws also enhanced the power of rulers who stood to gain from a sense of benevolent justice towards all their subjects. Herman Bennett has argued that as the Hapsburg monarchs attempted to assert greater—indeed absolute—authority over their American subjects, they encroached upon the master-slave relationship, strengthening competing legal administrations like Church and Inquisition courts to serve as checks to local power networks.[10] Indeed, Isabel Criolla's performance before Álvarez emphasized her true Christianity and her mistress's neglect in matters of religious paternalism—both supported by absolutist efforts.

As a *criolla* (creole woman: Isabel Criolla's "last name" is really an adjective fixing her natal birthplace in the Americas and not Africa), Isabel had learned about the nuanced limits to a master's power in the Spanish Americas in a way that her African-born counterparts might have found difficult, though not impossible. Some jurists in the medieval Arab world ruled that maltreated slaves had the right to approach the *qadi* (judge) and request to be sold to another master. Before her capture and sale to the Americas, Mariana may have heard of similar cases heard by *qadis* in the Manding empire from which she hailed (although how much

Shari'a law was honored in her homeland is difficult to assess). Juan's plea for Álvarez's intercession might have been informed by the patronage customs and laws regarding slavery and pawnship in the Kingdom of Allada, which had recently grown in power thanks to its economic alliances with European slave traders.[11] African societies had their own legal traditions that opened spaces for moral protest, some certainly comparable; furthermore, many coastal Africans were aware of European legal and moral frameworks regarding slavery.[12] In both New and Old Worlds, such appeals to officials like Álvarez gave them power over slaveholders to "investigate and ascertain whether the charge is true," and to do what was necessary to penalize the excessively cruel master by selling his slaves "in such a way that they never can be again placed in the power" of the master.[13] Culturally aware performances like Isabel Criolla's, by engaging in the rituals and rhetoric of Christian law, shaped the practice and theory of slavery in the colonial Spanish Caribbean.

The historiography on Atlantic slavery has long recognized the uniqueness of these legal opportunities for enslaved peoples in the Iberian colonies. The classic work of comparative slavery, Frank Tannanbaum's *Slave and Citizen* (1946), emphasized the ameliorative character of Hispanic legal traditions compared to the more restrictive legal codes established in North America. More recent studies of black populations in the Spanish Americas have worked around and beyond the Tannenbaum thesis, most notably by exploring the agency of African actors in shaping the legal landscape of opportunity.[14] The Catholic Church in Spanish America had worked to Christianize, creolize, and educate Indian and African "pagans" about their subordinate position in the New World order. However, scholars interested in subaltern resistance have shown that giving Amerindians and Africans access to the language of universal Christianity also offered pathways to shape social relations and challenge colonialism's totalizing power.[15] And so it was for Isabel Criolla and many others like her in Cartagena, who learned to resist the terms of their enslavement by understanding Spanish Church and society's concerns with the salvation of souls and maintaining Christian norms of piety and charity. Both of these issues could trump the seeming impunity of Spanish American masters, whose very remoteness largely protected them from both monarchical and Church control.

Cartagena de Indias and its environs is an especially rich site to investigate the intersections between imperial power and individuals on the margins who sought to harness communal protections against the everyday violations of their everyday lives. The sea and fluvial pathways between this rich Caribbean port and the inland town of Santa Fe de Mompox where Isabel was captured symbolize the increased commercialization and cosmopolitanism of Spanish Caribbean cities, crucial hubs in the transportation network that linked Spain to its inland riches (not to mention targets for plundering pirates).[16] The province of Cartagena and the Rio Magdalena were also highly vulnerable—it was here that the Spanish empire had to defend itself against the persistence of native resistance, and the growing numbers of independent, bellicose maroon communities, as well as Northern European smugglers and pirates. Spanish American security thus lay not only in the strict discipline of any of these three offenders, but in a pragmatic policy alternating between repression and lenience—one never knew when the empire might need to rely on one of these groups as loyal allies rather than as enemies.

Thus, although Gregorio Álvarez, as *alcalde* of Mompox's Holy Brotherhood, was assigned to recover runaway slaves in order to maintain orderly social relationships between masters and slaves, his position as head of this local religious society also required him to take care that all souls (even in such degraded, rebellious vessels such as Isabel's) were recognized as worthy of spiritual redemption.[17] The ten-peso fines that Álvarez required masters to pay before collecting their runaway "property" were used not only to fund further disciplinary expeditions against maroons, but also to build a new church of San Francisco for the city of Mompox, where masses would be said to release captive souls from purgatory. Masters and mistresses whose form of control was seen as sadism, as anti-Christian barbarity, could thus find themselves disciplined for putting both public safety and the "order" of a Christian republic in peril.

This chapter follows the spatial, emotional, and legal journeys on which Isabel Criolla and her Spanish advocates embarked, exploring the social, economic, and religious landscape of the Spanish Caribbean. Using the story of Isabel's petition to propel our narrative journey through Cartagena de Indias and its hinterlands in the early seventeenth century, Chapters 1–3 occasionally pause to analyze not only the unique aspects of her case but also its points of comparison with other secular and Inquisition cases dealing with cruelty to slaves. This chapter explores attempts to limit abuse through appeals to shared Christian values. It illuminates the great power wielded by religious and imperial institutions in Spanish urban social hierarchies, and the role of spiritual transculturation in helping slaves articulate protests against the worst abuses of the master-slave "contract." Chapter Two continues by discussing the difficulties Isabel and her imperial protectors faced in their attempts to successfully curb abuse—especially difficult in cases like the one brought against Camargo, where the shadow of sexual violence and unspeakable sins served as barriers to effective policing of social relationships in Spanish slave societies. Finally, Chapter Three breaks down some of the legal and moral dynamics of everyday contests between master and slave, colony and metropole—power plays that helped to define the limits of coercion and cruelty in Spanish America. We begin with a journey to Cartagena—a journey that traces the scenery and cultural milieu of this regional center for justice and commerce, allowing us to better envision the choices and limitations that marginal individuals like Isabel navigated in early seventeenth-century Spanish colonial society.

On May 8, 1639, Isabel Criolla likely boarded a canoe or river raft (*champán*) rowed down the Rio Magdalena from Mompox towards the Caribbean Sea, from whence they would travel southwest along the coast to Cartagena. A letter written by Álvarez accompanied Isabel, describing her to the governor of Cartagena as "one of the good Negroes that this town has had, a good Christian"—a direct contradiction of his official first sentence, which had labeled Isabel and other persistent runaways of being "prejudicial to the republic," and sentenced to banishment. Perhaps the change in Álvarez's perspective began when doña Eufrasia Camargo and her husband complained that they wanted Isabel back, that their prerogative as property owners had been slighted. Don Ortiz filed appeals stating that being denied a voice in the judicial process left him "aggrieved"; doña Eufrasia was less civil in her insults against the head of the Holy Brotherhood—she had told him "that if it cost her all her estate and all the slaves she owned, she'd see the bones and blood" of her former slave Isabel. In his letter to don Melchor de Aguilera, the province's governor and captain general, Álvarez wrote that "he could not in [good] conscience" hand Isabel over to her owners, and asked Aguilera, as the "superior judge" in the region, to "carry out that which is best for God our Lord and His Majesty."[18]

When Isabel Criolla and her guard entered into Cartagena, a city of roughly fifteen hundred Spanish *vecinos* and nearly double that number of African-born or Afro-creole slaves,[19] they would have disembarked in one of the busiest ports in the Americas, an official way station for the annual *flota* and one of two licensed ports for the importation of African slaves into the Spanish Americas. With the pull of untold wealth in the mainland interiors of Mexico and Peru, many of the old population centers of the Spanish Caribbean (like the island of Hispaniola, Columbus's first colony) had lost much of their population over the course of the sixteenth century. Cartagena, however, remained a thriving center thanks to its importance in imperial commerce and transportation. In Cartagena's docks, Isabel would have seen ships being loaded and unloaded, and likely also a few of the hundreds of passengers who arrived yearly from Spain, those who stayed a few weeks or months in Cartagena on their way to or from the administrative centers of New Granada, Quito, Mexico, or Peru.[20] If the port was as busy this year as it was in 1633, Isabel also might have seen one of a dozen or more slave ships (*negreros* or *armazones*) owned by Portuguese contractors.[21] Most had come from West Central African nations like Angola and Kongo, although many were from Cabo Verde or São Tome, other well-established Portuguese trading colonies that served as consolidation centers for war captives and slaves from the areas inland along the Rivers of Guinea (from the Senegambia region to Sierra Leone).[22] She may have seen priests gathering on the docks, walking among the severely ill slaves recently unloaded from the pestilent ships, their captains eager to avoid losing valuable "pieces" of merchandise to mortal illness. The priests tending to the skeletal slaves with dead eyes would have been mainly Jesuits from the city's mission Colegio, perhaps also lay brothers from the hospital order of San Juan de Dios. The Jesuits may have been accompanied by one of a dozen or so African-born translators they employed to communicate with the weakened arrivals. For those whose physical and emotional trauma was too great to admit speech, the priests tipped a small vessel of liquid over their heads, muttering incantations in Latin, a tongue foreign to all its recipients, baptizing them "in the name of the Father, the Son and the Holy Ghost."[23]

Amid the shouts of merchants and peddlers, Isabel and her escort would have walked into the city's bustling central market, the Plaza de Aduanas, through the Gate of the Half-Moon. Here nearly everything could be found for sale, including African slaves, oiled and groomed to appear healthy and fetch the highest price. Some, mostly women and children, were purchased by wealthy Cartagenero *vecinos* or churchmen to serve in their city palaces, boosting their small army of servants to better reflect their masters' status and wealth.[24] Local Spanish or *mestizo* artisans may have purchased a few youths from Africa for more laborious tasks, appraising the less expensive slaves for their potential strength, dexterity, and aptitude to learn the basics of their trade, leaving their masters time to establish themselves in more "honorable" pursuits.

The rest would have been sold in lots to wholesalers who would stand to make a hefty profit marching them further inland to mine owners in the Kingdoms of New Granada, Quito, and Peru, or agricultural producers and ranchers, always hungry for new laborers to replenish their hard-worked crews. Twenty-four slave warehouses near Cartagena's wharf supplied the voracious colonial appetite for labor, as did dozens more privately owned baracoons scattered throughout the city, down the main avenues and within sight of city landmarks like the Cathedral and the convent of St. Augustine.[25]

Governor Aguilera was particularly interested in Isabel's case, having heard about it while passing through Mompox, and had ordered his lieutenant to look into the matter. Upon their arrival, Isabel Criolla likely was taken straight to the administrative buildings that ringed the city's main plaza to arrange an audience.[26] There Isabel might have had a chance to pause and gaze around her at the other buildings situated in the Plaza Mayor: at one side, the imposing height of the cathedral's bell tower; directly opposite, the *palacio* of the Holy Inquisition, the headquarters of the third such tribunal to be established by the Spanish in the Americas. These symbols of the intimate relationships between church and state would have reminded Isabel of the power and wealth of the institutions to which she would have to appeal—the Plaza Mayor had been designed as a physical representation of the ideal Spanish ordered society, and in order to convince colonial officials of the justice of her plea, she would have to present herself as part of that ordered society, not against it.[27]

Depending on the gate from which Isabel exited the city center, she would have passed at least one of the seven convents (five run by male orders, two female) and a half dozen churches that dotted Cartagena's urban landscape. Without question she would have seen some of the more than forty secular clerics and confessors employed in meeting the residents' spiritual needs (dozens of friars were also employed in the city's regular orders).[28] If she followed the street to the left of the Inquisition Palace back towards the Customs Square (Plaza de Aduanas), she would have passed another imposing church compound, the headquarters of the city's Jesuit Colegio, to which some of the same priests she saw at the docks may have been returning with their African translators, intently discussing their plans to capture the souls of this new shipment of slaves.

Among those priests were likely the Colegio's rector, Alonso de Sandoval, and Pedro Claver, who had gained saintly reputations for their

FIGURES 1 & 2. Modern views of Cartagena de India's central cathedral (left) and main entrance to the Inquisition Palace (right), the latter of which has been recently converted into a museum and archive to preserve the city's history. Photos by the author..

charitable and ministerial work among the African populations in Cartagena. Their innovative and extensive use of African translators to explain the rudiments of Christian doctrine and teach its attendant rituals to the newly arrived enslaved meant that Africans from many regions had access to a fairly uniform explanation of their place in the Spanish colonial worldview.[29] Claver was canonized as the "saint of the slaves"[30] shortly after his decease, but it was Sandoval who had founded the mission after having worked with poor black and Indian populations in the regions surrounding Cartagena, Panama, and the mining districts of New Granada during the first decades of the seventeenth century. Claver was sent to help Sandoval in his efforts, so that the elder Jesuit might retreat to his cell to compose his magnum opus—a treatise entitled *De Instauranda Aethiopum Salute* (1627) that compiled his ethnographic investigations into the customs of different African regions and set out an ambitious agenda for turning unacculturated Africans (*bozales*) into good Christian slaves (*ladinos*).[31] Claver, meanwhile, took on the day-to-day operations of the African mission, preaching to open-air crowds with a small painting of hellfire "and the soul of a very beautiful woman being tormented by the demons," as well as small medals and rosaries to pass out to slaves who could repeat the tenets of the faith.[32] Black and white witnesses who testified in the case for his beatification spoke of his tireless mission to sponsor slaves who wished to marry and live within the bounds of Christian matrimony (for which he often raised the ire of local slave owners, who could not break that institution for a convenient sale), and described his attempts to banish *amanecimientos*, ritual dances slaves and free blacks often held on feast days or at night, threatening those he caught with beatings and imprisonment for their continued adherence to "superstition" and "licentious dancing."[33]

Next, if the governor had decided that the "old runaway but good Christian" was not a flight risk and he wanted to spare the expense of locking her up in the common jail,[34] he might have sent her to be lodged in a barrio called Getsemani, well beyond the opulence and security of the walled portion of the city. Exiting through another fortified gate leading towards *la otra banda* (the "other side"), Isabel may have observed crews of black and sunburnt men laboring in the hot sun and oppressive humidity to build more fortifications to protect the city from pirate attacks.[35] There she might have watched military leaders exercising their troops, preparing them for the assault they feared could come any day, as Dutch and English ships employing pilots familiar with Spanish coastlines multiplied in number and daring throughout the Caribbean.

FIGURE 3. The three-story Jesuit Colegio
and adjoining church loom over a plaza
which has been renamed in honor of San
Pedro Claver, now decorated with artwork
and memorials in honor of the "Saint of the
Slaves." Inside the church, Claver's bones
repose in a glass coffin below the altar. Photo
by the author.

The threat was seen as so severe that city officials had organized a regiment of black freedmen to swell the numbers of able-bodied soldiers who could defend the city—given Spanish military values of honor and lineage, these would have been seen as a less-desirable fighting force, but nonetheless necessary to this particularly vulnerable Caribbean hotspot. That same year, Governor Aguilera had reported to the Council of the Indies in Seville that he employed 65 *mulatos* and 103 free blacks in the local militia.[36] Perhaps one of those groups had been among those assembled for exercises that day as Isabel continued her weary journey to her night's lodging.

FIGURE 4. Engraved portrait of Pedro Claver
by Marcus Orozco, which appeared in the 1666
hagiographical biography, *Apostolica, y penitente
vida de el V.P. Pedro Claver, de la Compañia de
Iesus* (Zaragoza, 1666). Image courtesy of the John
Carter Brown Library at Brown University.

This imagined journey with Isabel through Cartagena helps us think
of the ways that authority and hierarchy—on display in the layout of
public spaces, in the preponderance of religiously affiliated persons and
institutions, and in the demonstrations of power and race in social interactions—might have informed the mental processes that subjected persons like Isabel considered in order to assert herself as part of the social
order. Next, we imagine Isabel's physical movements and interactions
to explore how the city and its social relationships may have "spoken" to
Isabel (and can speak to us): about common patterns in relationships between enslaved women and white men, about conflicts between enslaved
women and elite mistresses, about the religious and social limits put on
white women's authority in the mastery of their slaves.

In Getsemani, Isabel would have entered into a typical urban Spanish
barrio, complete with its myriad *castas* (castes) and *forasteros* (literally,

FIGURE 5. Plan of the city of Cartagena, showing the most important government and church buildings (below), and the barrio of Getsemani (above), where mainly lower-class people of color and foreign merchants resided. Although both sections of the city were well-fortified by the time this 1735 plan was made, in the seventeenth century the commercial district of Getsemani was much more open to military attacks. Image courtesy of the John Carter Brown Library, Providence, Rhode Island.

outsiders): Portuguese and Flemish merchants, *mestizos, mulatos,* free blacks, and lower-class Europeans of all nationalities who served in the city as artisans, ship-workers, or street vendors. Here were fewer overt signs of the Spaniards' religious institutions, although the Franciscans had established a convent in the neighborhood, and the brothers of San Juan de Dios operated a hospital for sailors and the poor.[37] Here, too, the neat hierarchies of the ideal Spanish city fell apart. Many sojourners to the city found lodging "in the homes of *mulatas*"—these freedwomen ran respectable inns and boarding houses as well as brothels that rented the bodies of poor and enslaved women to both local and transient men who came to Cartagena on business or who found themselves flush from gaming or an unexpected payday.[38] Black and mixed-race female slaves were often more numerous than men of African descent in cities throughout the Spanish empire.[39] This predominance of enslaved women of color, combined with the intimacies of urban lodging and interaction, gave masters the opportunity to exercise their power of coercion to command or persuade black women to yield to sexual relations—interactions that more often than not resulted in the birth of children who would become slaves like their mothers (no matter the shade of their skin).

In the day and night before Isabel was brought back to the walled city to repeat her testimony before the governor, she may have gathered with other residents of Gesthemani in the Plaza de la Yerba,[40] listening to local gossip and sharing her story with local residents. Those who heard her story with sympathy might have reluctantly shared with her other commonplace tales of masters in Cartagena who were notorious for their brutality, and the sad plight of their abused slaves. They probably would have told her not to hope for justice—just five years before, one woman working as a clothing peddler, a slave of Catalina Pimienta Pacheco (the widow of a powerful Italian resident merchant), had found temporary refuge from her mistress's cruelties in the home of a wealthy and well-connected churchman who had even tried to help her sue for her freedom.[41] Juana Zamba pulled out of the suit shortly after the judge ruled she should return to her mistress's home for the duration of the lawsuit, and Juana had not been seen out of the house since. Small wonder she dropped her complaint—her lawyer had written in his first petition that Juana had been beaten so badly that she was left crippled, her face burned so badly that she was nearly blind. The free *morena* Isabel Rodríguez, on the other hand, told anyone who would listen that Juana was fine: even she had admitted to being disgusted with the whole thing, that the lawsuit "had been a matter between white people (*una cosa de blancos*) and she had never gotten involved in it nor asked for it." Others said Juana was just getting back at her mistress: after all, they had argued over how much Juana owed Pacheco from her peddling. Some of the older residents, remembering Juana's previous mistress and her reputation for viciousness, might have believed that the ugly scars were remnants of that earlier era (at least that was what Pacheco contended as she defended herself against "slander"). If Isabel had met the local midwife, she might have confided how she had nearly wept to see scars in Juana's "shameful parts" when she delivered a stillborn child.[42] Who had damaged Juana most, and why, must have been a subject of speculation for some, while others would have preferred that the whole issue not be discussed at all.

Silence and obfuscation was indeed the most important aspect of colonial and religious control in Cartagena de Indias. Given the close quarters of the typical urban household, sexual dalliances between masters and female slaves were rarely a secret. Isabel would have seen at least some pregnant women among the many enslaved street vendors, washerwomen, cooks, and maidservants accompanying their mistresses through the streets of Getsemani. Seeing the swollen bellies of those women, Isabel might have met their gaze to bear silent witness to their predicament, for she herself had borne a *mulata* daughter named Juanita while living as a slave in the Camargo-Ortiz household. She did not wish to speak of who the father was or how he made her yield—and besides, no one wanted to hear about it. In the record of Isabel's case, the very markers of her daughter's mixed heritage were nearly elided—only in the final appeal at the end of more than two hundred folios was Juanita marked as a *mulata*.

Even when a lighter-skinned child was born to an enslaved black woman in Spanish colonial society, this very evidence of sexual coercion almost always went unacknowledged. Once Eufrasia Camargo had referred in her testimony to whipping her female servants "to avoid offenses against God," but she made no further distinction as to *what* offenses she might have felt the need to curtail.[43] The palpable silences intimating the sins of extramarital sex, of rape, and of the vulnerable female body could only engender guilt, shame, and recrimination if dealt with honestly—but the patriarchal society in which these acts occurred was no moral utopia when it came to such matters. These remnants of the archive remind us of how sexualized torture and violence could be avoided, even normalized, by the men who authored and edited official documents such as Isabel's and Juana's court cases.

The best hope for enslaved women who suffered sexual abuse came in the form of special favors (in the form of material comforts or the promise of manumission) to ease the bitter gall of intimidation and shame, to transform the inequality of their relationship into a fictional accord of mutual benefit, and to ease their masters' consciences. The worst they could expect was repeated and brutal rape, or to be exposed to the rage and humiliation of their master's wife. Juana Zamba's lawyer asserted that her 10-year-old daughter Isabelina had died two months after being beaten savagely with a tarred whip until it broke open her flesh, then further tormented when the dust of wild barley was applied to the wound; in another legal brief, he referred to the murder of another of Juana's daughters, Faustina.[44] In this context, the multiple references in Juana Zamba's and Isabel Criolla's cases to miscarriages, the scars Juana bore in her "shameful parts," the savage beating that had led to her daughter Isabelina's death, and the welts on the buttocks of doña Eufrasia's slave women strongly suggest that enslaved women's coerced sexuality and reproduction had been transformed into a narrative of black women's "sinful" promiscuity by Spanish mistresses.[45]

It seems likely that elite Spanish women were more susceptible to charges of un-Christian cruelty than their male counterparts. First, elite Spanish women were seen as guardians of the Catholic faith in the domestic sphere. Secondly, women whose rage was motivated by jealousy or sexual competition (implicit in the acts of violence against sexualized areas of female slaves' bodies) came dangerously close to exposing colonial society's moral double standard and their husbands' sins of sexual coercion. When elite white women transgressed the circumscribed boundaries of their proper role—as exemplars of piety, chaste wives who turned a blind eye to their husbands' indiscretions—their behavior threatened not only the ordering of their individual household but also the structure of society.[46] In the 1634 proceedings against Catalina Pimienta Pacheco, Juana Zamba's lawyer argued for the necessity of bringing this mistress and others like her to justice, no matter their social station, citing as precedent another case that royal officials in Castille had recently prosecuted against "a titled Lady (who out of respect will not be named) who had taken a firebrand and burned one of her servants below her skirt." The lawyer informed Cartagena's judge that this elite Castilian woman had faced banishment and a fine of twelve thousand *ducados* for her crime. The cases weren't exactly equivalent, he admitted—the Spanish case had involved a free servant (*criada*), not a slave—but Señora Pacheco, even if she was of a "very prominent" family, was no noblewoman. The law exempted no one, Juana's lawyer argued, from the kinds of "atrocious" tortures and violent punishments committed, and he hoped that the guilty party would be banished from their "Christian republic."[47]

If Isabel had thought to point out to residents of Getsemaní that her mistress was particularly un-Christian in her treatment, residents might have told her what she doubtless already knew—that Spaniards held their own to a different standard of religiosity than they did those not part of the *república de españoles*. In fact, singling out individuals of African descent for religious discipline was an important function of the city's Inquisition—unlike Amerindian neophytes who received exemptions from the full rigor of their inclusion in the Catholic Church, black "New Christians" were subject to the same scrutiny and standards of orthodoxy as Protestant pirates and crypto-Jewish *converso* merchants.[48] Residents of Cartagena and the surrounding cities were probably still talking about the previous year's spectacular *auto de fe*, and although the biggest group of *reconciliados* paraded through town in 1638 had been crypto-Jews from the wealthy Portuguese merchant elite, individuals of African descent held positions of symbolic importance at the fore and rear of the *auto*'s solemn procession of penitents.[49]

If she had asked for details of this inquisitorial spectacle, Isabel might have gained some new perspective on the importance of religious language in struggles for power. The first to be paraded through the city was the *mulato* Vicente de Paz, a convict sentenced to labor in the building of Cartagena's new fortifications. De Paz had tried to escape, looking for a better life (or at least a night of freedom), and when he was caught and ordered to receive a whipping, he looked to a sin of heresy to bring him before the Inquisition. Before the punishment began, "the said *mulato* cried aloud that he renounced (*renegaba*) his baptism and the holy oil he had received" as well as the "Most Holy Virgin."[50] The Inquisition regularly saw these sorts of cases, in which slaves cursed God, the Virgin, the saints, or their baptism when faced with the lash—thirty-four were registered in Cartagena's Tribunal over the course of the seventeenth century, and the crime was just as common in other American Inquisition Tribunals.[51] The phrase *"reniego a Dios"* (I renounce God) was common enough as profanity went in early modern Spain, at least in the masculine sphere, where it was delivered as an offhand frustration when one's luck turned bad in a game of cards or dice.[52] Prior to 1638, three whites had been questioned by inquisitors about renouncing God in this way, but two were released without any physical chastisement—Antonio de Cabrera because he claimed that when he had uttered "the said blasphemies, he had been drinking a great quantity of strong spirits to relieve an extreme pain in his stomach," and Portuguese pilot Manuel de la Rosa, who wouldn't even admit to the allegations, saying that in the stress of trying to land his ship, he might have cursed "the father who made him and the mother who bore him," but swore he could never renounce God "if he was awake and in his sound judgment."[53]

By contrast, when slaves like De Paz uttered these words—especially since they often did it when being punished by their masters—the curse against God (and the authority He had given to masters) posed a much more serious challenge to the colonial order. As slaves began to face arrest and punishment for this offense, many learned that they might escape the brutality of their enslavement (at least temporarily) with a theatrical renunciation of the Christian god. Additionally, as Cabrera's and De la Rosa's cases illuminate, charges of blasphemy carried certain escape clauses that could also be manipulated by those savvy to the technicalities of heresy laws. Almost all slaves charged with blasphemy claimed they hadn't meant to say those words, that the cruelty of their master (or the beating they were receiving) had made them desperate and crazy. Vicente de Paz, like Cabrera, argued in his defense that he had been drunk, "out of his mind, and that he was very sorry for having said it."[54] Nonetheless, such protestations of contrition or insensibility due to pain did little to expiate the crime of blasphemy for slaves brought before the Inquisition. The multiracial residents of Cartagena had likely flocked to the square to watch De Paz at the head of the procession of penitents in the 1638 *auto de fe*, or watched from their doorways as he received one hundred lashes through the city streets—the ceremony of suffering and atonement prescribed for all slaves who dared to use the Lord's name to defy the social order.[55]

Envisioning this spectacle, Isabel must have considered again the care she would have to take in using Spanish legal and religious conventions to protest her mistress's mercilessness. Imagining Isabel Criolla's inner life requires seeing the world through her eyes: what she saw, whom she spoke to, how her experience related to or deviated from that of other enslaved individuals living in isolated urban ports of the seventeenth-century Caribbean. She would have learned—from the people she met, from comparing the structures of the "ideal" Spanish city with the relative disorder of outer *barrios*—that denunciations of cruelty, like performances of religious belonging, called for careful modulation. She would need to capture her judges' moral convictions of how the world *should* be while being careful not to challenge how colonial society really worked.

2 / Imperial Intercession and Master-Slave Relations in Spanish Caribbean Hinterlands

Isabel Criolla's journey to Cartagena likely gave her ample time to think of how she would represent her dilemma and that of the other women in Camargo's control before Cartagena's governor. As an American-born enslaved women, Isabel's life was deeply marked by the processes of creolization that occurred in spaces across the Atlantic World—perhaps especially intense for her, for she had negotiated and survived her subordinate status in Mompox's urban settings and then integrated herself into the very different politics of the maroon enclave.[1] As a creole woman, Isabel may have been especially adept at translating her personal conflicts into larger issues requiring the community's attention; she may have learned from other blacks born in the Americas about Spanish ideas regarding the supposed proper ordering of colonial society, or had seen concrete evidence of others who convinced churchmen, rival elites, or imperial officials to intervene in "disordered" master-slave relationships.[2] Isabel had already done an excellent job persuading Gregorio Álvarez to deviate from his principal responsibilities of recovering runaway slaves for local property owners. Her reference to her mistress's wanton destruction of valuable "pieces of slaves" and her disregard for the spiritual well-being of her human chattel made Álvarez consider his other societal responsibilities to the church and empire. Isabel was so successful that Álvarez seems to have disregarded her long-standing relationship with the maroon communities that threatened public safety and Álvarez's own desire as a property owner to keep his own slaves from knowledge of such "bad influences."

When Isabel was called back to the government buildings on May 18, she knew she must repeat her success with Cartagena's governor. Asked to confirm her earlier testimony about the four slaves of Camargo's who died without confession, Isabel swore it was all true, and she was eager to elaborate. She now added testimony about how Camargo blended her sadism with disordered faith, for after she had ordered the slave women tied down for their daily lashes, Isabel recounted, "her mistress would take her time, praying an entire rosary very slowly, pausing at times to do or order some things, and in that way the said punishment continued."[3] Isabel asserted that they were "dying" in their current estate, and that four more women currently in Camargo's service had seen exactly what she had, but "didn't dare to say it for fear of their said mistress and if they would have said it she would kill them."

This chapter explores several of the groups who participated in defining the boundaries of un-Christian cruelty in colonial Spanish societies. First were slaveholders, whose reputations for Christian respectability were upheld by public opinion, or whose penchant for extreme cruelty scandalized their neighbors. Next were churchmen and imperial representatives who tried to restore peace to a troubled household through moral suasion, and if unsuccessful, by pressing the legal option of re-sale on angry masters. The enslaved participated in the process through their recourse to neighbors and mediators, and by their decisions to stay and fight a moral battle or to flee their tormenters, constantly weighing the consequences of their actions in the balance of power between their master, the community, and outside intervention. As we will see, local oligarchies perhaps played the strongest role in protecting the prerogative of slaveholders. They insulated elites charged with cruelty from outside inquiries—by appealing to personal relationships between clients and patrons, and by intimidating witnesses or encouraging their non-cooperation. Creole elites could, in many instances, dismiss the spiritual resonance of cruelty charges by drawing on their personal power to squelch attempts at imperial intercession.

Isabel alleged that everything she had said "is very public and notorious in the town of Mompox, and everyone knew that in the execution of the cruelties she used with her slaves she had more sophisticated methods to imprison [them] than were in the jail: shackles, handcuffs, and bits to put in their mouths."[4] To give strength to Isabel's claims that Camargo's excessive cruelty was "notorious," two free residents of Mompox, Nicolas de Castrellon and Miguel Navarro, also presented their testimonies to the governor in Cartagena. Castrellon said it was true, it was public knowledge that four of Camargo's female house slaves had died without confession, and that she whipped her slaves "every day of the year," usually for three or four hours at a time—"until she left them with the hides stripped from their bodies and almost dead."[5] Navarro, who lived next door to the Camargo-Ortiz household, recounted that "one day, leaving his house, he heard that [Camargo] was whipping a *negra*, so out of curiosity he stopped underneath a tree near doña Eufrasia's house and began to count the strokes of the whip." Even beginning his count midstream, Navarro tallied a total of 194 or 196 strokes. Navarro's proximity to the scene meant he had gotten personally involved, and he shared the story of how one night a desperate Isabel had knocked on his door, begging him to take off her shackles "because she couldn't take such excessive and long punishment anymore." Navarro admitted that he, "sympathizing with the said Negro, took them off . . . and gave her some *bollos* [a type of bread] and told her to go with God."[6]

Like Navarro's well-wishing salute, the most lurid details that Castrellon gave the judge in Cartagena were those that emphasized Camargo's aberrance from implied Christian norms—like his corroboration of Isabel's tale that her mistress marked their beatings by prayers on the rosary.[7] Castrellon reported that people like his friend, the master carpenter Pedro de Vargas, had shared gossip about how Camargo even forced her slaves to eat their own excrement or to drink cow's bile. Castrellon said that his friend had tried to reprehend Camargo when he witnessed the latter offense, trying to shame her by declaring that "even in Barbary one couldn't use like cruelty."[8] Given the proximity of the *Reconquista* in the Iberian imagination, this reference to the perceived barbarity of North African captivity was one of the strongest rhetorical condemnations one could make. Castrellon continued the characterization of Camargo as a sadist driven by her venomous rages, sharing how she had reacted to the news that Álvarez had merely banished Isabel by calling for the hanging of her renegade slave and demanding the authorities should instead "give her [Isabel's] head to hang in the patio of her house so that the children could throw stones at it, which would make her very pleased and contented." Some of the city's citizens were disturbed by these sentiments, and Castrellon reported that the parish priest Father Francisco Ortiz "Chiquillo" (Jr.) had even offered to pay four hundred or even five hundred pesos in alms to sell Isabel or free her, "moved that [Camargo] not kill the said slave with blows."[9] When news reached doña Eufrasia that Isabel's testimony had led Álvarez to initiate a cruelty investigation, she vowed vengeance, punishing Isabel's daughter Juanita more often, "saying that she would have to pay for her mother."[10]

What compelled Governor Aguilera to continue in this case? He certainly recognized the danger posed by runaways and the need to keep slaves disciplined. But clearly there was something seriously wrong in Camargo's household that raised the question of whether anything could excuse such treatment of the woman before him, her daughter, and others like them. If Aguilera had taken the time to consult with spiritual men of the city, what advice might they have given him? The well-respected Jesuit rector Alonso de Sandoval had written in his treatise that a good Christian slave should "patiently suffer the sorrows and afflictions unjustly caused by the fury of his master."[11] While rejecting the slave's recourse to protest, Sandoval also warned masters to act in all things with paternal moderation, reminding them that God "is the Creator of [both] lords and servants . . . who are of the same nature (*en la naturaleza son iguales*)."[12] Sandoval's associate Father Claver also followed this mixed policy, acting both as an enforcer of the colonial hierarchy and, as his alias suggests, a "saint to the slaves," an intercessor on their behalf. According to one of his close associates, "If [Claver] knew that some Negro or Negress had fought with their master or had been put in jail," he would bring the offending slaves to the Colegio

> where he would [first] scold them very harshly for not paying attention to the service of God and their masters as they ought to; and if in these [cases] there had been anything to reprehend concerning mistreatment that [the masters] gave to their slaves, he also did that (if it was necessary and advisable), using kindness and love, not just reproach. And if it was not possible to attain it [peace/better treatment], he asked them to sell [their slaves] and send them away from this land; for it could be that in another place they could find masters to their liking.[13]

Governor Aguilera must have believed that his intercession was necessary, taking seriously Isabel's claims that her life (and her soul) would be in danger if she were returned to Mompox, for he not only ordered that she remain in Cartagena, he also sent an independent investigator to Mompox to look into these very serious allegations of mistreatment. *Licenciado* Lorenzo de Soto, a royal scribe, was appointed for the task, and he set out on his journey at 5:00 a.m. on May 21, retracing Isabel's steps back to Mompox, carrying with him orders to arrest Eufrasia Camargo, freeze her assets, find any material evidence related to the case, and question witnesses—both those who had already testified in Gregorio Álvarez's preliminary inquest, and anyone else who could confirm or deny Isabel's claims.[14] De Soto had special instructions to bring Isabel Criolla's daughter Juanita back to the capital and report back within twenty days.

Judge de Soto might have boarded a small ship as he embarked on his journey to Mompox, moving skittishly along the Caribbean coast towards the mouth of the Rio Magdalena, where mariners would have to remain alert to the possibility of foreign pirate attacks.[15] Entering the mouth of the Rio Magdalena (also called the Rio Grande for its centrality to regional transportation networks) would have put him at ease, but even in this more placid waterway, he and other passengers might have had occasion to spot one or two small Indian pirogues, vaguely threatening in their silent passages to unmarked inlets along the densely vegetated shoreline.[16] If during the two-day journey he had time to review the *autos*, the bundled collection of testimonies and legal motions related to the case, De Soto might have observed these watercraft with special interest, noting that Mariana Mandinga had escaped to the opposite bank of the Magdalena with the help of Indians.[17]

The crew likely passed many other rafts and other larger watercraft manned by enslaved and free black rowers (*bogas*), who had, since the beginning of the century, replaced Indian guides, their people decimated by disease and the abuses of the *encomienda* system.[18] Such work offered these men of African descent remarkable mobility and an intimate knowledge of the unsettled terrain that bordered the Magdalena. De Soto might have remembered from the case file that Francisco Angola, the maroon leader captured in Álvarez's raid and later executed, had been able to move freely in these waterways as a result of his stint as a sailor in Cartagena, and Juan Arará, before escaping his master to live in the nearby hills "as a vassal of God," had been a *boga* working the Magdalena.[19] Sir Francis Drake had sparked a wave of paranoia about collusion among maroons, Indians, and Protestant pirates after his successes in co-opting both groups in Panama in 1572–1573. Reinforcements from Mompox had gone to the defense of Cartagena in 1597 when "El Draque" threatened to conquer the Spanish there by the same means.[20] Even without such conspiratorial alliances, Cartagena's maroons could disrupt trade routes along the Rio Magdalena, and were feared as a powerful fifth column if slaves in the Zaragoza mines rebelled.[21]

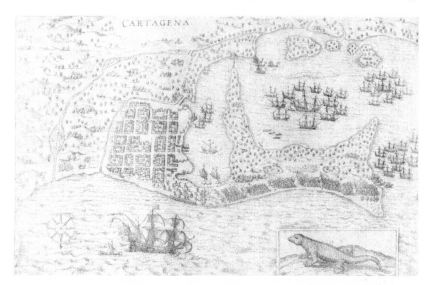

FIGURE 6. Engraved view of Drake's attack of Cartagena by Boazio, 1588. "Expeditio Francisci Draki eqvitis Angli in Indias Occidentales a. M.D.LXXXV." Image courtesy Hans and Hanni Kraus Sir Francis Drake Collection, Library of Congress American Memory Digital Collection.

Indeed, since the mid-sixteenth century, Spanish officials in Cartagena province (as in other regions where slaves had been imported in large numbers, especially in the Caribbean) battled against these communities of African and Afro-creole runaways, termed *palenques* after the stockades they erected to protect residents from outside attack.[22] In 1616, Mompox's mayor (*alcalde ordinario*) Captain Diego Ortiz Nieto, one of the several *encomenderos* who held grants to diminishing Indian labor in the region, had organized an expedition against the threatening maroons, pushing many of them further into the dense forests and rugged mountains back from the Rio Magdalena.[23] In 1631, Gov. Francisco de Murga sent an expedition against a *palenque* "next to the Rio Grande of the Magdalena"—but when the Spanish arrived at the village, the huts and food stores had been abandoned, so they burned the place.[24] Two years later Governor Murga sent out another attack against the maroon stronghold of Limón, located in the mountains of María to the west of the Rio Magdalena. When this expedition succeeded, authorities hung the leaders in the Plaza de Yerba (back in Cartagena, the main square in the lower-class Getsemaní district), then quartered their bodies and displayed their heads at the Puerta de Media Luna (the main portal into

the walled city) as well as back on the principal streets of María.[25] Gregorio Álvarez, who knew the terrain around Mompox due to his frequent
journeys to find runaways, had gleaned from his interrogations in 1639
that there were at least two *palenques* in the region, called Detapia and
Gualmaral, and De Soto may have talked with other passengers about
the likelihood of attack.

When Lorenzo de Soto safely disembarked and entered the town of
Santa Cruz de Mompox, he may have noticed that this lively port city
bore at least some resemblance to Cartagena. By virtue of its strategic
position along the Rio Magdalena, Mompox was another imperial thor-
oughfare through which Spain funneled its material goods and officials
towards the large administrative centers of the Kingdoms of Santa Fe
(Bogotá) and Quito.[26] It was also a thriving center for contraband, and
between legal and extralegal trade, its residents had accumulated great
wealth.[27] Governors appointed to cities upstream from Mompox were
daily migrants in the flow; priests, too, made the journey to Santa Fe de
Bogotá for study in its university, as did Pedro Claver in 1613, returning
again to Cartagena through Mompox in 1616. Spain's religious institutions thrived in the city—secular clergy there directed the activities of
27 parishes reaching down to Cáceres in Antioquia, and an Augustin-
ian convent had been in place since 1606. In 1611, just one year after the
founding of Cartagena's Inquisition, a *comisario* had been appointed in
Mompox to oversee the referral of heretics there to the Holy Tribunal
for justice.[28] Intimately tied to imperial and Caribbean religious and
commercial networks, Mompox needed to be brought under control,
disorder punished in order to ensure security.

A royal investigator bringing an arrest warrant for doña Eufrasia Camargo must have been quite the event for residents of Mompox, for as
Álvarez had hinted in his letter to Governor Aguilera, the lady was no
ordinary citizen. Reconstructing her family connections cited in this
case and information from local histories showed that Camargo was
clearly part of Mompox's oligarchy. Her father had arranged marriages
for two of his daughters, joining them to the venerable Ortiz and Nieto
families (surnames also prominent among Cartagena's elite): doña Eufrasia had married don Alonso Esteban Ortiz and Eufrasia's sister Ventura wed don Alonso's cousin, Captain Diego Ortiz Nieto.[29] Despite her
status, Judge De Soto recorded that he arrested doña Eufrasia the same
day he arrived, and detained her in one of the riverside warehouses belonging to don Pedro Sanchez Dominguez, ordering her to remain there
or pay a penalty of one thousand pesos, finally placing an embargo on

the sale of her goods.[30] There was no time to spare—De Soto had much more to do.

Next, to corroborate the maroon woman's testimony, he set out to find the other women that Isabel Criolla had cited as fellow servants of Camargo. Lorenzo de Soto first questioned Mariana Mandinga and Susana Angola a second time (they had already given statements after they were captured in the mountains by Gregorio Álvarez), and then took the statements of Gracia Conga and Inez Criolla. Sworn in by the sign of the cross, all of the women confirmed Isabel's story of the "rigorous punishments" their mistress regularly ordered, and which sometimes lasted over an hour, "their feet and hands tied to a chair, and with a whip and crop made of very hard rawhide."[31]

Because the testimony of slaves was often inadmissible against their masters, De Soto needed more than just the women's version of events. Just like the *alcalde* Gregorio Álvarez had done to confirm Mariana's and Susana's testimony when they were captured, De Soto recorded the results of his own visual inspection of Inez Criolla, noting that she carried fairly fresh ulcers and that "in some parts her body [appeared] dappled, and the buttocks carried even more marks [showing] where the black flesh had taken off."[32] We should be wary of reading such recognitions of bodily pain as positive confirmation of the slave's humanity in the eyes of the state—such comments also show the observer's subconscious categorization of the enslaved as little more than a "criminal(ized), wounded body, or mortified flesh."[33] These recordings of de Soto's visual examinations of Inez and other enslaved women, written down and preserved in the colonial archive, served as a form of surveillance and display of imperial power over the bodies and fortunes of all its subjects. Furthermore, although de Soto was charged with seeking justice in cases like Isabel Criolla's and Juana Zamba's, he did so by stripping the enslaved woman of their markers of Christian modesty: "forcing her to uncover herself" for an "*inspección ocular*"[34] was the only way to verify the master's crime and consider (with the appraising eye of the white male authority) the extent and severity of damage to the enslaved body and thus to the commonwealth.

As Judge de Soto's questioning continued, all four slave women testified to the depths of their physical and psychological torment. In more than one statement, when the judge asked why they were punished, he heard that Camargo's whippings were ordered out of minor incidents of everyday dissatisfaction. Mariana said that her mistress "had no better reason to punish them than to say that the *bollos* that the said Catalina made for the slaves were poorly ground, and said that the said Phe-lipa . . . washed [the clothes] badly, and for the others, whatever they did in the kitchen or with the sewing, and for other trifles."[35] They also testi-fied that the four slave women who had perished in Camargo's service—Phelipa Angola, Catalina Conga, Sebastiana Criolla, and Isabel Angola—had been treated with equal severity prior to their deaths. Nevertheless, under questioning, several of the enslaved women, beaten down by the years of unjustified torture, parroted to the investigator their mistress's "official" reasons for their fellow workers' deaths (just as a few almost believed that their beatings were just punishments for poor work). Inez testified that she had been forced to endure one of the most humiliat-ing acts, saying that her mistress "had also subjected her to another se-vere and disgusting punishment, which is that many times while being whipped, unable to bear [it], she had soiled herself, and [doña Eufrasia] had made her put the filth in her mouth."[36] The women spoke of their mental and physical exhaustion, and how their attempts at flight proved only a temporary release, for Mariana said that they were treated with even "more rigor" after they were caught again.[37]

Three women testified they had become so desperate that they had turned to eating dirt, which they did because "it was understood that later they would fall down dead (de susto)."[38] Inez said she and the others ate dirt to escape from "the continuous and very severe punishments . . . in-stead of throwing themselves in the river, as they had many times been desperate to do." Slaveholders throughout the Americas portrayed dirt-eating as pathological and unhealthy—resulting in weakness, swelling of the body, general despondency, infertility, and even death. They feared that the practice was a deliberate attempt by slaves (at the very least, a pernicious custom brought from Africa) to deter slaveholders' economic goals and personal authority.[39] Mariana, Inez, and Susana supported this interpretation by testifying to their deliberate choice to seek an end to their tortured lives. But only Susana Angola linked their actions to a Christian framework, saying that they preferred this prolonged death to drowning themselves in the river, for "by this method they would have the opportunity to confess as Christians."[40] Like Isabel, Susana seems to have recognized the value in pointing out her own desire to die as a bap-tized Christian, to have one last chance to confess her "sin" of despera-tion. However, De Soto strangely neglected to investigate deeply on is-sues relating to Camargo's or her slave women's "Christianity." Inez, the other creole slave in the household, was the only one questioned about her mistress's use of the rosary as a disciplinary device, and she claimed ignorance of the specific event, saying that from the room where she worked she couldn't see into the corridor where doña Eufrasia sat and listened while whippings were being performed outside.[41] The enslaved women, wisely perhaps, were reluctant to categorically denounce their mistress for the unconsecrated deaths of Phelipa, Catalina, Sebastiana, and Isabel Angola—uncertain of the judge's ability to do anything to change their situation. Gracia did say that both Phelipa and Catalina had died "suddenly." But Sebastiana, she said, had died from a bout of dysentery (*cámaras*), not from mistreatment; Isabel Angola had also died of natural causes, exposed to shock (*pasmo*) after rising too soon from her bed after birthing a child. Gracia added that it was possible that Phelipa also died of shock and not from the beatings.[42] Mariana said that Sebastiana had confessed before her illness overcame her.[43] These technical, overly specific answers convey not only Camargo's authority to dictate the ostensible reasons for her slaves' deaths, but also the women's underlying fears of the consequences of their testimony if they were returned to Camargo's power in the future.

When De Soto turned to the question of Camargo's husband don Alonso Esteban's involvement in the whippings, the women's caution was heightened. Inez said their master sometimes stopped punishments when he was at home, and never whipped them himself;[44] likewise, Susana said he never ordered them punished, and would even take off their chains at times, providing some measure of relief when he was around.[45] However, no one elaborated on *why* Ortiz was relatively protective—none of the women offered in-depth answers, and De Soto did not press for answers. Here again the specter of sexual coercion and the shameful connotations of sexual sin take the form of repressed silence and complicity. Sharon Block has employed an analysis of the "strength of mastery" in her study of the rape of enslaved women to describe how masters could redefine rape as consent—forcing enslaved women to choose between assent and any series of unacceptable options: separation from their children, threats of physical violence, etc.[46] This same "strength of mastery" and narrative privilege belonged to mistresses like Camargo who, concealing their rage at sexual relationships between their husbands and enslaved women, could reinterpret the torture and punishment they inflicted on black women as legitimate chastisement for poor work or a disrespectful attitude.

After so many inconclusive answers about Camargo's responsibility for her former slaves' deaths, a surprise witness suddenly appeared. Another of doña Eufrasia's slaves—Isabel Criolla's son Pedro—approached

De Soto to admit that he had recently run away from the city, leaving his mistress's home in order to avoid a whipping that Camargo had ordered for a minor youthful transgression (he had snuck away "to the plaza to watch a bullfight"). Evidence of the speed at which news traveled from Mompox into the maroon-controlled hinterland, Pedro said that he had come out of hiding when he heard that a judge was taking testimonies about the deaths and punishments enacted by his mistress. Although the women who regularly faced Camargo's wrath were wont to downplay her responsibility (suggesting that at least some of their former comrades, though poorly treated, had died of natural causes), Pedro did not equivocate. He stated clearly that although Isabel Angola had died of "shock" (*pasmo*) shortly after giving birth, she bore ulcers from whippings "between her legs," and those were the reason for her demise without confession. Likewise, Sebastiana had been overcome by dysentery (*cámaras*), but he blamed the "beatings and captivity" his mistress ordered as the cause of the "mortal . . . illness."[47] Pedro confirmed that all of doña Eufrasia's female slaves bore many scars on their "back and buttocks and legs"—scars he was all too familiar with because he had been forced to whip them almost every day, watching their tortured bodies swell with "pestilent sores." At the end of his statement, Pedro beseeched De Soto "for the love of God" to protect him from the cruelty of his mistress.[48] Pedro's confident denunciation serves as a contrast to the cautious testimony of the other enslaved women, who had been beaten down by the years of unjustified torture—though deep down they must have recognized that those "trifles" didn't merit their ultimate punishment. As an enslaved man, Pedro did not have to suffer the sexual advances of the master nor his mistress's subsequent rage. Although he had always protected himself by complying with Camargo's demands that he use his strength against her latest victims, he now knew he could escape and survive—perhaps he hoped that his strength of testimony might avenge the abuses of his mother, sister, and his other *compatriotas*, still so fearful for their own safety.

When Judge De Soto turned to white Momposinos for help in figuring out the case, he found his path blocked at every turn. As part of Lorenzo de Soto's administrative seizure of Eufrasia Camargo's goods, he had searched her and her husband's homes for chains and shackles, but could find none.[49] De Soto was probably warned of this difficulty beforehand—when he had questioned the slave women about Camargo's modes of punishment and imprisonment, several noted that their mistress borrowed her disciplinary tools, especially the stocks, from neighbors and family members.[50] What was more, many of them said they hadn't seen the tools of their torture lying around recently—Inez said she understood that some of her mistress's slaves had hidden them.[51] Word got out that Eufrasia's sister, Ventura de Camargo, had urged that some townspeople find and hide the evidence. De Soto followed the gossip trail to question Inez Noble, a free *mulata*, who admitted that she had secreted two chests holding the "iron chains and shackles" from doña Eufrasia's dispensary with the help of the enslaved woman Dominga Conga, another witness who had apparently escaped De Soto's first inventory of Camargo's seized property (including household slaves).[52] Inez testified that she took the box to the kitchen of next-door neighbor doña Andrea de Varela, the wife of another *regidor* of Mompox, and then one of doña Eufrasia's nieces came to tell doña Andrea to send the boxes to the house of doña Ventura, Eufrasia's sister. Obstructing justice was nothing new in the battles between local elites and imperial administrators; patronage networks between upper-class Spaniards, their servants, and other clients often served to hinder royal investigations into colonial malfeasance.[53]

Though Lorenzo de Soto threatened legal action against Ventura Camargo, and even threw some of the offenders in jail, he could get no one to turn in the concealed evidence.[54] Several days later, he decided to follow the trail himself to search among the wooden beams being used to construct a wall on doña Ventura's property—there De Soto found "an iron chain fifteen *varas* in length and a ring of a screw (*una argolla de tornillo*) to pin to the foot, and a nail with which to fasten a ring around the neck (*para canpanilla*), and some shackles, but nothing more."[55] His efforts to seek out more witnesses with knowledge of the case were equally frustrating. The one person De Soto was able to compel to testify was master carpenter Pedro Vargas, who had been cited in Nicolas Castrellon's statement made in Cartagena. A close reading of the testimony reveals Vargas's caution in his phrasing. The artisan affirmed that yes, he had seen all four of Camargo's slave women in chains and bearing fresh wounds; and yes, she had a reputation for being cruel. However, he averred, she only punished her slaves for running away or for being careless in carrying out her orders. Yes, he answered, he had seen them being whipped, but couldn't say for sure how long the beatings lasted. Yes, he said, he had once seen Camargo make one of her slaves drink bile—as a remedy for eating dirt—but had never even heard that she forced her slaves to eat their own excrement.[56] Far from Castrellon's retelling of Vargas's brave confrontation of Camargo for her cruel and un-Christian treatment—"even in Barbary one couldn't use like cruelty"[57]—the master carpenter, subjected to colonial rules of deference to the "dons" and "doñas" of Mompox, seems to have been unwilling to register any stronger sentiments to an outsider.

As for earlier reports that the "whole town" knew of Camargo's cruelty, that may have been the case, but no one was talking—not even Father Ortiz, who allegedly had himself offered to redeem Isabel from the hell of her mistress's household. Spanish high officials charged with special investigations of colonial elites were largely ineffective given the imbedded loyalties of local politics and power. Even with all the force of Church law, civil law, and Cartagena's governor behind him, De Soto's attempt to get to the truth of Camargo's cruelty was compromised by the community's greater fear of what might happen to them personally if they were to cross the powerful Camargo-Ortiz families.

3 /   Law, Religion, Social Contract, and Slavery's Daily Negotiations

By the time Lorenzo de Soto returned to Cartagena to deliver his report to the governor, news had yet to reach the Americas that earlier that year, Pope Urban VIII had publicly condemned the slave trade, calling it "a means to deprive men of their liberty."[1] His decree echoed medieval conceptions of the foundational importance of freedom: "All creatures in the world naturally love and desire liberty, and much more do men, who have intelligence superior to that of the others, and especially such as are of noble minds, desire it."[2] The *Siete Partidas* had long asserted that although slavery was a condition "contrary to natural reason," it had been used since ancient times as an alternative to executing war captives, and as it became part of social custom, slavery became a hereditary status, passed on from enslaved women to their children.[3] The papacy had generally viewed participation in the Atlantic slave trade as an opportunity to Christianize "pagans" in Africa. But Pope Urban's remarks had potentially radical ramifications, for they suggested that the African slave trade was not dealing in legitimate war captives, and thus intimated that its Catholic participants were responsible for rationalizing a moral evil. Although we tend to think of papal decrees as mandates accepted without question (especially by the "most Catholic" Spanish monarchy), history tells us that Urban VIII's denunciation of the slave trade had little effect.

Indeed, although mostly silent today, it is important to know that Spanish American slavery in the early seventeenth century prompted

numerous moral, legal, and physical negotiations. The master-slave social contract was not only based on multiple legal interpretations, but
was compounded by the religious and economic localism of Spanish
American colonies, which pitted peninsular officials against American
creoles, and the hierarchical prerogatives of state and household man-
agement against more generous mandates of Christian charity. Struggles
over the definition of this social contract also took place on the ground,
in daily exchanges—physical and verbal—between slaves and their owners. Arguments written down by lawyers and powerful churchmen who
were interested in the question of slavery are our most direct evidence for
this process, but everyday confrontations also worked to define ideas of
the acceptable treatment of Christian slaves by their Christian masters.

After Bartolomé de las Casas's famous denunciation of Amerindian
enslavement, some Spanish jurists and theologians had written skeptical
inquiries into the "just conquest" and enslavement of Africans. Nonetheless, their occasional denunciations of the growing trade in African
slaves never reached the same level of public acclaim.[4] Cartagena's Jesuit
rector Alonso de Sandoval was one of those who admitted that he had
been "perplexed for a long time" on the question of whether the Africans
shipped to his city had been captured in just wars; he read the works of
prominent jurists like Luis de Molina to try to help inform his counsel to
sailors and shipmasters who came to him with a "troubled conscience"
regarding what they had seen in their slave trading voyages.[5] In his 1627
treatise, Sandoval explained how he tried to answer his doubts by way of
inquiry into the international Jesuit networks of his day, writing in 1610
to Father Luis Brandão, Rector of the Jesuit College in Luanda, Angola.
Father Brandão assured Sandoval that he should shake off his scruples in
the matter, denying that the commerce in African slaves had ever been
considered illicit by anyone "of good conscience" in Portugal, not even
the learned bishops and educated Jesuits who had visited the African
entrêpots of San Tomé, Cape Verde, and Luanda. The Luandan rector
may or may not have been telling the whole truth, but his condescend-
ing response to Sandoval's earnestness reveals commonly accepted Iberian beliefs about the legality of enslaving Africans as captives of "just
war." Brandão wrote: "no Negro will admit to be a just captive, so may
Your Reverence not ask them whether they are fair captives or not, because they will always say they were stolen or captured under a bad title,
understanding that in this way their liberty will be granted." Though
acknowledging that some slaves were likely procured through illicit
means, Father Brandão asserted that it would be impossible to search

out innocent victims among the thousands who left port annually, and it "seemed [to him] not to be much to the service of God" to pursue justice for so few when so many more souls could be saved in sending Africans to Christian lands.[6] Father Sandoval continued to discuss the theological justifications of European trade in African slaves with other clerics he knew to have first-hand knowledge of the issue,[7] but he seems to have implicitly accepted Father Brandão's reasoning. When composing his treatise for publication, Sandoval suppressed his own struggles of conscience and encouraged others to do the same, concluding his brief statement on conscience in his tract by stating simply: "it will be good that we maintain circumspection and reserve in this problematic business. . . ."[8] Adriana Maya, a Colombian scholar of the African-descendant community in colonial New Granada, has asserted that Sandoval's regular allusions to the "monstrosity" of African bodies and souls, and his belief that Christianization offered their only hope for salvation, effectively contributed to the era's "deafening silence" on the issue of just war and African enslavement.[9]

As Isabel Criolla's case confirms, Iberian secular and canon law's multiple interventions into the master-slave relationship afforded slaves the opportunity to seek the assistance of local authorities in cases of severe cruelty to "investigate and ascertain whether the charge is true," and to punish an excessively cruel master by selling his slaves "in such a way that they never can be again placed in the power" of the master.[10] Canon law afforded similar protections, and offered sanctuary for those escaping violent conflict. In Juana Zamba's bid to secure her freedom, her lawyer pointed out to the governor that "the slave has the right to betake himself to the church [in case of] the cruelty of the master and enjoy its asylum (*ymmunidad*)," and that a slave could be set free as compensation if there were any person or persons willing to pay the price of his or her sale. Juana's lawyer planned to appeal the case's initial dismissal by proving that Juana's mistress had kept her locked up in the house, preventing her from engaging in the Christian duty of confession during Holy Week—both offenses against the Church for which masters could be held accountable.[11]

In these practices of competing discernment and legal intervention in the master-slave relationship, local representatives of Church and State held enormous power. Not surprisingly, in attempting to contravene the "complete authority" of masters over slaves by enforcing this clause in the law, these officials could evoke the ire of local property owners. We already heard how Eufrasia Camargo railed against Gregorio Álvarez's circumvention of her rights over Isabel Criollo; her husband also filed a brief in an attempt to override the *alcalde*'s decision to send the slave to Cartagena. Strident legal battles over the right to jurisdiction were commonplace in the Spanish Americas, and were especially ferocious when it came to the right to control labor. Creole Spaniards had defended their right to determine the proper course of action in the far-away Americas, propounding the legal fiction of "I obey but do not comply" (*Obedesco pero no cumplo*) since the first days of conquest.

When Judge De Soto returned to Cartagena, he found the defendant busy trying to find a way to assert her rights as a slaveholder. Doña Eufrasia had contracted a lawyer with a proven track record—her choice, Diego de Horozco, had successfully defended Juana Zamba's mistress, Catalina Pimienta Pacheco, in her 1634 bid to retain control over her human chattel when accused of excessive cruelty. Horozco immediately petitioned for his client's freedom of movement, secured copies of the case file against her, and arranged for her to testify in her own defense.[12] In Camargo's statement to the governor, she categorically denied Isabel's accusations, countering that she punished only those slaves who "were runaways or thieves, or to avoid offenses against God," and that her punishments were absolutely routine and ordinary. In Horozco's written briefs defending his client, he argued that there were practical distinctions between the state of slave society "in the Indies," and the forms of enslavement legislated in Europe. The main difference, he said, was that

> ... in these parts, the Indies ... there is no service by freedmen, and the forced labor of slaves must be used ... [therefore] it is advisable to keep them subject and under pressure, not only for the public good and the conservation of the state of Spaniards (*vecinos* and naturals of the Indies), but in particular for [the sake of] their very own masters ... [who] run the risk of their lives. Other unfortunate mutinies and uprisings could occur if they do not keep them subject, under pressure and punished, even with greater rigor (apart from their lives and Christian piety) than that which their offenses normally merit.[13]

Horozco cited legal precedents in Peru and New Spain that allowed for severe punishments.[14] He pointed out to Governor Aguilera that not only was it lawful to have chains to keep slaves restrained, but it was customary in this region.[15] Juana Zamba's mistress had bolstered this argument in her own statement of defense, testifying that it would set a bad precedent if "runaway and thieving slaves" could be allowed to get away with their crimes.[16] Nearly everyone among the Spanish elite agreed. Franciscan preacher Father Geronimo de Chavez defended his friend Eufrasia Camargo by testifying that in his many years of experience in the Indies, "he knows . . . that if the Negro slaves are not kept occupied by their masters, they are no good for service . . . in order to have service from them it is necessary to be very careful and vigilant with them."[17] Camargo's lawyer capitalized on this perception, reminding the court that slaves were considered "false by nature and liars, easily conspiring," and that in legal terms, officials couldn't "give credit" to accusations against their masters because of the "foremost hatred (*odio capital*)" they held for their social superiors."[18]

But the case was also about Camargo's negligence in her obligations to uphold her duties as a Christian head of household, and the governor had a responsibility to his imperial master as "Most Catholic King." Camargo responded vigorously to these charges—she first gestured to her honor, the biggest card in her favor. She asserted that she was "not only the daughter of Old Christians and nobles (*hidalgos*), but [also] a good Christian, fearful of God and her conscience; neither through fault nor negligence would she let her slaves die without confession."[19] Answering to the specific details of each case, Camargo testified that a confessor had been brought to Sebastiana's bedside when it appeared she would not recover from the dysentery that had weakened her to the point of death, and that she had done the same when Isabel Angola became ill (though she admitted that Isabel's state of shock (*pasmo*) had kept her from the act of confession by the time the priest arrived). Confession had also been impossible in the death of Phelipa Angola, who doña Eufrasia alleged "fell down dead [suddenly], just talking in the kitchen with her *compañeras*." She had an excuse for Catalina Angola's exclusion from last rites, for Catalina had hung herself "without anyone giving her cause for it, unless she was tricked by the devil."[20] Indeed, Camargo's lawyers filed court papers from 1621, confirming that an enslaved woman named Catalina had taken her own life shortly after an unsuccessful attempt at escape. By shifting the responsibility for Catalina's desperate suicide from the brutal treatment she endured to the perceived susceptibility of Africans to the forces of evil, doña Eufrasia engaged in the most common strategy for slaveholders to contest church and imperial efforts to limit their power of mastery, citing the cultural superiority of Christian Europeans to justify legal liberties.[21]

Just as elite creole Spaniards contested the coercive powers of the imperial Catholic order as they tried to shape laws "in the Indies" to suit their purposes, smaller-scale contests over proper treatment occurred every day between masters and slaves, and both groups used legal arguments to attempt to control the other. We can reconstruct how these everyday struggles were played out by closely reading the Inquisition and secular cases included in this chapter—in descriptions of confrontations that led to legal action, we can see how slaves actively contested their masters' justifications for punishment. Both Juana Zamba's and Isabel Criolla's cases expose everyday negotiations with parish priests or wealthy neighbors who they thought might intercede, either through purchase or sponsorship in legal action. Furthermore, in confrontations that led to blasphemy trials before the Inquisition, slaves verbally called upon the Christian god and his representatives to intercede, to set down limitations on those acts of violence and cruelty that their masters tried to uphold as customary.

One element of these daily contestations can be seen in slaves' familiarity with a provision in the "Law of Bayonne" (*Ley de Bayona*), which appears to have allowed masters to tie slaves to a chair or ladder to restrain them in the course of a whipping.[22] Knowledge of this particular law suggests that legal contestation was not only the purview of lawyers and their courtroom briefs, but rather was something debated in daily life—when slaves protested the cruelty of their bondage and the force of the lash on their bodies, masters responded by citing the legal codes that authorized their physical domination. In Isabel Criolla's first declaration to the governor of Cartagena, she alleged that her mistress's unprovoked beatings were normally performed by binding them "to a chair *according to the law of Bayonne.*"[23]

References to this particular law show up frequently enough to suggest that such debates were part of everyday life—even African-born slaves learned about the law's parameters. In 1633, the freeborn black Domingo Canga came forward voluntarily to Cartagena's Inquisition Tribunal to confess that he had renounced God when Father Antonio de Cifuentes, who tried to claim him as a slave, had ordered that he receive three hundred lashes, first binding him "according to the Law of Bayonne." When Father Cifuentes further called to someone else to bring "a cane with molten tar . . . to tar him," Domingo resorted to blasphemy to protest what he saw as cruel and undeserved punishment which broke the boundaries of reason and justice.[24] Based on both Isabel's and Domingo's experience, it seems that when slaves challenged their masters to explain the legitimacy of their severe punishments, their masters would invoke their rights stipulated under the Law of Bayonne. If slaves felt that the punishments they were ordered to receive were illegitimate or went beyond the letter or spirit of this law, they could appeal to a higher power, calling their own masters to judgment for their moral transgressions against the social contract.

In fact, slaves regularly utilized narratives of their membership in the Christian community as a verbal reprimand in their daily confrontations with their masters, especially to challenge slave owners' physical domination and torture of their bodies. In the first place, slaves could verbally press for a master's attention and better treatment by invoking "the love of God and the Virgin" in their pleas to rein in violence.[25] Eufrasia Camargo's female slaves told Judge De Soto how they often beseeched their mistress with these symbols of Christian charity, and both Isabel Criolla and her son used the same language in their appeals to the Spanish judges. Blasphemy cases before the Inquisition provide even more numerous instances. Juan Antonio, a Christianized Berber slave who had been denounced in Panama, related in his first audience that, "his master cruelly punishing him, he asked him to let him be, for the love of God . . . "[26] These appeals show how slaves tried to ward off their pain and desperation by calling upon the most-respected symbols of the Christian faith to protect them from their masters' disorderly, warped rage, acts that they tried to masquerade as legal chastisement.

When such appeals to Christian compassion didn't provide results, renouncing the Christian god became a powerful curse against him who allowed such treatment to persist. Both European and African cultures remained deeply defined by the power of oral speech, especially as it related to magic and religiosity.[27] The Inquisition's punishments of those who dared curse their God illustrate their recognition of the symbolic power of such blasphemies. Unlike the everyday blasphemies and renunciations that slipped from the mouths of ordinary citizens every day, slaves' blasphemies were considered a serious offense against the faith "because they derived from 'a desire to obtain revenge.'"[28] Even if slaves later claimed that their statements didn't come "from the heart" or were made when they were "beside themselves" with pain or anger (both reasons that lessened the power of blasphemous oaths), their actions nonetheless challenged the social order of the Christian god.

As we have seen, renunciation cases often had as much to do with on-the-ground power plays as they did with appeals to the supernatural. Juan Chico, an enslaved tailor owned by Francisco López Nieto, a notary working for Cartagena's Inquisition, was so abused by his master that Chico tried to bargain with his master to be sold to another. When once their confrontation escalated to the point where Nieto ordered his slave chained and muzzled as punishment, Juan told his owner to release him, "or if not, he would have to renounce [God]." Later, before inquisitors, Chico claimed that he had blasphemed out of desperation, "not in the sprit of renunciation but only to free himself from the things he was suffering."[29] During the trial it came out that this was Chico's second blasphemy offense in a decade—Chico complained that he had been subject to constant "bad treatment" during this time period, and the lawyer assigned to him by inquisitors actually went to the trouble of questioning 15 witnesses, some of whom agreed that Chico's blasphemies had been the result of his maltreatment. This case seems to have been one of very few cases where inquisitors deviated from their standard punishment of one hundred to two hundred lashes and public shaming—although Chico was ordered to receive one hundred lashes in public, his master was also ordered to sell him away from the city.[30] Another slave who was spared lashes and later banished from Cartagena (a *de facto* way of ordering a slave to be sold) was a Berber slave from Portobelo, whose master responded to his pleas "for the love of God" to leave off whipping him so cruelly with an equally passionate reply, "saying to the Negro who was whipping him, 'Give it to this dog until he renounces [God].'"[31] Juana Zamba's lawyer had argued that in fact, cruelty among masters was such a grievous problem that it led to death "and many renunciations and blasphemies against God our Lord, of which the Holy Tribunal of the Inquisition has seen fit to punish in the sight of the entire city."[32]

Several scholars of these blasphemy cases have noted that "in the case of renunciation, the spoken word became one more weapon in the [slave's] resistance against the dehumanization" that led to their enslavement.[33] Since inquisitors were slaveholders, too, they were naturally concerned by slaves' use of this stratagem to resist their subjugation. When inquisitors heard the blasphemy case of a *mulato* named Salvador in 1627, his audacity towards his master became a matter for discussion. Salvador had allegedly addressed those administering his lashing with a veiled threat, saying "Leave me be—don't make me say more of those crazy things (*disparates*) like I said on the ranch (*en la estancia*), because if you whip me I'll have to say them." In tribunals throughout the Iberian world, inquisitors were conflicted about how to deal with these threats from subordinates, realizing that "black and mulatto slaves renounce [God] and blaspheme in order to put fear into their masters when they punish them."[34] In reports to the Suprema in 1619, 1627, and 1628, Cartagena's inquisitors remarked that it was unfortunately still frequent "in these parts" that slaves like Salvador used "this infernal means to tie [their masters'] hands and are not punished."[35] After 1654, the solution seems to have been to move these penitents to private *autos de fe* to reduce the visibility of the strategem, punishing slaves the same as ever.[36] Despite the Inquisition's continued severity in punishing this deliberate blasphemy, slaves continued to use the Inquisition as a weapon against their masters when other alternatives proved futile—until around the 1670s the Tribunal simply stopped prosecuting slaves for this particular crime against the faith, leaving the matter of punishment in the hands of masters.[37]

Beyond the religious negotiations of everyday master-slave struggles and the creolization that provided enslaved individuals with the tools of protest, this investigation of Isabel's legal battle has hinted at how enslaved individuals in the Spanish Americas coped with physical pain, the struggle against desperation, and the tragedy of despair. For most Spaniards of the seventeenth century, cruelty and barbarism in enslavement were cognitively related to Barbary captivity—the fear of being stolen away and sold as a slave to a Muslim master on the other side of the Mediterranean Sea, where Christians might be tempted to apostatize to Islam to escape the daily torments of their degradation and slavery. For this reason, even in the Americas, the psychological weight of cruelty and sadism was applied almost exclusively to these powerful enemy, religious Others. Only in extreme cases could it be applied to Christians.[38] But for slaves in the Americas, none could look forward to the arrival of an African merchant, envoy, or religious organization to redeem them from captivity.[39]

In the Iberian West Indies, selling Africans into slavery was not the legacy of religious crusading, but was rather a business dominated by Christians, defined by royal monopolies and international trade networks. In this world, although the transport of Africans to the New World was tied at least rhetorically to a Christian mission, they had become defined primarily as commodities in Caribbean ports like Cartagena. When witnesses were questioned in Juana Zamba's case, one elite Cartagenero remarked that the slave's deceased master, Portuguese merchant Captain Julio Evangelista, had a strict policy of disciplining his slaves "with moderation—since they cost him his money he would not wish that they would run the risk of their lives."[40] The danger in cases of excessive cruelty was less about the risk to the soul of the enslaved than a loss of profitability (for the owner) or the good order and security of the larger society (for the empire).

Enslaved individuals like Isabel Criolla rejected their commodification when they held up their souls to public view. Whether demonstrated as Isabel's direct appeal to her captor, an act of humble ingratiation with a churchman who could act as an intercessor in a tumultuous household, or in blasphemous tirades against the Christian god who allowed their masters to treat them with inhumanity, the overlapping legal systems of Spanish colonialism opened "jurisdictional breach[es which] provided Africans and their descendants with opportunities to navigate the households, institutions, and imposed practices that were intent on defining them as chattel, vassals, and Christians."[41] Called before Gregorio Álvarez de Zepeda to be judged for her marronage, Isabel Criolla saw a breach instead of a judgment, an opportunity to record her grievances for posterity. Educated in the fundamentals of Christian morality, she understood how to craft an effective "pardon tale"—by declaring in the most evocative, persuasive way she knew how about her belief in the white man's god, and the certain loss of her soul if she were to become a slave to Eufrasia Camargo once again.[42]

In the end, Governor Aguilera handed down his judgment on September 15, 1639, in the "complaint and criminal case against doña Eufrasia de Camargo regarding the rigorous punishments and maltreatment of her slaves, of which have resulted the deaths of some of them without confession and the other sacraments," finding doña Camargo culpable in two of the four deaths, fining her four hundred pesos. As for the female witnesses still considered Camargo's legal property, Aguilera ruled that Gracia, Susana, Inez, and Mariana should all be sold in the Mompox marketplace, with strict orders not to be returned to her power; Isabel and her daughter Juana were to be sold in Cartagena, at a greater distance from the vindictive reach of their former mistress.[43] Notwithstanding this favorable outcome, Eufrasia Camargo still held remarkable power—she appealed the case to the Superior Court of New Granada, which moderated the ruling in favor of Camargo's property rights. Although warning her to act humanely in the future towards the four slave women from her household who had testified in the case—or be "severely castigated"—the superior court overturned the ruling requiring her to sell the four women who had been witnesses, and also allowed that Isabel and her *mulata* daughter might be sold "in the town of Mompox or where [Camargo] might see fit." The only physical protection Isabel and Juanita would be granted was that of being deposited "with a person of honor" in the interim.[44]

Such a ruling offered no guarantees that Isabel and her daughter would remain clear of Camargo's abusive hand, or if they did, that their future master would be kinder. Would doña Eufrasia still try to ensure that she would see the "blood and bones" of the rebellious Isabel? Would one of don Alonso's relatives purchase the mother and daughter together, or might they be separated in retaliation for Isabel's brazen attempt to disrupt the social order in Mompox? Would Isabel try to escape again and take her daughter with her to one of the *palenques*? Depending on the good will and consistent enforcement of Church and imperial law by local officials was always a gamble—after all, churchmen and colonial officials were usually embedded in elite networks of patronage, many of them slaveholders who also had a stake in protecting their property prerogatives. Gracia, Susana, Inez, and Mariana had been right to equivocate in their testimony to Judge De Soto, wary of what fate awaited them if Camargo escaped punishment in time to avenge her public humiliation.

One can imagine how swiftly the news traveled from Cartagena to Mompox, up and down the Magdalena, after Governor Aguilera pronounced the good news for Isabel, Juana, Mariana, Gracia, Inez, and Susana—and then the sobering news months later when the higher court restored several of the women to Camargo's control. As slaves shared the stories of successes and failures to take advantage of juridical opportunities, they also shared advice about other alternatives. In a region marked by constant movement, slaves and ex-slaves also spread the news about the best ways to take control of their lives, whether as part of Spanish colonial society or outside of it. They could follow Isabel Criolla's example, and take their chances with the institutions that claimed to speak for the Spaniard's all-powerful god. Or they could reject the Christianity that defined their domination, cursing the Spaniards' god and his saints, and the baptism that dictated their obedience—redefining "blasphemy" as a sacred act that called the gods to witness their suffering.

But in the Spanish Caribbean hinterlands, simply evading one's master was often the easiest and best option. Bustling urban circum-Caribbean cities like Cartagena de Indias or Mompox presented multiple opportunities for mobility and escape. Juana Zamba had absented herself temporarily from her mistress's service, first in the rural outskirts of the city, then sheltered in the home of a sympathetic clergyman in the urban center itself. Isabel Criolla and others, knowing they could not hide for long in the smaller city of Mompox, sought a more permanent escape from their sufferings. Isabel ran away repeatedly until she found her home among the maroons, and stayed among them for eleven years before her recapture. Near the end of Eufrasia Camargo's trial, Isabel's son, Pedro Criollo, absconded from Mompox a second time. While the investigation proceeded, Pedro had been briefly imprisoned "for some thefts," but he soon evaded captivity. Most of the townspeople believed that Pedro had gone to "the savannas of Tolu" to find employment in the wide-open prairie ranches.[45]

Perhaps someday in the future Pedro would seek refuge in one of the *palenques*. The constant movement of Afro-creole populations within the urban spaces and along the transportation arteries of the Spanish Caribbean—enslaved and free, runaways, convicts, messengers, rowers—produced astute Atlantic creoles whose powers of observation and exchange built a foundation of knowledge that helped to inform their decisions about how to negotiate or resist their current status. Slaves worked for freedom through active and passive resistance and juridical protests; in many cases, they also displayed "a resistance of the soul," a rejection of Christian mores that allowed European religious elites to designate Africanized spiritual practices mere "witchcraft, sorcery and quackery (*curanderismo*)." The proliferation of maroon communities throughout the circum-Caribbean presented perhaps the largest challenge to imperial security and authority during the early modern period.[46]

Many Spaniards had decided that slaves were key to the successful exploitation of their colonial posessions—and where there were slaves, there would always be runaways. One year after the death of the man who would become San Pedro Claver—the saint to the slaves—Governor Zapata balanced his raids on palenques in the Rio Magdalena region with diligent efforts to baptize "the children and older Negroes who were without baptism."[47] The Spanish could never feel secure with an armed presence so nearby, and over the course of the seventeenth century began to search for ways to deal with maroon populations, implementing policies both of brutal repression and incorporation, an extension of the medieval model of reconquest, but also of incorporating enemies too powerful to defeat into the fictive community as the king's vassals, with Christianity as the homogenizing glue for the new order. In the Spanish American world, religion was one of the most powerful tools to control the enslaved; it also provided slaves with the best opportunities to evade that control.

PART II

NICOLAS

"To Live and Die as a Catholic Christian"

> Vitel. *I wonder sirra*
> *What's your religion?*
>   Gazette. *Troth to answer truly*
> *I would not be of one that should command mee*
> *To feed upon Poor John, when I see Pheasants*
> *And Partridges on the Table . . .*
> *. . . I would not be confin'd*
> *In my beliefs, when all your Sects[and?] sectaries*
> *Are growne of one opinion; if I like it*
> *I will professe my selfe, in the meane time*
> *Liue I in England, Spain, France, Rome,*
> *I am of that Countryes faith.*
>
> —PHILLIP MASSINGER, *THE RENEGADO*
> (London, 1624)

4 / Northern European Protestants in the Spanish Caribbean

In October 1651, Inquisition officials from Cartagena de Indias traveled to Jamaica to investigate the murder of the island's governor, don Pedro Caballero, who also held a position as an Inquisition official, meaning that his killer would be tried under their jurisdiction. Inquisitors focused primarily on the servants and associates of Jamaica's previous governor, don Jacinto Sedeño, Governor Caballero's sworn enemy. One of the men in Sedeño's cadre who witnessed the murder was especially interesting to officials from the Holy Tribunal: Nicolas Burundel, a reputed English-man and alleged heretic who had scandalized residents with his anti-Catholic blasphemies. Several months later, appearing before the Lord Inquisitor in Cartagena, Burundel tried to straighten things out for the record. He said he was French, not English, and that he had been bap-tized a Catholic in his native Calais, where he never had anything to do with heretics. The first misidentification might have had something to do with Nicolas's curly blond hair or his broad northern accent, which made it easier for him and his Parisian wife to communicate with one another in Spanish. But those who knew the couple identified them both as French. The second misidentification had probably been linked to the first—if he was English, than it followed that he must be a heretic (after all, England was for the Spanish the most stereotypically Protestant na-tion of the period.) As for his reputation as a heretic, well, Nicolas admit-ted that his religious education had been a bit lax—he had lived at sea almost exclusively since age ten—but he firmly denied accusations that he was "an apostate heretic, nor does he know what it is to be a heretic because he is a Catholic Christian, by the grace of God a descendant of Catholic Christian parents and grandparents."[1]

Nicolas Burundel was one of at least 39 Northern European interlopers in the Spanish Caribbean to be brought before Cartagena's inquisitors over the first 50 years of its foundation as the third American Tribunal of the Holy Inquisition (1610–1660).[2] The decision to found this third American Tribunal in or near the Caribbean had been based on complaints that

> [in]to all these called the Windward Islands come many heretics, both Lutherans and Calvinists, with their ships loaded with goods to trade . . . the grave damage they cause . . . is not only of temporal things, but also the spiritual [ones, for they] pervert souls with the false doctrines they profess . . . [3]

The Spanish Inquisition's mission to uphold Catholic orthodoxy against Protestant challenges of the sixteenth and seventeenth century was tied to the absolutist pretensions of Hapsburg Spanish rulers, who had defined themselves as defenders of Catholicism and rightful rulers of the Americas since Pope Alexander VI's bull of 1493. This section's investigation of Northern European Protestants before Cartagena's Inquisition continues to emphasize that institution's importance in shaping religious and secular hierarchies in the Americas, defining and disciplining a wide range of foreign populations.

Unlike African and Afro-creole slaves and their threat to order and religious purity, most Northern Europeans traveled across the Atlantic "with their ships loaded with goods to trade." By the early seventeenth century, the Spanish Caribbean had largely degenerated into a sparsely populated frontier, distancing Caribbean settlements from the regular trade and transportation networks that linked the empire's more valuable inland administrative centers. In Caribbean outposts like Hispaniola and Jamaica, many Spanish residents continued to trade illegally with French, Dutch, and English interlopers; the seventeenth-century proliferation of Northern European settler communities in the Caribbean helped foster even more durable contraband networks. European empires continued to challenge these cooperative relationships, hoping to monopolize the terms and profits of America's wealth, but in the early to mid-seventeenth century, many royal officials were distracted by affairs in Europe or were simply too far away to police the Caribbean as closely as they might wish.[4]

Northern European sojourners like Nicolas Burundel who helped turn the wheels of the Caribbean inter-imperial cooperation and conflict were bit players in larger struggles over the pursuit of wealth and cultural conformity. Men like Nicolas faced marginalization and coercion (though of a less totalizing kind than racialized enslavement) in their interactions with Spanish Caribbean societies. They crossed over to Spanish American territories—as sailors, runaways, smugglers or prisoners—but their freedom of movement and economic opportunities depended on attaching themselves to powerful patrons in their new environs. These men (in my sample, all were men) were rarely wealthy, but instead, like Nicolas, came from humble backgrounds: sailors, fishermen, tailors, peddlers, carpenters, coopers, or bricklayers.[5] In this situation of economic dependency, foreigners found that the articulation of a Catholic conversion served as a means to overcome the cultural divide that designated those of their nations not only as heretics, but as illegal aliens and rapacious enemy "pirates."[6] Local officials, like the former governor don Sedeño, Burundel's patron, often encouraged these cultural crossings to legitimate their own position by co-opting potentially subversive forces, attuned to the benefits of collaboration with foreign contrabandists and would-be mercenaries. This chapter will explore how local conditions, operating in a dialectic with Old World conventions of religious conversion, produced scripts for successful performances. Participating in these mutually beneficial rituals of conversion and incorporation went beyond crass or utilitarian profiteering, for in the process, the two sides began to reshape the meaning of interdenominational Christianity in the Americas—moving from deep-seated antipathy to practical tolerance. The Spanish Inquisition stood at the crossroads of post-Tridentine Catholic orthodoxy, the Hapsburg Empire's efforts at hegemony in Europe and America, and market-driven demands for tolerance.[7]

The historian faces challenges in reconstructing these complex collaborative relationships between Spaniards in the Caribbean and foreigners like Nicolas, many of them Protestants. Given the fact that most of the available evidence for the seventeenth-century Caribbean is found in imperial archives, we should not be surprised at the small amount of evidence there—Spanish officials in the Caribbean had ample reason to hide their illicit relationships with Northern European "pirates" and "heretics" from imperial oversight. However, royal officials occasionally submitted investigative reports charging economic malfeasance and improper relations with foreign traders, providing interesting anecdotal information on individual local elites whose activities managed to rouse extraordinary suspicion. Records from Cartagena's Inquisition—because their primary focus was on religious sentiment and its associated everyday behavior—offer an excellent view of daily negotiations over conversion and social integration. It is unfortunate that the full corpus of Cartagena's Inquisition records have not survived, as they have for tribunals established earlier in Mexico City and Lima, but the Spanish Inquisition's Supreme Council in Madrid kept copies of all annual reports (*relaciones*), as well as copies of individual cases that local Tribunals found difficult to resolve; these are now housed at the National Archives in Madrid. Nicolas Burundel's trial was one of only three involving Protestants for the period under investigation for which we have a full trial transcript, and thus provides rich details about everyday life for Northern Europeans in the Spanish Americas. His case is in many ways very different from the other cases brought against Protestant "apostates" during the period (the reason why local inquisitors sent the *Suprema* a copy of his case file in the first place), but his life before being brought before the Tribunal *was* fairly representative.

Nicolas Burundel is a perfect example of European mobility between Old World spheres of influence where both trade and religion mattered greatly. As the son of a Calais cloth merchant, Nicolas said he had lived much of his life at sea, serving on ships sailing between European ports: Dunkirk, Lisbon, cities along the Bay of Biscay. His life at sea had been interrupted after he was taken captive by North African "Barbary" corsairs and sold in Algiers to a French renegade (the contemporary term for a convert to Islam). Redeemed by his father after three years, Nicolas returned to Calais, and at the age of twenty, began to represent the family in trans-Atlantic journeys to Caribbean settlements to sell clothing and other supplies to French colonists. On the island of Guadeloupe, he said, he fell in love, but finding some opposition to the match, ran away with his sweetheart to Puerto Rico; they lived for a time in Cartagena before finally settling in Spanish Jamaica.[8] Likewise, at least one-third of the other 38 individuals under consideration had traversed the waters and coastlines of the North Atlantic and Mediterranean—from Majorca to Tripoli, Algiers to Cadiz—before learning the inlets and shoals of the West Indies' island chains. Such navigations (both literal and symbolic) provided opportunities for many to become conversant in dealing with Spanish culture, whether in the seas of the Old World or the Caribbean, "Sea of the New World."[9]

This chapter will first examine the extent of post-Reformation confessional culture in the Caribbean, and how Protestant and Catholic formulas for heartfelt conversion were used to express allegiance. In Chapter Five, I analyze how the accused men learned to manipulate the

Spanish Inquisition's diplomatic and bureaucratic concessions to foreign Protestant merchants. Finally, drawing on the cultural tropes of maritime danger and religious pollution that existed in both Mediterranean and Caribbean realms, in Chapter Six I examine the psychological clash between toleration, conversion, and coercion in American zones of "Christian" influence. This final chapter in Nicolas's story in particular extends Ira Berlin's definition of Atlantic creoles beyond the bounds of the Atlantic slave trade to include linkages between inter-European affairs and the struggles between Christians and Muslims during the early modern period.[10] While Berlin's creoles developed out of African coastal commerce, similar attempts to define commercial relationships and overcome cultural differences happened in the Mediterranean. In this contentious world, many Europeans who would become Atlantic creoles had first learned how to be Mediterranean creoles.

Aware of the opportunity for duplicity among individuals like Nicolas Burundel, Inquisition officials listening to the Frenchman's proclamations of his Catholic identity were unconvinced—he had given very few satisfactory answers to mitigate the testimony of witnesses who claimed he was a heretic. What was more, suffering from the isolation of life in the secret prisons, the Frenchman began to show signs of madness . . . or was it demonic possession? One night four months after his arrest, Burundel woke the whole prison with shouts and banging, yelling that he would kill anyone who dared enter his cell. The next morning when the jailer reported the unusual event, the visiting inquisitor, Pedro de Medina Rico, personally went to the Frenchman's cell to investigate. What he found inside was shocking:

> . . . having opened [the cell], [Burundel] was found on his knees upon the floor (*tarima*) facing the wall, asking for mercy and praying Our Fathers and Hail Marys in Latin, his entire costume dirty with urine and excrement from his chamber pot, which was broken in various pieces and the excrement spilled on the floor, and a brick from the floor pulled out and broken into three parts . . . the Lord Inquisitor . . . ordered that he come with him to the Audience [chamber], which [Nicolas] entered quietly, still weeping and with his hands clasped. The Lord Inquisitor ordered that a bench be brought to him and that he sit on it, which he did, and once seated the Lord Inquisitor asked him what was wrong (*que tenía*), to which he replied that 'the Devil had tricked him [into believing] that the

fathers of the Company [of Jesus] and all the priests were coming to kill him with shotguns (*escopetas*).[11]

That night would begin a new phase in the Frenchman's proceedings, as Nicolas began to tell the inquisitor and others around him that he "wasn't himself"—he said he felt like he was drunk all the time and complained especially of a pain in his chest "from the navel upwards."[12] In succeeding audiences, the scribe noted that Nicolas would often breathe heavily, "with anxiety and fatigue, as if something was bothering him inside his chest," and recorded Nicolas's assertion that he wasn't able to finish even one Our Father or Hail Mary without getting distracted.[13] When asked what was happening, Burundel claimed that "his lordship [the inquisitor] should know what he had in his body—God was punishing him."[14] Was it madness, was it possession, or was it (as the inquisitor feared was a third possibility) a calculated attempt to have them all believe he was possessed and/or mad? Seeing as how the Frenchman had failed to convince the Tribunal of his "Catholic Christian" identity, it is not surprising that he was also unconvincing as a madman.

Nicolas Burundel's attempts to perform the madness of possession may seem a poor comparison with the 38 other cases of Protestants before Cartagena's Holy Tribunal who chose to perform Catholicism instead. However, the idea of the performance and/or belief in supernatural illnesses *was* a reflection of the European tradition of demonology, a theological convention shared by Protestants and Catholics alike.[15] By comparing the evidence taken from other foreigners' cases with Burundel's odyssey through post-Reformation Continental Europe, the watery reaches of the early modern Atlantic and Mediterranean Worlds, and his more than ten-year sojourn in the Spanish Caribbean, we can better understand the politics of profit, tolerance, and religious antipathy in the seventeenth-century Caribbean.

Scholarship on sixteenth-century Europe has elaborated deeply on the processes of confessionalization and religious renewal, processes which aimed to convert the fundamentals of Catholic and Protestant doctrine into an essential *identity* for men and women from all levels of society. Protestant and Catholic orthodoxies were defined through a dialectic that depended on oppositional politics—Catholic identities thus were built around devotional practices that upheld doctrines most firmly opposed by Protestant reformers (for example, Mary's immaculate conception, the true presence of Christ's body and blood in the Eucharist, the veneration of saints and relics, etc.), and vice versa. By the early seventeenth century, such hallmarks of Protestant and Catholic identity had become fairly ingrained, even at the lowest levels of faraway colonial society.[16] Confessional identity helped to define acceptance in Spanish Caribbean society, and individuals and religious institutions worked to punish those identities deemed unacceptable. Articulations of Counter-Reformation Catholicism provided Northern European outsiders with opportunities to witness and model their new Catholic identities through the rehearsals and rituals of conversion, whether their audiences were local elites, churchmen, creolized slaves, or the inquisitor himself.

In Jamaica, Nicolas Burundel could thank the legacy of the Catholic Reformation for his denunciation and prosecution, which might never have come to light were it not for the willing cooperation of witnesses from all strata of Jamaican society—slaves and free *mulatos*, established Spanish citizens (*vecinos*), convicts, and respectable maidens. A creole-born enslaved woman named Marcela Perez was the first to denounce Nicolas—she overheard him utter blasphemies while arguing with his wife, and so Perez rebuked him, calling him a "heretic dog." When the Frenchman tried to silence her, calling her a whore (*puta*), Marcela took her complaint to her local Inquisition officer (*comisario*).[17] Within several months, the *comisario* had more fuel to add to the fire. Rumors that Burundel was a heretic had begun circulating widely, and respected *vecinos* Diego Navarra de Lara and Francisca de Espinosa joined the list of official witnesses. Navarra wrote a letter from his ranch to report that he had once employed the "Englishman" as a laborer, and that one day, conversing with Nicolas about the reverence due to saints, Nicolas said that he didn't believe in wooden saints (*santos de palo de la tierra*), only God in heaven. Navarro, scandalized, reproached Burundel, but he "remained obstinate" and so Navarro said "he was obliged" to resort to physical violence, kicking his worker to the ground.[18] Francisca de Espinosa testified that she had often comforted Nicolas's wife Ana in the wake of the couple's frequent arguments. Ana railed against her abusive husband, and confided in Francisca that Nicolas had told her she shouldn't call Mary "virgin," but only recognize her status as the mother of God—"for if the Virgin had given birth, how could she be a virgin?"[19]

After Burundel was arrested by the Inquisition constable on October 2, 1651, his wife was questioned, and two Spaniards and two mixed-race creoles were also called upon to testify. Ana defended her husband's orthodoxy to the *comisario*, saying that in France, "she had lived among many heretics and would have known if he was one"; nonetheless, her protestations couldn't overpower the testimony of her neighbors. Doña Isabel de Prado, a Spanish maiden who seems to have been another of Ana's confidants, reported that one of her family's slaves told her one day after visiting Burundel's home that Nicolas had mocked his wife's urgings to go to confession, responding with a dismissive "'Go on, get out of here—I'll confess with Juan,' pointing to another Englishman who was there, 'and Juan with me.'"[20] The slave in question, a girl named Jacinta, was called in by the *comisario*—she confirmed that Nicolas had uttered this blasphemy "with much laughter and delight," and that he had also bragged that "he didn't go to the Holy Friday procession to watch it, but just to make fun of the penitents."[21]

Although Burundel's patron, the convicted ex-governor Jacinto Sedeño, seems not to have paid much attention to his lackey's irreverence (indeed, Nicolas had plenty to say about Sedeño's many blasphemies), the Frenchman's hot temper and disagreeable manner pulled him into conflictual relationships with people around him, and his imprudent comments against Catholic teaching made him an easy target. Spanish citizens were understandably hostile to men like Burundel: more often than not captured as pirates, held as prisoners, or entering their territories clandestinely, they were classed as enemies not to be trusted. If they hoped to find protection in this hostile land, they needed to attach themselves to powerful men. In a 1648 investigation of Jamaica's chief cleric, abbot Mateo de Medina Moreno, Cartagena's inquisitors were upset about his frequent unlawful licensing of baptisms and reconciliations for "many heretics of different nations."[22] One man said he had seen the previous governor, don Francisco Ladrón, encourage hastily performed baptisms of some English and Irish sailors who had deserted from the English privateer William Jackson's fleet after they had sacked part of the island. Governor Ladrón had said that those Englishmen "were Christians, and wish to submit themselves (*reducirse*)" to the Catholic Church. Turning to one of his solders nearby, Governor Ladrón allegedly said, "Go with his lordship and take this Englishman with you. I don't remember if he also wanted to convert (*reducirse*), but tell them to give the license to *licenciado* Alonso Tellez so he is absolved with the rest."[23] This kind of cavalier attitude signified to the witness that government officials not only tolerated but also encouraged hasty, perhaps blasphemous, conversions to Catholicism.

Churchmen like Father Tellez were the lynchpins of these alliances. As representatives of the secular and spiritual powers in the colonies, their mediation between sacred and secular was powerful enough to ritually erase at least one aspect of enemy identity. Upon receiving the deserters, Tellez admitted he had been reluctant at first, arguing with the officers who presented themselves as godparents that if their godchildren had come to Jamaica with "the wish to be baptized, they could not have taken up arms against us." He was suspicious that the Englishmen may have requested baptism "to devalue the sacrament, for he had heard it said that they were already baptized." However, facing the "tears and other afflictions" of the hopeful converts, and ordered by his superior, Abbot Medina, to proceed, Tellez capitulated. Trying to maintain some semblance of order, Tellez said he consulted a "Roman Manual" for the format of the ceremony—reconciling those who had some Catholic education, and baptizing the others *sub conditione*, ensuring that they were first instructed "many days" in the faith and knew how to pray.[24]

In addition to Tellez's skepticism, at least one other person felt he should register his scandal at these baptisms. Diego Nuñez Rosa said he left the cathedral "with great anguish" when he saw the first three Englishmen brought to the baptismal font, "not believing that it could be possible among Christians to carry out such a great sacrilege."[25] Rosa said he complained to everyone he saw, then went to the *comisario* and told him that it was common knowledge (*se decía por público*) that one Englishman had been baptized two or three times before, saying that "wherever they caught him he got baptized because they gave him clothes [for the occasion]."[26] But these and other questionable baptisms were more often met with rejoicing than skepticism. A long-held crusading ethos seems to have combined with Counter-Reformation spirituality to induce many Spaniards to accept at face value the triumph of the One True Faith over heresy. The prestige of being affiliated with these seemingly miraculous signs of God's power led nine of the island's leading men, nearly all military and administrative officeholders, to offer their pious support of the baptisms, which celebrations were witnessed by nearly everyone on the island. Even if Father Tellez did not quite believe he was redeeming lost lambs, he might have consoled himself that those heretics could only be bettered by their instruction in Catholic beliefs and the good example of Spanish society (like Alonso de Sandoval did with his acceptance of Africans' "just" captivity and enslavement). Faced with his prelate's orders and the insistence of foreigners' godparents, "the most principle residents of the place," Tellez could sleep with a clear conscience—he just had been following orders.[27]

Building on the credulity and good will of Spanish Catholics, Protestant foreigners who expressed a desire to become part of the local community nonetheless had to convincingly perform their conversions for the populace. A few described with curiosity how priests adapted the sacrament of baptism for these adult converts. The ceremony, "which seemed longer and different than those normally used for children," began outside the door of the church, where the men kneeled on the ground and waited to be recognized by the priest. When the priest asked "What did they want?" the men were coached to reply, "Baptism," and to affirm they had never before received the Sacrament. After this ritual exchange, Father Tellez allowed the converts to enter the sanctuary. Next, converts participated in a brief demonstration to prove they had been well instructed—some were asked to explain the meaning of the images in the church (some representing the saints) or made to recite the Creed aloud. The penultimate act before receiving the holy oil of baptism, the men had to lie prostrate on the floor, "and with acts of humility beg forgiveness."[28]

Participating in, witnessing, or retelling rituals like these provided foreign initiates with ready-made scripts for conversion. We can better glimpse the transmission of similar ritual memories by looking at the case of Thomas Cox (alias Drac alias Gales), an English royalist fugitive who traveled widely in the Spanish Caribbean in the late 1640s. Denounced for "pretending to be a Catholic," Cox testified before Cartagena's Inquisition in 1652 that he had been encouraged by some Irish comrades from Santo Domingo to convert to the True Faith—they knew some priests in that city who spoke his language and could facilitate the process. Arriving in Santo Domingo during Lent, Thomas said he borrowed some texts from a Flemish chaplain of the city's garrison, and then (like a good Protestant) spent the next seven weeks comparing them with the Bible, "and he discovered everything to be true." Confirmed in his new beliefs, Cox said the chaplain sent him to a Dominican friar who, for 30 *reales*, would "make a bull of the Holy Crusade to clear him of [his] excommunication." Payment complete, Cox explained that

> the said cleric and friar ordered him to strip to the waist, which he did, believing they wanted to whip him harshly for his sins. The said friar took a book and began to read in Latin while the cleric gave it to him gently on the back with a little rod (*una barica*) and in this manner (as they told him) they absolved him.

It was such a "great consolation," Cox recounted to Cartagena's inquisitors, to receive the license that would give him permission to enter the island's churches, that he joined a religious procession outside, and went to mass that day (Maundy Thursday) and every day thereafter until the celebration of Easter Sunday.[29]

An inspiring story, indeed. But in the following audience, Thomas Cox had a real confession to make: he wished to say that he had been honest in every respect, "except it wasn't true, that is to say it was false," about the ceremony performed by the Dominican friar. The scribe in the Inquisition chamber then noted that the accused "asked for mercy, dropping to his knees, his hands raised in the air."[30] Cox tried to explain, saying he had lied out of fear, and later shared that he had gotten the idea for the story from seeing a similar ritual performed by a Franciscan on a French convert in Venezuela.[31] This admittedly rare admission of a counterfeit conversion is likely representative of what must have happened quite regularly when foreigners were asked to explain their Catholic identity to others. It is a telling reminder of how easy it must have been to "fake" a conversion—all one needed were regular participation in the rituals of Catholic life (such as processions and confession) and a dramatic story of conviction (many of the cases examined here were accomplished by proclaiming they had been "struck through the heart" by God or had been convinced by the superiority of priests' arguments against their old Protestant errors). Cultural chameleons like Cox relied on sophisticated storytelling to cultivate sympathetic relationships, resorting to physical articulations of remorse and verbal cries for mercy when their stories were challenged.

To avoid these challenges, foreigners learned to keep parish clergy and members of the regular orders had at arm's length, for their education in spiritual matters made them more apt to see through a hastily constructed façade of "true" Catholic belief. Nicolas Burundel seems to have been exceptionally wary of getting involved with priests. Though he attested he "gave proof" of his Catholicism before Cartagena's bishop in order to gain a license to marry his wife Ana when they first settled in that city, he was aware of the risk of such interactions, for at first, "with respect to [the fact that] he spoke a very closed French and Spanish not at all," the bishop had called him a "heretic and a barbarian (bozal)."[32] From then on, Burundel seems to have limited his contact with priests to the occasional brief exchange with the Jesuits, who ran a sort of early modern "soup kitchen" for the poor, funded with alms collected from Cartagena's citizens. He said that he had confessed once with a priest in Jamaica, but didn't remember what he had said—maybe a good thing, he thought, because he later saw the same priest "drunk . . . in a tavern (pulpería)"—such intemperance spoke poorly of his trustworthiness as a confessor.[33]

Though foreigners appear to have convinced some sectors of Spanish society of the sincerity of their conversions, the longer the term of residence, the more risks such suspect outsiders faced. Language acquisition had much to do with the level of vulnerability. As long as individuals remained on the margins of society and only revealed their derision or suspicion of Catholic practices with one another, they were generally safe. But when long residence gave way to regular communication in a shared language—as in Nicolas Burundel's case—Old World conflicts were more likely to break out. For Thomas Cox, his native tongue failed to protect him, for English was a common language among the substantial community of Irish and English Catholics who had fled to Spanish territories during the tumult of England's Civil War.[34] Cox told inquisitors he suspected his informers had been an Irish captain and English priest with whom he used to get drunk in Santo Domingo, and he cautioned the Tribunal not to give credit to the tales of those drinking buddies, for they were no longer friends.[35] As for the deserters from Jackson's fleet, no one could tell yet how long they would last. In his investigation, Jamaica's Inquisition *comisario* neglected to question them, explaining that of those who were still around, "none [are] acculturated (*ladino*) and understand our tongue."[36] Guillermo Obrey, one of the Frenchmen living in Jamaica, said that even though he was born a Catholic, he had to wait to get a license to confess "until he was more *ladino* and could be understood." When asked if it was possible that any of the other foreigners on the island had been baptized before receiving the sacrament in Jamaica, Obrey said it was certain they had been, "because in his land everyone was."[37]

Cartagena's inquisitors must have torn their hair out at the Jamaican abbot's negligence. In an act dated March 11, 1648, they reminded Jamaica's clergy that *only* the *comisario*—the Holy Office's offical representative—could reconcile heretics in such cases, and that they must adhere to the Tribunal's official instructions for doing so.[38] Indeed, located at the heart of the Spanish Caribbean commercial and imperial power, Cartagena's Holy Tribunal of the Inquisition held supreme responsibility for enforcing Counter-Reformation orthodoxy throughout its Caribbean and New Granada jurisdictions. Manned by highly trained administrators conversant in canon law and theology, this institution took their "inquisitiveness" into all sorts of heresy quite seriously. In cases against Protestant offenders, they consulted with theologically trained clerics to "qualify" charges, to determine whether their past acts could be categorized as formal heresy or merely superstitious, ignorant, or disrespectful.

In Nicolas Burundel's case, inquisitors also employed educated priests as consultants to uncover whether his "madness" was just an act. Inquisitor Medina Rico had already warned the Frenchman that "the devil couldn't make an assault on him, and that he shouldn't fake madness or that he was being tricked by the Devil, for in addition to being a grave sin, he would be punished for it."[39] But three judges (*calificadores*), Franciscan friar Martin de Velasco, and Dominican friars Pedro de Achurri and Francisco de Vargas, were informed of the case as it currently stood against Burundel. They were to visit Nicolas periodically, offering him the "comfort" of a rosary to pray with or the "consolation" of confession, hoping to draw out Burundel's true beliefs as they conversed about his past and how he had practiced his faith in places like France.[40]

Nicolas saw through the charade of such duplicitous "consolations" and tried to avoid serious conversation with his priestly visitors. Burundel refused to make confession with any of the three, insinuating that what he confessed would be reported to Medina Rico, despite confession's supposed secrecy. After a few frustrating visits, Father Vargas reported that Nicolas wasn't demented, but was faking his physical ailments to distract the Tribunal from his heresy, and only tolerated their visits because he was lonely in his cell.[41] Velasco claimed he had uncovered the Frenchman's secret identity as a heretic, revealed in their conversations about Catholic doctrine and Nicolas's mocking responses.[42] Though Burundel would later claim he had done his best to treat these priests with the respect due their station, he insisted he didn't have to confess with them or let them instruct him in the faith, saying "I'm not here to be taught."[43]

Indeed, punishment was the more common—and accurate—definition of the Inquisition's function. As the foremost defender of the faith, the Spanish Inquisition was, for many Northern Europeans, the most powerful symbol of Reformation antagonisms, and its powers most clearly demonstrated in the spectacular ritual of the public *auto de fe*. Though Protestants composed only a small fraction of those reconciled as repentant sinners in these theatrical rituals, their symbolic position was much greater. Two of the three most lavish *autos* mounted in Cartagena's public square during the Tribunal's first 20 years (in 1614, 1622, and 1626) highlighted the Inquisition's power to conquer the Caribbean's menacing Protestant threat.[44] Reconciliation at this level required more than mere protestations of faith or humble supplication—it required punishment.

Bringing together individuals from the furthest reaches of the Tribunal's jurisdiction and all levels of society, *autos de fe* were shining demonstrations of Spanish Catholicism united against heresy. Chronicles of the 1626 *auto de fe* describe this sense of coming together, beginning with a pronoucement in early April by Inquisition officials "that upon the arrival of His Majesty's galeons, an *auto de fe* would be celebrated." Officials also proclaimed that all citizens of the port city and surrounding areas should be in attendance, for which they would gain papal indulgences.[45] First, a surveyor chose a design for the theater, deciding on one that closely approximated an *auto de fe* he had seen mounted in the Canaries; next, three infantry captains and aldermen (*regidores*) were chosen to direct the construction of the project, and they called upon the entire populace to help gather the wood necessary to build the three massive stages necessary to visually demarcate the tiered hierarchies of the Crown, Church, and Society. When the fleet arrived in Cartagena on June 10, the armada's generals joined their efforts to the production, ordering their common seamen and convict laborers (*forzados*) to hoist 42 masts from the ships to the main plaza where they would form a dramatic awning for the main stage, rising "like pyramids of wood . . . to compete with the clouds." Everyone with homes along the parade route was ordered to hang their most expensive draperies from the balconies and to sweep their properties.

Cartagena's citizens may have awakened before dawn on the anticipated day of festivities to watch that year's penitents march through the city streets, led by members of the city's religious orders who processed behind a "cross dressed in mourning with a black veil, grave signs of the sadness and emotions that our mother the Church [feels] when her children deny her." By mid-morning, they jostled into the main square to watch the head of the city's Dominican order raise the Host in celebration of high mass, and listened to a sermon preached by a learned Franciscan, who used St. Paul's rebuke to the errant Christian community of Galatians as his scriptural homily. At the end of this particularly fitting exhortation, the crowd watched as the Holy Tribunal's secretary took the pulpit and instructed everyone in attendance to make the sign of the cross. With him they swore "to defend the faith, obey and execute all the commands of the Holy Office and defend its ministers." As a reward for their attention, the secretary read the pope's bull, which bestowed indulgences and his thanks to those co-protectors of the faith.

Mirroring Geertz's insights on religion and ritual, these ceremonies of inquisitorial authority gained potency the more the populace participated in official definitions of orthodoxy, providing a sense of unity against the heretics-penitents. Perhaps a shiver of anticipation passed over the crowd—it had been only four years since the last *auto de fe* when an English Protestant had been burned at the stake.[46] This year, Frederico Cuperes, a Fleming from Antwerp, was the first to climb atop the platform, wearing the shameful *sambenito* which carried the symbols of his Calvinist heresy. After the Inquisition secretary read the charges of which the Fleming had been convicted and his abjuration of the same, the secretary proclaimed the price of his reconciliation—one hundred lashes in the city streets. For one moment Cuperes went "off script," taking his time on stage to threaten the witnesses who had denounced him, protesting that he had been coerced, that out of fear he had confessed that which he had not committed. But the show went on, despite the Fleming's protests. Insincere confessions could be as dangerous as insincere conversions. By playing his part (as a penitent) in the inquisitorial process, Cuperes accepted the Tribunal's legitimation of the Catholic worldview, and his protest at this late stage likely did little to challenge inquisitorial authority.

With these sorts of examples of the Inquisition's stern treatment for heretics, it is not surprising that Nicolas Burundel viewed the Tribunal's investigating clerics with distrust, fearing that any admission of sins that took him outside the bounds of Catholic orthodoxy would only expose him as a liar. With the help of his court-appointed lawyer, Burundel submitted a petition that reiterated his innocence, saying he was by nature "a coarse man of little intelligence in these [religious] matters; he hoped his unintentional faults could be pardoned." Interviewing the Frenchman after his petition was registered, the inquisitor inquired as to whether a priest had seen and "consoled" Nicolas at all; Burundel responded that he didn't need consolation from anyone "if it wasn't from the Lord Inquisitor himself."[47] But his longed-for consolation was far from forthcoming—Medina Rico had already received his partner clerics' determinations on Burundel's state of health. Not only did they believe that the Frenchman was faking his real or imagined ailments, but they raised more questions about his orthodoxy, claiming he had scorned their talk of sacramental confession and transubstantiation, and asserted that his outward comportment betrayed a deep scorn for Catholic institutions and their emissaries.

By the seventeenth century, confessional antipathies were so engrained at all levels of European society that even in the relatively lax religious atmosphere of the Caribbean, they contributed significantly to religious xenophobia. Notwithstanding, Spaniards at all levels of colonial society generally believed their faith could do miracles—even transform heretics into good Christians. This confidence gave support to would-be converts, who could counterfeit an emotional display of being "tricked" by their old doctrines or "moved by God" to see the light and learn about the truth from Catholic priests. But like Burundel's disastrous results with demonology, following the wrong script could be a dangerous prospect indeed.

5 / Empire, Bureaucracy, and Escaping the Spanish Inquisition

On September 28, 1652, Nicolas was brought to the main audience chamber to hear the Tribunal formally charge him with the crime of Calvinism. The accusation alleged that he must have been comprehensively educated in the very fundamentals of this "damned" heresy to say the things he had. Medina Rico gave credence to the clerics who believed that Nicolas had consciously decided to fool them with a performance of madness, "hoping in this way to get out of prison without being corrected."[1] After all 21 charges were read, the Frenchman was asked to respond in his own defense. Although he began by reiterating that he was "fearful of God and his crimes," Nicolas faltered, overwhelmed with the magnitude of his predicament, and then could only think to say "that he was here, and they should do with him what they wished." But the inquisitor tried to hold back Nicolas from his descent into despair, saying, "Don't lose hope, this Holy Tribunal is like God our Lord, and will treat with great mercy those who are good penitents—who confess their offenses and repent of them." He further told Nicolas that he still had "time to prove himself worth its mercy."[2]

But instead of following the suggestion that compliant confession and conversion might (even at this seemingly hopeless stage) be to his advantage, Burundel shut down. He refused to respond to the rest of the charges against him, and he resisted the mandatory consultation with his lawyer. Three days later, as the inquisitor consulted with other learned officials about the next step toward uncovering the truth—torture—he also ordered that Nicolas be transferred to the relative comfort of a common cell. Having tried and failed to get priests to draw the Frenchman out of his shell, Medina Rico instead tried enlisting the aid of two other inmates with whom he would be sharing his new quarters.[3] Burundel's first new cellmate was Francisco de Murillo, a Franciscan priest who had stolen the alms he had been collecting for his monastery in Bogotá and ran away to Venezuela with the money, trying to escape his past by abandoning his vows of celibacy for the vows of holy matrimony.[4] Juan de Noguera was a Portuguese medic *cum* charlatan living near the Pacific coast, whose dubious services for hire included the use of a divining rod which allegedly helped find lost items.[5] Burundel, rejecting any deviance from his testimony before the inquisitor, had been astute to mistrust the priestly *calificadores* sent to probe his true beliefs, but he should have thought to be more circumspect in his conversations with these new cellmates. He was not. Over the course of two months, from early October to early December 1652, Noguera and Murillo gave regular statements to Medina Rico, offering their observations of Nicolas's behavior and their recollections of conversations with the Frenchman. (Of course, such testimony has to be taken with a grain of salt, for both men had incentive to lie—they might hope their reports would create tacit promises of leniency in their own cases. As such, I have placed more emphasis on testimony in which Murillo and Noguera, in their separate reports, corroborate one another's stories about Nicolas.)

Both of these informers' initial reports emphasized Burundel's overwhelming depression and despair. One day he glimpsed his wife in the square through the tiny window in their shared cell "and began to shout loudly, saying, 'Wife, I am already dead!'"[6] Murillo had to force him away from the window, and Noguera reported he was behaving "like a crazy, desperate man,"[7] one time begging them to kill him . . . he was only "dog meat" and wouldn't feel anything . . . "he pardoned them for his death. . . . " To prove his point, Nicolas grabbed at his own throat "with both hands," and told them, "look, look, I don't feel it!"[8] then "squeezing with all his might." Murillo and Noguera intervened to wrest his hands from his neck when it looked as if he would choke himself. The reason for such despair, so Nicolas asserted, was that "his case was more dire than all the others, for he had killed a man who was the governor of Jamaica." Murillo, knowledgeable in the Spanish Americas' complex and overlapping bureaucracies, tried to dissuade him, telling him that the Inquisition didn't arrest people for murder, and suggested that he might find some relief if he begged the Tribunal's mercy. But Nicolas insisted his case was hopeless, that "he didn't want mercy in this life, for he'd already asked the Tribunal and God for mercy." Remembering his supernatural symptoms, he added, "who else should he ask [for help], the Devil?"[9]

Nicolas's behavior certainly seems to have reflected a tormented state of mind, at times desperate and suicidal, at other times angry and manipulative. Though his symptoms of madness had been deemed simulations in the *consultadores'* damning reports, Nicolas kept insisting that he was an "Apostolic Roman Catholic Christian" and that his labored breathing was not faked, but was rather a "trial God gave him for his sins and desperation."[10] Perhaps his judgment had been clouded by nightmarish tales of the Spanish Inquisition. Perhaps he did wish to die. What *is* clear is that he was not able to see the opportunities afforded to him by inquisitorial legal procedures, nor was he attuned to the changes to inquisitorial policy that, over the seventeenth century, provided increasing protections to certain groups of foreign Protestants. Nicolas seems to have been unable to see beyond the confines of his cell, and his inferences about how he might successfully secure his freedom were fundamentally flawed, pushing him down the path from struggle to despair.

In a European diplomatic context, the seventeenth century was a period in which the power and will of the Spanish Inquisition to wipe out all vestiges of foreign heresies was on the decline; those aware of these changes could unmoor the Tribunal's legal apparatus from its mystique and terror. As the Hapsburg Empire's hegemony dwindled over the course of the seventeenth century, it was forced into a series of unfavorable treaties requiring concessions to the demands of Northern Europeans, some of them religious. International relations demanded diplomatic tolerance, and powerful mercantile interests made toleration a profitable option. Although legally a separate entity from the monarchy, the Spanish Inquisition and its affiliated Tribunals were forced to change its policies towards foreigners in accordance with the Crown's international treaties and agreements.

The biggest policy changes were enacted beginning with the 1604 Treaty of London, in which Philip III was forced to concede toleration to Protestant English sailors and merchants. To encourage the renewal of friendly trade relations, the Spanish Inquisition was barred from prosecuting English subjects during their visit to Spanish ports, as long as they didn't "give scandal" to the Catholics living there. The newly united Dutch Provinces pressed for, and received, the same concessions as the English when they signed the 1609 treaty with their former Hapsburg overlords. The Inquisition agreed to comply, but in 1610 determined that they would only exempt foreign transients (such as sailors); charges could still be brought against those merchants and factors who maintained more permanent residence in Spanish territories. Toleration policies were erased in the 1620s, first in 1621 when the Dutch treaty expired, and then in 1626, when war broke out with England. During this time of renewed conflict, Philip III ordered the cessation of commercial relations with enemy nations, and authorized the confiscation of enemy estates and the prosecution of heretics found in Europe and the Americas. However, in 1630, with peace restored between England and Spain (and for the Dutch, after the Treaty of Munster in 1648), the Spanish Crown reinstated earlier privileges and made more concrete guarantees for domiciled foreign merchants, who—unless they became naturalized citizens—were not to be considered residents.[11]

Inquisition officials again complied with international law, but reserved the right to prohibit Protestant books and pamphlets, performing *visitas* of arriving ships in order to confiscate seditious religious contraband. Although foreigners' religious beliefs were officially protected, they were not exempted from surveillance. Toward this end, the Suprema instructed all Tribunal heads to appoint their "most intelligent, learned, and trusted" *comisarios* to meet Protestant nations' vessels soon after disembarking in order that they might offer a "cure . . . for [their] souls." In this new plan of investigation, *comisarios* were instructed to "listen [to them] with much gentleness," and question them about the "errors [that exist] in the sects of Calvin, Luther, and other heresiarchs, in the foreign lands where they are from." Protestants who "came of their own volition to reduce themselves to our Holy Catholic Faith" would be joyfully reconciled; they would be exempted from the shameful garb of the penitent and the financial penalties usually levied against heretics, and inquisitors were to assign them only "some spiritual penances."[12] Thanks to these diplomatic and bureaucratic transformations and normalized peacetime trade, the numbers of foreigners prosecuted for Protestant heresy declined dramatically, and the horror of burning at the stake became a true rarity.[13]

Cartagena de Indias's Holy Office followed these new procedures faithfully—surprising since we often think of the Inquisition as merely an arm of the imperial state, a state that officially prohibited foreign settlement in the Americas and ignored peace treaties "beyond the line" of amity. Adhering to the letter of the law did *not* excuse all foreign heterodoxy, however. In July 1619, the Tribunal's administration ordered the arrest of an English spice merchant named Adán Edón, who had been residing among the Spanish in Caracas and Cumaná since smuggling himself on board an Indies-bound vessel earlier that year. Fourteen witnesses testified to the "great scandal and gossip" that this Englishman had caused in the province with his irreverence for Catholic practices: on the voyage, Edón had refused to contribute alms to pay for the recitation of masses for a good voyage, and by absenting himself from Sunday mass, Edón further condemned himself in the court of public opinion. Transported to Cartagena to stand trial, Edón defended himself by saying that his peninsular Spanish trade partners had already paid a 1,000 *ducat* surety to the governor of Cumaná for his good behavior and that "it [was] false that he didn't hear mass, because he heard mass many and diverse times, and when he passed by the churches when people were present, more often than not he removed his hat so as not to give scandal." Despite his proclaimed adherence to the terms of the international agreement (avoiding behavior that would "scandalize" Catholic populations), inquisitors could point to Edón's semipermanent residence to justify their prosecution. When, after many sessions with learned priests and confessors, Edón refused to be "reduced" to Catholicism. Although urged to think of "the great danger . . . of losing his temporal and eternal life," he accepted his sentence of "relaxation" to secular authorities, and was burned in a public execution at the 1622 *auto de fe*.[14]

But during times of peace between European powers, most foreign merchants who took up residence in Iberian Catholic trade ports—Seville, Cadiz, Madrid, Lisbon, and especially the Canaries[15]—found ways to work out their religious differences in more pragmatic ways. In these commercial frontiers where Spaniards interacted regularly with "heretics," Protestant merchants and ships' crews learned to present themselves "spontaneously" (*espontaneamente*) to the local Tribunal to register their desire to become Catholic, for which the prescribed sentence was not (as we have seen) an extensive investigation of past heresies and sins against the Church, but simple procedures in which, after a requisite three hearings, converts might be absolved *ad cautelam* (with caution). In commercial ports from Seville to the Canaries to Galicia and the Basque coastline, the procedure happened so frequently that it appears caution was only a euphemism. In the Canary Islands alone, the local Inquisition Tribunal reconciled 121 foreign Protestants over the course of the 1600s, 118 of them "*espontaneos*."[16]

In Cartagena de Indias, the singularity of Edón's obstinate refusal to change his confessional identity is highlighted by the fourteen cases (one-third of the total in seventeenth-century Inquisition registers) of voluntary self-presentations *for* conversion. An additional one-third

might be categorized as pseudo-spontaneous, in which foreigners requested reconciliation *after* inquisitors had gotten wind of their heresies,
turning themselves in. Others held in the common gaol appealed to religious authorities to mitigate their fates as enemies and heretics. In many
cases, the tactic seemed to work. Five English sailors rowed into Cartagena's harbor in April 1620, saying that they had fled the mistreatment
of their English captain "and the bad life" of piracy, hoping for a better
life among "Christians." Indeed, the governor and the city celebrated the
pirates' repentance, but after finding them taking hand-measurements of
the cannons and counting the number of artillery pieces that protected
the walled city, he threw all five in prison as spies. There they languished
until a Jesuit priest visiting the prisons took notice of their plight. Juan de
Arsell, a teenager in their group, took the lead in conversations because
he could speak a bit of Spanish, which he had learned when his father
"sent him from his land to the Island of La Palma (Canaries) [to live] in
the home of some merchants." Arsell's two-and-a-half-year stint in that
mercantile entrepôt may have prepared him to coach his friends as they
"made demonstrations of wanting to become Christians" before their
Jesuit visitor.[17] Brought before the Inquisition Tribunal, Arsell and the
others spoke of their desire to convert, and swore they meant it "with all
their heart[s], without fear of prison." Although common sense dictates
that at least some of these conversions were insincere, inquisitors nonetheless followed official instructions, absolving these willing converts *ad
cautelam*, and according to procedure, mandated only a light spiritual
penance, sending them to be instructed in a city convent, warning them
they must confess their sins with a priest at the end of their education.[18]

No further "spontaneous" presentations were recorded until the mid-
1640s, when a series of seven Englishmen and a Scot came before the Tribunal to request conversion. These fresh arrivals all required the services
of English-speaking translators (most of whom were English Catholics
already living in the city) who helped their compatriots follow the script
for voluntary conversion laid out by the Suprema, vowing "to live and
die" in the Roman Catholic faith.[19] The first four cases were spaced out
over the course of several months, from May to August 1643, but given
such an abrupt upsurge in interest in the procedure, inquisitors wanted
to communicate to the Suprema that they had been appropriately rigorous. They pressed the fourth voluntary convert of the year, Thomas
Maren, to recognize that there were fundamental incompatibilities between Catholicism and his old beliefs. Maren responded to this implicit
statement of doubt by saying that of course he understood, and wanted

"to live and die in the Catholic faith—if he didn't believe it why would he come to this Holy Office?—for it was only to that end, for the salvation of his soul, that he had revealed himself [in hopes of] a remedy."[20]

In June and July 1645, three more Englishmen approached the Tribunal to register for their Catholic "citizenship," but in these cases inquisitors recorded how the converts were asked to affirm that they had not "converted to our holy Catholic faith in any other time but the present." In response, each penitent ratcheted up the anti-Protestant rhetoric, one asserting that he "detested and [wished to] separate himself from that sect of Protestants." The final case of "spontaneous" conversion prior to 1660 was that of Isaac Doni, a 26–year-old shoemaker who appeared before inquisitors "to testify [against himself, regarding] the errors and heresies that he had been following." Emphasizing his simple nature and ignorance, Doni spoke affectingly of the "great pain [he felt] in his heart" when he realized "he had been deceived" by his old faith. The notary wrote that Doni "made demonstrations of repentance and the desire to be a true and faithful Christian." Although an uneducated man, this convert had learned how to combine the formulas afforded by treaty stipulations with a convincingly heartfelt performance to earn his "cautious" absolution.

Despite their cooperation, Cartagena's inquisitors seem to have been a bit disgruntled with how the treaty loopholes for English and Dutch nationals were being employed. By 1648, Juan Federico, a Dutch "captain of a frigate that was preying on these coasts" (likely involved in contraband trade) was captured, and officials of the coast guard complained to the Tribunal that Federico had caused scandal by his open confession of Calvinist beliefs and refusal to show deference to Spanish religious symbols. Inquisitors wrote to the Suprema for advice on how to proceed with this man's case, which they believed should not be exempted from prosecution as "the new peace with the Dutch" might require. Federico, they said, was a "pirate thief" who had gone outside the "law of man," renouncing his vassalage to his law-abiding Dutch sovereign when he and pirates like him "infest[ed] these coasts, robbing and doing such damage to the estates and lives of the vassals of His Majesty." Federico's illegal status, they argued, conferred justice on their proceedings. Citing precedent in their 1622 proceedings against Adan Edón, they added "many more reasons" to go forward with prosecution: not only were Catholic souls in danger, but their patron the Crown also suffered, and so they urged the Supreme Council to allow them to punish Federico so as "to put a brake" on piratical activity. Finding himself potentially devoid of legal protections, the Dutch captain took matters into his own hands in the interim, and late the night of January 25, 1648, he "fled with another eight Dutch or English in a canoe."[21]

The debate did not end with Federico's flight, however, but stretched on until 1659, when the Suprema finally weighed in on the matter. In the meantime, two related cases came before Cartagena's Tribunal. In the first, concerning an English tailor resident in Caracas who remained obstinate that he would "live and die" as a Protestant, local inquisitors decided to release the accused on a sort of extended bail, prohibiting him from leaving the city upon pain of 200 lashes "until some other thing be ordered."[22] The second dealt with a Flemish or French pirate, Juan L'Grafe,[23] who was denounced in 1655 by captive Spaniards who had been humiliated and aggrieved when L'Grafe mocked a flag on their ship depicting St. John the Baptist and the Virgin Mary. Through signs and some words that crossed the language barrier between them, L'Grafe had allegedly expressed delight at the idea of beheading the painted figure of John the Baptist, if it were not for the image of the Virgin Mary ("a pretty whore") on the other side. Members of the local inquisitorial board debated about the case. One said that L'Grafe should be released because of the Peace Treaty and their instructions received in 1654 that "the Dutch should not be asked about their religion . . . if they haven't committed an offense against the faith . . . in the kingdoms of Spain or in their adjacent islands, beaches, ports, or bays, anchored there"—but what jurisdictional protections should be afforded to those caught at sea, and not anchored at any port? Another argued that the articles of peace didn't protect the pirate because the comments he had made against Mary's virginity had caused scandal among Catholics.

After nearly a year had passed since commencing his term of imprisonment, L'Grafe issued a series of petitions to inquisitors, trying to secure his release with arguments that he was a burden on the system, "surviv[ing only] on alms." That approach got him nowhere, so after two more years had passed, he requested an audience to express his desire

> to be Roman Catholic and separate himself with all his heart from the sect of Calvin that he had followed, because he had been blind and because in the three years that he was imprisoned among Roman Catholics he wanted to become like the rest.

Understandably suspicious at this about-face, Cartagena's officials wrote again to the Suprema, and in July 1659, more than four years after his initial arrest, the Supreme Council affirmed that L'Grafe should be accorded the same privileges as any other Protestant foreign national who wished to convert. They continued that although Cartagena's officials would be justified in proceeding against him for blasphemy, it would be "such a religious deed" if they would show mercy and instead assign him a light, spiritual penitence and admit him to formal reconciliation. They attached another copy of the 1630 instructions on "The Style to be observed with 'spontaneous' heretic nationals."[24]

Like these and other foreign Protestant nationals who were an increasing presence in Spanish port societies, Nicolas Burundel found himself vulnerable due to his extended residency. He had not refrained from "giving scandal" to the Spanish populace of Jamaica, nor had he (at least not that we know of) made any attempts to register his conversion, "spontaneous" or otherwise.[25] Though he was from a merchant family with ties to port cities where the Inquisition was active, Nicolas did not seem to be aware of procedural loopholes that treated with lenience Protestants who declared their wish to convert or be reconciled, knowing that a simple vow to "live and die as Catholics" carried enormous practical and cultural weight. Most likely Nicolas, out of ignorance, fear, or obtuseness, could not comprehend the inner workings of the Inquisition's bureaucratic machine, which spread, like the Hapsburg Empire, across Europe, the Mediterranean, and into the American continent.

At odds with Old World desires to neutralize religious tensions for the sake of mercantile cooperation, the popular idea of the Inquisition as an instrument of terror, of arbitrary cruelty and politically motivated vengeance continued to hold immense cultural currency.[26] The secrecy of the Inquisition's proceedings and the difficulty of securing release without confessing one's crimes—real or invented—enlarged the Tribunal's reputation for irrational zealotry. The possibility that those charged would be tortured to extract a predetermined confession, or even executed by fire, has contributed to the Black Legend's historical longevity. Nicolas Burundel, already depressed and desperate, would have little time to calm down before facing yet another ordeal. Because of the Frenchman's intransigence, the inquisitor and his consultants had voted to approve the use of torture "to know the truth."[27] This method of extracting confessions was accepted in European judicial and military interrogations, and was a commonplace in inquisitorial practice, since theologians assumed that physical suffering was the only way to gain access to the inner truth trapped inside the sinner's mind.[28]

On Monday, October 7, 1652, Nicolas was brought to the torture chamber, where he was warned he had one last chance to answer the

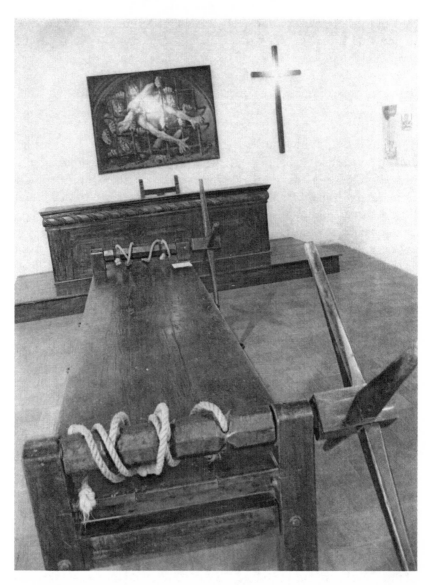

FIGURE 7. This montage of Inquisitorial torture and coercion is on display at Cartagena's Inquisition Museum, housed in the original Palacio of the Holy Inquisition, downstairs from the city's new archive and historical center. Photo by author.

charges against him. Frustrated, he burst out with a blasphemous "God be plagued! Why couldn't his lordship order him whipped or hung?" He averred that even though he had asked God and the Holy Virgin for mercy, he couldn't imagine "what truth or lie" he could say that would convince them of his word. Strapping the Frenchman onto the rack, the inquisitor proceeded by reading the Holy Tribunal's standard disclaimer about how it would be Burundel's own fault if the day's session resulted in death or injury. Nicolas interrupted, "Señor, it doesn't matter if you read [the charges] or not, there are the garrotes," but before the first turn of the wheel, the inquisitor calmly asked why he wished to "see himself in the pain of torture." Wouldn't cooperation be preferable? With the certainty of agony before him, Nicolas capitulated to the demands of the terrible bureaucracy, agreeing to answer their charges, and was taken down from the rack to be questioned in the main audience chamber.[29]

6 / Conversion, Coercion, and Tolerance
in Old and New Worlds

After bowing to the Tribunal's serious threats to employ torture, Nicolas returned to his cellmates with a story. Juan de Noguera reported that when Nicolas came back that morning, he was quieter than usual. Murillo said that Nicolas later joined the two at the table to eat, then confided, rather dramatically, "that he had seen a place no other Christian had [ever] seen." Nicolas proceeded to describe in great detail how during that morning's audience, he had been left alone in "a small chamber, without any windows." A writing desk, lit by only two candles, sat in front of an apparatus Burundel called the "torture mule." Adding a touch of drama to his role as hero, Nicolas claimed that he "voluntarily" climbed atop the device to show he wasn't afraid of death.

They began to discuss Nicolas's exchanges with the inquisitor concerning the charges levied against him, and he inquired about some points of doctrinal heresy he didn't understand—but Murillo and Noguera had been warned not to instruct Burundel in anything, so they feigned ignorance. Rather abruptly, Burundel shifted to a new topic, posing a seemingly unrelated question to his companions: "If you, going about this sea [that is, the Caribbean], were to come upon a ship of Moors and were to capture them and bring them to this city, what would you do with them?" Murillo responded without hesitation, saying that those they didn't sell, they would "make use of (*servirse dellos*), and seek to teach them so that they would become Christians." Nicolas probed further, "You wouldn't oblige them to become Christians by force?" referring to the beatings to which a reluctant convert might be subject.[1]

What element of Nicolas's past drew him from his tale of torture "never before seen by a Christian" to the theme of Mediterranean captivity? Since Nicolas Burundel had been captured and brought to North Africa to serve a "renegade" French Muslim in his youth, he would have been aware that coercion and conversion often went hand in hand. Likely Nicolas had himself faced some pressure to convert to Islam during his three-year stint as a captive in Algiers—young Christians like him were especially susceptible to both the coercive demands and persuasive powers of Muslim masters on the Barbary coast (his French master had chosen that very path to economic security and advancement).[2] The latest study on Mediterranean captivity by Robert C. Davis estimates that between one to one-and-a-quarter million Europeans were at least temporarily enslaved on the Barbary coast between 1530 and 1780, about 35,000 per year during the peak of North African corsair raids from 1580 to 1680.[3] In the seventeenth century, Mediterranean battles expanded rapidly into the Atlantic, affecting large numbers of Northern Europeans whose presence in Atlantic entrepôts was part of both long-established and growing international trade.[4] The ongoing struggle between Cross and Crescent in the Greater Mediterranean profoundly affected early modern European conceptions of conversion and apostasy, from the stories of redeemed captives like Nicolas Burundel to the many more who vicariously experienced "Barbary captivity" (often called Barbary slavery): by donating to redemptive societies, consuming the widely available print and oral tales of miserable slavery and daring escapes, or observing stage depictions of Barbary captivity. Frequent travelers and residents of coastal regions might have even more direct connections to these individuals and their tales. For European Christians of all persuasions, conversion to Islam was a dangerous—albeit fascinating—threat, one that needed to be carefully defused. Rituals of reconciliation were required to reintegrate returning captives and repentant apostates into European society; dramatists portrayed staged narratives of renegades repenting of their apostasy, fictions that belied the reality that a return to Christianity was rare indeed.[5]

Atlantic creoles from Protestant Europe brought with them to the Caribbean not only a keen sense of how they might manipulate Inquisition bureaucracies, but also practical knowledge about the complex politics of Mediterranean commerce, captivity, and conversion. In the American Antilles, Northern Europeans also sought lucrative markets and faced the danger of capture by an enemy Other (the Spanish) whose extraordinary cruelty was portrayed as flowing from a warped, anti-Christian religious zeal. Like in the Mediterranean, men who negotiated the boundaries of Caribbean Spanish captivity were faced with serious spiritual temptations, exemplified by the expediency of conversion. The similarity between these Mediterranean and Caribbean maritime analogues is worth analyzing, for beyond a surface comparison of the geographic semblance of these inland seas, several striking commonalities in strategies for conversion and re-conversion emerge from the records.[6] First, many had been able to compare the two spheres personally: data on the individuals brought before the Inquisition in Cartagena from 1610–1660 reveals that at least one-third (and the real percentage was likely much greater) had been educated in Old World maritime realities. Some, like Thomas Cox, prior to "faking" his Catholic conversion in the Caribbean, had taken part in "pillaging the Turk" through privateering ventures aimed at Muslim foes. (He might have also attacked shipping sponsored by European Catholics, but would have been smart enough to keep that story from inquisitors). Others, like Nicolas Burundel, translated their challenges as prisoners of the Inquisition through the lens of previous adventures in Barbary captivity. Like those privy to inquisitorial loopholes on voluntary conversion, European Catholics returning from North African captivity were aware, by example or rumor, that Inquisitors dealt relatively kindly with those who voluntarily confessed of being coerced into apostasy.[7] Inversely, if an apostate was redeemed (or escaped) from Barbary but waited for others to denounce him to Inquisition Tribunals, he faced a protracted ordeal, first of enumerating and confessing every one of his spiritual infractions, and then trying to disprove the witnesses who had testified against him, racking his brain to name all enemies who might have said something incriminating in the case. Trials lasting two to four years were not uncommon. But in coming forward voluntarily—again, *"espontaneamente"*—redeemed captives could craft their own narrative of events, and inquisitors rarely pushed for details or corroborating testimony in their haste to reunite another lamb with the Christian flock.[8] This pattern was clearly applicable to Cartagena as well, for only one case of voluntary conversion (Juan L'Grafe's delayed change of heart) took longer than one week to be processed.[9]

When savvy converts paired their voluntary self-denunciations with assertions that their former religious identity had been coerced—especially in the case of youths—they mirrored the essential elements of Mediterranean-style repentance and reintegration.[10] This phenomenon is best seen in a series of cases in 1615 against a group of Frenchmen routed from a Huguenot settlement in the Amazon and brought to Cartagena to facilitate their banishment back to France. The first of those to present himself "spontaneously" was Pedro Mozón, who testified he had spent five years of his youth as a Barbary captive. Perhaps sure that the Catholic Church would be lenient towards him, as it was towards returning captives who had been forced to convert to Islam, he admitted that he had been baptized and raised as a Catholic, but fate stepped in at the tender age of 12—his parents died, forcing him "to make his living" serving a French Huguenot captain who owned a privateering ship (*un navio con que andaba robando por la mar*). When his employer told Mozón he, too, must follow Huguenot practices, "seeing himself poor and defenseless, he acquiesed to his master." Although he claimed to have persisted as a Catholic for many years, Pedro admitted that recently he had succumbed to formal conversion—but was heartily repentant that he ever abandoned his natal faith.[11]

Mozón's lead was quickly followed by two more with "spontaneous" confessions. Both claimed, like many other youthful apostates to Islam, that they had always been faithful Catholics "on the inside," but had followed Huguenot practices out of fear they would be put in jail or that their wages or lands would be taken away. David Mingan had been raised a Huguenot but claimed to have been converted to Catholicism by Capuchin missionaries who had visited their settlement. Nonetheless, he continued to go to Huguenot services "out of fear of the governor, who was a great Huguenot heretic, and if he became a Christian and was discovered, [the governor] would take away all that his father, who had died there in Marañón, had earned as his wages."[12] Jacques de las Fontanas said he had lived as a Huguenot for three years because his master "told him that since he was his servant (*criado*) and lived in his house, he would have to be present at their prayers (*preces*)"; he argued that he had gone to Huguenot services only out of "curiosity and duty," and that some Capuchin fathers had assured him he could confess his sins without fear once he returned to a "Christian land."[13] The politics of power and the casuistry of religious identity—disguising one's "true," interior faith with a necessary exterior show—was a cultural trope that worked as well in the Caribbean as it had in the Mediterranean.[14]

Inquisitors, too, responded to repentant Christians in the Caribbean the same as in the Mediterranean. Inquisitors severely reprimanded Mozón and Las Fontanas—they, having been raised as Catholics, should have known better—but only required that as punishment they be sequestered for the remainder of their time in Cartagena in one of the city's monasteries for instruction. The Tribunal sent the Protestant-born

Mingan to join the other two for religious tutelage, but provisionally absolved him of any taint of heresy. One on the council argued that in a perfect world, he should have renounced his false faith as soon as he was convinced by the Capuchins; however, considering his limited exposure to Catholic teaching, his youth, and willing cooperation, they could accept his excuse that he had not followed through with his Christian obligations "out of fear he would lose what he and his father had earned in service of their king."[15] Understanding the coercive demands of converts' subordinate positions and the financial stakes involved in such hierarchical societies, local inquisitors opted for a benign approach to rescue these transient apostates from damnation.[16] Back in Madrid, however, the members of the Suprema remarked on their suspicions of former Barbary captive Pedro Mozón's polished performance (perhaps having seen too many like it among Muslim apostates on the peninsula), writing on their copy of Cartagena's yearly report that the inquisitors should have put him "to the test of torture . . . regarding his motives."[17]

Nicolas Burundel had already faced the threat of torture, and despite the fact that such practices of physical violence and intimidation were common practice in early modern law enforcement, he expressed his surprise and outrage at its use. He was equally shocked by his cellmates' responses to his query about whether North African Muslims would be forced to convert to Christianity if they came to Cartagena. Juan averred that one had to become a Christian voluntarily, and Francisco said that it was true—he remembered that some "Moors" had lived in that city unmolested by Inquisition officials (likely they were royal captives sent as forced laborers in the Caribbean naval galleys or assigned to building the city's defensive walls).[18] Nicolas was outraged: "Why then do they make those of other faiths/laws (*leyes*) turn Christian?" Murillo and Noguera tried to explain that "only heretics, who had strayed from the law they professed in baptism," were subject to the Tribunal's punishments. To Nicolas, this logic defied reason—frustrated, he demanded to know "which is worth more, to be a heretic or a Moor?" His cellmates repeated that only baptized Christians were subject to the penalties of the Holy Tribunal, so Nicolas answered his own question (which seemed patently ridiculous), declaring it "better to be a heretic than a Moor."[19]

Nicolas's assertion of the difference in value between Christians (Protestant heretics included) and "Moors" was in fact a distinction that the Spanish Inquisition and other institutions of the Catholic Reformation shared. Because the Mediterranean's imperial and religious politics were so complex and challenging, inquisitors tried to prioritize

which heresies were most worth their time. Catholic apostates or secret practitioners of Judaism or Islam came first; Protestants—who, like
Burundel, erroneously called themselves Christians—came next. Like
Nicolas, many people today are ignorant of the fact that the Inquisition
only prosecuted Christians or those who had converted to Christianity—they had no jurisdiction over Muslims, Jews, or even Amerindian
"New Christians."

This reality is encapsulated in the story of seven war galleys that departed from the Spanish coast in May 1616 to do battle against Muslim
corsairs and other enemy vessels in the Strait of Gibraltar and the coasts of
Spain. In that expedition, General Gabriel de Chaves captured three vessels allied with North African forces—the third a light vessel captained
by a well-known English "pirate," Thomas Shelley, who ran raids out of
Algiers with a crew of 30–odd men, mostly also English. After bringing
their prizes back to port, Spanish officials condemned six of the leaders
to death, but before carrying out the sentence, turned the inmates over
to Jesuit fathers from Cadiz—including one English Jesuit—for spiritual
redemption. The fathers of the Company celebrated soon thereafter the
"Remarkable Conversion" of all 36 English corsairs taken in this raid,
and composed a memorial of the event for publication that same year.
They must have sent the tract to many of the order's far-flung missions
and urban schools—one copy made its way to the library of the Jesuit
colegio in Bogotá, another likely molded sitting on the humid shelves of
Cartagena's *colegio*.[20] The text, written in stirring military metaphors,
emphasized the ease with which a variety of English heretics—compla-
cent Anglicans, ardent puritans, even renegade Muslim converts—were
swiftly conquered by the Jesuits' "Christian stratagems."[21]

Meanwhile, the 120+ "Turks" taken in General Chaves's raids were
kept chained to their vessels off the Christian shore, likely destined to
serve as oarsmen in Spain's coastal galleys, perhaps to be shipped to
America to serve in *guardacostas* patrolling the shores against enemy
intruders. Muslim corsairs were not pressed to convert to Catholicism,
but were instead immediately sent as rowers to the galleys, a backbreaking sentence to be sure, but one which might allow them the opportunity
to escape back to their homes in North Africa if their ship was later captured by Ottoman or Moroccan allies. Following this logic, renegade Europeans sometimes insisted that they had been born "Turks" or "Moors,"
as did one English renegade among the captured corsairs, "thinking to
escape his death under the disguise of a Moor, and remain a royal slave
in the galleys."[22]

Spanish Catholics observed the line of demarcation between European Christians, more deserving of redemption (both their lives and their souls) than the imminently enslaveable, polluting proto-racial Jews and Moors who had been expelled from the peninsula.[23] Nicolas Burundel was likewise attuned to his superior position above those religious and racial inferiors. At one point during his imprisonment he had insulted a Berber prisoner whose cell was down the hall from his, calling him a "mulatto dog." Another time, Nicolas asserted that the jailer had been giving him saltwater to drink, perfidious behavior indeed: "he was not a Moor or a Jew—why should they treat him in such a manner?"[24] Nicolas clearly thought of himself as somehow superior by virtue of his status as a white Christian, and thus insisted that to be a Christian (even if a heretic) should distinguish him from those "Moors" and "Jews" he imagined to be the legitimate objects of inquisitorial judgment. A week after his troubling exchanges with his cellmates, Nicolas was still fuming. He told Murillo and Noguera again "that one heretic was worth more than 100 Moors"—baptism should confer more protections on European Christians, not fewer! He also disparaged the Holy Office for "obligating men by force to become Christian," and told his cellmates proudly that in France there was "liberty of conscience"—no one there was arrested for heresy.[25]

Burundel's increasingly suspicious statements would soon lead to more startling revelations. Even though Nicolas didn't like talking about religion in general (it made him angry, and when he got angry, he started breathing in that affected way to which he had become accustomed), he couldn't avoid the subject with cellmates determined to curry favor with the inquisitor by recounting Burundel's indiscretions. Murillo reported that when he suggested to the Frenchman late one night that praying his rosary might bring some relief for his afflictions, Nicolas snapped at him in frustration, telling Francisco that

> those rosaries were no good, that those in his land were different . . . Asking him what differences there were . . . he wouldn't
> say but just insisted that they were different. [Murillo] said to him,
> "Well, if they're different, it must be that there's a different God in
> your land," to which he responded, "Yes."[26]

Such comments may have spurred Murillo, who had been born in Muslim-controlled Granada, to recall the similitude of Muslim prayer beads and Catholic rosaries. "Are you a Moor or a heretic?" Murillo challenged, aghast. Juan de Noguera corroborated the account of this unexpected revelatory exchange, as well as Nicolas's angry reply: "I'm not a Moor; I am a heretic."[27]

Nicolas was clearly playing with the definitional boundaries of Christianity, and he and his cellmates seemed to be speaking "past" one another when they used the term *Christian*. In fact, because we only have a record of these conversations from the point of view of Burundel's cellmates, we don't really know for certain when Nicolas used the term *Christian* or *Catholic,* or if he ever used the term *Protestant* or *Huguenot.* Much of the uncertainty stems from his cellmates' seeming inability to distinguish between Christians (Protestant and Catholic) and heretics (Muslims, Jews, or Protestant dissidents)—not to mention their incentive in reporting back a particular type of story to the inquisitor. The experience of captivity in North Africa may have convinced some European Christians, forced to huddle together into an indistinguishable "infidel" mass, that they had much more in common with one another than they had previously imagined. In Barbary, captives like Nicolas from Protestant lands had more contact with Catholics than they ever had at home, and learned about the congruencies in their faiths, similarities obscured by nationalist, anti-Catholic polemicists.[28] Such exchanges generated the conditions for the creation of common identities, the circulation of conversion strategies, and the exchange of international gossip. In one study of Northern Europeans interfacing between Islam and Catholicism, by the mid-seventeenth century, it seems that English captives brought before Spanish Inquisition Tribunals as Barbary renegades felt comfortable instead asserting their convinced Protestant identity, admitting they had converted to Islam merely out of expediency. Perhaps because of the networks of knowledge that operated among captives in North Africa, they knew enough about Hapsburg diplomatic concessions to take a confident stance, stating bluntly that they did not wish to betray "the religion of their parents" and become Catholics. Thanks to the century's treaty protections, many were simply shrugged off with a safe-conduct pass to their home countries. Such a tactic was not without peril, however. One adamant Protestant had his goods confiscated, and another was sentenced to one hundred lashes. The latter decided to opt for the path of least resistance and request Catholic instruction.[29]

After Murillo and Noguera had related to the inquisitor their triumph at finally getting Burundel to unmask himself as a heretic, the two began to embark on a new campaign to taunt their surly cellmate. Francisco began the game by casually asking Juan one day "if he'd ever seen anyone burned by the Inquisition in his land." Juan replied that yes, he had seen many Jews and heretics brought to the stake in Portugal. At this, Noguera said, Nicolas got up out of bed, and interrupted to ask if they had been Christians or Moors. Murillo thought Nicolas was asking about those who staged the *auto de fe*, and responded that they were "Christians, defenders of the faith." Noguera thought Nicolas's question was in reference to those "men of flesh and blood" sent to the stake, and said they weren't Moors, but rather Jews or heretics. "What did they mean by heretics?" Nicolas wanted to know. Discussing the matter at length, Murillo claimed that the "principal errors" heretics were known for were their denials of confession and communion. But Nicolas shouted them both down after the argument grew heated on conflicting definitions of penitence and the efficacy of confession to priests, insisting that no Christian could burn another in the name of religion "if God didn't order it" and that the fires of hell were reserved "only for devils and men who weren't Christians."[30] Over the next several weeks, the tension grew palpable between Nicolas and his cellmates. Nicolas's surprise revelations about his real beliefs (interspersed with more assertions of his possession and other mocking provocations) only caused new tension in the cell—the Frenchman one day averred that he was "a better Christian" than both his cellmates, even if they did spend most of their days kneeling in prayer before an image of the Virgin in their cell. He rejected his companions' offers to share their rosaries with him or teach him Catholic prayers.[31] Murillo reported that the prayers Nicolas claimed to recite in bed were really murmured maledictions against "his wife, and his children, and himself, and the person who locked him in prison, and the minute he touched foot on Spanish soil."[32]

In this period of reflection (and perhaps regret), Burundel began to expound from an even more radical perspective on religious tolerance and the proper response to heresy. Telling his cellmates that even "in Moorish lands they don't do as they do here—arrest men," he recalled the similarities between bi-confessional France and the practical toleration afforded to non-Muslim foreigners in North African cities. Heresy was just a label, he told the others, explaining that someone considered a heretic by one group "called those of the other [sect] heretics and viewed them as errant . . . "[33] It was unclear in Juan de Noguera's testimony if Nicolas was referring to French Protestantism or North African Islam when he explained how "if one wanted to convert to their sect they would accommodate [that person] and act with kindness (*lo regalaban*); but if one didn't wish [to convert] one wouldn't be compelled, but would rather be left to live in the law that [person] wished."[34] In Nicolas Burundel's final analysis, liberty of conscience in the way it had been mandated in France since the 1598 Edict of Nantes was best. However, he also may have been suggesting that the Spanish Inquisition had sunk so low that it was even better to reside in "the land of the Moors," where the use of persuasive, rather than coercive, powers were used to effect conversion.

The levels of cruelty and violence employed to achieve religious hegemony in Europe's early modern religious wars seemed out of touch to men like Nicolas Burundel. To them, the use of the Inquisition's controlled violence seemed more than anything like the abhorrent tactics that propagandists described as common among sadistic, irrational, anti-Christian tyrants forcing their captives to convert to Islam. Frenchmen who had witnessed the establishment of official toleration in their homelands, and who for years had been protected by the Gallican ban on the Inquisition in their country, were especially apt to criticize the Holy Office's strong-arm tactics. One French peddler living in Cartagena was arrested for his opinionated banter with clients, including such blasphemies as calling the Inquisition's officials "Turks and heretics," saying that "the French weren't fools for refusing to admit the Holy Office in their lands."[35] Juan de Noguera overheard Burundel muttering after yet another frustrating audience with the inquisitor that "this wasn't the Holy Office, but the Holy Devil."[36] One month later, when Burundel came begging the inquisitor for the "consolation" of "life or death," he responded calmly that Nicolas had only himself and his disorderly behavior to blame for the delays in his case.[37] Six months later, the case had come to a standstill as Nicolas continued to claim possession by a supernatural being (which he had begun calling a familiar of the Holy Inquisition), so officials ordered another round of torture. This time, Nicolas could stand only one turn of the screw before he promised full cooperation, although in subsequent questioning he remained steadfast in his claims that he was not "a heretic, nor was he raised in heresy—but [was] an apostolic Roman Catholic."[38]

Foreign Protestants were not the only ones to pronounce the Tribunal's hold over their lives and consciences a cruel parody of Christianity. After Burundel was removed from the cell he shared with Murillo and Noguera, it seems they turned on one another. Of course, we can't know whether they were telling the truth when they informed on one another, especially since Nicolas was not asked to serve as a corroborating witness. Juan de Noguera reported to the inquisitor in November that Francisco had said that "if he were a powerful man," he would try to persuade the pope and the king of Spain to do away with the Holy

Tribunal, "because the Inquisitors were no more than thieves whose only purpose was to steal the estates of those they arrested." Murillo allegedly believed that the inquisitors, who "worshiped money," automatically judged all inmates guilty (so they could confiscate their estates), and that their spy-mongering and torture were inspired by the Devil, carried out "under the cloak and name of God." Francisco told Juan that he might just run away—he had already proved himself an expert escape artist. What would he do then?

> He would go over to Holland and bring some Dutchmen to conquer this city, and the first thing he would do would be to take control of this Holy Office and call before him the Lord Inquisitor and say to him, "how is it that you are doing this and that? why did they put you here?" and then put him in a cell and give him coarse bread (*bollos*) to eat.[39]

Caribbean Spanish residents certainly knew the menace presented by the Dutch and their sea rovers in those waters. Murillo's belief that he would find allies against the Inquisition among other European Christians, and his distaste for the institution's use of torture and reliance on prisoners to betray one another, suggests that his conversations with Burundel about the value of Christian lives and consciences might have had some effect.

From European Christians' religious-commercial-political entanglements in the Mediterranean, to their battles to define and control New World imperialism, many came to believe that fostering commerce (and tolerance) were the keys to survival. Such utopian ideals might have been especially persuasive in the Caribbean, far from the true threat of Ottoman and North African Islam, a space where European colonists of many nationalities were more likely to think of their common religious superiority compared to "idolatrous" Indians and "heathen" African slaves. Northern Europeans may have fit more easily into the upper echelons of Spanish America's evolving racial hierarchies—at least they were fellow Christians who had some respect for the ritual of baptism, and they *did* make trade and commerce quite profitable . . . but far from both the military and religious threat of North African Islamic clout (and far from the protection of metropolitan military support), Protestant interlopers also took on the role of the fearsome, threatening Other.

The process of Protestant confessionalization—especially as Reformed Churches fractured into smaller and smaller denominational units—required the *experience* of conversion, making it a performable act. The transferability and ubiquity of such acts varied widely from place to place, individual to individual. However, in certain areas of Northern Europe it was normal to be conversant in multiple theories of conversion; when asked by an Inquisition *calificador* how he knew so much about Calvinism, Nicolas Burundel replied, "having been raised in a land with so many sects, I know them and can speak them all."[40] Mobility, cross-cultural contact, and polyglotism—shared by many European Atlantic creoles—all enhanced the transfer of religious knowledge, providing even unlettered men with an education in faiths beyond the one to which they were born. Through the commercial and religious transformations of the seventeenth century, Northern Europeans drawn into trade and conflict with Catholic and Muslim powers—from Algiers to the Canary Islands, from Lisbon to Malta—learned to become religious chameleons, and learned too that compliance or duplicity were preferable to conflict or the pain of coercion.

But despite the adage that money makes the world go round, it is worthwhile to remember that even as European colonists sought out commercial opportunities as planters or privateers in these islands, they did not leave their religious convictions behind. We cannot speak with any certainty about the "truth" of the many conversions to Catholicism registered in the reports of Cartagena's Inquisition during the seventeenth century, nor can historians ever access the silent space of those men's minds. Inquisitorial procedures, as well as the Tribunal's sheer power to coerce and shape (false) testimonies, means that historians can only see these men's stories through a glass darkly.

Although Caribbean versions of Christianity may be interpreted as especially cynical, it is clear from the evidence that although Northern European "pirates" and their patrons put aside confessional boundaries at times in their everyday social and economic dealings, they were rarely hardened or indifferent to the spiritual resonances of confessionally defined morality or justice. Nicolas Burundel's one small voice actually challenges the easy conclusion that religious compunctions were shed at the slightest provocation. After reading Burundel's case many times— reading between the lines and listening for its silences—I believe his vacillating stories reflected his desperate attempt to maintain a Calvinist faith underneath official protestations of his "Roman Catholic Christian" identity. One day, shortly after the Frenchman had confessed to his cellmates that he was a heretic, Nicolas turned to Francisco Murillo and asked why he kept praying day after day to the images of Christ and the Virgin, which had been placed in their cell. Burundel suggested that those prayers might have more effect if directed to "St. Nicodemus." For modern readers, this reference may seem strange, but as a lapsed church-man, Murillo would have understood it right away. Nicodemus appears in the Gospel of John, a Pharisee to whom Jesus had preached of the need to be "born again" in the Spirit. Nicodemus was swayed by those words, and he helped to bury Jesus's body when it was taken down from the cross. However, Nicodemus, a "Christian" convert, performed the burial in secret, fearing the derision of his Pharisee peers.[41] Religious leaders from the medieval inquisitor Nicholas Eymerich to Protestant reformer John Calvin wrote about the moral perfidy of religious dissimulation— Calvin denounced Protestants who tried to argue that secular laws man-dated that they separate their inner beliefs from outward conformity to Catholicism, calling them cowardly Nicodemites.[42]

Were Burundel's own prayers to St. Nicodemus answered? We can-not know the content of his silent prayers, but it is certain that his pleas for the speedy conclusion of his case were denied. In March 1654, more than two and a half years after his arrest, Cartagena's officials were still uncertain as to how to proceed against the recalcitrant Frenchman, and so they wrote to the Suprema in Madrid for advice. The Suprema wrote back in September of the following year, calling Burundel a "genuine spy" who should be dealt with accordingly (neither what type of spy-ing they suspected him of, nor the necessary consequences, were spelled out); the Suprema's letter would not be received in Cartagena de Indias until July 1655. Finally, in October 1656, and again in March 1658, the Frenchman was brought into the audience chamber, where he was re-quired to renounce his severe crimes (*abjuración de vehemente*) before receiving the sentence mandated by the Tribunal: for the crime of her-esy, three years of unpaid labor on the city's fortifications, followed by another three years of instruction with the city's Dominican fathers; for his complicity in the death of Governor Pedro Caballero, five years in the galleys and perpetual exile from Jamaica, Cartagena, and Madrid.[43] Did Nicolas survive and thrive after his release from the Inquisition prisons or was he "already dead," beaten down by the psychological stress of im-prisonment? Did he find Ana, perhaps escape? Others had been known to do the same. We find the Englishman Thomas Cox (who had confessed to making up a fake story of conversion in Venezuela) several years af-ter his release residing in the English half of St. Christopher, where he volunteered to help a puritan military expedition attack the Spanish in Hispaniola (the subject of Part III); Cox had survived twelve years in Hispaniola and several more in Cartagena's Inquisition prisons, only to meet his death during one of the first of many disastrous skirmishes on that island.[44] Life was brutally short, even for the most resourceful.

In Nicolas Burundel's Mediterranean and Atlantic worlds, performance and deception were necessary survival strategies, unsavory though they might seem from a stance of religious orthodoxy or moral absolutism. His extended experience with the Inquistion in Cartagena helps us recognize that religious identity in the early Caribbean was paradoxical, both easy to perform and deeply felt. Burundel knew that being a Christian—even a heretic Christian—gave him and other sojourning foreigners in the Caribbean a certain sort of privilege, given their embeddedness in contraband networks that subordinated the mandates of the Church to that of easy profits. Because of the privilege tacitly extended to Nicolas as a man of European descent—a "white" Christian—he and others came to see the use of violence to enforce religious conformity as a crime in itself. Like enslaved individuals who protested cruelty using the language of spiritual belonging, Protestant Northern Europeans shared with one another strategies for calling on the power of their shared religion (Christianity) and their racialized privilege to help mitigate the negative effects of their otherwise uncertain lives.

PART III

HENRY

"Such as will truck for Trade with darksome things"

The Spaniard we have hinted is the Pope's supporter, and the Treasure of the West-India's is the Spaniards strength. These Silver Sinews, and Golden Nerves, are the strength of the Man of sin; as to his external part, which is to destroy is (instrumentally) the work of the Sword: Cut but in twain that Silver thread, and Babels brats will murther one another; stop but the current of this Silver stream, and they all die with thirst.

. . . can we not face Frontiers, and look in the mouths of Cannon as well abroad as at home[?]: But grant wee do march . . . having a care that the Dust of the Gold get not into our Throats (by vertue of a conceit) and cause a greater thirst then our proportion of Water will satisfie.

—*A DIALOGUE, CONTAINING A COMPENDIOUS DISCOURSE CONCERNING THE PRESENT DESIGNE IN THE WEST-INDIES*
(London, 1655)

7 / Cromwellian Political Economy and the Pursuit of New World Promise

The day after Christmas 1654, Henry Whistler, a man of considerable sailing experience, waited aboard a ship anchored on the Thames as the cannon fired, a signal to call passengers on board. Whistler took advantage of the lull before the journey to begin composing what he titled "A Jornal of a Voaidg from Stokes Bay: and Intended by Gods assistant for the West Inga [Indies]." As he watched the ship slowly fill up and the tearful goodbyes on the docks below, Whistler's imagination was sparked by how much the scene before him resembled a passage in a book he had read recently, recounting the sailing of another fleet to the Americas. Borrowing (or rather, plagiarizing) some rather humorous phrases from the book, Whistler copied how the ship's departure warning shot was taken by many as "a worning for them to hid[e]." Others wept, he wrote— "yong men that had intangelled them selues in loue with some yong virgin"—as they bid their sweethearts good-bye, "bequeathing unto them sume pledg of Thayer wanton love; receaveing from them sume Cordiall against sea sicknis: as Capes, and Handcerchifes, and shertes, to eye and ware when Neptune should most appose them." Called away from his literary appropriation to his sailing duties, Whistler finished the day by recording the work of getting all the fleet safely out of the port, where about midnight they caught "a fair gale" from the south-southeast.[1]

Whistler, like many other men living in Cromwellian England, was drawn to one of the best sellers of 1648, *The English-American, his travail by sea and land*, written by a Protestant firebrand named Thomas Gage who had been raised by his English Catholic family in Spain. This retrospective of Gage's life opened with his missionary journey to the Americas in the habit of a Dominican (the passage that Whistler copied contained Gage's satirical comments on the lewdness of some Spanish friars he met, who wept openly as they took leave of their sweethearts, "young Franciscan Nun[s]").[2] Gage's hugely popular narrative recounted his peregrinations in Mexico and Guatemala and his journey back to England, where he converted to Protestantism. The popularity of anti-"popish" (especially anti-Spanish) literature was one element of Gage's literary success[3]; the other was the rarity of first-hand narratives from the Spanish Americas. And Gage's story dazzled! Not since the Inquisition survival narratives of Miles Philips, Job Hortop, and Robert Tomson at the end of the previous century had English readers felt both their curiosity about the Americas satisfied and their sense of Protestant superiority confirmed.[4] Gage's conversion/travel narrative encouraged the English to challenge Spain's precedence in the Indies by force, and he would repeat that suggestion in a private petition to puritan leader Oliver Cromwell, who had taken on the title of "Protector" of England in 1653 at the close of a Civil War that had divided the nation for nearly a decade.[5] This current fleet's voyage, with Henry Whistler above-deck navigating and Thomas Gage below in the chaplain's quarters, would test England's imperial pretensions. Just as the young English Catholic Thomas Gage had three decades earlier defied Hapsburg decrees barring foreigners from the Indies, this expedition defied tradition as England's first officially state-supported military campaign against the Spanish in the Americas.[6]

Known to subsequent generations as Cromwell's "Western Design," this offensive served as a brash advertisement of English Protestant imperial ambitions and Cromwell's millennial belief in the righteousness of an all-out religious crusade "beyond the line."[7] Convinced by Gage of Spain's weakness in the Americas, Cromwell ordered an assault "upon some of the Islands, and particularly Hispaniola, and St. John's Island [Puerto Rico], one or both."[8] The plan went that England would first occupy the fortifications of their captured islands, and then use them as a base from which to launch attacks on key Caribbean ports like Havana and Cartagena. In the final victory, Cromwell imagined that England would "Be master of the Spanyards Treasure which comes from Peru,"[9] and Gage promised that America's "Indians" would "willingly and freely invite the English to their protection," thus transferring "just right or title to those Countries" to English government.[10] However, such plans came to naught. Despite numerical supremacy, the expeditionary forces' first attack on Hispaniola was easily rebuffed, the army being hit hard with casualties and illnesses. The expedition's second attack on Jamaica, a sparsely populated frontier outpost, succeeded—but only marginally so—for the island's Spanish and black inhabitants (free and enslaved) retreated to the hills and began a drawn-out series of guerrilla attacks against English forces weakened by disease and poor provisions. England would have to pump money and migrants into the island for nearly five years before it could be secured.

This chapter examines the vicissitudes of the Cromwellian-era political economy, from its millennial promise to make England a nation flowing with American milk and honey, to its embattled defense of a colonial policy that failed to deliver its economic promises.[11] The logistical missteps and unexpected setbacks of the Western Design disrupted the cohesiveness of the expeditionary forces and their sense of cultural and religious unity, pitting "godly" officers against their "unregenerate" troops, divisions that often followed lines of socioeconomic status more than any measure of religious conviction. These failures and divisions prompted many—both in England and the West Indies—to accuse leaders of religious hypocrisy, of using the language of godliness to mask the "avaricious Intents of some (more than ordinary) Men, who desire rather to heap up to themselves Abundance of Treasure, enjoy fair Houses, rich Plantations, and all Things suitable thereunto, [rather] than to glorify God in their Actions."[12] As the campaign struggled to hold on in Jamaica, new questions about political and economic justice travelled from the Caribbean to England, as it appeared that the Cromwellian regime was exploiting the labor of Englishmen, making them "slaves" and thus disrupting the nascent racial hierarchies of Caribbean colonialism. Many Englishmen influenced by (if not completely accepting of) the radical republicanism of the Interregnum period following the execution of Charles I came to protest the "tyranny" and "slavery" that Cromwell and his merchant allies imposed on Englishmen sent to Jamaica. By the end of the Interregnum, various sectors of the English populace would unite to protest the forced labor of their countrymen in the West Indies, and a new sense of the rights of "free-born Englishmen" emerged, one which rejected the language of puritan exclusionary practices and forged a naturalized idea of English privilege (implicitly defined as Protestant and white).

Imperial historians who have studied the Western Design in the past have focused primarily on the strategic mistakes of the expedition: the mismanagement of supplies, the problems of illness and poor discipline among the troops, the quarrels between officers, even judgments of the commanders' perceived character flaws.[13] More recent treatments of the affair by British historians have endeavored to answer questions about Cromwell's goals for foreign policy, and have scrutinized the balance between religiously and economically defined motivations for expansion during the Protectorate.[14] A few scholars have seen the failures of the Western Design from a class perspective, believing that the expedition unleashed a particularly "Atlantic" culture of republican liberty.[15]

These approaches certainly have great value, but analyzing the influence of gender and race on the religious politics of the Western Design brings into sharp relief Englishmen's emerging sense of their political and economic clout in the Caribbean, their authority based on concepts of their own Protestant privilege and racial exclusion.[16] The execution of Charles I had severed the nation's (god)head, unleashing radical new ways of thinking about state power, hierarchy, and patriarchy—much of it through the idiom of religious identity and millennial expectation.[17] The social and religious tumult of the Civil War period created a "world turned upside down," challenging fundamental English societal norms from divine right to patriarchal authority. Contemporaneously, the solidification of English plantations in the West Indies offered the opportunity to challenge Spanish Catholic dominance in the Americas. Part of that solidification, the wholesale adoption of African slave labor, also helped define how the English saw themselves as a nation. Tied to traditional early modern categories of belonging like nation and religion, the struggle to define new gendered norms and racial categories in the Caribbean helped define English exceptionalism.[18]

This story offers a new perspective on this transformation as it centers on the experience of men like Henry Whistler and the common seamen and soldiers who formed the majority of this expedition. We see how they defined themselves as Protestant men, and as white men, whether that definition came from first-hand experience or inherited preconceptions of the Caribbean. The colorful specificity and unique interpretation of events in Whistler's narrative is the closest we can get to the experience of the thousands of unnamed and unsung men-at-arms.[19] Although Whistler left the Caribbean shortly after the initial capture of Jamaica, my research in Spanish archives revealed other never-before-seen stories of men who, like him, were disgusted by the expedition's puritan leadership, especially their demands that soldiers till the land, a humiliating sacrifice in a region where Africans, not Europeans, were defined as "natural" slaves and drudges. The soldiers' masculine self-conception was built more around conquest, valour, and survival than their superiors' rhetoric of pious paternalism and providential fortitude.

However, this story is also (of necessity) about Thomas Gage and other men favored during the Interregnum, of puritan elites who dreamed of a Protestant crusade against Spain's overseas domination and the Catholic agendas supported by its wealth. The fact that we know Whistler was reading Gage's narrative—and found it interesting enough to copy—means that we can assume that he, and many other ordinary Englishmen, found Gage's ideological Protestantism and tales of Spanish American decadence to take pride in his contributon to an attack against Spanish holdings in the West Indies. Although scholars have tended to see the Western Design as a battle between religious and secular motivations, I would like to propose that we look at the nuances that drew together concepts of England's imperial mission with the spiritual rhetoric of economic rights. Gage's narrative and Cromwell's instructions to his commanders reflect this unity: they believed that easy profit and control of American riches would be England's providential reward for success in this venture. Whistler was as cognizant of this promise of wealth as any other young man who had read Hakluyt and other chroniclers. He had his own dreams of American treasure. These intertwined ambitions—religious victory and American prosperity—would define the goals and expectations of those who participated in the Western Design. In seeking out prosperity in the unexpected succession of failures and setbacks that the expedition's participants faced, especially when it came to race and opportunity, theye would come to critique the religious leadership's broken promises.

Cromwell's vision of political economy was inextricably linked to the popular belief that Protestant England was providentially suited to triumph, in Europe and throughout the world.[20] We can see this conviction in the commissions Cromwell issued to General Robert Venables and Admiral William Penn, joint heads of the Western Design's military offensive. He first called them to remember the "cruelties and inhuman practices of the King of Spain exercised in America, not only upon the Indians and natives, but also upon the people of these nations inhabiting in those parts. . . . " (meaning the West Indies).[21] Cromwell also referred to the Spanish Inquisition's jurisdiction over foreign merchants—a legal point Cromwell had tried to negotiate with the Spanish ambassador just months prior, demanding of him "that liberty might be granted to the said [English] merchants to have and use in Spayne English bibles and other religious books." Don Alonso de Cardenas recoiled at this request and the Protector's insistence that free passage be granted to Englishmen traveling to the West Indies, saying that to concede these points would be "to ask his master's two eyes."[22]

Thus was born Cromwell's justification for war, a war that took on millennial import. In popular English puritan conception, Spain was seen as handmaiden to the pope (the Antichrist himself), so Cromwell's reference to Spain's spurious "claim . . . to all that part of the world by colour of the pope's donation" took on apocalyptical resonance.[23] Cromwell consulted with the puritan reverend John Cotton on the spiritual aspects of his plans, and together they read the prophesies of the seven seals in the Book of Revelation. Cotton encouraged him to act, saying that "to take from the Spaniards in America would be to dry up Euphrates."[24] Now Cromwell did not so much wish to dry up the Euphrates—that symbol of the Spanish Canaan's wealth and fertility—but rather to divert its flow to English coffers. Taking up the point that Spain had time and again tried to push the English out of the Americas, Cromwell asserted his "just grounds to believe that [Spain] intends the ruin and destruction of all the English plantations, people, and interest in those parts." Basing his military aims on a providential model of Protestant duty, he ended his commissions with a call to arms: "[we have], for these and several other reasons, with advice of our council, prepared and set forth a fleet . . . into America, with an intention to assault the said King of Spain and his subjects there."[25]

Despite the clear goal of divesting America's wealth to England, the "mission" of this assault was also expressed as a plan to "save the Indians" from Spanish cruelty and Catholic aberrance, appealing to England's imagined role as Protestant avenger.[26] The "Black Legend"—a narrative of Spain's unmatched greed, cruelty, and hypocrisy—was commonplace in English nationalist thought from the Elizabethan period; propagandists had eagerly exploited tales about the unjust enslavement of Native Americans from writers like Bartolomé de las Casas. In fact, Cromwell and those military and civilian commissioners he would charge with carrying out the expedition imagined Native Americans as one among several groups of potential allies in the Americas. Like several generations of puritan colonial propagandists, Gage's entreaties to attack underscored the unhappiness of Native America's inhabitants. Beginning in his prefatory dedication and throughout his narrative, he referred to the multitudes of "oppressed people" he had encountered during his time in the Spanish Americas. Across cities and town in the Mexican and Guatemalan territories, his narrative continually referenced examples of Spanish inhumanity against Indians, who were kept in "slavish bondage" because of their European masters' covetousness. Continuing in the vein of "the enemy of my enemy is my friend," Gage referred to yet another group who would gladly accept England's benevolent leadership: communities of African descent likewise enslaved by the cruel Spanish, not to mention those who, "for too much hard usage, have fled away . . . from their Masters unto [the] woods, and there live." In Guatemala, he asserted, there were two or three hundred maroons living just outside the urban centers: "These have often said that the chief cause of their flying to those mountains is to be in a readiness to joyne with the English or Hollanders, if ever they land in that Golfe; for they know, from them they may injoy that liberty, which the Spaniards will never grant unto them . . . "[27] In the search for war justifications, a multitude of allies (Indians, black slaves, even Spanish creoles) proved convenient.[28] England's rhetorical hopes for interracial alliances with Indians and Africans assumed, in a way, that these communities could be incorporated into a puritan New World Order. However, as we will see, these fantasies were silent on exactly how English Protestants might achieve spiritual common ground with peoples still considered "savage" in popular imagination.

The most famous examples of interracial utopian dreams come to fruition could be found in narratives of Sir Francis Drake's exploits, especially the time he had co-opted disgruntled maroon and Amerindian groups to help raid Spanish holdings, culiminating in his capture of the mule train carrying silver across Panama in 1572–1573. These tales were revived in the era of the Western Design. For more than two generations, the English public had read about Drake's exploits in Hackluyt's volumes and periodic reprints. In 1653 a new tract entitled *Sir Francis Drake Revived* was published, recounting Drake's fortuitous Panama landing in the midst of a siege of Nombre de Dios by armed maroons, who introduced his men to friendly Indians off the coast near Tolu and eventually assisted him in intercepting the silver train.[29] When Gage spoke of Drake's exploits, he remembered not only his sacking of the great port of Cartagena, but especially his confederation with the "Blackmores" from Nombre de Dios: "the like was never by any other attempted, and by the Spaniards is to this day with much admiration recorded."[30]

Cromwell's plan for imperial expansion—his "puritan" political economy—was designed not only to destroy Spanish Catholic hegemony, but also (as with Drake) to redirect the wealth of the Indies to England and give God's Chosen People the economic standing to rule hemispheric affairs. As Cromwell dreamed of building a New Jerusalem,

FIGURE 8. Portrait frontispiece to *The world encompassed by Sir Francis Drake, being his next voyage to Nombre de Dios formerly imprinted* (London, 1628). This plate was reproduced again in the 1653 publication, *Sir Francis Drake Revived.* Image courtesy Hans and Hanni Kraus Sir Francis Drake Collection, Library of Congress American Memory Digital Collection.

Gage offered an intriguing tidbit about Spanish prophesy which (though tainted by Catholic superstition) surely had something to say to those with providentialist predilections: "It hath been for these many yeares their own common talke, from some predictions, or (as they call them) prophesies . . . that a strange people shall conquer them, and take all their riches from them."[31] Cromwell's military and economic millennialism envisioned first establishing English troops in the Caribbean, weakening Spain's grip on the mainland, and finally winning English conquest of a land presumed so rich it might be mistaken for "Mahomets Paradise" (according to Gage, the appellation the Spanish had applied to Guatemala).[32] The success of a providential political economy depended on Gage's final words of advice to the Protector. It was imperative, he cautioned, to send godly men, men who could resist the temptations of American treasures. In his narrative, Gage continually commented on how Spanish American "liberty" from metropolitan rule and the many opportunities for easy riches served to corrupt—even pious friars full of religious zeal soon fell into anti-Christian economic oppression of America's native peoples. Before returning to the subject of a potential puritan religious mission to the Indians, Gage counseled Cromwell to be sure that "such as goe thither . . . be well principled in points of honesty; otherwise they may soone bee snared, and fall from God . . . "[33]

Both of Cromwell's commanders, General Robert Venables and Admiral William Penn, seem to have met his standards for men who would prize the ideals of a religious mission over the lucrative possibilities of personal gain. Penn, who had served in Parliament's naval campaign against the Irish during the 1640s, had dismissed his father's appeals to return to more profitable private commerce, arguing that his efforts and funds in the campaign had been "well, very well spent . . . for the maintenance of so good, so just, so pious a quarrel.[34] Venables, a Parliamentarian taken with rather strict puritanism, would later claim he had accepted the paltry commission Cromwell offered him "to let the World know it was the Promotion of the Gospel and the Service of our country we chiefly did propound to ourselves"—not the money.[35]

What about the rest of the men who would end up joining the campaign? What dreams motivated them to offer their skills as soldiers and sailors? Some of those who enlisted likely came from the ranks of the New Model Army, either those disbanded after Cromwell's rise to power or those left without work after wars with the Irish and Dutch; many more seem to have been recruited from among the slums of London, swollen with uprooted refugees, the poverty-stricken, many of whom would later be labeled "Cheats, Thieves, Cutpurses, and such like lewd Persons." The truth was, London's "masterless men" saw few opportunities to make a living outside of soldiery, and many must have hoped that by going abroad they might avoid debtor's prison or the dole.[36] Given the religious and political tumult of Britain's preceding decades, a general anti-Catholic campaign was appealing, but with few economic opportunities at home, the promise of American riches was an even more compelling incentive to join.

In Barbados and St. Christopher, another roughly three thousand troops were recruited, mainly from the ranks of struggling freedmen and servants hoping to escape their indentures. They, too, fantasized that knocking Spain out of its place in the Caribbean would open up new opportunities for wealth and self-sufficiency. In the 1630s and even the 1640s, some men of slight means who came to the English Caribbean had been able to fulfill their dreams for property and prosperity. But to do so, they first had to survive the "seasoning period" and then, if they were servants, to survive their masters' hard usage, since wealthier planters could buy replacement servants cheaply and "had little reason to exercise restraint in their efforts to extract more work from them." But by the 1650s, with a "boom" in sugar prices encouraging planters to buy up most of the island's arable land, servants in Barbados who served out their indentures rarely had the chance to make their dreams of trans-Atlantic prosperity come true—so a campaign such as this offered new opportunities for optimism.[37]

Barbadian planters initially resisted cooperating with the expedition's orders for recruitment, for the intensification of sugar production necessitated the expansion of African slavery, and consequently the need for a robust militia to police a potentially rebellious enslaved population. They feared that the absence of so many white freemen and servants would open up the island to attack by internal enemies, not to mention the threat of Spanish reprisals if Cromwell's expedition was successful. Barbadian elites also grumbled about being forced to house and provision troops during their several months' stay on the island. Cromwell's orders to confiscate the cargos of foreign ships (mostly Dutch vessels engaged in "illegal" trade) created more dissatisfaction, for the commissioners required Barbadians to buy those goods at well above market prices.[38] While the expedition's soldiers and sailors challenged the expedition's "godly" reputation by enjoying themselves (as soldiers were wont to do), the frustrated commissioners painted the island's planters as driven only by their private interests. Cromwell's puritan designs faced significant resistance in the business- and greed-oriented West Indies, problems that would only grow worse when it became clear that ordinary soldiers and sailors would not reap the wild profits they had come to associate with manly conquest and colonial success.

8 / The Politics of Economic Exclusion: Plunder, Masculinity, and "Piety"

Leaving the English islands for their chosen target of Hispaniola, the commanders of the expedition tried to refocus the company on their religious mission, ordering a day of fasting and waiting on the Lord. As their stomachs growled, the soldiers likely took part in each ship's program of preaching, joint prayer, and other encouragements to reflect on their sins and the dangers of battle. For those men like Henry Whistler who were literate and had happened to bring along a small prayer book, such as the pocket-sized *Manual of Devotions*, they might have read "The Soldier's Devotion" privately or with others. In it was outlined the divine approval for war: "If the ground be good; as either to maintain true Religion, therefore is warre against Antichrist commanded: or else to recover that which the Enemy hath unjustly taken away . . . "[1] Those who brought with them a Bible might follow the verses cited in the text's margins to find more concrete evidence of God's will for war. Sailors perched in the crow's nests watching for enemy ships, as well as navigators steering clear of damaging underwater reefs, would have been called to mind of the larger importance of watchfulness—of their sins, of evil outside forces—on such a strange, becalmed day of fasting.

The fleet arrived off the coast of Hispaniola, and on Sunday, early in the morning, the company joined again in prayer to ask God's blessing on their undertaking. Perhaps Thomas Gage preached extemporaneously about how they were following in the glorious steps of fellow Englishman Sir Francis Drake, the great Protestant pirate who held the city of Santo Domingo for ransom in 1586; he might have elaborated on the providential import of capturing this island, "the Spaniards first plantation," a sign of providential favor which would doubtless cow the "superstitious" Catholic enemy into submission.[2] Gage and other ministers would have found it fitting to lead the company in reciting "The Soldier's Prayer":

> O Almighty God, who hast stiled thy selfe a man of Warre, and hast now called me to be a man of War; I beseech thee teach my hands to war and my fingers to fight; Give unto me, and every one of my fellow Soldiers, the strength of Sampson, the courage of David, and the Wisedome of Solomon . . . And because Death is Before our eyes, give us grace to be mindfull of it, and prepared for it . . . Take our Bodies into thy protection, and defend us; Take our Souls into thy tuition, and sanctifie us, that though we return not home, we may be received into Heaven, through Jesus Christ, Amen.[3]

This solemn moment of reflection on a Sunday morning before marching to defeat the great Catholic enemy is one that anthropologists like Geertz would clearly see as a community-building religious ritual—meant to solidify a sense of common identity and purpose, meant to sustain those for whom death and suffering would surely come.[4]

But for the officers who had attended that morning's private War Council, a note of discord already threatened the mood of spiritual unity. The commissioners told officers before landing that they would be charged with enforcing one particular order: that "noe Souldeger . . . plunder any plas that they should take, vpon paine of death, and that all plunder or goods that shall be taken . . . shall be put into a public stor for the car[ry]ing on of the Desine." The officers greeted the news with dismay—several of them had debts they wished to recoup through their traditional right to pillage. Whistler seems to have overheard this turbulent congress, and so recorded the protests of a few who exclaimed, "had not me Lord Protector promisd them and thayer Soulders free plunder whare soeur thay did goe, thay would not haue come out of England . . . thay had promised Thayer souldgers for to incoraidg them to come with them[!]"[5] Yet Cromwell's commissioners could not be moved to grant the right to plunder, promising only that each man would receive six weeks pay upon taking the island. Reflecting on this dispute, Whistler might have remembered another passage in his pocket prayer book, a meditation on just war that warned the soldier to beware: "If I take up arms and goe to warre for mine own private ends; either for covetousness, and to grow rich thereby . . . I am not lawfully called unto war."[6] In any case, he wrote in his journal with displeasure, "Now when we should haue bin ascking the lord to giue vs this place: Wee . . . ware asharing the skin before wee had Cached the foxx."[7]

Despite disagreements, the commissioners prevailed upon the officers, saying that such limits were necessary if the expedition was to have specie on hand to purchase provisions to support the army. Venables and Penn together drafted a policy against looting. Designed, they wrote, to satisfy both "Reason and Religion," the chief officers justified the unpopular ruling with reference to the biblical King David, who had made it "a Military Law (1st Sam. xxx.24), to give equal share to every person of the Army though not present." In this statement, they styled themselves as Old Testament patriarchs who aimed to "rectifie so great a disorder, crept so far into Modern Armies" that

> the Men that usually performed the Service of the day lye Slain, Wounded, or have the Enemy still before them, so that without imminent ruin they cannot seek after Spoil, [yet] the persons whose deserts merited little or nothing in the Service of the day carry away the profit of the whole success.

Penn and Venables put the charge to their immediate subordinates to distribute pillage "according to every Mans quality and Merit."[8] Soldiers would have been sure to note the contradiction between these quotes. The biblical promise of "equal share[s]" versus officers' discretionary privilege spoiled the fantasy of free riches, replacing it with a form of puritan social control that seemed uncomfortably close to the exclusions of Old England's hierarchies.

One can imagine the dismay that must have appeared on the men's faces when they heard the orders upon disembarking in Hispaniola. Indeed, the commanders could sense a palpable silent fury, and a few threatened mutiny. Whistler recorded how "some said that [the General] was but one Man, and could not hang all the Army, and that whilst they had no Pay they would have all they could get."[9] (Back in England after the campaign had failed, General Venables claimed he had never supported the idea, "fear[ing] it would disgust the Army, and turn them against me . . . this was so contrary to what had been practis'd in England," but he tried to shift the blame to greedy and selfish officers who hungered for plunder in "a country where they conceiv'd Gold as plentiful as Stones.")[10] With promises of extra pay for taking the city of Santo Domingo quelling this protest, the army was convinced to proceed, but as they marched, issues of plunder and moral mission remained foremost in soldiers' minds.[11] Passing by two abandoned plantations, the troops made sure to despoil the "popish trumperie" in Catholic chapels and homes. At one site, the men "brought forth a large statue of the Virgin Mary, well accoutered, and palted her to death with oranges"; they scoffed at "a black Virgin Mary" they discovered, imagining it a popish connivance "to enveigle the blackes to worship."[12] Whistler's account of another episode of such despoiling juxtaposes these performances of iconoclasm with rueful notes on wealth denied:

> This day they met with a monestorie, but all the Ballpated friors ware gone, But thay lef all thayer Imedges behind them, sum of our souldgers found plate hear: and one among the rest touck the Virgin Mary vpon his head, and brought her among the Armie, she wase most richlie clad: But the souldgers did fall a flinging of orringes att her, and did sodainelly deforme her, she had Crist in her armes, both these Immadgs ware very rich.[13]

Such observations, jumbling together anti-Catholic performances with references to the value of religious images and the discovery of silver "plate," suggest that the ban on plunder frustrated many who wished to do more than just enact symbolic desecrations and appropriations. These acts of vandalism on "richlie clad" statues and other religious relics were no doubt signs of soldiers' raucous bravado, but such acts also served to demonstrate their Protestant allegiance to their commanders: those who had been set over them as judges of their merit, those who watched for any surreptitious pocketing of valuable trinkets.[14] That night they gorged themselves on sugared orange juice (little else was available for provisioning), but doubtless slept little, distracted by the anticipation of a triumphant march into the city and the rich rewards that awaited them.

Those dreams did not become a reality. Within a week, the English had advanced and had been twice repulsed by Spanish and creole mixed-race fighters. Disease and hunger had broken out in full force among the English invaders. Suffering from dysentery, lack of potable water, and their disappointing lack of military prowess, the expedition's participants found themselves grasping for answers. The commissioners turned to their beliefs in divine providence to explain their inexplicable failure: God was displeased with them—for their confidence in their own strength, for their sinfulness and disorder. When victory in Santo Domingo was denied a third time, officers announced that "the hand of God" had dealt them this terrible blow. Penn and Venables cited their

men's lack of bravery ("being only bold to do mischief"), their reputed
contempt for religion, (and their lack of discipline as having "drawn this
heavy affliction upon us, [this] dishonour to our Nation and Religion."[15]
These final critiques of cowardice, impiety, and "dishonor" flew in the
face of the upright Protestant manliness imagined to help propel England to new heights in international strength.

The soldiers, on the other hand, created their own narrative of who
was culpable for their losses, contesting their leaders' construction of
masculinity as flawed. The loudest grumblings charged General Venables with a lack of manly courage on the battlefield and weakness as a
master-planner. Whistler was especially partisan, claiming that in the
first attack the general "very nobelly rune behinde a tree," leaving the
regiment of seamen to step forward as heroes who "put the ennimie to
flie for Thayer liues." As the English regrouped from the attack, Whistler
said, Venables reappeared from behind his tree, "very much ashamed,
but made many exskuces: being soe much prosessed with terror that
he could hardlie spake." [16] This presumed incident of cowardice was
linked to growing rumors that Venables had been unmanned because
of his wife's presence in the fleet.[17] The general would later defend his
decision to bring along his wife, referring to Cromwell's blessing on his
plans as head of a holy household. Since "His Highness only did intend
a Plantation, where Women would be necessary," he wrote, "I proposed,
if the Climate were not my Enemy, to stay there."[18] But while Venables,
weakened by a tropical fever, could recuperate in his privileged space
on board (and tended to by his loving wife), the men were left to suffer
without any comforts. Whistler described the sentiments of many when
he wrote:

> . . . haueing a good ship vnder him and his wife to lie by his side,
> [he] did not fele the hardship of the Souldgers that did lie one the
> sand vntell the Raine did waish it from vnder them, and hau-
> ing littell or noe vitelles, and nothing to drink but water. But the
> Gennerall did not consider that, But resolued to stay 2 or 3 dayes
> more, pretending to refresh them, but the lieing heare did doue
> the armie more hurt than Thayer marching, ffor the fresh meat,
> and the abundant of frut that they did eate, and lieing in the raine
> did ca[u]se most of them to haue the Bluddie-flux, and now Thay-
> er harts wore got out of Thayer Dublates into Thayer Breches, and
> wos nothing but Shiting, for thay wose in a uery sad condichon, 50
> or 60 souls in a day [perished]. . . . Now the Souldgers did begin to

Murmur at the Gennerall liing abord with his ladie, and keeping them ashore in this sad condichone."[19]

Knowing sailors' lore about women being unwelcome passengers, it is perhaps unsurprising that the seamen should blame Venables for bringing his wife along. But the puritan model of a godly colonial society meant that women were necessary, and Mrs. Venables's presence was part of Cromwell's puritan ideal that a heaven-sent victory over the Spanish would transition seamlessly to a godly plantation modeled on the "natural" order of that most stable of structures, the family.[20] In Barbados, the officers and commissioners had even agreed to transport "Soldiers Wives (who offer to carry their own Provisions)... to take care of sick and wounded men."[21] However, given the context of the failed expedition and divisiveness in the ranks, Mrs. Venables's presence only served to accentuate the wide gulf between the expedition's leadership and its men in terms of social and economic opportunities. Combined with the officers' proclamations against plunder, Venables's privileged distance from the suffering of battle and camp life highlighted the stark contrast between haves and have-nots in England's social hierarchy.

It also highlighted the ways in which lower-class men like Whistler saw their contribution as men to the project of colonial expansion. Under traditional English models of masculinity, men could become masters and "complete" men only after they acquired the wealth and position to marry and become the head of a household overseeing children and (ideally) servants or journeymen of one's own.[22] Such ideals were increasingly difficult to attain over the course of the late sixteenth and early seventeenth centuries, with economic shifts that pushed lower-class tenants off the land and into itinerant labor.[23] Alexandra Shepard remarks that this nationwide trend "intensified the pressure on patriarchal definitions of manhood which attempted to stigmatize subordinate men as unmanly." Those who fell outside the category of household heads did not have to passively accept their emasculation, however; they could champion alternative definitions of masculinity: "violence, excess, bravado, prodigality, collectivism, and contrary assertions of independence."[24] We can see such independence in the threats of mutiny before marching, violence and bravado in the desecration of Catholic objects, and collectivism in the grumblings of soldiers and sailors about a superior officer's undeserved female comforts—we can imagine that Nicolas Burundel and sailors like Henry Whistler could bond over such scorn and resentment for their social betters.

In the Caribbean, the resistance to traditional patriarchal norms was intensified. There, opportunities for marriage and traditional pathways to mastery were even scarcer than in England. Skewed sex ratios favored women's advancement through marriage, in what some might consider a mockery of traditional femininity: Whistler was shocked that women in Barbados who would be considered "bawds" or "whores" had become wives ("if hansume")[25] to successful colonists who sought female companionship and legitimate heirs to secure their family fortunes. By contrast, most freemen in early Barbados had more difficulty crossing class lines—they often had to work their way up the social ladder by establishing partnerships with other unmarried men, sharing accommodations and the credit risks involved in setting up profitable but capital-intensive enterprises. In the early years of settlement on Barbados, these joint ventures allowed some British freemen (including a few former indentured servants) to make tidy profits by growing tobacco and cotton, working their land either in partnership with others or (preferably) with the help of hired or slave labor.[26] Many ambitious but poor male migrants in the skewed demographic picture of the West Indies must have been frustrated by their female counterparts' easy advancement. Men in the Caribbean therefore defined their manhood in a way that made sense given their own circumstances. The harsh disease and labor environment meant that men who endured colonial transplantation could claim their mere survival as an indicator of their mastery and superiority. The ostensible reward for outliving the competition in the Caribbean was imagined as riches and leisure, but Venables's privilege, constitutional weakness, and disregard for his men produced a rift in the expedition's tenuous unity.

Officers, seeing themselves as patriarchs charged with disciplining their subordinates, set up punishments to remedy laxity and disorder. Venables denounced the bulk of his army as "the most prophane debauch'd persons that we ever saw, scorners of Religion, and indeed men kept so loose as not to be kept under discipline, and so cowardly as not to be made to fight."[27] He ordered judgments for military misdemeanors (Adjutant General Jackson was cashiered for cowardice and sent to swab the decks) and capital offenses (a sergeant from another regiment who had tried to run away was hanged).[28] However, chastisements for moral transgressions were also part of his campaign to cleanse the army of ungodliness. Jackson's demotion was not only for his shameful battlefield performance, but also for his reputation for moral disorder—having been cited "for whoring and drunkenness at Barbadoes," he was discovered by his superiors in Hispaniola with a woman not his wife "lodging in one Chamber together and not any other person." Venables wrote that he had ordered to remove Jackson from the scene, "lest he should bring a curse upon us, as I fear he did . . . "[29] Officers, urged on by the high commanders to do more than admonish their companies for swearing or drunkenness, made amends in part by targeting women (who could always be blamed for corrupting men's efforts).[30] Reminiscent of the emasculated rage voiced by Whistler's critique of Venables, officers first exposed "some women found in mens apparell"; later, they sought to root out "all suspected whores" in their camp, intimating that the latter group was substantial ("Barbados & those plantations yielding fewe else.")[31] Targeting cross-dressing women and prostitutes allowed the company's men (of all ranks) to unite in shaming and disciplining two groups of poor women whose attempts at financial independence kept them free of the subjugation of traditional marriage, and whose wartime opportunism siphoned off the potential earnings of the humblest of soldiers.

The army then shipped off from Hispaniola, the campaign in danger of total collapse—short on rations, thousands already dead and many more sick, their dreams crushed. One petty officer lamented as he looked back on the island: "Sir Francis Drake tooke it, Anno Domini 1586, with 1000 men the same day he landed, kept it a month, and sold it for about 700[li] sterling, because for want of men he could not inhabit it."[32] The company's dreams of fabulous wealth and providential victory had melted away. En route to Jamaica, the commissioners ordered a day be "sett apart . . . for to seeke ye Lord in." One ship captain sorrowfully wrote in his log, "the Lord, I hope, will pardon & amend all ye Imperfections, & defects therein, & [for] his mercy, & loving kindnesse sake owne us Guide us & protect us. Amen."[33] But since few now believed that the expedition's failings were solely due to the hand of God, the commanders endeavored to put better checks on their soldiers, issuing orders against runaways "that his next fellow should kill him, or be tried for his own life."[34] To supplement a lack of funds, the commander of the fleet also collected fines for blasphemy, swearing, and drunkenness—if men did not have the sugar or coin with which to pay, they would pay with their broken flesh.[35] Even in Hispaniola, such stringent moral discipline had prompted some dissatisfied men to vote with their feet and abandon the expedition.[36]

These disciplinary measures did little to improve morale, even after the landing of a small party on the shores of Jamaica to parley with the

Spanish when it seemed that their enemies would surrender without a fight. (Despite Spanish Jamaican officials' attempts to spur the defenses and economic development of the island, their main "urban" center, Santiago de la Vega, remained a sleepy hamlet defended by a meager five hundred militiamen in possession of fewer than three hundred working arms.[37]) Whistler remarked on General Venables's optimism after his first meeting with the "the Chefe men of the Iland," in which he and Gage (serving as a translator) spelled out English demands for surrender, "the same ... that they gaue our English vpon Providenc [Island]," a reference to the allowances made for puritan settlers ousted from their homes by the Spanish in 1641. These severe articles allowed residents no more than safe passage off the island, while their "goods, and all Money and plate, with thayer Negors, and all other slaues" would revert to English hands. Whistler hinted at the darker thoughts of some who foresaw that their officers' triumph would be the ordinary man's loss.

> Gen^ll Venabeles wos much puffed vp with the thoughtes of thos termes that the ennimie ware like to sine to, he knowing that it would be much for his aduantaig; for if our Armie did fight, then our souldgers would get all the plunder and Riches; But if thay did yeld upon Artickles, then all wos in his hands to doue as he did pleas: but this is our mild thoughts of him: god grant it may not proue a truth inded.[38]

Meanwhile, Spanish residents of the city watched from afar as their planned celebrations for the day of the Holy Trinity were converted into Protestant ceremonies of possession. Thomas Gage assumed the pulpit in the cathedral church, preaching a rousing sermon to incite the army to further Protestant victories.[39] But again, God's providence seemed set against the English forces. Instead of accepting the terms of surrender, the Spanish leadership chose to retreat into the inland forests and mountains, praying that reinforcements would arrive to redeem their city from the heretic army. Back at the English camp, fevers overtook the army, and they could not catch enough cattle or pigs to supplement the fleet's severely shortened rations. Forays into the countryside to hunt game soon grew dangerous due to enemy raids, and troops were reduced to eating dogs and horses. Both the expedition's leaders left for England within a few weeks of occupying the island: General Venables to recover from his fever, and Admiral Penn to defend his reputation. When they arrived in England, Cromwell threw them both into the Tower, and then turned to self-recrimination. Cromwell was said to be unsettled by discovering within himself the "sin of Achen"—a biblical reference to one of Joshua's war captains who raided Jericho's riches against God's explicit command to offer up the first plunder to him as an offering. Although many continued to blame the expedition's failures on the sins of "ungodly" soldiers, others would come to believe that Cromwell's own secret core of greed had caused God to withhold His blessing from the expedition.[40]

Reinforcements sent from England a few months later were even more disappointed. One officer who had been in Jamaica since the first invasion expressed his pity for those "poore men . . . all their imaginary mountaines of gold are turned into dross, and their reason and affections are ready to bid them saile home againe already." Though lean from half-rations, he tried to maintain an upbeat tone in letters to relatives, asserting that his character and his faith had been strengthened by hardship. "I doe not repent of my coming this voyage hitherto" he maintained as he tried to reassure his loved ones, perhaps even to convince himself. Many of the lower-class recruits stuck in Jamaica during these hard times may have felt that their faith, too, was being put to the test. Ministers and ordinary people of the era often framed matters such as sickness and setbacks in providential terms. But a significant proportion of those soldiers remaining on the island seemed to have turned against the idea that impiety had led to their downfall. It was the cowardice and poor leadership of General Venables! some must have complained. Continued discord was enmeshed in the problem of shortened funds, and the expedition's straits meant that soldiers were "bound to take land in payment," a far cry from the bonus cash pay all had been promised for forsaking plunder. Later this officer wrote, "wee expect noe pay here, nor hardly at home now, but perhapps some ragged land at the best, and that but by the by spoken for, for us generall officers not a word mentioned."[41]

If even regular officers were denied good land as compensation, then what did the average soldier gain or lose in the final accounting? Within months, English officials had equipped a fleet of sea rovers to police their new possession, authorizing raids on enemy vessels and settlements to raise money and intercept news of the Spanish treasure fleet's planned route. Many soldiers and seamen eagerly volunteered to join these privateering teams. Their early efforts were not very lucrative—the English failed to intercept that year's *flota*, and even raids on cities in Hispaniola, Cuba, and the mainland (they sacked the city of Santa Marta, near Cartagena, three times between 1656 and 1658) yielded slight returns. One commentator in Jamaica wrote that news had come to them that

"¾ of the plunder went to the State, being all sold publiquely, att which the souldiers grudg exceedingly, and I wish it spoile not the whole designe . . . "[42] In 1659, Captain Christopher Mings succeeded in capturing £200–300,000 worth of pillage from the treasure fleet and raids on Spanish settlements like Cumaná, Puerto Cabello, and Coro, but Captain Mings was soon suspended and sent back to England "for disobeying orders and plundering the hold of one of the prizes to the value of 12,000 pieces of eight"—the alleged "plunder" Mings argued was an executive decision to distribute money among his officers and men before registering the prize with Jamaican officials.[43] Even these occasional opportunities for profit were limited to very few men—most conscripts were instead sent to the fields as laborers to plant and harvest provision crops. One officer who wrote from Jamaica in late April 1656 continued by blaming the moral failings of the army:

> the soldiers were much bound up with thoughts of their own
> strength, not considering the power of God's ability, and with cov-
> etous expectations of Indian treasure. As yet no planters are come
> down to them, our soldiers are too much addicted to sloth, and
> would rather famish than use means of preservation.[44]

Nearly everyone involved felt cruelly disappointed, cheated out of their Caribbean dream. Jamaica had turned into a space of harsh military discipline that served to heighten the widespread discontent among the soldiery—they had not come to till the ground but to rule over it! In the West Indies, as they had noticed, hardly any white men were subjected to such menial labors—such work was fit only for "savages" and "brutes." Combined with earlier moves to restrict men's access to Spanish plunder, this new development only heightened what many had said in England about the campaign's private interests promoting ungodly greed and unfair distribution of enemy loot.

Commander Edward D'Oyley, who had been left to manage affairs on Jamaica, seems to have been aware of the consequences that might arise from unequal distribution of resources, and looked for means to restore a sense of cohesion to the struggling forces. He took it upon himself as much as possible to remind the troops of their common cause as Protestants. In his journal, D'Oyley bemoaned the fact that "almost all the chaplains and ministers are dead, whereby we are much deprived of the benefit of preaching of the Gospel among us."[45] In August and again in September, he recorded the distribution of more than two thousand Bibles to the troops, and took special care to award salaries to men who had agreed to serve as ministers on the island.[46] He knew that their military endeavors (especially in times of hardship) would succeed only if they addressed the "the general good of all." In July, when "the scarcity of provisions for the Army, & the approaching fear of want" brought tensions to a breaking point, D'Oyley tried to shame officers who brought in false, inflated lists of those still alive in their companies, "aiming at their own private ends." This ploy to secure a larger share of the rations was reprehensible, and D'Oyley claimed that it was "the intention of the Commander in Chief [himself] and principal officers, to starve altogether, if the Lord in his providence think best . . . "[47]

But admonitions to Christian charity and Protestant unity did little to curb the dissatisfaction that soon roiled up to revolt. We know of at least one major plan for mass desertion of men who resented being forced to till the Jamaican soil. Retribution for such willful disobedience was swift—three of the ringleaders were hung as an example.[48] In the following years of continued hardship, soldiers were subjected to involuntary servitude for minor offenses. One soldier named Betts had stolen "five shillings and 6 pence, and a new pair of shoes" from a fellow soldier who had managed to pull together a small plantation. As punishment the (now barefoot) Betts "was ordered to serve the sd. Philipson in his plantation two months." More extended labor contracts were imposed for moral offenses—in 1659, Francis Hildenham, "heretofore of the Army of Jamaica, being formerly detected and punished for a drunkard and swearer, and afterwards dismissed from the army and island," was sent back by the governor of Tortuga "for speaking Treasons against his Highness the late Lord Protector." Hildenham escaped the death sentence only because Cromwell and his son had died in the interim, and with a new wind blowing in England, D'Oyley remarked that instead, he "thought fit that the said Francis Hildenham labour for his living."[49]

Many men who had had enough of repressive martial law ran away, taking their chances with passing Spanish or Dutch ships. Arnaldo Isassi, still holding onto the title of acting governor of Jamaica, had captured some English prisoners. In a letter to the governor of Cuba, Isassi remitted an English prisoner who had bargained for his life to be spared, but decided to keep another, "a little lad who waits on me." From these two, he had learned that English troops were begging to be released from the "slavery" of life in Jamaica, offering to go to St. Christopher and serve out three years of indenture there, and that many of their wives had petitioned Cromwell on the same terms.[50] Several of these deserters appear in manuscript testimonies taken by Spanish officials, their military intelligence circulated throughout the Spanish Caribbean and back to Seville. In one set of testimonies taken from runaways from Jamaica, a German soldier, "Ricardo Ope," and a Scotsman, "Thomas Quinarte," identified themselves as Catholics, and freely offered details of the army's condition, emphasizing the sickness, hunger, and low morale that prevailed in the English camp. Ope said that he had been sentenced to death for fighting, but ran away before the sentence could be executed—he judged that only two thousand men remained of the nearly eight thousand who had first landed. Characterizing the English troops as fearful in the face of a dearth of supplies and high mortality, he suggested that many would defect to the Spanish if offered good terms of surrender by an invading force.[51]

Perhaps the most bitterly disgruntled runaway was a Dutchman named Richard Caer. This engineer had emigrated from Brazil to Barbados sometime during the 1630s (perhaps one of the first to introduce sugar technology to English planters), where he took up residence, bought land, married, and accepted the commission of captain in the local militia.[52] This man clearly had achieved the level of mastery and economic independence that signaled success in traditional European hierarchies. He was also a devout Protestant, proudly (and in passable Spanish) claiming his confessional identity at the opening to his testimony, swearing the truth of his statement as a fellow Christian, a believer "in almighty God and in Jesus Christ our Lord who suffered passion and death to redeem sinners." Despite his partisan religious politics, Caer had renounced his role in Cromwell's design, given its failure to live up to its economic promises. When asked why he had left the English camp, Caer responded that "in all the time he had been in Jamaica" (about six months), "they hadn't given him more than one-weeks' pay and had denied him leave to go to his home in Barbados." He had planned his escape with two comrades, and said he left behind the corpses of nearly six thousand dead who had perished "from hunger occasioned by necessity and overwork." Caer promised that those who remained "were disgruntled and disconsolate"—their chief complaint was that their commanding officers "made them work as if they were slaves." Again, the aversion to involuntary labor brought up the specter of slavery, a fate so intolerable it could push Protestants to defect to their Spanish archenemies.

Cartagena's Governor Zapata recognized the potential use value of the skilled engineer before him, interjecting at the moment that Caer seemed most dissatisfied with the injustices meted out by his co-religionists. Zapata smoothly suggested that he presumed "that fortune brought [Caer]

FIGURES 9 & 10. Views of Cartagena's San Felipe fortifications, including clever engineering that makes individuals ascending stairwells visible to defenders above, but not vice versa. Photos by author.

to serve the Protector Cromwell and not his inclination," then reminded the Dutchman of the economic benefits he might gain by staying a while in Cartagena. As a "master engineer and a man of reason," surely Caer would know there was peace between Spain and the Dutch States. Would he therefore be amenable to an offer of a salary, clothing, and freedom of movement as an employee of the governor?[53] It seems that Caer accepted the opportunity, for today, docents leading tours of Cartagena's majestic San Felipe stone fortifications tell visitors that many of the structure's innovations were thanks to this same Dutch engineer.

Caer's willingness to essentially betray his Protestant allegiance for economic opportunity, much like the men in Part II who willingly converted to Catholicism, reflected tendencies among Caribbean men to downplay antagonistic confessional identities and to create advantageous relationships based on the mutual benefits of economic collaboration and common European Christian sensibilities. Caer, by rejecting the false promises of Cromwell's millennial political economy, also rejected a hierarchy that included making anyone of European descent labor "as if they were slaves." This Dutchman thus proves the archetype of Caribbean masculinity: survival and the search for individual advantage.

9 / Anxieties of Interracial Alliances, Black Resistance, and the Specter of Slavery

Caer's comments about his fellow Protestants being forced to work "as if they were slaves"[1] are worth closer attention, for they hint at subterranean anxieties about the politics of labor exploitation and race that plagued Interregnum attempts to implement its colonial political economy. This chapter considers the revolt against what the Western Design's participants imagined to be the cause of their relegation to the status of "slaves" in the West Indies: their own countrymen and co-religionists' profit-seeking, not the machinations of cruel, foreign, "popish" enemies. This expedition fostered a sharp turn in the evolution of English thought on New World wealth and labor. Early in the campaign, when participants imagined Spanish riches easily falling into their hands, puritan providentialists cast people of all ranks and "nations" as allies and beneficiaries of the Protestant New World order. However, accepting some of those groups as allies and fellow fighters—especially blacks, who were increasingly seen by West Indian colonists as "natural slaves"—destabilized the Caribbean's nascent racial order, an order that defined those who would gain from the region's profitability and those who would serve as disposable labor. The providentialists who took part in the expedition also had trouble coming to grips with Jamaica's black population's seeming allegiance to Spanish Catholic forces, further weakening the campaign's ideological legitimacy. In the end, no one even dared to contemplate how to incorporate African "pagans" into the English Protestant community in Jamaica. The English invaders turned from imagining blacks as allies to insisting on their subjugation, casting them as rebellious slaves who needed to be hunted down by force of arms (a process that would continue well into Jamaica's eighteenth-century Maroon Wars). Meanwhile, "white slaves"—frustrated soldiers forced to labor in Jamaica, along with scores of political prisoners sold into West Indian bondage—vented their frustrations with Cromwellian political economy by rejecting its religious language, preferring instead to fight for their hereditary rights as "free-born Englishmen."

To untangle this complex shift, we return briefly to the fantasies of cross-racial cooperation that informed the expedition's religio-political visions of millennial victory. Cromwell, Gage, and other planners clung to the vision—exemplified by tales of Sir Francis Drake's alliance with Panamanian maroons—that non-Europeans oppressed by Spanish "cruelty" would happily surrender their fealty to English "liberators," automatically recognizing them as just and benevolent overlords. In the first heady marches on Santo Domingo, these fantasies seemed to be coming true—a few blacks enslaved by the Spanish approached the English invaders to offer their assistance. Such appearances, most notably the arrival of one unnamed black man—"a negroe who had formerly served Sir Thomas Warner, Governour of the Iland [of] St. Christophers, and was taken [and] enslaved by the Spaniards"—fed English hopes of success.[2] This particular alliance was especially heartening, given that this man knew the city and surrounding terrain, and that he could also communicate his knowledge with ease—thanks to his dual experience of enslavement, he "spake good English and Spanish."[3] Furthermore, his familiarity with at least two colonial cultures during his lifetime meant he was an archetypical Atlantic creole. His ability to recognize and confirm English cultural principles played into his performance of alliance: the Spanish, he reported, cowered with fear at their enemy's approach, and "confesse ye Lord fighteth for us."[4] However, despite this portent and the arrival of a few more ex-slaves from Santo Domingo, the army's "hopes of more negroes comming in . . . succeeded not."[5] Despite the disappointment, General Venables rewarded their assistance and valor in accordance with his instructions. The first runaway to arrive, one wrote, received "civill entertainment and the Generall's protection."[6] As the army advanced on the city, this handful of black allies fought side by side with English troops when attacked. Warner's former slave, it was reported, "beaui[d] himselfe stoutly in this days work, kild one & wounded another, calling out to our men, Give ye dogs no quartr."[7] General Venables honored his promise of "freedome" as reward for such valor.[8]

Yet the fact that such preferential treatment was remarked upon so often reflects the reality that "civill entertainment," "protection," and "freedome" were very rarely awarded to blacks, and that these few unnamed "negroes" were exotic anomalies. More pervasive at this time were competing narratives that depicted Africans as "an exotic, alien and slavish incarnation of the dark side of the soul . . . [or] as a commercial object, a commodity to be bought and sold."[9] The English were greatly influenced by Iberian attitudes toward Africans in the Americas, where although the Church frowned upon cruelty, the assumed baseness of African peoples allowed their subordination as "natural" slaves who must expect that their lot in life would be toil and unhappiness. As a result, European Protestants living in Iberian port cities (like Nicolas Burundel) expected to receive preferential treatment over Jews, Moors— and especially *negros*—on account of their perceived racial (and religious) superiority. English soldiers and sailors visiting the West Indies for the first time had a chance to compare what they had read about in books imagining Africans and colonial slavery. During the fleet's brief stay on Barbados, Henry Whistler had commented on the incredible diversity of the island's multiethnic population, but paid special attention to its preponderance of "miserabell Negors borne to perpetuall slauery thay and thayer seed." Instead of expanding on the misery—the pitiable wretchedness—that so often defined race-based slavery in the Americas, Whistler instead focused on other connotations that the word *miserable* carried: lowly, living in penury, contemptible. He remarked on the value that the offspring of Africans could gain on the market (about five pounds sterling for a newborn) and the low maintenance required for young human chattel ("they cost them noething the bringing vp, they goe all ways naked: some planters will haue 30 more or less about 4 or 5 years ould").

Whistler was able to make this shift from adult misery to the economic benefits of black children's "nakedness" by referring to how planters "allowed" their slaves multiple sexual partners—this was not an effort to accommodate African ideas of polygamy, but rather a sense that blacks' perceived animalistic tendencies justified a program of "breeding." Before thinking of black children's value, he stressed the physicality of sexual reproduction. Black men, he said, were given access to "as many wifes as thay will haue, sume will haue 3 or 4, according as they find Thayer bodie abell." These assumptions implicitly justified selling slaves "from one to the other as we doue sheep," and provided a tacit justification for the "perpetuall slauery" and "misery" that Africans and their

American-born children endured.[10] Together with stories from English voyagers to West Africa that denigrated those societies' polygamy, the realities of planters' exploitation of black women's fertility nourished familiar stereotypes of African savagery, especially related to their perceived promiscuity.[11]

Such perceptions of Africans as being contemptible, nearly outside the bounds of humanity, merged with the demand for African laborers within the English Caribbean after Barbados' sugar boom during the 1650s, and the expedition's leaders had to confront early on the contradictions in their estimation of black bodies. While blacks encountered in English territories were automatically commodified (starting with the 244 Africans confiscated from Dutch ships trading in Barbados in defiance of the Navigation Acts, sold for £5,162 to local planters to help provide funds with which to provision the army),[12] blacks in Spanish territories were supposed to be allies, elevated to the status of men who would fight for a cause (revenge in this case). In the early stages of the fighting, leaders seem to have lived with the cognitive dissonance. In the case of Capt. Warner's "servant," later "enslaved" by the Spanish, the semantics of voluntary and involuntary subordination promoted a useful fiction that allowed commentators to recognize the human agency—though not the personality nor even the name—of this one "negroe" who proved himself worthy of freedom from enslavement.[13]

But in skirmishes with Spanish forces on both islands, the English could hardly deny the reality that substantial numbers of blacks were among those defending "Spanish" territory from English invasion. In one of the first encounters in Hispaniola the English killed about thirty Spanish fighters "they being most of them Negors," which Whistler noted seemed to "friten many that did think that thay would not fight but a rune . . . but thay now find it other wayes."[14] Soon, troops scavenging for provisions on Hispaniola disappeared, captured or killed by enemy fighters. To redeem themselves from charges of "base cowardice," observers derided the "savagery" of their attackers—drawn from the ranks of criminal "cowkillers" (the early buccaneers), and especially the "Negors and Molatos" that the English characterized as "thayer slaues."[15] Shaken by surprise attacks that decimated entire companies, English commentators especially showed their fear of engagement with enemies skilled in the use of pikes or lances.[16] In these encounters, English troops were at a distinct disadvantage, for they had only been outfitted with half-pikes (the best that Barbados's remaining stands of woods could supply). English soldiers had to deal with the additional humiliation of the fact that scores died on the battlefield from pike wounds in their fleeing backsides—another literal and metaphorical stab at their already wounded masculinity. The skill and determination with which multiethnic forces attacked English troops in Hispaniola struck fear in the hearts of men who still imagined themselves trampling degenerate Spaniards, taking their gold, and even celebrating a Protestant victory over Catholic domination. It seems at the very moment at which English soldiers were most unmanned by their military failures in Hispaniola—their officers cowards, their fellows unwilling to fight, the whole army brought low not by an epic battle with the enemy but by the "Bluddie-flux"—at this moment, the true threat came from the fighting prowess, independent valor, and physical hardiness of African and mixed-race Caribbean men.

Indeed, black soldiers seem to have brought out exaggerated fear among English troops. Despite the fact that a few blacks had joined the English forces, by the time their several advances had been thwarted by surprise raids, unseasoned English troops had so linked black men with dangerous aggression that the simple appearance of "2 of our owne negroes" who came to drink at the riverside threw the English into a panic: "some of them spying [the black men] cried 'the enemy,' upon which all immediately threw away their armes, and ran for it, some for feare leapt into the river, whereof 3 were drowned, soe much were we cow'd and daunted."[17] Although running from "naked pagans" (as one critic later referred to these African-descended forces on Hispaniola) could be portrayed as shameful cowardice for Christian warriors, in the Caribbean, flight served to protect men from danger, giving them an opportunity to live (or seek vengeance) another day.[18]

One reality of which the English forces seem to have been unaware— or were reluctant to recognize—was that in Hispaniola, nonwhites were a substantial majority of the island's free population, fighting not only on behalf of Spanish interests, but to defend their own lives and lands from foreign encroachment. By mid-century, only about one-third of the island's inhabitants were categorized as white, and the garrison was manned by fewer than two hundred regular soldiers. In the face of such a huge invading force, the Spanish required all able-bodied fighters to defend the island—as in Cartagena, these included black and mulatto recruits from the urban center of Santo Domingo, but also African-born fighters skilled in the use of lances. A Congolese defender of Santo Domingo named Juan Garcia Fernandez described his military regiment as composed of "Indian mestizos and other different mixtures, like *mulatos* and blacks from Congo, Angola, Arda [Allada], and other African coasts, and the captains of the *lanceros* are creoles, 'natural' in color (*de color natural*), strong and lusty men of the countryside, and even white laborers." For his faithful service during the English invasion, Fernandez was promised a post as head of a black militia in Santo Domingo. Such extraordinary service to the Spanish empire and the island oligarchs had its reward—manumissions had swelled the numbers of black and mixed-race inhabitants of Hispaniola over the course of the century.[19]

But rather than recognize or even consider that men of African or mixed heritage could be fighting to defend their own lands and liberties against foreign aggressors, the English puzzled over the gap between what they had expected to find and the reality: why might oppressed, reviled slaves fight *with* the Spanish? Several wondered if it had to do with religion. The English knew, through Gage's narrative, that the Spanish required enslaved and free blacks to adopt Christianity, but since they also painted Spanish Catholicism as illegitimate, superstitious, and irrational (in anti-popery vitriol, a perfect magnet for weak minds), it made sense to them that Africans, also imagined as superstitious and barbarous, would be attracted to this aberrant form of Christianity. English officers doubtless remembered the statue of a dark Virgin they had destroyed in Hispaniola, which they imaged to be part of a Catholic plot to make Africans worship their corrupt and disordered religion. In Jamaica, some Englishmen who joined the expedition after living among the Spanish (probably the runaways from Jackson's privateering raids mentioned in the previous section) explained it as religious indoctrination. These renegade Englishmen said that Spanish priests had tried to crush ideas of capitulation or desertion: "the priests do terrify the negroes and the Spaniards amongst them by saying that [the English] do deny God, and that when any cometh to us we do put out their eyes."[20] Whistler also believed that the Spanish who commanded the island's multiethnic forces relied on religious superstition (wearing papal bulls as talismans against death and damnation) and spread rumors of terror and cannibalism to compel their subordinates: "to thes thay did proclaim freedom if they would fight, telling them that if they would not fight that we would take and eate them as fast as wee take them, and this did greatly incoridg them to fight."[21]

All such rumors and assumptions, however, depended on fictions of African superstition and tractability. The expedition's leaders clung to these fictions even in Jamaica. As Spanish leaders secretly planned their flight while promising capitulation, they tried to dissuade the English forces from coming near their camp, saying that "their Mullatoes" might do harm to stragglers. Venables dismissed the veiled threat, replying that those "Mullatoes . . . were their Servants, and at their Command, and neither durst or would do any hurt [to English troops] but by their Command or Connivance."[22]

In Jamaica, the continued collusion of Spanish and maroon guerilla fighters after the English occupation frustrated any attempts at securing the island. English leaders did not know if the black fighters who continued to catch their soldiers unawares were allied with the Spanish or not, but they did know that their enemies' intimate knowledge of the island's geography made them frustratingly elusive.[23] Governor D'Oyley heard one proposal that would grant soldiers "three years service of all such Negroes and Mulattoes as they should take prisoners," but rejected that plan, thinking that it might be better if cash rewards were given to soldiers like William Crane, "a Trooper . . . for taking a Negro."[24] D'Oyley sent out raiding parties against the maroons, ordering his officers to "find out by Intelligence . . . or any other means; where any of their Quarters or Habitations are; And to use his utmost to infest and disturb them . . . "[25] Another officer wrote home to request that his family send "a couple of whelps of the blood-hound strain to make draught-dogs of them, or if possible one ready made . . . I can deem no way like unto this to clear the black rogues from this place."[26] In these early, uncertain years, a handful of black and mulatto men, former allies of the Spanish, seem to have lived in relative peace with English residents of Spanish Town, but people of African descent were generally treated as subhuman enemies to be "hunted down" or subjected to a more "natural" state of slavery.[27]

What was the acknowledgment of all these difficulties back in England? Though many languished in Jamaica, others, like Henry Whistler, had been able to return to England (Whistler left with Admiral Penn soon after General Venables to make sure his name wasn't sullied in the recounting of events). Certainly Whistler would have heard that Cromwell shut both commanders in the Tower for their failings. Though the Protector was chastened by the expedition's outcome, he and other interested parties meant to secure Jamaica, a new plantation that promised a fresh round of profits for those able to get in on the ground floor. Back in London, Henry Whistler may have wandered to the Cockpit Theater in Drury Lane to watch one of the few licensed spectacles authorized under Cromwell's iron fist. William D'Avenant's opera-masque, *The Cruelty of the Spaniards in Peru*—one of several propagandistic texts designed to inflame Englishmen against the Spanish in the Americas—featured

FIGURE 11. Illustrated frontispiece to *Tears of the Indians* (London, 1656).
Image courtesy of the Robert Dechert Collection, Rare Book and Manuscript
Library, University of Pennsylvania.

Peruvian natives who sympathized with English mariners put to the rack by officials of the Spanish Inquisition.[28] As Whistler would have likely been recruited for one of the return expeditions to ship reinforcements to Jamaica, he may have picked up a book to help him pass the time, perhaps the 1656 translation of Bartolomé de las Casas's classic tale of Spanish cruelty dedicated to Cromwell. Gruesomely illustrated, *The Tears of the Indians* opened with a preface calling on "all true Englishmen" to take up arms "against your Old and Constant Enemies, the SPANIARDS, a Proud, Deceitful, Cruel, and Treacherous Nation, whose chiefest Aim hath been the Conquest of this Land, and to enslave the People of this Nation."[29] Faced with this renewed onslaught of propaganda, English audiences might be forgiven for believing that English suffering was primarily due to the perfidy of their old Spanish enemies.

But they also knew that ungodly greed had been a problem in their latest failings. As stories circulated about the Caribbean following the Western Design, more and more people had become aware that the search for West Indian riches led some to wealth and others to perdition. In 1659, just after Cromwell's death, a published petition addressed to parliament alleged that "free-born Englishmen" were being "Barbadosed" and unjustly sold as "slaves" to West Indian planters.[30] Several men presented their experience of being captured under pretense of having participated in Royalist plots, after which they were secreted away in the dark, dank holds of transatlantic vessels, and upon arrival, sold to planters who treated the laborers as another piece of property, housing them among animals, even "attached as horses and beasts for the debts of their masters."[31] Their published pamphlet called on "the Honourable the Knights, Citizens, and Burgesses assembled in Parliament" to redress the enslavement of the "Free-born people of this Nation." The petitioners exposed their suffering through comparisons to religious Others: one called Barbados "the Protestants Purgatory"; another referred to hard usage by "unchristian Janisaries"; the primary petitioners referred to misery "beyond expression or Christian imagination."[32] These religiously tinged references continued in their appeal to parliament as the "Angel of their Deliverance" from covetous West Indies traders painted as "merchants of Babylon." An Old Testament command against slavery was featured on the title page (Exodus 21:16 "And God spake all these words, saying, He that stealeth a man and selleth him, Or if he be found in his hand, He shall surely be put to death"). Marcellus Rivers and Oxenbridge Foyle, the captives' primary petitioners, reminded English readers that "to sell and enslave these of their own Countrey and Religion, much lesse the Innocent" was "a thing not [even] known amongst the cruell Turks."[33]

Not surprisingly, this pamphlet, designed to create a public outcry, took more than a few rhetorical liberties, employing the metaphor of "unchristian" cruelty to build on the critiques of religious hypocrisy displayed in the Western Design. Just as the experience of serving in the New Model Army helped create a political consciousness among the "common man," those who experienced military failings and labor coercion in the West Indies mobilized political opposition back in the metropole. The knowledge of the Western Design's continued failings opened a small window to argue for some measure of moral protection against the exploitative threat of mercantile expansionism in the Americas.[34] This was perhaps not, as labor historians would have it, a blanket protest against West Indian slavery, but rather one that served to define more clearly which sectors of the global labor force might face spiritual and physical dehumanization (already seen as the fate of enslaved Africans and their progeny, also the more barbaric of the "wild Irish") and which would not (those defined as "free-born" Englishmen, presumed to be both Protestant and "white").

This shift away from the language of religious justice to political and economic issues becomes clearer when reviewing the parliamentary debate on Rivers and Foyle's petition. One of several MPs who moved to strike the petition from consideration on grounds that it was a rebel plot aimed at destabilizing the government was Martin Noell. A merchant who had invested heavily in promoting West Indian enterprises at mid-century, Noell had been among those whom Cromwell had consulted in the planning of the Western Design—some said that he was to blame for the expedition's inadequate provisioning. He scoffed at the deportees' charges of deprivation and rough usage, saying of the plantation system: "The work is mostly carried on by the Negroes. . . . It is not so odious as it is represented."[35] But he had been named in the complaint as one of the "Merchants that deal in slaves and souls of men," that is, one of those who had colluded with corrupt officials to better profit on the market for indentured servants. Others were alarmed by efforts to discharge the bill, arguing that "slavery is slavery," and that if they, as representatives of the English state, would not hear the petition, "none but God in heaven" might redress the situation.[36] Sir John Lenthall averred:

I hope it is not the effect of our war to make merchandize of men. I consider them as Englishmen. I so much love my own liberty as to part with aught to redeem these people out of captivity. We are the freest people in the world . . . They are put to such hardships, to heats and colds, and converse with horses. If my zeal carry me beyond its bounds, it is to plead for the liberty of an Englishman, which I cannot hear mentioned but I must defend it.[37]

But Mr. Boscawen stated things more bluntly: "If you pass this, our lives will be as cheap as those negroes."[38] Certainly issues like party politics were at stake, but in the debate, it seems clear that MPs knew that the underlying issue was not a matter of religion, it was about putting in place a morally defensible political economy that yielded profits—the plantation model—one increasingly defined by racialized labor. At the same time, MPs engaged in creating a moral economy that addressed the intertwined issues of religion and race in the colonies, in which "Christian" or "white" servants were to be uniformly treated with more humanity than Africans and their descendants. Perhaps considering an overtly religious justification for protecting white "slaves" too reminiscent of Cromwell's hypocritical moral economy, they silenced both questions of race and religion and emphasized the more neutral "rights of Englishmen."

The mutinies and desertions of lower-class recruits in Jamaica and the metropolitan protest against allowing the "enslavement" of Englishmen in the West Indies reflected both England's general dissatisfactions with Cromwell's puritan political economy and recognition on the part of the political and mercantile classes that West Indian labor conditions had to be handled with care. Radical Protestantism had not served to unify the nation at home or abroad, but had instead become a byword for tyranny masquerading as piety. The lure of personal profit lay at the heart of this mental transformation—indicting unruly soldiers and covetous officers for their lack of manly courage, revealing Cromwell's hidden lust for power and the perfidy of West India merchants who hoped to gain from his pretensions. Cromwell's grand scheme to drive the Catholic Spanish Antichrist from the Indies did not launch a great unifying national project, but instead disintegrated, as lurid tales of human trafficking and labor exploitation drove a wedge between English participants, discrediting leaders' pronouncements of their Protestant mission. The disillusionment felt by soldiers in Jamaica who deeply resented being forced to till the soil like vile slaves mirrored the anger among other servants transported to the West Indies under coercive, perhaps illegal, circumstances. Together they forced their superiors in the islands and the metropole to provide both protections and incentives for those who risked their lives hoping to gain their fortunes, lest they abandon the massive effort at colonial expansion.

Despite the bitterness left in many men's mouths after the first failures of Cromwell's great experiment in colonial political economy, there were still a few who saw hope for a continued geopolitical battle with Spain in providential terms. They turned to those old fantasies of saving the Indians from Spanish cruelty, and thereby enriching themselves from an alliance with the Americas' native inhabitants. While questioning Spanish prisoners, English officials noted with interest news of a revolt in the mines of Lima in 1658; Spanish officials also heard from an English prisoner about the excitement generated by a Floridian chief who had approached them for passage to England to treat with Cromwell for protection against the Spanish.[39] After the Restoration of King Charles II to the throne in 1660, politics changed, but little shifted in terms of colonial rhetoric. The royal seal authorized for the new Jamaican settlement included a vignette of two Indians presenting fruits to the reinstated monarch, and an image of two more natives supporting a cross inscribed with the text "Behold! Another has offered its branches," projecting, as one scholar has recently argued, "an image of Jamaica as a gift willingly given to the English nation by an indigenous people who had long since ceased to inhabit the island themselves."[40]

At Charles II's accession, he and other colonial advisors took a moment to consider the place of Jamaica in England's economic and religious imperial objectives. Charles fought hard to maintain possession of the island during treaty negotiations with the Spanish, well aware of its economic potential. As he moved to reassert his authority over American colonial possessions, Charles was not insensitive to religious imperatives—in his instructions to the Committee for Foreign Plantations, the king wrote that the committee should order that baptism be offered to both Indians and slaves, thus fulfilling England's religious/civilizing mission.[41] But the damage had been done—the failure of the Western Design's religious rhetoric to unite Englishmen in a Protestant success against the great Catholic enemy had left faith greatly discounted in the Caribbean. Those in Jamaica who still believed in a puritan errand to the Indies could only sadly note that "Profession of religion makes people suspected to be knaves."[42]

What would England's newest Caribbean possession become in such a jaded climate? By the 1660s and 1670s, the city of Port Royal transformed itself into a haven for opportunistic pirates and privateers hoping to enrich themselves at the expense of the Spanish.[43] In time, governors of the island would try to curtail such individualistic enterprises so as to funnel the riches of the Indies into state coffers or other authorized commercial networks—including trade with Spanish merchants in Cuba,

Hispaniola, and elsewhere. In these dealings, religious antagonisms were swept aside for mutually profitable trade enterprises between Christian nations. One Spanish merchant wrote to London officials in 1660 to recommend that some of the ousted Spaniards be allowed to resettle in the English territories of Jamaica, asserting that "security and just government, combined with personal and religious liberty . . . will attract many, to the prosperity and increase of population of the island."[44] Such increase of population and prosperity was the real challenge for Jamaica. Although as many as 12,000 English had come to Jamaica by the time of the Restoration, fewer than 2,500 men and one thousand women and children survived; while the fledgling colony had managed to put roughly 2,500 acres under cultivation, they had been able to procure only about 500 enslaved blacks to work those fields.[45]

In the 1670s Jamaica's productivity and population began to take off, mainly through the licensing of privateers and the large-scale importation of African slaves by the Royal African Company; by the eighteenth century Jamaica would become the slave-dominated sugar island of popular fame. In this and other Caribbean islands dominated by sugar and slaves, few thought to protest the moral injustice of enslaving thousands of Africans, especially when keeping white immigrants loyal to the defense of imperial holdings meant allotting them privileges they may not have enjoyed in the Old World. Local officials did work to stem the tide of Irish servants, anticipating the dangerous consequences of allowing Catholics to serve as militiamen (though the islands needed as many white defenders as possible with growing slave majorities), fearing that their religious loyalties might turn them into allies of Spanish or French enemies.[46] Englishmen had always placed great stock in their "freedoms" as established under the Magna Carta, and after the burst of popular republicanism of the Civil War years, they articulated this sense of inalienable rights as a kind of universal human rights. Their new "natural philosophy" was, however, not religion- or race-neutral. Great Britain's tradition of religio-political exceptionalism required that privileges be granted primarily to men unhampered by "popish" superstition or the hint of racial slavery. The unspoken association between the rights of "free-born Englishmen" with Christianity would silence any concerted attempts to establish puritan-style evangelization missions for Africans. Slave labor was considered so essential to the success of England's—and ordinary Englishmen's—colonial efforts that to allow Africans to acquire Christianity might put that unspoken assumption in jeopardy.

PART IV

NELL, YAFF, AND LEWIS

"He hath made all Nations of one Blood"

Poor Affrick groanes her Groanes assend on high
The AEthiopian [L]aments his Xtian Slavery
Beeing wth more then Israels bonds oppressed,
Whn ye Aegiptian stratejems Destressed.
The Heathen then did on Gods people trample
But why? alas use we ye like Example.
to those, and yet p'fess those rules denyit,
Whom ffamine nev'r Drove to our Dyit.
Objects of Pitty who can but Lament
the Innocent Cause of the Poor Ignorant:
Whom our amased Xtiandum Exclude
from future bliss, beyond all Lattitude
What Cruell heart so hard them to Deny
the Enjoying temporall felicity,
whom God possess'd wth rights & Liberty.

—POEM WRITTEN ON A LETTER FROM RICHARD HILL, JR.,
TO JAMES DICKENSON (London, 1698)

10 / Quakers, Slavery, and the Challenges of Universalism

When news reached Barbados that Cromwell's troops had failed in Hispaniola and were struggling to survive in Jamaica, Colonel Lewis Morris of Ape's Hill must have said a silent prayer of thanks to God that he had declined Cromwell's commission to command a regiment for General Venables. It had been a flattering offer, he knew, a reward for his loyal service to the parliamentary cause, and in recognition of his experience in the Caribbean. As a young indentured servant, Lewis had much in common with the masses of poor servants and younger sons described in the previous section who came to the Caribbean in search of their fortune.[1] Morris had risen quickly in this land of opportunity, beginning as an indentured servant for the puritan-funded Providence Island Company in the 1630s, rising to the position of trusted interlocutor for the Company's negotiations with Moskito Indians on the coast of Honduras; then he was made a shipmaster, and later named second-in-command to Captain William Jackson during privateering raids against the Spanish in 1638–1640 (he may have been involved in the sacking of Spanish Jamaica and the city of Tolu near Cartagena). Allying with Caribbean projects serving the Protestant cause helped Lewis gain the skills and esteem necessary to call himself "Captain" and later "Colonel" Morris. He had been lucky enough to buy into the landed class with investments in sugar planting and shipping, and had even been named a parish vestryman in July 1655. He likely wished to see the Spaniards brought low, but something had held him back from joining the Cromwellian expedition. It seems he did not completely buy into Penn and Venables's promises of a rich reward, and allegedly demanded that his price for joining the expedition was "a hundred thousand weight of sugar, that he may pay his debts, and leave his estate clear to his wife." Financial insecurity worried him greatly—he would not risk his newfound prosperity.[2]

Lewis Morris represents the competitive spirit of early British commercial expansion, especially among those poor and middling classes of Caribbean migrants wary of Protestant rhetoric that promoted unity but failed to produce rewards. Doubtless he had been an enthusiastic participant in anti-Spanish projects like Providence Island, the Moskito trade, and Jackson's "puritan" privateering ventures. But a breach of trust between himself and Captain Jackson in 1640 over the division of plunder had led to Morris's brief arrest for debt.[3] The courts agreed that Jackson's case was weak and freed Morris, who returned to Barbados with his privateering profits and invested heavily in new sugar refining and processing machinery introduced by the Dutch and Portuguese Jews ousted from Pernambuco.[4] Within ten years his land had succeeded in producing roughly sixty thousand pounds of sugar, and he started building his own fleet of ships to transport it more cheaply to European markets.[5] He didn't forget his roots, though. Captain Morris was a member of the Barbados Assembly when they voted to pass a 1656 law "for the Relief of such Persons as lie in Prison, and others, who have not wherewith to pay their Creditors."[6]

It seems that Morris's search for moral security in the years following his refusal to join Cromwell's expedition prompted a crisis of faith, especially after several radical Protestants from England who had begun to call themselves Children of the Light visited Barbados.[7] These individuals spoke of the leveling of society, addressing everyone in the familiar address of "thee" and "thou," and rejecting the honor of doffing their hat to any but God. Many Britons who scoffed at the group's confrontational public harangues called them simply "Quakers" for their tendency to fall into trance-like ecstasies during their strange, silent meetings. This religious sect, also known as the Society of Friends, has been well-studied for a variety of reasons: as an exemplar of the explosion of religious radicalism in Civil War–era England, and as among the first proponents of religious toleration in North American settlements (especially in William Penn's founding of Pennsylvania). Barbados's reputation for religious tolerance—Whistler had marveled at the "libertie of contienc[e] which wee soe long haue in England foght for"—made it possible for Quakerism to flourish. Indeed, only two short decades after the first missionaries arrived in Barbados in 1655, Quaker leaders referred to the island as the "Nursery of Truth" for the more than one thousand

Friends who resided there.[8] Perhaps most famously, Quakers are known as abolitionists *par excellence*—so to many it is a surprise that in Barbados, Quakers embraced, rather than rejected, slavery. Quakerism had grown in numbers and acceptance on the island in large part because influential men like Colonel Lewis Morris—some of them planters and office holders, others merchants, and over 80 percent of them slaveholders[9]—became not only converts to the Society but also its patrons.

This final microhistory brings us back to the life of enslaved Africans in the English colony of Barbados following its first sugar "boom." Barbados achieved slave majority status by 1660, and ten years later, blacks outnumbered whites two to one.[10] Among the thousands of West Africans who were born on or were brought to that island during the second half of the seventeenth century, roughly five hundred men and women were named as individuals in the wills of Barbadian Quakers—Mingo, Tom, Hannah, Addoe, and so many more. As we saw in Part III, few individuals of African descent ever took on complex personalities in the English mind, and Quakers of this era thought no differently. Slaves were viewed as objects to be bartered and traded, sold and mortgaged; they were treated as livestock, sometimes even given the same kinds of pet names. Most lived and died without any record, without names, and so they often become invisible to historians.[11]

But the lives of these enslaved people, though largely hidden to us, were necessarily shaped by their masters' own positions on money and morality. They were watching when Quakerism's spiritual "father" George Fox visited the island in 1671, heard their masters discuss with Fox the controversial premise of bringing "Ethiopian" slaves into their Society of brotherly love. The English had followed the Spanish example of enslaving Africans, but not their practice of extending them a place in the Christian community—in part because of the Protestant emphasis on biblical literacy, in part because of a growing conviction explored in the previous chapter: that Christians should not be enslaved, and by the same logic, African slaves (whose lifetime labor seemed to be the key to colonial success) should not have access to the same redemptive possibilities as white Christians. Many Quaker converts must have agreed—but not all. Visitors like Fox pressured Englishmen to exercise their responsibility as slaveholders to "save" Africans from their heathen darkness. Even Admiral Penn had, during his stay in Barbados, taken up the cause of one African named Anthony, impressed that he "seemed to have a desire to become a Christian."[12] As we will see, Lewis Morris held similar aspirations to share his faith.

But to put the story in richer perspective, I have also chosen to bring to life the story of Yaff and Nell, an enslaved man and woman who were targeted by their master's evangelical mindset. Their names do not appear in any documents prior to the year in which Lewis Morris wrote his will, where he designated both as "faithful" servants destined for future privileges: Nell to receive freedom after the death of Morris's second wife, and Yaff bequeathed as a servant to guide the next great Quaker leader, Admiral Penn's son William, "provided the said Penn shall come to dwell in America."[13] Such sentiments suggest that a sense of reciprocal responsibility had grown over many years, that Yaff and Nell had become an integral part of Morris's life. They, no less than Colonel Morris, had to figure out how to respond to deepening racialization stemming from English colonists' desire to build an ever more efficient labor force for their plantation colony; they watched (and protested) as Christians worked to justify an economic system that denigrated many for the profit of a few, one that reduced Africans to mere commodities.

This chapter, an introduction to these three individuals, explores the rise of Quakerism in Barbados during the second half of the seventeenth century. Lewis Morris and others embraced a faith that challenged them to question traditional hierarchies and to acknowledge the greed and injustice of their world. Household slaves like Yaff and Nell bore witness to the Society's evolution, sensing the advantage in fostering an affective kin link to the white community. Chapter 11 explores the years immediately after Fox's visit, as the promise of evangelization stalled because of concerns over security, stability, and discipline—both within the Society's ranks and on the plantation. Finally, in Chapter 12, we return to the cautious exchanges forged between Quakers and enslaved men and women like Yaff and Nell, whose proximity to their masters meant they were most likely to receive the greatest rewards in performing loyalty and dedication to their masters' mores. Sadly, the imperative to build stable, profitable colonies for Friends in Barbados and elsewhere led them to promote a racialized "Protestant ethic," a paternalistic, pro-slavery ideology that would be replicated throughout the British Atlantic World.

Cromwell's Western Design helps us understand the concerns and experiences of men like Lewis Morris, but how does one begin to trace the histories of enslaved people like Yaff and Nell in West Africa? Where did they, or their parents, come from, and what influences did they bring with them across the Atlantic? Historians' search for African "roots" or "retentions" have engendered much healthy skepticism and debate in the past decades, so my imaginative focus centers on the historical possibilities, with answers based on informed, *plausible* speculations. Data on the origin points of slave trading journeys is rather sparse for Barbados before 1656, in the decades when Morris would have likely purchased a large gang of slaves to put his first sugar works into production, and also—as befitting an up-and-coming "gentleman planter"—an African youth to be his personal servant.[14] Even Yaff's name is not necessarily a vital clue. Since English colonists did not adopt the use of ethnic "surnames" as the Spanish did, any speculation on his place of birth is rather difficult; however, drawing on one database of African names from the nineteenth century shows that "Yaff" (sometimes also spelled Yafe) appears in naming patterns in Senegambia or Sierra Leone, both regions that had begun to yield significant returns for Northern European slave traders by the middle of the seventeenth century.[15] Yaff may have arrived on the *Peter and Mary*, a ship sponsored by a London merchant who had taken up African captives from the Cape Verde Islands and the coasts of Senegambia and Sierra Leone before arriving in Barbados in 1644.[16] If he had come from an independent township among the stateless Diola communities in modern-day lower Senegambia and Guinea-Bissau, his family may have perished in the violence and displacement of the Koonjaen civil wars, or been pushed into such poverty that they could not redeem him (either with goods or political connections). Just as in the previous section the English parliament moved to exempt English Christians from enslavement in the Caribbean, leaders from that region had decided that, in order to avoid the negative spiritual consequences of capturing and selling individuals from powerful kin groups, only already alienated captives would be handed over to Mandinka or Luso-African traders in exchange for goods that would strengthen their own communities, providing protection against future attacks.[17] Did Yaff respond to the traumas of losing all who were dear to him, to the sickening horrors of the Middle Passage, by holding onto the name he had been called so often with affection?[18]

Nell's single recorded name makes her more of an enigma, thwarting any sort of speculation on her roots. Among enslaved populations, as in early modern societies in general, the woman's experience is most elusive. (The same is true of European women: all we know of Lewis Morris's first wife, Anne Barton, was that she was a widow when they married in 1637.) Whether Morris purchased an African woman like Nell or her mother as a wedding present for his young wife, we do not know.[19] The Morrises would have been expected to maintain a significant household staff in order to emulate their peers, providing lavish hospitality to guests.[20] Nell may have been the daughter of Lillee or Jane, two women with small children whom Morris acquired in 1655 for a thousand-plus pounds of sugar and several hundred of indigo.[21] Though we have no markers to give Yaff or Nell real roots, knowing about their possible backgrounds allows us to think more deeply about how they might have responded, individually and collectively, to their master's conversion and spiritual life, and to the Quaker missionaries who first appeared on the island in the late 1650s. Our vision of the Caribbean's moral economy becomes richer and more nuanced if we attempt to "see" as anthropologists the draw of Quakerism for men like Lewis Morris, and how the faith might have also appealed to the enslaved people living in converts' households.

The political turmoil and warfare of mid-seventeenth-century England, as in many parts of West Africa, seems to have pushed men and women to seek stability, often through a search for religious renewal, the restoration of a "purer" symbolic authority uncorrupted by time and human agendas. Quakers were among many new sects that proliferated in the power vacuum of England's civil turmoil of the mid-seventeenth century; some converts had been Cromwellian soldiers who, like Henry Whistler, had become jaded by puritanism's exclusionary hypocrisies. Quakers' belief that everyone had access to the Inward Light of Christ led some to denounce the authority of the Anglican Church, others to deny the false performances of social deference; a good number even accepted women as preachers and visionaries. Moreover, many became "convinced" (a Quaker coinage that became synonymous with conversion) that their way of looking at the world must be spread in order to change a world gone wrong. Dozens of ordinary men and women from all ranks and classes felt called to embark on mission trips to Holland, Ireland, the Levant, Constantinople, and also the Americas.

Among those who headed west across the Atlantic were two religiously liberated women, Anne Austin and Mary Fisher, who disembarked in Barbados a few months after the Penn/Venables forces had left the island.[22] Although men often subordinated women in religious matters both in West Africa and European Christendom, flexibility along gender lines was quite possible at the local level, and in moments of crisis women could transgress ordinary limits on their own power. In some parts of West Africa, women played key roles in addressing social chaos through religious renewal. At the start of the eighteenth century, the charismatic noblewoman Beatriz Kimpa Vita channeled the spirit of the Catholic St. Anthony (figured as a black man) to lead the Kongolese people out of increasingly disruptive civil wars to political and religious unity.[23] Likewise, during the English Civil War, women came out in force as mystics and leaders of new and diverse restorationist and radical spiritual paths.[24] English residents of Barbados would likely have been surprised at the liberty of Austin and Fisher, but they seem not to have challenged the women during their mission visit. On January 30, 1656, Fisher wrote from Barbados to George Fox with the good news that "here is many convinsed & many desire to know the way."[25]

Personal interactions would often determine those early conversions—the forging of a spiritual connection to another's charismatic, shamanistic power. We do not know if Lewis Morris or his wife Anne were among those to whom Fisher referred, but they seem to have been at least curious. When Henry Fell, a relative of George Fox's new wife Margaret Fell (also an early Quaker champion) arrived a short time later, Morris invited the visitor to accept hospitality at Ape's Hill. But on his walk to Colonel Morris's plantation, Fell was accosted on the road by islanders upset that he had earlier interrupted an Anglican Sunday service. Yaff may have helped the bloodied visitor up the steps to the house, and Nell and Anne may have tended to his bruises while he recounted the incident to Lewis. Whatever transpired after these conversations, Fell wrote to his mother back in England that Morris had been "much troubled" by the incident, and helped his Quaker guest to be heard by his friend, Governor Searle.[26] The bonds of intimacy and connection fostered in the aftermath of the attack likely aided Morris's attraction to Quakerism.

Those same personal bonds, forged in the intimacy of everyday interaction, would have included enslaved people like Yaff and Nell. As we have seen in the Spanish Caribbean, overlapping patron/client relationships structured the contours of social power and cooperation; the same dynamics in Africa are often referred to as landlord/stranger relations. Indeed, the British Caribbean was not so different, and thus we must think about the proliferation of Quaker conversions as reflecting an early modern ethos that privileged personal connections over abstract forces or institutional pressures. Col. Morris may have been introduced to Fell by another Providence Island Company veteran and sugar planter, Lieutenant Colonel Thomas Rous (whom Fisher and Austin had inspired), and he later brought into the Society his neighbor Ralph Fretwell, another influential planter, Assembly member and judge.[27] In such a personalized world, ritualized kinship created social order. As in Part I, familial connections and "rituals" of island hospitality practiced by local elites provided for the quick growth of the

Quaker community, as patrons like Morris sheltered the Society from governmental suspicion.[28]

Likewise, experience with "godly" patriarchal models from England (like those espoused by Penn and Venables in Part III) would color Morris's relationship with Yaff and Nell, for both Europeans and Africans inhabited relatively hierarchical worlds where masters' responsibilities included caring for "client" groups, protecting them from the violence of exclusion. Outsiders (clients, slaves, or strangers) also saw kinship as a comfort in unequal relationships. Although Yaff and Nell couldn't escape the flattening negative label of "Negro" any more than Nicholas Burundel could the stigma of "heretic," for Nicolas and other Northern European sojourners, religious conversion was a strategy to mitigate their exclusion; Yaff and Nell must have seen their master's religion as one way to forge a sense of kinship across the racial divide, something to supplement the material and emotional support they received from their other chosen collectivities—their shipmates, their countrymen, or those they worked alongside.[29]

In these personal exchanges, Yaff and Nell may have marveled that Quakers rejected their society's rules of deference; they addressed everyone with the informal pronouns "thee" and "thou," and men would not take off their hats in the presence of superiors, claiming it was an honor reserved for God alone. Lewis Morris may have been particularly drawn to the ways that this faith encouraged people to show respect for men of lesser means, since he had been one, too. He likely played a part in making sure that Friends of all strata were welcomed with open hearts (one-third of Quakers who appear in the island's 1680 census possessed insufficient acreage or labor to run their own independent sugar works).[30] But Yaff and Nell might have remained ignorant of many of these peculiarities if Colonel Morris had acted like some of his planter neighbors and barred his domestic slaves from the room during moments of religious exchange, "As if there were some secret Charm, or power of doing mischief in Prayers." Even if excluded, Yaff and Nell would have understood their master's ritual peculiarities as characteristics of a familiar institution. Secret societies in Africa were open only to the initiated, and Christianity as a whole probably seemed to many enslaved Africans as little more than a set of puzzling but important rituals.[31]

Yet if they had been allowed a glimpse into Quakers' emerging Society, a new connection might have formed. The thing that had made Quakers so distinctive from other Civil War–era religious sects was, of course, their trancelike "quaking" and public theatrics calling the wicked to judgment, and so the enslaved may have understood their masters' faith as a type of possession cult or spirit mediumship.[32] Scholars have noted how people of African descent were drawn to the more emotive forms of religiosity popularized by Protestant evangelicals in the eighteenth- and nineteenth-century transatlantic Great Awakenings, and how likewise, the enthusiastic bodily responses of black onlookers stimulated some whites to approach their faith with more displays of outward emotion.[33] The same may have been true for early Quakers: William Penn's report of his first religious stirrings as an adolescent came after listening to a sermon so evocative that "a black servant of the family could not contain himself from weeping aloud." One Penn biographer asserts that this servant was Anthony, the black youth whom William's father Admiral Penn had bought in Barbados on his return from Jamaica, hoping to bring him to Christianity. Although Anthony may have been weeping for any number of reasons (the pressures of enslavement, loneliness, etc.), Penn felt a sympathetic bond and a stirring of spiritual catharsis.[34] These moments likely happened in Barbados, too: writing of her 1681 mission trip, Joan Vokins said that her "Soul was often melted" as she experienced the divine presence in Barbados gatherings, "*even* in the meetings of the Negro's or Blacks, as well as among Friends."[35] An ethos of bodily religious experience in a space of spiritual equality might have offered Africans and Quakers a way to interact in a way that temporarily transcended the psychological distance of racializing boundaries, the resentments and abuses of power of Atlantic slave societies, a way to promote mutual healing.[36]

Quakerism's appeal to both black and white on Barbados may have been strongest when they explicitly denounced aspects of a plantation culture that, as the young convert John Rous (the son of Colonel Morris's friend Lieutenant Colonel Thomas Rous) put it, delighted in "Pride, Drunkennesse, Covetousnesse, Oppression and deceitful-dealings."[37] These sins were rampant within the Atlantic World's expanding commercialism and unequal distribution of wealth. Those merchants and planters who had, like Colonel Morris, succeeded in this economy, must have been aware that one bad crop or ill-timed investment could destroy their gains, and that God's providence humbled the proud. Quakerism's uncompromising message of the approaching Judgment certainly made some of the newly rich consider their own place in the afterlife: those who live easy in this world, their Bibles said, could find themselves barred from the Kingdom of Heaven. Wealthy Barbadians like Rous, heir to his father's considerable sugar estates, seem to have been affected by this strain of Quaker rhetoric. Part of the Society of Friends' attractiveness to Britons also rested on their acknowledgment of the moral dangers of economic entanglements, and their Society provided clear moral prescriptions: the duty to keep one's word in business affairs, to avoid unnecessary debt that would endanger families and business partners, and to eschew the vindictiveness of legal prosecution against debtors, replacing litigation with "loving" admonitions to one another as "Friends" to resolve any conflicts over money.

In Barbados, the spiritual dangers of investment and temptations of a competitive marketplace were intimately tied up with callous and dehumanizing treatment of laborers and the poor. Rous joined another visiting missionary Richard Pinder in prophesying that those who gained wealth "by violence and oppression" would find themselves subjected to a fate similar to their laborers in the afterlife.[38] Continually calling Barbadians "hard-hearted," John Rous and Pinder's declamations created a rhetorical parallel between the suffering of Barbados's laborers to the Exodus story, where Pharaoh hardened his heart to Moses's call to recognize the sufferings of the enslaved Israelites, until it was too late to repent—God struck down the Egyptians' firstborn sons.[39] The young Rous warned his wealthy friends and neighbors that "the cry of the oppressed is intred into the ears of the Lord of Sabbath, who will speedily come to pour forth his plague upon you . . . you that trust in your riches and despise the poor."[40] Planters in hard financial times might be tempted to cut back on provisions for their laborers, but Quaker missionaries Pinder and Rous denounced the disregard for human misery as an unholy reflection of man's greed,

> who to get of the earth into his possession, and increase his unrighteous Mammon, (which is his God whom he serves) cares not what murder is committed by him to fulfil his unrighteous and covetous ends, (I speak concerning you, who like unnatural beasts have been the death of many of your Servants, by withholding from them convenient food, for want of which many have perished under you) . . .[41]

Such denunciations must have struck at the "tender" hearts of planters like Morris who saw the like callousness in themselves. Efforts to make amends would have allowed enslaved people like Nell and Yaff to see the Society of Friends as a sort of "healing" cult.

George Fox, the Society's most charismatic spokesman, articulated a more direct spiritual response to the state of alienation between planters and their enslaved laborers. His Epistle of 1657, "To Friends beyond Sea, that have Blacks and Indian Slaves," and his subsequent visit to the

FIGURE 12. This engraving depicts the reality that not all Quakers had the capital to invest in the sugar boom, and thus tried their hand at other popular commodities like tobacco, here as in Virginia, gathered with the help of enslaved laborers. Image courtesy of the I.N. Phelps Stokes Collection, Miriam and Ira D. Wallach Division of Art, Prints, and Photographs, The New York Public Library.

island of Barbados in 1671, would challenge many planters, including Lewis Morris, to consider how their faith related to their practices of slaveholding.[42] Fox must have been disturbed by reports from returning missionaries Anne Austin or Mary Fisher, or perhaps the ardent young John Rous (who had shown an interest in Fox's stepdaughter, Margaret Fell Fox), that new converts in the Americas were reluctant to act in a spirit of universal love when it came to the enslaved. His first call to faithful Friends to remember that God "hath made all Nations of one Blood," urged them "to love all Men, for Christ loved all."[43] Did Fox's letter prompt Barbadian Friends like Morris to question their modes of thinking about African and American Others? To someone like Lewis Morris, this epistle may have pushed him to attempt an overture to slaves like Yaff or Nell, especially if they had shown interest in their master's ablutions, for Morris had himself been a captive and "slave" in 1639. That year, en route to a Providence Island Company privateering expedition, he and everyone aboard the *Mary* found themselves captured by Barbary corsairs; they would suffer "Chaynes and hunger" in Algiers alongside other Christians until their ransom in February 1640. Certainly Morris had experienced the weight of being "othered" with the label of infidel. We don't know much about his material conditions during the more than six months that it took for the PIC directors to negotiate their servants' ransom, but he may have been forced to labor in the city's public works or have been chained to other slaves in the coastal galleys. If he saw some captives there casually and cruelly whipped (or experienced it himself), he may have also seen others who were well treated, even given privileges when they willingly converted to Islam (or as the captives' petition to the PIC trustees put it, if they in "despair, [turned] their backs on Christ").[44] What kind of a master did he want to be?

In 1668, Morris's memories may have been refreshed yet again by a second captivity, this time for two years by French Catholic authorities who claimed that he had been involved in unlawful "depredations by sea." The allegations were shameful: the French charged that in 1663, Morris had negotiated a secret deal with Amiwatta Baba, a Carib lord on St. Lucia, bribing the Indians with money and plying them with liquor to induce them to accept an English "alliance." The French also claimed that Colonel Morris and some associates had, for private profit, invaded St. Lucia the following year, and with the help of Baba's Carib subjects, dispossessed the French settlers there. It is very possible that Yaff was with Lewis during this period of captivity, at least for part of the time.[45] Did Lewis admit to him any personal fault in the matter, or did he insist, as in a later letter (the only written in his hand and orthography), that his captors were "weked and unjust" in their accusations? Yaff may have spoken to his master about the spiritual significance of captivity, perhaps recalling his own fears when he first arrived in the tropical lands of the Christians, "a Strangar in a strang land." Yaff might have shared how he had hoped to be ransomed through his kin networks (as had the young Lewis from Algiers) or rescued by a powerful patron from a situation where a wicked man had captured him in "hoeps of enriching himself" (as Morris would characterize the situation to his patron and rescuer Lord Arlington). Did Yaff ask Lewis if he had considered converting to Islam during his captivity in Algiers? Yaff may have known people bought by Mandinka traders, captives who often saw the wisdom of securing spiritual kinship with their Muslim masters. We will never know the content of their conversations: all that remains is Colonel Morris's pious letter to Secretary of State Arlington, in which he gave "Prayes to God and thankes to thee as the Enstrument by which I was Delivard from unResnable men."[46] Morris might have just as well used the same providentialist language with Yaff, urging the young African to count himself fortunate that he had been taken from Africa, a land of pagan darkness, and brought to a kind and generous Christian master (not to French or Spanish popish cruelty), by which means he might be delivered from eternal damnation. How much was spiritual kinship possible between such different, unequal parties? Only sporadic moments between individuals could have made possible a spark of spiritual connection between black and white, but those sparks could just as quickly turn to ash. Although we often think about faith as a matter of belief or doctrine, its impulses were in the everyday moments. Conversations could bring about a mutual recognition of kinship, or encourage a shared way of seeing the world—or they could accentuate differences.

In 1671, George Fox and a dozen other Quaker luminaries from the British Isles set out across the Atlantic to unite a faith community held together by fragile bonds of correspondence, marriage, and commerce, but still rather heterodox in opinion. It would take the considerable force of Fox's personality to formalize his somewhat contentious ideas about interracial fellowship. Nell may have heard gossip from household slaves at Lieutenant Colonel Thomas Rous's plantation about the much-anticipated visit of these strangers, including young John's famous father-in-law, George Fox. They spoke of him with reverence, and indeed Fox did seem to have uncanny power. Barbadian Friends had doubtless begun to whisper about the mysterious death of one John Drakes, a notable young man from the island, whose plans to marry an orphaned daughter of Quaker parents had been squashed by Fox who, as her guardian, had refused the match. Drakes had been furious, and hearing that Fox's visit to Barbados was imminent, reputedly threatened that "if he could possibly procure it, he would have [Fox] burned to Death." Instead, a mere ten days after uttering this threat, the thwarted suitor found the tables turned: he was "struck with a Violent Burning Fever," from which he soon perished. Word travelled that "his Body was so scorched [sic], that ... It was as black, as a Coal," a curious reversion of his blasphemous threat. The funeral had been held only three days before Fox and his party landed.[47]

When the much-anticipated party aboard the *Industry* landed in Bridgetown, they would have heard this marvel, and shared their own miraculous story: Fox and some of his fellow passengers wrote in their recollected journals how three weeks after leaving England a "Sally-man of War . . . seemed to give us Chase," making the passengers and crew "very apprehensive of the Danger." These stories would have thrilled listeners who shuddered at the chilling prospect of Barbary captivity—again, perhaps a more visceral memory for Colonel Morris. As the ship drew nearer and nearer, Fox said he urged the crew to take this apparition as a "Trial of Faith," and later, in prayer, received a revelation in which "the Lord shewed me, 'That his Life and Power was placed between us, and the Ship, that pursued us.'" The ship's crew begged Fox to pray for them that they might avoid capture, but they were still amazed when the ship disappeared one moonless night, an incontrovertible sign of spiritual deliverance. The next day, Fox would write, "being the First-Day of the Week, we had a publick Meeting in the Ship . . . and the Lord's Presence was greatly among us."[48]

Two more stories, two opportunities for interaction on the basis of shared worldviews: both West Africans and Christians of the time placed much stock in dreams and other portents, and believed that some people had special access to the divine. Did Nell reveal to her mistress what her mother had taught her about people like Fox, blessed by the gods with second sight and magical powers? Did Yaff share with his master how other Africans were discussing this man's powerful sorcery—not quite comprehending that for Europeans, witchcraft was always considered to be evil? If they had become comfortable with some sort of interpersonal exchange, these conversations very well may have happened. Colonel Morris would have tried to explain that men themselves had no such power, that these were instead judgments meted out by the hand of Almighty God, signs to the world that Friends were blessed by Him.

In the first seven weeks of his stay, Fox did little but rest, for he had become very ill. Others in his entourage went out to preach in his stead—but to see this supposedly great man's weakness may have dampened the earlier sense of enthusiasm. Certainly, Friends had heard that his constitution had been damaged by several lengthy imprisonments in England fighting for their liberty of conscience, and would have assumed that he might also be affected by the tropical fevers that struck so many on their arrival in the West Indies. For many West Africans, however, sickness was not only physical. It was a manifestation of one's lack of care for the tutelary spirits, or the result of an enemy's witchcraft or malediction.[49] Had Fox been cursed by another, more powerful enemy? And how could such a weak, pale figure maintain a great following? Fox himself knew that he was troubled by something beyond familiar aches and pains, beyond tropical fevers: "And indeed, my Weakness continued the longer on me, by reason, that my Spirit was much pressed down at the first, with the Filth and Dirt, and Unrighteousness of the People, which lay as an heavy Weight and Load upon me."[50] While others among the visitors gathered Friends together into meetings, and set about explaining the new meeting structure that they had all agreed would best support their Society's stability and righteousness in the years to come, Fox observed life on his in-laws' plantation—attended no doubt by an army of enslaved men and women like Yaff and Nell, who bathed him and brought him gingered water to soothe his stomach. Perhaps even an African healer who knew of roots and herbs came to his bedside, trying to diagnose the witchcraft that had weakened him so.

After his condition improved, Fox spoke before Barbadian Friends gathered at his son-in-law's place of birth, urging them to purge their meetings from rancor, to regulate marriages and burials, to record the same, and also to compile a list of "such, as went out from Truth into Disorderly Practices." Linking the figurative to the literal, Nell may have been called upon to carry out Fox's command to Friends to "sweep their Houses very clean; that nothing might remain, that would defile."[51] In a later address to a large group of men charged with overseeing the Society's flock in Barbados, Fox turned decisively to the matter of slavery. Armed with biblical examples, Fox warned the white, largely slaveholding audience of men that they risked their souls if they continued to "slight them, to wit, the Ethyopians, the Blacks now, neither any Man or Woman upon the Face of the Earth, in that Christ dyed for all, both Turks, Barbarians, Tartarians and Ethyopians."[52] The main theme of Fox's sermon, later published under the title of *Gospel Family Order*, was to encourage heads of household to establish a "Government of Families according to the Law of Jesus" modeled on the extended households of biblical times, which included those "bought with money" (i.e., indentured servants and slaves). They should be like the Old Testament patriarch Joshua who, Fox reminded them, decisively affirmed his spiritual dedication: "As for me *and my house*, we will serve the Lord."[53]

While (as I have suggested throughout this chapter) the possibility for individual interactions between masters and slaves on the subject of religion had always existed, here Fox *required* it of those attending this first official Men's Meeting—if they thought of themselves as Friends. They must do more to distinguish themselves on this issue of evangelical outreach. Nonetheless, a ripple of unease must have passed through the hall. Yes, surely it was the right thing to do—but what about the consequences? Lewis Morris for one would have known of the resistance likely to be met from local slaveholders, whose opinion it had always been that encouraging widespread Christian conversion was unadvisable: would they not need to make any Christian converts free? Or would slaves seek inclusion only for special favors? Others would protest that they couldn't spare laborers from fieldwork every Sunday for instruction. Most were also fearful of slaves congregating in large numbers, or gaining a command of English, which might help them foment insurrection.[54]

Rumors of this danger that Quakers would "teach the Negars to Rebel" made it out of the meetinghouse and to the ears of the island's governor. Other misconceptions—that Quakers didn't believe in Jesus's divinity, or that they had no use for the Scriptures (both foundational to Church of England theology)—made their potential religious instruction of slaves even more troubling. When the summons came for Fox to come before the governor to speak his piece, Lewis Morris and Thomas Rous agreed to accompany him.[55] Colonel Morris would have surely reminded Fox of the need to remain silent before the governor about any radical ideas. Fox would have known that to be taken seriously here in Barbados he had to maintain a sense of unity with local Quakers, families like Morris's who relied on African slavery as their key to economic stability. Intending to placate his audience, Fox approached the governor as a godly patriarch, saying simply that "Negars & Tawny Indians make up a very great part of Families here on the Island, for whom an Account will be required at the Great Day of Judgment."[56] Futhermore, Fox used strong language to register how much he and other Friends "abhor[ed] and detest[ed]" ("the Lord Knows it") anything that might encourage slave unrest:

> that which we have spoken and declared to them is, to exhort and admonish them, To be Sober, and to Fear God, and to love their Masters and Mistresses, and to be Faithful and Diligent in their Masters Service and Business; and that then their Masters and Overseers will Love them, and deal Kindly and Gently with them: And that they should not beat their Wives, nor the Wives their Husbands; nor multiply Wives, nor put away their Wives, nor the Wives their Husbands, as they use frequently to do: and that they do not Steal, nor be Drunk, nor commit Adultery, nor Fornication, nor Curse, nor Swear, nor Lye, nor give Bad Words to one another, or unto any one else. For there is something in them, that tells them, That they should not Practice those Evils . . .[57]

Thanks to Fox's introduction by Morris and Rous, both well respected by this governor, the conversation that followed Fox's speech was civil, and afterwards they all dined together before Fox accepted the invitation to stay with Colonel Morris at his plantation, travelling first by boat, then on horseback up to Ape's Hill.[58]

There Nell may have ministered to Fox if he still felt weak or feverish, and Yaff and others in Morris's household would have had an opportunity not only to see a famous religious leader but to understand some of the politics and contentiousness that embroiled the Society—for Fox was only one voice in the evolving discussion about the directions in which to take their faith, and in Barbados, local planters like Colonel Morris would be the ones who would definitively shape the sect's engagement with slavery. We don't know whether Yaff and Nell were brought into any of those conversations, as perhaps they had opportunity before, but certainly the dynamic would have shifted to the "leading" men who had ultimate power to define evil and to set standards for the Society's future evangelization efforts.

11 / Evangelization and Insubordination: Authority and Stability in Quaker Plantations

With George Fox and several others in attendance, Colonel Morris's household would have been a flurry of activity. The topic that reportedly occupied most of the visitors' time was how Friends might best "settle" their membership in a more "disciplined" way.[1] Lewis Morris had impressed them. He and six other local Quakers were entrusted "to hold a Correspondency wth all ye Governors, Major Generalls, Judges & Justices in America" to better represent the Society's grievances to civil authorities (they especially needed a way to conduct everyday legal business without swearing oaths).[2] Pleased with the "settling" of affairs in Barbados, some of the visitors prepared to leave the island for mission points further afield. Two of them, William Edmundson and John Stubbs, found themselves "moved of the Lord to visit the Leeward Islands, and Col. Morriss, of Barbadoes, would go with us." They first stopped in Antigua, where Edmundson reported that "we had great meetings, and many were convinced and turned to the Lord." One of the puritan Winthrop family, Colonel Samuel Winthrop, a prominent sugar planter in Antigua and a personal friend to Lewis Morris, invited the party of missionaries to continue on to Barbuda and Nevis in his ship, "with himself, Col. Morriss, their waiting-men and seamen."[3] Yaff may well have been one of these "waiting-men" who accompanied his master through the Leeward Islands, and would have listened as this trio of leading Quaker allies discussed plans to bring more people to the Truth, and more discipline to those who claimed it.

Winthrop and Morris felt confident that they would be good stewards of the Society's interests, for they had been part of the Caribbean's ruling planter class for a while now, and knew the force of their own prosperity and reputations. This self-importance seems to have rankled Edmundson, who complained that upon arriving at Nevis, the men took an inordinate amount of time in "dressing, and trimming themselves, as they and such Persons use to do . . . [to] be taken notice of as being Great Persons."[4] Edmundson had a point. By the time that Yaff and Colonel Winthrop's manservant finished with their masters' toilette, a government official arrived to inform the group that they would not be allowed to disembark: "We hear that since your Coming to the Caribbee-Islands, there are Seven Hundred of our Militia turn'd Quakers, and the Quakers will not fight, and we have need of Men to fight, being surrounded by Enemies."[5]

Although the Society of Friends had gained a substantial following in the Caribbean, they came to be seen as detrimental to England's colonial order at a time of increasing military pressure from competitor France (the new continental Catholic superpower) and internal threats to security in their plantation colonies (recurring slave and servant rebellions). Quakers' growing wealth and prestige was seen as increasingly dangerous, especially considering their militant pacifism (their refusal to serve on militias) and their new mission to the enslaved.[6] At any other time, Colonels Morris and Winthrop might have tried to prevail with Nevis's governor by using soothing words—in fact, in Jamaica, Friends had agreed to pay to have other white men serve in their stead on militia days—but Edmundson was among those metropolitan Friends who wanted his co-religionists to stop prevaricating with the Society's key doctrines of "conscience." England's far-flung colonial holdings had made the job of disciplining new converts and upholding orthodoxy more difficult (it is exactly for this reason that sprawling empires like Spain had introduced the Inquisition—policing cultural conformity helped the monarchy maintain its authority). Whether or not an active evangelization campaign would become one of those principles central to Friends' identity was still an open question, but Colonel Morris would have been among those Friends in Barbados who defined the possibilities and restrictions.

In the Caribbean, the threat of disorder was simply intolerable. During the 1670s, leading Quakers felt their sense of religious order and personal authority threatened—both within the Society's emerging group of local leaders and with the plantation economy. Despite having given up fighting, Colonel Morris and other leading West Indian Friends did not give up their military titles (a sort of West Indian "gentry" honorific); they were as dedicated to disciplining the Society's membership, their families, and their plantation "households" as they had formerly been to maintaining

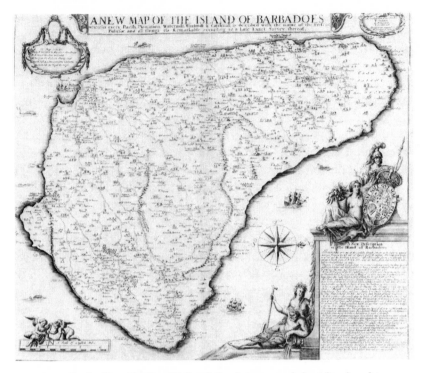

FIGURE 13. Barbadian Quaker Richard Forde surveyed the island and produced this elegant map engraving published in 1675. Out of religious scruples, Forde did not portray Anglican churches or military fortifications. Image courtesy of the John Carter Brown Library at Brown University.

military and social order in the Caribbean.[7] The Society's new emphasis on "discipline" would have allowed Yaff and Nell to observe how people in their master's religious community disagreed and argued about leadership issues. Although they held firm to many unconventional beliefs and practices, Quakers also found ways to modulate any messages that threatened secular authority, hoping to secure religious tolerance in the public sphere.[8] Conservative trends in denominational matters suppressed Quakerism's earlier radical tendencies, and must have worked to reify social and racial hierarchies on the plantation.

Some of the biggest unanswerable questions in considering the effect of Fox's Gospel Family Order challenge concern the mechanics of evangelization: understanding how Barbadian friends modified Quakerism's particularly open, democratic Christian message to suit their highly hierarchical society. These conversations have largely been lost to historians—no monthly or quarterly meeting records survive for seventeenth-century Caribbean Quakers, relatively few published or manuscript works mentioned the evangelization program, and even then only in passing.[9] The types of dialogues that may have previously taken place on an individual level now needed to be communicated en masse, or at least in a more formalized way. John Stubbs, one of the visitors to Barbados in 1671, admitted that having meetings with blacks in attendance seemed "a great cross at first," and that it had taken some time before he felt "the Lord's presence and power in that service."[10] This discomfort may have prompted Fox to write a follow-up letter of 1673, in which he advised the Men's Meeting that Friends with slaves should "let them have two or three Hours of the Day once in the Week, that Day Friends Meeting is on, or on another Day, to meet together, to wait upon the Lord." He provided no specifics on whether "waiting upon the Lord" might follow the form of silent meetings or some sort of preaching and instruction.[11] What message might they begin with? Planters may have looked to Fox's 1660 catechism for children, which hammered home Quakerism's central philosophy that the universal Light of Christ "doth enlighten every man that cometh into the World."[12] Fox had written more on this issue after his return: he firmly held that Christians should recognize that even the world's "heathens" had an innate capacity for righteousness and spiritual wisdom.[13] Had Fox attempted, like Fathers Alonso de Sandoval and Pedro Claver, to question individuals like Yaff about the religious beliefs of their homelands, to identify their shared divinely inspired roots? Or did Morris do the same so he might be made aware of the specific "errors" of African religions that most needed correction? Did Yaff decide to flatter their pretensions, agreeing that Christianity "undoubtedly surpasseth all other Religions in the World, as much as the Sun's Light doth that of a Glow-Worm"?[14] Or did he offer his doubts about the commensurability of their belief systems? We must assume that some blend of the two characterized early Quaker missionizing.

If planters allowed for some sort of open exchange, Quakerism's focus on dreams and other personal revelations may have allowed Africans raised with a similar spiritual ethos to have a voice. In many parts of West and West Central Africa, a comparable focus on "continuous revelation"— the interpretation of dreams and visions by ritual specialists or in community discussions—could provide moral healing in times of distress.[15] For Quakers, dream revelations "plotted courses for people to take in their everyday lives on earth," and Europeans, too, used the remembering and retelling of their dreams to help resolve personal and group dilemmas.[16] But although Fox himself had drawn on dreams as his inspiration for preaching, Quaker leaders increasingly urged Friends to be wary of the sources of their dreams: they could be related to stress (the "multitude of business" that distracted the mind). Dreams might be the "whisperings of Satan." Only rarely were they truly the voice of God "speaking . . . to man."[17]

Problems also arose when one person's inner revelations challenged the ruling group's assumptions or sparked disagreement about what it meant to be a Christian and a Friend. The inherent instability of continuous revelation created rifts and threatened to challenge authority. As Friends had discovered in their own denominational growth, too much democratic exchange of revelations, too much looseness, could introduce "disorder" into the Society and encourage "Dark Spirits." It had already happened in the 1660s, when one Quaker charismatic, John Perrot, seduced audiences in Europe and the West Indies with his stirring tales of missionary adventure, but he was disgraced soon after his "hat heresy."[18] Perrot, early on one of the shining stars of Quaker missions, had stubbornly adhered to a personal revelation (opposed by Fox and others) that men need not uncover their heads during prayer, a scandalous challenge to the idea that humans owed deference to God above all men. Perrot's relocation to the Caribbean and the continued rebellions he and other separatists mounted against Fox's leadership made efforts at unity difficult during the second half of the seventeenth century.[19] Colonel Morris, who would have been exposed to Perrot's influence in the West Indies, must have wondered what might happen if enslaved Africans—on the grounds of personal revelation—began to refuse the rituals of deference that supported plantation hierarchies.

The new Quaker meeting structure put in place during Fox's visit was designed to firm up the Society's doctrinal positions, unify its public message, and help restrain unruly members. Quaker leaders began to publicly disown those they called "Dark Spirits." They explicitly frowned upon extemporaneous preaching by women and outbursts from other "weak vessels." Silent meetings were to be a curb to the unruly mind rather than a prelude to visionary "quaking." Lewis Morris and his wife would have been part of local efforts to curb "excess" and "Ranterism," negotiating any local disagreements on the right way to live out Quaker principles, policing their enslaved neophytes with the same rigor. These ideological controversies continued among the Society's membership during the 1670s and '80s, doubtless distracting many Friends from the sticky business of evangelization.[20]

If Yaff and Nell heard some of the bitter invective associated with these squabbles, they would have been dismayed at the new uses being made of allusions to "Egyptian slavery." Leaders like Edmundson sternly admonished those who had escaped "the [spiritual] Bondage of Egypt," but fell away from unity before reaching the "Land of Promise."[21] In response, separatists spoke of their consciences being "Inslav'd or kept in Bondage" by the new forms and rules that Fox insisted upon, and even painted themselves as the biblical Joseph, the youngest and favored son of Jacob, betrayed and sold by his jealous brothers into Egyptian slavery.[22] To Quakers who remained faithful to the "Foxian party," separatists' "misuse" of Egyptian metaphors might have provoked fears that the Dark Bodies of those enslaved people among them (those so far removed from the Light of Christianity) could also become Dark Spirits, seduced from impressionistic principles of Christian love and charity into vanity, presumption, and bitter, warlike words. The enslaved who suffered under literal bondage every day of their lives, on the other hand, might have felt that their masters had since turned from their suffering, falling prey to the complicity and "hard-heartedness" that early missionaries had warned against.

But these are mostly philosophical speculations—again, the formal tenets of Quakerism would have been secondary to the spirit of engagement between individuals on matters close to their hearts. In times of financial hardship for Friends' estates, slaves themselves must have used the venue of religious meetings to protest the potential sale of their comrades, shipmates, or blood relatives—to protect and honor their own complex kinship networks in the same way Friends protected others within the Society. Some evidence suggests this concern was seen as legitimate. For instance, when Colonel Morris's kinsman Thomas Morris had died in Barbados shortly before Fox's visit, Lewis was instructed to help the widow ensure that none of the other slaves would be sold off or disposed of in any way.[23] Wills—the most comprehensive and personal of the extant sources for Quakers in Barbados—do not reveal motivations, but within their silences we can infer possibilities for interaction with the enslaved. For instance, Robin, Pegge, and Jack, three slaves held by Quaker George Foster, may have somehow influenced the remarks in his will stipulating that they should stay at his plantation "on the Cliff" and that any of their children designated as bequests to family members "shall not be by any of them sold, mortgaged or alienated."[24]

Ordering intimate family relationships, especially those of marriage and reproduction, were central to Quaker leaders' efforts to promote theirs as a respectable denomination. As Friends worked to bring order and respectability to the Society, they insisted upon careful record keeping of births, marriages, and deaths, a process that involved Friends of both sexes. Quaker critics, and some Friends themselves, condemned the extraordinary freedom of many women within the Society, especially the missionary travels of women like Anne Austin and Mary Fisher, often without their husbands.[25] Societal assumptions of women's weakness of the flesh (especially in sexual matters) made these women's spiritual freedom a liability. Fox relied on local leaders like Colonel Morris to intervene if they heard of any "disorderly walkings," for the Society's reputation suffered damage when "svch stinking stves [stews]" became public knowledge. One piece of gossip concerned "Mary A—— of Long-Island" who reportedly "left her Husband to exercise her Talent in Barbadoes, and became Pregnant in that fruitful Island, and returned to her Husband with Increase."[26]

The reference to illegitimate and shameful "Increase" was often used to refer to children of enslaved women, a marker of animalistic "breeding." Indeed, some Barbadians had evidently jested about Friends' unique marriage ceremonies (in which the congregation, not a minister, served to solemnize the couple's vows), calling them marriages "after the Negro fashion."[27] Indeed, Friends wanted to completely erase the stain of illegitimacy from the Society, even as they held firm to their doctrinal positions. In Fox's Gospel Family Order sermon, he went so far as to advise that "if any of your Negroes desire to marry, let them take one another before Witnesses, in the Presence of God, and the Masters of the Families . . . [vowing] not to break the Covenant and Law of Marriage (nor defile the Marriage-Bed) as long as they lived . . . and so to record it in a Book."[28] Yaff or Nell might have approached Colonel Morris or his wife to indicate their interest in marriage partners, and (if their masters took the requests seriously) they might have asked other slaves about the "clearness" of both partners from other claims, as well as both partners' willingness to be joined.[29] White and black alike would have gained bonds of kinship by "allowing" and recognizing marriage.

Moreover, careful record keeping was needed to legally legitimize Quaker unions, especially in a place like the Caribbean, where disease and property concerns prompted hasty marriages that went unrecorded in Anglican parishes.[30] As when refusing Cromwell's commission in 1655, Colonel Morris had his own marital and inheritance concerns to deal with. We know that sometime in the 1670s, Lewis Morris remarried (because local

Quaker records have been lost, what happened to his first wife Anne remains a mystery, as does the date of Morris's second marriage). In 1677, one "Marie Morres" was listed as a member of the Women's Plantation Meeting, the Quaker gathering place near Speightstown.[31] Lewis Morris's biographer believes that this woman, also referred to as Mary (Marie and Mary were often used interchangeably at the time), had herself been a servant in Colonel Morris's house. Like his first wife, Marie had likely arrived in Barbados as an indentured servant, another of those who were able to raise their station through marriage to newly wealthy planters.

By the time of the island's 1680 census, Quakers had some of the most stable family networks in Barbados.[32] However, most Quakers seem not to have followed through on officially recognizing slave unions. The language in Morris's will, like that of almost all wills sampled in my study, carries not a hint of a suggestion that he had taken care to promote the spiritual bonds of matrimony among enslaved people he considered both "property" and (potentially) part of his "family." Plantation owners everywhere balked at conferring too much stability on slave families, for a bad economic turn could require the sale of a newborn, or if a slave should become troublesome, the separation of a "married" couple. Unlike in the Spanish Americas, in the English Caribbean the strength of private enterprise and religious toleration meant that only slaveholders—not the Church, not colonial officials, and certainly not black men themselves—could claim rights over the "increase" of enslaved women.

What might have happened if Mary and Lewis tried to discipline their households using Christian definitions of marriage? Mary's position on sexual propriety may have been compromised if she had used her feminine charms to tempt Lewis to marry her, and even if that was not the case, Nell would have been justifiably offended if Mary had read at the dinner table a recent epistle from Edmundson about the need "to take great Care to Restrain and Reclaim [Negroes] from their former Courses of their filthy, unclean practices, in defileing one another."[33] Fox urged plantation mistresses like Mary to use their authority to "endeavour to break ym off of yt Evil Custome among ym of runing after another Woman w[he]n married to one already"—but how could Mary exercise such authority when she had so recently been little more than a servant herself?[34]

Enslaved members of Quaker households like Yaff and Nell must have been disappointed that Fox and other missionaries focused so much negative attention on the evils of polygamy and sexual (rather than familial) relations among enslaved members of their household. Perhaps Yaff revealed to Lewis that several of the leading African men on the plantation had had more than one wife at home, where their power depended on showing they could support a large household. Most Africans who arrived in Barbados would have seen polygamy (even polygyny in some places) as natural arrangements that allowed leading families to create complex bonds among the most successful and best-connected lineages. Quaker families certainly arranged marriages to strengthen their religious "kin" group, but with slaves, crude references to "breeding" and the repetition of negative stereotypes like Henry Whistler's from Chapter Nine naturalized this rhetoric of inferiority and uncleanliness. Enslaved people might have been legitimately puzzled by the prohibition on polygamy if they had heard Lewis Morris read from Fox's 1670 *Primmer and Catechisme for Children*, in which he described how the biblical patriarch Jacob married two sisters, Leah and Rachel, serving two terms of seven years to their father to secure both women in marriage. Why the double standard?

As in the case of Isabel Criolla in Part I, the conversation might have been tense with sexual rivalry—especially if Marie suspected or knew that Lewis had gratified his lusts with Nell before and after their marriage. Some enslaved women may have encouraged a physical relationship with Colonel Morris, a decision that to us today seems simultaneously empowering and troubling given their legal powerlessness as well as white men's certain coercion (subtle or overt).[35] Women like Nell were hardly alone in negotiating such situations, seeing little with which to protect themselves. In many parts of Africa formal concubinage between a slave woman and her master was not only tolerated, but often helped raise the status of the woman. In some regions, women who became "Mother of the [master's] Child" (*umm al-walad*) would have had recourse to legal protection under Muslim law.[36] Perhaps Nell, either out of confusion or to prove her power over Marie, asked her mistress to explain why Abraham, believing his wife Sarah to be barren, agreed to raise as his own a son borne by the "bond Woman" Hagar. Lewis and his wife had no children of their own to secure his legacy. To Nell, Hagar might seem a bittersweet example, for she was consequently made a free woman and their son Ishmael shared equally in his father's inheritance. Fox's depiction of the Old Testament story in his educational primer for children even acknowledged that Abraham grieved for Hagar at her death.[37] These secret jealousies and anxieties over authority, although absent from the extant sources, were certainly part of everyday insubordination, fodder for vindictive discipline by plantation mistresses.

Quakerism's program of evangelization, despite its pretensions to spiritual fellowship, was in many ways only a "softer" form of spiritual colonization. Despite, or perhaps because of, the increased interactions promoted

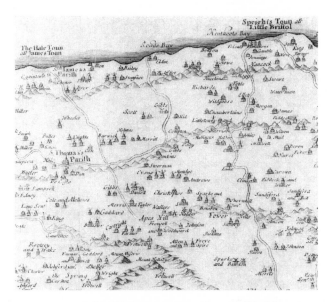

FIGURE 14. Colonel Morris seems to have still held various
properties up from the main roads out of Speightstown
and Holetown [Hale Town] leading towards Apes Hill in
1675, as shown in this detail from Forde's map.

by Quakers' mission to the enslaved, personal betrayals and false promises
would have cut all the deeper. Economic pressures only intensified the
sense of alienation. Profit margins on Barbadian sugar were on the decline by the mid-1670s, and so planters like Colonel Morris were forced to
make drastic cutbacks or take on an intolerable burden of debt themselves.
The enslaved would have faced hunger from the rising cost of foodstuffs:
to keep costs down, slave gangs would have been worked even harder to
compensate for the high cost of "unnecessary" additional laborers. Certainly, the harsh regimes of sugar planting and the intolerable cruelty of
discipline would have prompted some, as in Part I, to curse the god of their
Christian masters and overseers. Did Yaff or Nell approach their master
and mistress with complaints of their suffering? How did Lewis and Mary
respond? Were they defensive, as Quaker leaders had come to be towards
those who questioned their doctrinal authority?

Clearly, dialogue alone would not mend the injustices of plantation
slavery. In June 1675, in a plan three years in the making, vanquished warrior "Coromantees" brought to Barbados from the Gold Coast called on
their own gods for protection and strength to rise up and kill "the Bac-
cararoes or White Folks." These soldiers allegedly planned to rule as kings

over other "stranger" Africans, expropriating their former masters' wealth and women.[38] Yochoe and Adoe, two men from the Gold Coast who had worked on the nearby plantation of Lewis's kinsman Thomas Morris, may have been forewarned of the attack.[39] Yaff and Nell, on the other hand, would have likely remained ignorant of the conspiracy, given their dangerously close relationship to whites. Indeed, according to one account of the incident published later that year, the plot was exposed by a female slave who overheard two of the conspirators quarrelling: one Coromantee youth had refused his orders to kill all the whites without exception. Anna, who later called herself Fortuna (perhaps a reference to the freedom which she was granted for her aid) revealed the secret, allegedly because she believed it "a great Pity so good people as her Master and Mistriss . . . should be destroyed."[40]

Certainly the slaves in Morris's household would have quickly learned of the plot's unmasking, for Speightstown and Holetown, the nearest ports to Morris's plantation (to which they traveled often to bring muscovado sugar and molasses for export) were the main theaters for swift and painful justice against the conspirators. In the first wave of reprisals, investigators ordered the execution of 17 individuals, 6 of them "burnt alive, and Eleven beheaded, their dead bodies being dragged through the Streets . . . afterwards burnt with those that were burned alive." As the investigation broadened, 25 more slaves were sentenced to execution, 5 of whom hung themselves first. Such acts of destruction and despair must have shaken the more than sixty slaves still imprisoned in Holetown awaiting trial, as well as their loved ones who had not (yet) been implicated.[41] The pervasive scent of the executed men's burnt and rotting flesh, which may have drifted inland towards the Morris plantation, would have served as a visceral reminder of the consequences of questioning the island's dedication to white supremacy.

Friends' meetings in the aftermath of the conspiracy would have likely been characterized by hushed conversations, avoiding the eyes of their own slaves in attendance. Were potential murderers among them, bathing them, preparing their food? Colonel Morris must have recalled his own role in disarming Irish servants and rounding up bands of runaway slaves in the summer of 1657, when the numbers of Protestant white men at arms had dropped with attempts to bolster Jamaica's fledgling population. He had been given carte blanche to "kill and destroy" any slaves who could not be apprehended otherwise, but how much should violence be part of the solution now that he was a Quaker?[42] Mary and Lewis must have wondered if it was wise to try calming the jittery household slaves with the reminder at daily prayers that those who accepted their station in life would be exalted at Judgment Day, and the wicked ones punished. In later years, annual epistles sent to regulate and standardize Friends' meetings in the Americas instructed that in "Family meetings among your servants . . . every Master & Mistress [should] warn, & strictly admonish ym from all Plots, & Conspiracies, wch is out of ye peaceable Truth of God."[43] Would they perhaps have also criticized Barbadian officials' unnatural cruelty?

Yaff and Nell would have understood that this sweep of more than one hundred suspected conspirators was meant not just to strike fear into the hearts of other slaves who might wish to mount the same kind of attack, but was also an opportunity for island planters to use "spiritual terror" to destroy the psychic and spiritual bonds that allowed sectors of the African population to mount challenges to Caribbean plantation regimes. Barbadian Christians knew that if the enslaved rallied around a cause born not of a splintered ethnic solidarity but of common frustrations as "Negroes," their shared beliefs in magic and spirit resurrection might also provide the ideological strength to orchestrate more powerful attacks. One tale of an exchange between two of the convicted conspirators at the execution pyre in Speightstown reveals the power of silence and shared spiritual strength in the face of death. One of the two seemed to have been persuaded to "confess the depth of their design" before dying, but before he could speak,

> The next Negro Man chained to him (one Tony, a sturdy Rogue . . .) was heard to Chide him in these words, *Thou Fool, are there not enough of our Country-men killed already? Art thou minded to kill them all?* Then the aforesaid Negro that was a going to make Confession, would not speak one word more. Which the spectators observing, cryed out to Tony, *Sirrah, we shall see you fry bravely by and by.* Who answered undauntedly, *If you Roast me to day, you cannot Roast me tomorrow* (all those Negro's having an opinion that after their death they go into their own Countrey).[44]

Europeans may have mocked their slaves' assertions that they would "return to their own country" at their death, but some might have been shaken by Tony's bravery in the face of a torturous death. What did Yaff and Nell witness of this incident, and how did they speak of the rebellion, both among themselves and before their masters? What did they believe about the afterlife, and the final judgment of Tony and his countrymen? Yaff, sickened by the spectacle, may have whispered his fervent wish that he could fly back to his home village after his death. Did Fortuna, the woman who had uncovered the plot, resulting in such wanton destruction of human life, appear at the marketplace wearing a new dress, one "with a Badge of a Red Crosse on the Right Arme"? Lawmakers in 1661 had decided such garb should be given to slaves who turned over runaways to the authorities, that "hee may bee knowne and cherished by all good People for his good service to the Country."[45] Nell may have asked herself if she would do the same in Fortuna's place, whether her own master and mistress were such "good People" that they should be spared, or if it was too heavy a burden to wear the mark of collaborator on her sleeve.

Colonists remained in a tense stasis, searching for answers as to what might protect them from the "barbarous cruelty of Savage Heathens."[46] Then, only two months after the conspiracy, another calamity presented itself, a hurricane that destroyed nine churches, killing dozens and flattening houses and windmills. Many Barbadians took these events as a sign that "the Lord hath taken us into his own hand to chastise us" for their sins and lack of repentance.[47] Friends would have responded to these events with the providentialism that characterized most puritan worldviews, and may have been (more than usually) susceptible to intimations that their sins were to blame. William Edmundson, who had travelled with Colonel Morris to Antigua and Nevis in 1671, returned to Barbados and reported that "people's lofty spirits were down by reason of a very extraordinary storm, called a hurricane." Edmundson took the moment of crisis as an opportunity to seek out new converts to Quakerism, to encourage Friends to stay diligent in their "church affairs," and to promote Fox's Christianization program among island slaves. Given the tense racial situation on the island, Mr. Ramsey, a local Anglican minister, denounced Edmundson before Governor Atkins, claiming that the Quaker's preaching would not "make our Negroes Christians, but would make them Rebels and rise and cut their [Masters'] Throats."[48] Edmundson responded to the accusations by claiming that converting slaves to Christianity would rather

> keep them from rebelling or cutting any Man's Throat; but if they did rebel and cut their Throats, as [Ramsey] said, it would be through their own Doings, in keeping [their slaves] in Ignorance, and under Oppression, giving them Liberty to be common with Women (like Beasts) and on the other Hand starve them for want of Meat and Clothes.[49]

But in the paranoid climate following the slave conspiracy, few could tolerate Edmundson's assertion that humane treatment and Christian discipline were the best ways to create a docile work force. Authorities did not seem to look into the economic hardships that had pinched at the enslaved population in the preceding years, and although no surviving evidence even hints at a link between Quaker households and the conspirators, island officials found the Society of Friends an easy target.[50] Among a series of laws meant to rectify the problem of internal security on the island, in April 1676 the Barbados Council voted to approve an "Act to Prevent the People called Quakers from bringing Negroes to their Meetings," which mandated first that any slave found present at Friends' meetings was subject to forfeiture, and further that the head of household who sponsored any such meetings was subject to additional fines of ten pounds sterling per slave present at the gathering.[51]

Some Friends seem to have flouted the new laws to gain the esteem of their missionary co-religionists, and Colonel Morris was among them.[52] He and other Barbadian Quakers doubtless continued to discuss the obstacles to their evangelization program with visiting Friends like Thomas and Alice Curwen, who came to the island shortly after the Council's new laws had passed. Alice was disturbed by the attitude of one widow on the island, Martha Tavernor, who had complied with the law and kept her slaves from meetings, despite their assertions of being "convinced of God's Eternal Truth." After Alice's return to England, she wrote to Tavernor, admonishing her that "if they *whom thou call'st thy Slaves*, be Uprighthearted to God, the Lord God Almighty will set them Free in a way that thou knowest not."[53] This sort of verbal reproach poked holes in the very justification and definition of slavery and was precisely *not* what Barbadian Friends wanted their slaves to hear.

Lewis Morris may have been concerned about such opportunities for slaves and other Friends to protest his judgment as a patriarch, but economic stressors may have made things worse. He might have needed to invest significant time and money to repair one or more of the windmills on his sugar plantation (in December 1675 it was reported that 16 windmills in the area surrounding Speightstown had been destroyed, and 12 more "much damnified"). From 1674 to 1678 he suffered fines in excess of ten thousand pounds of sugar for his refusal to pay to support his local Anglican parish or send men and horses to the militia muster.[54] Colonel Lewis Morris, worried about more fines, may have considered it convenient to drop his adherence to evangelization, but he seems to have chosen the more difficult path, for in 1677 he and his neighbor Ralph Fretwell's names were turned over to authorities for bringing slaves to Friends' meetings. The informer, Thomas Cobham, had been eager to receive his reward, but Quakers reported that the *Manifest Hand of God* had reached out in retribution for his meddling:

> soon after [he] was taken with a Fever and Swelling in his Neck and Throat, which daily increased in a very strange manner; so that towards his latter End, he . . . said to his Mother, *She need not provide a Coffin for him, for he should be burnt up before it was made*; crying . . . *Now the Quakers will say, It is a Judgment fallen on me.* After this manner did this miserable man end his Days.[55]

What did Yaff and Nell think of what had happened? They might have considered, as after hearing the tale of Fox's power over life and death, that Quakers themselves possessed some obeah spirits. If so, could their master unleash that destructive power on them?

Although William Edmundson believed that during this second trip, "many of the Blacks are convinc'd and several of them confess to Truth," how many, and for what reasons, did slaves respond to evangelization in Barbados?[56] Two decades later, Friends claimed that discipline had always been their primary goal:

> most Friends that had Negroes set apart one hour or two once a week to instruct them according to their understanding, and to read the Scriptures to them, directing them to the inward Teacher, whereby they might be led out of Stealing, Murdering, Plotting, and of their Uncleanness and Adultery.[57]

Quakers in the Caribbean recognized the threat of rebellion as urgent enough to rewrite their reasons for evangelization—and to reconsider their religiously inspired refusal to participate in the local militia. Friends in Nevis and Barbados compromised with local officials, agreeing to participate in unarmed patrols of the island, promising to notify authorities if they suspected conspiracy was afoot or force was otherwise needed.[58] As long as intensive plantation slavery continued, insubordination had to be met with retribution, whether through violence or religious "discipline." For enslaved people living in Quaker households, some of whom may have been initially heartened by their masters' willingness to participate in spiritual communion, such authoritarian impulses and "hard-heartedness" carried seemingly insurmountable obstacles to true kinship and universal love.

Yet Yaff and Nell likely continued, cautiously, to seek a sense of sacred kinship with Lewis and Marie, for those personal bonds were the keys to a sense of security—salvation in the form of protection from the common rigors of their bondage. Despite the suspicion that many enslaved people in Barbados must have harbored towards the Society of Friends' evangelizing "discipline," some nonetheless found reasons to build on the positive connections that Quakerism offered. For enslaved people knew that they lived in an uncertain, brutal world, and that they needed to seek out shelter in whatever manner they could. No matter their flaws, slaveholding Friends like Lewis Morris had made promoting spiritual kinship into a part of their public persona: slaves witnessed some Quakers eschew violence, refusing to take up arms for the militia (for some, at great cost and pain);[1] they listened to missionaries like Edmundson shame slaveholders for allowing the cruelties and injustice that inflamed racial tensions on the island. Yaff and Nell might have been won over by Friends' public critiques of Barbadian officials, as when Quakers denounced the shocking callousness of Council member Alexander Ruddock, who believed that summary executions of suspected rebel slaves was a necessary evil ("What was it for Barbadoes to put twenty or thirty Negroes to Death yearly for Example-sake?" he had asked). Friends had even made the protection of enslaved families part of their critiques: in a petition to Governor Dutton in 1683, Quakers expressed their outrage that, in confiscating property to recover fines, some marshals had seized "our black Servants in an unnatural Way and Manner, viz. Husband from Wife, Wife from Husband, Father and Mother from children, and Children from parents . . . though the Produce of the Country and other Goods might be had."[2] Perhaps, Yaff and Nell must have thought, there was still a chance that they might create a common moral vision, that they could use Quakerism's virtues to further their own interests and associations.

Yaff and Nell would have been keenly aware that such altruism also served as currency in the Society's efforts to accumulate "moral capital." Highlighting Christian concern for the enslaved helped allow the Society of Friends to claim the moral high ground as they worked to secure tolerance and other concessions from the government. But to be taken seriously, Quakers' public positions had to be demonstrable, and so Yaff and Nell could claim some voice in whether the world would believe their masters' high-minded rhetoric. Perhaps they started by acknowledging Lewis Morris as a principled slaveholder. The famous eighteenth-century black abolitionist and ex-slave Olaudah Equiano had done the same when he praised his former master, an Antiguan Quaker by the name of Mr. King:

> He possessed a most amiable disposition and temper, and was very charitable and humane. If any of his slaves behaved amiss he did not beat or use them ill, but parted with them. This made them afraid of disobliging him; and as he treated his slaves better than any other man on the island, so he was better and more faithfully served by them in return.

King's Quaker faith doubtless shaped his "amiable disposition" and self-conception as a humane master, but his attitude also made slaves very aware of their disposability in a world where they were counted as commodities, where a displeased master might "part with" one slave and buy another without any personal loss or moral qualms. Given this reality, enslaved people had to *compete* to demonstrate their "faithful" service—Equiano perfectly articulated his unsteady position balanced between gratefulness and anxiety, wariness and trust. And so the promise of moral engagement required Yaff and Nell to suppress their own doubts, to accept the rules of their masters' game, a game rigged against their interests. The intensely personal bonds between master and slave may have allowed both sides to interpret, even perhaps *feel*, that their relationships were characterized by good faith, respect, and affection. But such illusory personal bonds could not stop the inexorable progress of Atlantic slavery and merchant capitalism, nor the attendant legal changes that led to the permanent marginalization of black people in the British colonial world: on the basis of religious difference, "cultural" distance, and ultimately, of race. Even Quakerism's small gains in offering religious inclusion made little difference to enslaved people like Yaff and Nell, for the Society was too focused on its own survival in the first decades of its development to risk dwelling on slavery's hypocrisies, especially since slave labor supported American Quakers' economic stability (and likely also the profits of metropolitan Friends).

The decades following Fox's visit to the Americas continued to be a time for leaders of the Society of Friends to push for social respect as well as legal and political concessions. Some Friends focused on cataloguing the injustices they "suffered" for their faith. As a prominent Friend, Lewis Morris likely took a role in collecting and forwarding evidence of Barbadian "sufferings" to the London Meeting for Sufferings, the administrative body that since 1675 had become Quakerism's public relations arm.[3] Other Friends took to public activism, disseminating pamphlets and other tracts defending their Society's positions. Anglican bishop Morgan Godwyn, who toured Barbados in the late 1670s, described how he was accosted by an unnamed Quaker in Barbados, insisting that Godwyn read a pamphlet that opened with a version of Fox's piercing question: "Who made you Ministers of the Gospel to the White People only, and not to the Tawneys and Blacks also?" Although Godwyn dismissed the larger issues in the Quaker's "Harangue," Friends would have been pleased that they were featured as the means by which a high-ranking churchman was moved to publish on the need for more active mission work to slaves.[4] Politically minded Friends used a wide variety of legal prohibitions, like the one forbidding them from including slaves in their meetings, as proof of their moral superiority.

This public relations campaign depended on getting Friends everywhere to live up to a standard of piety and loving engagement with their fellow man, demonstrating their dedication to "God, who call'd and gather'd you to be a People . . . as Lights in the World."[5] Therefore, when Public Friends like Edmundson, Alice Curwen, and Joan Vokins visited the island, including slaves in their revivalist gatherings served as a way to press local Friends to remain steadfast in their responsibilities, even when it made them uncomfortable. At times, missionaries called upon Barbadian Friends to consider what they would do "in the same Condition as the Blacks are."[6] Lewis Morris may have been reminded of his own time as an indentured servant when he heard Fox speak of how the ancient Hebrews freed servants "of their own Nation and People" after seven years' service and gave them land and herds to start new lives as freedmen. Could Friends "here in this Island or elsewhere," Fox had asked, show their New Testament spirit by allowing "the Negroes and Blacks, whom they have bought with their Money, to . . . go free . . . if they have served them faithfully"?[7] Fox's inspiration for encouraging manumission in his sermon at the Rous plantation may have come from conversations with Waide, Susannah, and George Nash, some of those slaves who had waited upon him in his sickness.[8] If Yaff stood in the adjoining hall when Fox made his manumission challenge, or Nell overheard Mary Morris discussing the issue at her Plantation Women's Meeting, they both would no doubt have spread the word in the slave quarters that "faithful service" might lead to real freedom from bondage. Having Africans serve the same limited terms as indentured servants was not without precedent in the English colonies, but Barbadian slaveholders would have considered it a steep price to pay, and one that would frighten rather than reassure their neighbors.[9] Certainly, Lewis Morris and other planters who prepped Fox for his visit to the governor would have warned him against any talk of manumission. Fox seems to have been content to wait and discuss the matter further with "weighty" Friends lest he jeopardize the larger cause of the Society's legitimacy.[10]

But the idea had been planted. Despite the traumatic conspiracy of 1675, some Quakers continued to consider ways that they might reach Fox's ethical high ground and showcase the transformational qualities of evangelization on those considered "faithful servants." Although Barbadians in general hardly ever freed their slaves (the best comprehensive study shows that only 2 percent of wills had manumission clauses), Quakers did so at a slightly higher rate—roughly 10 percent.[11] Here Yaff and Nell had an edge, for almost without exception, Quaker testators (like those in the wider study) awarded freedom to those with whom they shared close personal bonds. Perhaps Colonel Morris had assured Yaff at some point (as Mr. King had done to the bright young Equiano) that "he did not mean to treat me as a common slave."[12]

Slaveholders saw their relationships with select slaves as somehow unique—the exception that proved the rule of racializing difference and distance. Fox himself seems to have been involved in encouraging this competitive process of differentiating worthy individuals from the masses. Shortly after his first written plea to remind American Friends that God had made all men "of one Blood," he also asked Barbadian Quakers to send him a black youth to be made into a "free man" (at least in the spiritual sense).[13] But enslaved individuals also took part in the process. Like Anthony from Part III, who pled with Admiral Penn to become his master and spiritual teacher, other slaves must also have asked to be shown the meaning of Christianity in an effort to create positive bonds of reciprocity. Although nothing in the surviving archive tells us conclusively that slaves were manumitted because they showed an active inclination towards their masters' faith, or that they consciously manipulated Quakers' public positions to hold them to promises of freedom, we can assert with some certainty that religious tenets played a part in conversations largely hidden to us today.

One of the first conversations would have been about defining the terms for "faithful service."[14] Serving as a lady's maid from youth to marriage, staying at a master's side through illness, sharing a long span of life together—the fondness and intimacy that may have characterized the relationship between Yaff and Lewis, or between Nell and Mary, clearly reflected norms for lifelong "faithfulness."[25] But the benevolent language of manumission clauses may have hidden uglier realities of exploitation. First, manumission by will meant that slaves had to serve for many years, well beyond their prime. Secondly, when women were freed, the issue of sexual exploitation is highly suspected (this pattern, too, can be found in non-Quaker wills). We can imagine the motives behind Quaker planter Alexander Benson's decision to manumit only one slave ("my woman negro by name Jane") out of his considerable plantations in Barbados and Carolina, or conjecture the reasons why Ann Biswicke was compelled to write a clause in her will directing executors to "sett William Connell a mallatoe man free."[16] Nell's manumission suggests the possibility, indeed the probability, of her own exposure to and negotiation of her master's sexual advances. As even the most privileged servants like Yaff and Nell would have known, the tradeoff between "faithful service" and recompense was not always satisfactory or honorable. For most, the opportunity was never made a reality, for Fox's arguments for manumission (which he didn't make often, or loudly) remained unconvincing to the vast majority of Friends.

During the 1680s and '90s, Quakers aimed to secure greater tolerance and prosperity for themselves and their Society, and in the Caribbean, that meant they resisted questioning the racializing system of plantation slavery. Colonel Morris needed laborers to meet the demands of his expanding business interests. Around the time that Fox and his missionary train left Barbados for the northern colonies, Lewis had traveled to New York to take over managing his deceased brother's share of their

shipping business and farmland in what is now the Bronx.[17] The year of
the Coromantee conspiracy, his diversification included investing in an
iron works in East Jersey, where he worked out an agreement with colonial officials to exempt any white men there from the demands of militia
duty.[18] Lewis may have brought Yaff with him on any number of these
trips to serve as a valet and assistant, listening as he made labor arrangements and cut deals with local authorities. Nell may have heard Lewis
and Mary discussing their options as steep fines against Friends made
him and others consider leaving Barbados for friendlier climes. Morris
and other Quaker "Gentlemen-Planters" may have conversed about their
philosophical correspondence with Thomas Tryon, a London merchant
and freethinker who had lived for some time in Barbados, and who later
published several anonymous tracts of practical and moral advice.[19] In
one, Tryon advocated a move away from sugar production, imagining it
fundamentally doomed, for

> to be a Master Planter, is to be a kind of a King over great numbers
> of disobedient and troublesom Subjects, every day bringing fresh
> Intelligences of Tumults and Disturbances: In short, 'tis to live in
> a perpetual Noise and Hurry, and the only way to render a Person
> Angry, and Tyrannical too.[20]

Morris and his planter friends were frustrated: before moving permanently to New York, he helped pen one more complaint to Governor
Dutton. He and his co-religionists were being robbed, he complained, by
"Hypocrites . . . [who] spend our Estates upon their Lusts, and often ex-
ceed and abuse the Law also"— for nothing more than their consciences![21]

How much the enslaved took an active part in building their masters'
outward fortunes was one additional way that some began to engage in a
moral conversation about slavery, its limits, and its reciprocal exchanges.
Prospering in the West Indies meant, in the Society of Friends' official
worldview, aligning one's "inner" and "outer" plantations, so as to bring
God's blessings.[22] If slavery was to continue, then how might it be best
be managed in harmony with godly principles? Colonel Morris may
have been among those who hoped, like Tryon, that care in that matter would help him "stem the current of Sighs, Groans, Turmoils, and
doleful Lamentations of your Servants, converting them into a pleasant,
calm and serene Life of happy employments."[23] "Good treatment," respect for work, honesty, and non-violence would seem to align with the
Friends' pre-existing principles.[24] Several Barbadian Quakers centered
their colonial endeavors around an idealistic "family" purpose which

would include one's slaves. When one prominent Barbadian Quaker, Henry Jones, moved to Philadelphia from Barbados, he ordered that his entire family, including his

> wife Rachall and my sons Joseph John Samuell Henry Daniel & Richard Jones & Elizabeth Catherine and Mercie Jones my daughters together with all my negroes to wit Abai Apior Andrew Morris ___ George Pacu Acubah boys Kett Grace Joane Hagar C[uuke] and Bella and Black betty

should together work to improve their Pennsylvania plantation.[25] Scholars who remarked on Morris's relocation north have often cited that he brought his slaves with him when he left Barbados (most sources put the number at between 60 and 70), and many assumed that he was acting out of paternalistic concern for his extended "family." No sources provide a clear sense of his motivation, but Morris and Jones must have factored in the intangible economic benefits that came with continuity of the workforce, familiarity with one's laborers, and the workplace morale built on a sense of common purpose.[26]

Then there was the economic value of a large family. Tryon referred to Africans as "naturally as fruitful as most Nations," and planters recognized that slaves were self-reproducing investments. The inventory taken at Morris's death suggests that he may have encouraged "natural increase," for one-third of the 44 slaves on his Morrisania plantation in New York were youths or young children.[27] Women like Nell would have been especially important investments in this process, whether encouraged to reproduce within or out of wedlock.[28] As befitting a legal culture in which slavery followed the condition of the mother, black children were more likely to be associated with their mothers in planters' wills, but among Quaker wills from Barbados, only a few explicitly recognized conjugal bonds between enslaved partners.[29] Colonel Morris, like many others who became masters of slaves in Barbados, did not even distinguish maternal relationships in his will.

Was he among those men who refused to acknowledge his relationship to some of his enslaved progeny, using manumission as a shameful payoff? Perhaps. Among the children born on Morris's estate in the 1680s was a boy named Harry. In some undated seventeenth-century accounts from Colonel Morris's iron works a "Negro Harry" appears; more than 50 years later, a "Mulatto Harry" was listed among three elderly slaves still residing at the Morrisania estate, having been earlier granted (in his second mistress's will) the right to live out his final years with whomever he chose "in consideration of [his] past faithful service."[30] It is impossible to know so many things about this Harry (perhaps there were two separate men, since names were passed along so frequently). But like Isabel Criolla's daughter Juanita, it is clear he had a white father, and that his distinctive status as a "mulatto" was public knowledge, even if that fact was rarely acknowledged. All we know is that Harry was a slave, and that he died that way. Friends' moral mandate to keep families together seems positive in the abstract, but individuals like Black/Mulatto Harry would have also been a constant reminder to everyone in the household about the lines of freedom and sexuality that could and could not be crossed.

For women, opportunities to demonstrate "faithfulness" existed in dangerous parallel to sexual and reproductive exploitation, but for some men like Yaff, the expectations of "humane treatment" came at a different cost. Yaff knew, as did Equiano, that to ensure that he did not garner a reputation as a troublemaker he and other black men would have to ignore all sorts of "violent depredations on the chastity of the female slaves"—in effect, to collude in white men's privilege.[31] At least men like Yaff and Equiano could reap rewards by engaging in the world of work. Quaker masters seem to have been most impressed by enslaved men who demonstrated what we might today recognize as the Protestant ethic—hard work, frugality, honesty, reputability—linking spiritual significance to economic advantage. Men's role within the international Society of Friends had increasingly become tied, both in the Atlantic marketplace and in the local community, to their credit-worthiness and perceived competence in their work. The Society's strict rule of absolute honesty in business—"Speak Truth, act Truth" was Fox's early exhortation to merchants and husbandmen. "See that you are faithful in this outward Mammon, this outward Treasure of the things of this Life, of this World, faithful to your Word . . . faithful to your Promises in all your Tradings, Traffickings, Bargainings." This moral economy relied on men who could trust one another in the marketplace.[32]

Enslaved men like Yaff, men with proximity to their master's business, could capitalize on that privilege by performing their diligence as workers, demonstrating their honesty when engaging in their masters' interests. Lewis Morris and many other Friends in the Caribbean recognized that their slaves played a large part in their ability to get work done. We know this because they at times compensated slaves, fulfilling the biblical maxim, "The labourer is worthy of his reward" (1 Timothy 5:18). Just as with "Negro Harry," Morris's account ledgers for his New

Jersey foundry included several small payments to individual slaves.[33] For those demonstrating longer-term diligence, significant rewards were possible (though most fell short of manumission). Lewis Morris singled out several of his enslaved male laborers, including one named Ned, who evidently rose to a position of special trust, serving as Morris's agent in at least one business deal.[34] Toney, an enslaved cooper, cultivated a bond of respect by demonstrating his skill as a craftsman, and so Colonel Morris wrote in his will that Toney should receive 40 shillings salary annually after his death.[35] A Barbados planter, John Todd, likewise recognized in his will the work ethic of "a Negro man by name Hector, a Potter, who for several years past hath been a profitable servant unto me," and promised him continued incentives, directing executors to pay Hector 20 shillings out of every 20 pounds he earned.[36]

Enslaved men might have engaged more explicitly with the spiritual value of work, and none more so than among Africans brought to work in Colonel Morris's new iron foundry. After all, blacksmiths were held in high esteem in many parts of West Africa for their mysterious ability to create swords and tools from earth, air, and fire. The forge brought forth objects of great power—guaranteeing victory in warfare, and prosperity in agriculture. In Africa, blacksmiths were among groups of "craft specialists" set apart from other members of the community—they operated their own cults of spiritual leadership, controlling rules of kinship, descent, and initiation.[37] The sense of divine and earthly purpose that informed this particular profession might have offered Morris's African-born ironworkers with a way to respond to the human yearning to believe that the everyday actions of life *mean* something.[38]

Perhaps reflective of discussions of this sort of spiritual connection to one's labor is an extraordinary bequest registered in the will of Rowland Hutton, a planter from St. Philip. Since their plantations were near one another, Yaff and Nell may have been familiar with the six slaves Hutton mentioned in his will. Rowland directed his executors that after his death, "my poor negroes being in number four"—Jugg, Wambee, Gaskin, and Tombee—should be freed over the space of four years. Hutton designated that they should all

> have sufficient provisions and cloaths allowed them until they shall
> be all free and to remain in their houses where they now live and
> upon there [sic] freedom to have four acres of land lying altogether
> where my said negros shall appoint or as much as they can manure
> and timber to build them houses from and out of my plantation at

> Conger road . . . to have cloathing those that are not able during the
> term of their lives . . . [39]

Hutton left open the possibility that if his son were to die without heirs,
another pair of slaves, Pegg and George, "shall be both of them free and
to have their share and maintenance out of the said four acres of land
formerly bequeathed to my said four negroes." Whose idea was this ar-
rangement? Perhaps Jugg, Wambee, Gaskin, Tombee, Pegg, and George
had chosen one among them to approach Hutton, to tell him that to have
the most pride and ownership of their labor, they must be allowed to
build a life apart the same way that Quaker sons made the transition
to adult mastery. Especially since Hutton's will was written less than a
decade after Fox's visit, they must have discussed their mutual rights and
obligations frequently, and might have reminded Hutton of Fox's words:
"let them not go away empty-handed, this I say will be very acceptable to
the Lord, whose Servants we are, and who rewards us plentifully for our
Service done him, not suffering us to go away empty . . . "[40]

However, Hutton's former slaves would have faced formidable challenges once the bequest was fulfilled; indeed, nothing exists to prove
that Jugg, Wambee, Gaskin, and Tombee were able to collect on Hutton's
dictate. Even if Hutton chose to keep the agreement low-profile by only
agreeing to four acres (ten acres would have qualified them as freedmen
under Barbados law), Barbadians' suspicion of the destabilizing consequences of black equality might have compelled outsiders to challenge
any kind of legal property transfer. And of course, even the most honorable of agreements with Quaker executors could be denied or made
subject to unfavorable conditions. Perhaps knowing that his executors or
estate managers might react spitefully to Toney's economic opportunity,
Colonel Morris stipulated in his will that his cooper should not have to
forsake his modest salary to pay for the basic necessities of clothing and
food.

The vast majority of Caribbean Friends, not to mention their non-
Quaker neighbors, balked at conferring on enslaved men the means to
achieve self-sufficiency, to become masters of their own independent
households. By the end of the seventeenth century lawmakers in several colonies had stripped the enslaved black population of any hopes for
freedom or financial autonomy. In May 1683 East Jersey's council passed
a law "Agst tradeing wth negro Slaves," asserting that "it is found by daily
experience that negro and Indian slaves, or servants under pretence of
trade, or liberty to traffic, do frequently steal from their masters."[41] The

narrative of untrustworthiness was so powerful that even the most diligent slaves, as Equiano found, feared the constancy of their masters'
promises:

> When I went in I made my obeisance to my master, and with my
> money in my hand, and many fears in my heart, I prayed him to
> be as good his offer to me, when he was pleased to promise me my
> freedom as soon as I could purchase it. This speech seemed to con-
> found him; he began to recoil; and my heart that instant sunk with-
> in me.

Equiano may have faced more serious resistance if he had gone to Mr.
King without a white man who could vouch for his honesty and confirm that he had earned the 40 pound manumission fee they had earlier
agreed upon.[42] This experience corresponds to a number of Barbadian
wills that awarded individual slaves special favors, yet threatened that
what was given could also be taken away, a demonstration of white men's
ultimate control of moral and economic power. The enslaved potter
Hector, who had always earned a share of the profits from his work on
John Todd's plantation, was warned that if after his master's death he
was observed to become "negligent" in his trade, or "squanders away his
time, Then it shall be lawful for my Executors & I do hereby Impower
them to sell and dispose [of him]."[43] On Morris's New York estate, Toney
and Nell were required to demonstrate "faithfulness" to his widow to
perpetuate their favored status. His will sternly demanded that they continue to "yield all duty, full submis^n and faithf^{l}obed^{ce} in all respects as
become dilig^t serv^{ts} tow^{ds} my wife; otherwise, they are to enjoy no benefit
hereby, but their beq^{ts} to be void, as if never written or ment."[44] Threats
lurked beneath the legal terms of agreements like these, subtle coercions
that demanded continued subordination of "faithful servants" to their
former master's family (whether through proximity, the expectation
of gratitude, or the promise of future charity). And as long as laws on
the books prohibited property ownership and trading with blacks, even
manumission may have spelled little more than another form of paternalistic interdependence.

Enslaved people like Yaff, Toney, and Nell knew that their economic
value as chattel mattered more than any assertions of loyalty or of
Christian fellowship. By 1686 those Friends remaining on Barbados had
shifted the rhetoric of Egyptian slavery yet again, linking it to their own
material persecution:

> For as the Israelites could not easily make Brick without Straw, no
> more, as you well know, can we manage well our Estates, when the
> best of our Negroes and Draught-Cattle are taken from us, and
> that not for our Debts, or wronging of any Man, but only for Con-
> science-sake to God as aforesaid.[45]

When Quakers protesting against financial persecution painted themselves as Israelite slaves, the real slaves in Barbados morphed from
humans with souls into commodities essential for colonists' quest for
profit, and local officials became the cruel Egyptian taskmasters who
persecuted God's Chosen People where it hurt most—the bottom line.

Quaker slaveholders studiously avoided labeling enslaved individuals' religious identities in any of their legal documents—likely in part
because legal bodies throughout the English colonies continued to contend with Northern European Protestants' implicit fears about a link
between Christianity and freedom.[46] Although historians of American
slavery have long recognized such fears by tracking the legal hedges to
counteract such a link, I would argue that larger Christian debates over
conversion and free will informed questions about the consequences of
an enslaved person's religious identification or professions of loyalty.[47]
By its very nature, enslavement denied men and women the exercise of
their own agency. However, the Quaker term for conversion—*convince-
ment*—supposed that the convert in question was free to contemplate,
to assess, and to accept a new life for him- or herself. Without free will,
the foundation of both Christian conversion and the cultural transformation of Africans—enslaved men and women's seeming "acceptance"
of their masters' values—had to be viewed with suspicion. As long as
Africans were enslaved, they would never be able to prove their mastery
and free will, hallmarks of Protestant conversion.[48]

Although a few Quakers cautiously implemented Fox's most radical ideas
of freedom after a term of "faithful service," most joined the mainstream
culture in seeing their Christianity as a de facto *justification* for African slavery, and those enslaved people who negotiated tentative bonds
around spiritual dedication and work ethic would have been disturbed
and disillusioned by this latest trend in Quaker rhetoric. George Gray,
a Barbadian convert who had been fined repeatedly for noncompliance
with island laws on militia and church support, had moved to Philadelphia around 1691–1692, joining other Barbados transplants who hoped
to take advantage of the colony's utopian spiritual and economic promise. Probably responding to discussions with other Pennsylvania settlers

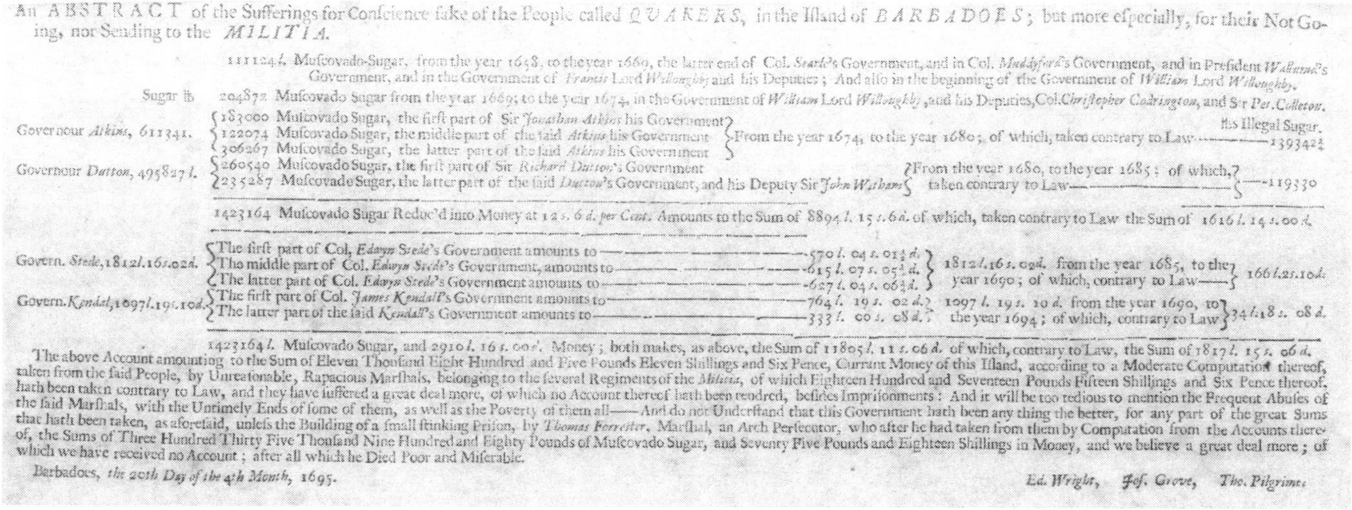
An ABSTRACT of the Sufferings for Conſcience ſake of the People called *QUAKERS*, in the Iſland of *BARBADOES*; but more eſpecially, for their Not Going, nor Sending to the *MILITIA*.

111124 *l.* Muſcovado-Sugar, from the year 1658, to the year 1660, the latter end of Col. *Searle*'s Government, and in Col. *Muddyford*'s Government, and in Preſident *Walrond*'s Government, and in the Government of *Francis* Lord *Willoughby* and his Deputies; And alſo in the beginning of the Government of *William* Lord *Willoughby*.

Sugar lb 204872 Muſcovado Sugar from the year 1669, to the year 1674, in the Government of *William* Lord *Willoughby*, and his Deputies, Col. *Christopher Codrington*, and Sir *Per. Colleton*.

Governour *Atkins*, 611341.
183000 Muſcovado Sugar, the firſt part of Sir *Jonathan Atkins* his Government
122074 Muſcovado Sugar, the middle part of the ſaid *Atkins* his Government
306267 Muſcovado Sugar, the latter part of the ſaid *Atkins* his Government
From the year 1674, to the year 1680; of which, taken contrary to Law —— his Illegal Sugar. 139342¼

Governour *Dutton*, 495827 *l.*
260540 Muſcovado Sugar, the firſt part of Sir *Richard Dutton*'s Government
235287 Muſcovado Sugar, the latter part of the ſaid *Dutton*'s Government, and his Deputy Sir *John Witham*
From the year 1680, to the year 1685; of which, taken contrary to Law —— 119330

1423164 Muſcovado Sugar Reduc'd into Money at 12 *s.* 6 *d. per Cent.* Amounts to the Sum of 8894 *l.* 15 *s.* 6 *d.* of which, taken contrary to Law the Sum of 1616 *l.* 14 *s.* 00 *d.*

Govern. *Stede*, 1812 *l.* 16 *s.* 02 *d.*
The firſt part of Col. *Edwyn Stede*'s Government amounts to —— 570 *l.* 04 *s.* 01½ *d.*
The middle part of Col. *Edwyn Stede*'s Government, amounts to —— 615 *l.* 07 *s.* 05½ *d.*
The latter part of Col. *Edwyn Stede*'s Government amounts to —— 627 *l.* 04 *s.* 06¾ *d.*
1812 *l.* 16 *s.* 02 *d.* from the year 1685, to the year 1690; of which, contrary to Law —— 166 *l.* 2 *s.* 10 *d.*

Govern. *Kendal*, 1097 *l.* 19 *s.* 10 *d.*
The firſt part of Col. *James Kendall*'s Government amounts to —— 764 *l.* 19 *s.* 02 *d.*
The latter part of the ſaid *Kendall*'s Government amounts to —— 333 *l.* 00 *s.* 08 *d.*
1097 *l.* 19 *s.* 10 *d.* from the year 1690, to the year 1694; of which, contrary to Law 34 *l.* 18 *s.* 08 *d.*

1423164 *l.* Muſcovado Sugar, and 2910 *l.* 16 *s.* 00 *d.* Money; both makes, as above, the Sum of 11805 *l.* 11 *s.* 06 *d.* of which, contrary to Law, the Sum of 1817 *l.* 15 *s.* 06 *d.*

The above Account amounting to the Sum of Eleven Thouſand Eight Hundred and Five Pounds Eleven Shillings and Six Pence, Current Money of this Iſland, according to a Moderate Computation thereof, taken from the ſaid People, by Unreaſonable, Rapacious Marſhals, belonging to the ſeveral Regiments of the *Militia*, of which Eighteen Hundred and Seventeen Pounds Fifteen Shillings and Six Pence thereof, hath been taken contrary to Law, and they have ſuffered a great deal more, of which no Account thereof hath been rendred, beſides Impriſonments: And it will be too tedious to mention the Frequent Abuſes of the ſaid Marſhals, with the Untimely Ends of ſome of them, as well as the Poverty of them all—— And do not Underſtand that this Government hath been any thing the better, for any part of the great Sums that hath been taken, as aforeſaid, unleſs the Building of a ſmall ſtinking Priſon, by *Thomas Forrester*, Marſhal, an Arch Perſecutor, who after he had taken from them by Computation from the Accounts thereof, the Sums of Three Hundred Thirty Five Thouſand Nine Hundred and Eighty Pounds of Muſcovado Sugar, and Seventy Five Pounds and Eighteen Shillings in Money, and we believe a great deal more; of which we have received no Account; after all which he Died Poor and Miſerable.

Barbadoes, *the 20th Day of the 4th Month*, 1695.

Ed. Wright, *Jos. Grove*, *Tho. Pilgrime.*

FIGURE 15. "An Abstract of the Sufferings for Conscience sake of the People called Quakers, in the Island of Barbados," in *A Short account of the manifest hand of God* (London, 1696). This detailed chart of cold hard calculations represented to officials how God's People had kept accounts in anticipation of the Final Judgment. Image courtesy of the John Carter Brown Library at Brown University.

about Africans' place in their utopian community, Gray felt "called by the Spirit" to present a testimony about his sense that slavery was a profoundly moral institution. He began by listing eight passages in the Bible related to issues of enslavement—many of the same ones Fox had used to argue for slaves' inclusion in the Quaker "family." Gray, however, used additional Old Testament verses to explain the justice of subjecting African "heathens" to *perpetual* slavery:

> (Levitt. 25 & 44) Both thy Bond men & thy bond maids which thou shall have shall be of ye Heathen that are round about you of them shall yee buy bondmen and bondmaids. Moreover of the Children of Strangers that do sojourn among you of them shall yee buy, & of their familyes that are with you which they begat in yor Land and they shall be your possession. And yee shall take them as an Inheritance for your Children after you to Inheritt ym for a possession, they shall be your bond men for ever, but over your brethren, ye Children of Israel, ye shall not Rule over one another with Rigour.

This passage in particular became a favorite among proslavery Protestants in the antebellum U.S. South. But Gray went even further in his push to paint slavery as a biblical tradition compatible with contemporary Quakerism, referring to one rather obscure passage in Exodus (21:5–6) that described servants whose bonds to their masters extended beyond mere duty. Perhaps he was fantasizing about the bonds of love between some faithful servants in his own "family" when he read a curious passage about Hebrew servants who professed their love for their master and thus voluntarily renounced their liberty in a ceremony of blood ties: "his Master shall bring him unto ye Judge & he shall also bring him to ye Door post and his Master shall bore his eare through with an Aul and he shall serve him forever." Gray did admit that he was a bit shocked by the barbarity of this Old Testament ritual, but he also seemed comforted by the idea that "if my brother an Hebrew be so served much more an ethyopian or black yt is a Heathen by Nature."[49]

How did enslaved individuals like Yaff and Nell respond to such sentiments? Certainly they would have been disheartened to hear the Christians' holy book used to validate the perpetual "possession" of the "Children of Strangers . . . and of their familyes . . . which they begat in yor Land," and depressed even more by the implication that although the Children of Israel should not "Rule over one another with Rigour," mercy did not seem to extend to those not designated as spiritual "brethren." Those who had chosen to defend their interests by association with their masters' moral code also entangled themselves with the economic interests and intimate affections of their masters. Did they ever think of those bonds as constituting a "love" so profound and complete that it erased dreams of freedom? Certainly for some, to stay near their families and others they had come to trust—both black and white—was a precious gift in an unstable world. Many enslaved people doubtless chose to define reward for their loyalties in different ways than we would today, creating complex, overlapping associations to protect their families and sense of autonomy. Faithfulness was never far from fear; it was characterized by a complex blend of respect, anxiety, enforced intimacy, even willing affection.[50]

While Quakers could "choose" suffering to prove their spiritual dedication, for Africans laboring in American colonies, suffering was a backbreaking reality, a consequence of the greed that spoiled human relations. The betrayal of moral principles doubtless slowed any preliminary success Quakers had in promoting conversion among enslaved Africans or their descendants. When slaveholding Friends did agree to collaborate on the missionary movement to blacks, it is certain they took on the task for a variety of reasons: some were doubtless spurred by idealistic evangelical dreams, others may have hoped to compensate for their guilt over acts of cruelty or exploitation, still others thought that in doing this Christian duty they might stockpile moral capital useful to point out their superiority over other competing denominations. Quakers' foray into evangelization briefly challenged racialized labor hierarchies and the evolving meaning of "freedom" in the English Atlantic, but their model of benevolent paternalism was caught up in the exigencies of plantation economies. Many Friends recognized the dangers. In 1690, shortly before his death, Fox wrote to Friends in the Americas:

> Let your light shine among the Indians, and the Blacks and the
> Whites, that ye may answer the Truth in them . . . Keep up your ne-
> groes' meetings and your family meetings . . . Take heed of sitting
> down in the earth and having your minds in the earthly things,
> coveting and striving for the earth; for . . . covetousness is idolatry.
> There is too much strife and contention about that idol . . . so that
> some have lost morality and humanity and true Christian charity.[51]

Fox and a few others had hoped to challenge the easy equation of white with Christian purity and black with heathen darkness, knowing that skin color was not a simple cipher for the soul. Solomon Eccles, who visited Barbados as a missionary and was imprisoned for a time for his

confrontations with local ministers, had made this point often by dark-
ening his face with ash, "to go as a Sign to this dark Generation, who
are as black within as the Ethiopians were without."[52] If one of Colonel
Morris's enslaved blacksmiths had been born in West Central Africa,
he might have told his master about how there they, too, believed in the
goodness of white things (milk, cassava meal, sacred *mpemba* clay). Perhaps holding up some of the charred pieces of wood slaves had cut and
burned that day to fuel the foundry, he might have shared how charcoal
markings were used in rituals to depict the spiritual blackness of greed,
sorcery, and murder.[53] These were not written indelibly on the body, but
they came to be so in much of the British empire, where the idea of the
impurity of black bodies and souls became a potent "truth" difficult to
erase. From the perspective of enslaved people, however, the worst betrayals may not have been of symbolic principles so much as in the realm
of personal relationships.[54] The blackness of greed seemed universal.

Modern historians who persist in digging for the past's ugly realities about this era of Quaker slaveholding are challenged by many archival silences—of obliviousness, arrogance, shame, or a simple neglect
to express in writing one's thoughts on noneconomic "essentials"—and
probably intentionally thwarted by nineteenth-century Friends' embarrassment of their Society's early complicity in Atlantic slavery.[55] As he
grew old and weak, Lewis Morris himself may have felt some nagging
guilt about his own past, for family lore in later generations had it that he
burned his papers before his death.[56] What did he have to hide? Interpreting those silences is a knotty issue, too uncertain for historians uncomfortable with speculation, but the psychology of avoidance is too powerful to ignore. In 1696, Barbadian Quakers received a letter from Friends
in Philadelphia (two signatories had formerly resided in Barbados) with
a request that slaves no longer be sold to the mainland. They seemed
concerned that replicating Barbados's reliance on a slave economy "may
prove preiudissial several wayes to us & our posterity."[57] Such vague language signaled disunity within the Society of Friends, acknowledging
that slavery's structural oppressions could overpower moral rectitude,
while it allowed Pennsylvania business associates to avoid offending
their West Indian co-religionists. Quakers largely sought the comforting
silences that distance from slavery would bring.

Historians looking for early examples of the Society of Friends' humane spirit have sought after stories like those offered by Yaff, Nell, and
Lewis. But seeing their relationships as exemplary unfortunately serves
to conceal the more accurate story of exclusion and distrust between

Quakers and their human chattel in this early period. Their stories are still valuable, not as some small evidence of religion's humanitarian spirit, but as a means for understanding the mechanisms of how religious groups (consciously or unconsciously) deal with their community's imperfections, how individuals trapped in a brutal world seek out symbolic ways to commune with their fellow man and the divine. Beneath the studied silence, however slight the evidence, historians *can* assert with confidence that Friends like Lewis Morris discussed with one another how to live out their faith. We must believe in the reality of lost conversations and phantom gesticulations that characterized exchanges between individuals—Yaff and Lewis, Nell, Anne and Mary—who lived and worked with one another. All those who lived in the Americas knew that financial gain was fundamental to colonial success, but they also recognized that the pursuit of profit carried with it many moral dangers. Would money or morality win out? Could the two coexist as godly endeavors, or would they forever be in tension? To explore beyond the dichotomies of piety and hypocrisy, to peer into Lewis Morris's and other Friends' ambiguous expressions of faith, is to illuminate the realities of human complexity.

Lewis Morris died in 1691, followed shortly thereafter by his wife Mary. His estates, including all those slaves counted as property, devolved to Colonel Morris's nephew and namesake, now a young married man who had decided to reject his uncle's strict Quakerism for the easy privilege of membership in the Church of England.[58] He may have honored his uncle's wishes for Nell and Toney's bequests, or he may have not. Of Yaff we know a bit more: William Penn came to collect his human legacy in accordance with his friend's encouragement, and Yaff continued to prove his exemplary work ethic and "faithfulness" to Penn's interests.[59] The politics of profit kept many generations of enslaved people in a state of stasis, their names appearing hundreds of times more often on property inventories than in Quaker tracts embracing common cause with "Negroes and Tawneys." Although unrecognized by their colonial masters, Africans and their descendants made their own cultural and personal legacies: around 1708, a black child was born into slavery at the Morris estate in New York, and someone decided to call him "Yaff."[60]

CONCLUSION

Cynicism and Redemption

13 / Religion, Empire, and the Atlantic Economy at the Turn of the Eighteenth Century

In 1720, a new pirate adventure by Daniel Defoe, *The Adventures of Captain Singleton*, became a best seller, bringing readers into the world of maritime captives and pirates, not to mention the first imagined journey across the African mainland.[1] Building on the success of *Robinson Crusoe* (1719), Defoe brought readers another pseudo-fictional narrative about ordinary men and colonial expansion. The story followed an English orphan whose early life sounds rather like that of Nicolas Burundel. Brought up from a tender age aboard various ships, Singleton survived traumatic experiences with exploitative masters and humiliating captivity in Barbary and Catholic lands, along the way learning mostly how to steal, lie, and live a dissolute life—a perfect preparation for mutiny and piracy under the very real Captain Avery, a pirate whose trial had become a *cause célèbre* during Defoe's time. About halfway through *The Adventures*, however, as the newly elevated "Captain" Singleton and his allies grew in strength and numbers, a new character appeared, a Quaker surgeon by the name of William, whom the pirates "forced" to accompany them in their marauding. (William regularly proved happy to advise his captors how to get "money without fighting," in accordance with his religious scruples.)

In one of the most dramatic scenes of the crew's adventures, they came upon an unmoored slave ship full of Africans, the only survivors of a shipboard revolt. True to his humanitarian self-conception, Quaker William prevailed upon his pirate friends not to massacre the ship's inhabitants, persuading them "that the negroes had really the highest injustice done them, to be sold for slaves without their consent." Defoe quickly exposed this thin veneer of moral superiority, for after the Quaker surgeon had effectively humanized the Africans, healing their wounds and teaching them enough English to acknowledge their stories of rape and debasement, William offered to assist the pirates in recommodifying the captives. In a routine familiar to contrabandists in the Caribbean and beyond, William, masquerading as the slave ship's owner, landed on the Brazilian coast under pretense of needing repairs after a storm. There he engaged with local planters and succeeded in disposing of every last African, returning to the pirates with nearly 60,000 pieces of eight. William prevailed upon his comrades to make him captain and owner of the sloop he had purchased with the slave profits, and promised to continue to serve them, but only as a provisioning agent, or "Victualler"—thereby distancing himself from the distasteful violence of both piracy and the slave trade without eschewing their rich rewards.[2]

Defoe's novel is a perfect example of the cynicism that accompanied nearly every early modern narrative of colonial unscrupulousness and ill-gotten gains. Turning William's cunning trick into a wry commentary on people who presume morality, Defoe's indictment mirrored common perceptions of Quakers as hypocritical, self-interested, deceitful, even "Jesuitical."[3] For despite his pretensions to be above violence, William was no better than either degenerate pirates or cruel planters who disregarded their fellow man to feed their greed and gluttony: his air of piety barely concealed his self-interested hypocrisy.[4] This trope was especially pronounced in metropolitan writings about the Caribbean that blamed the "tropics"—the land, climate, or air—for causing people to lose their moral compass, of stimulating greed and cruelty in ostensible "Christians."

The Caribbean crucible of empire, slavery, and piracy similarly mocked European pretensions to the moral high ground in colonial expansion. In critiquing the seemingly "natural" degeneracy of the West Indies' moral climate, however, commentators in Europe were blinded by the fact that the moral universe had shifted under their own feet no less than those of their colonial counterparts—a shift based on the links between imperial secularization, racialization, and intensified commercialization in the Atlantic World. Sociologist Max Weber famously tied the early modern world's "disenchantment" of religion to the rise of rationalization and secularization[5]; this basic premise can be tied to several others. Afro-Caribbean theorist Sylvia Wynter has argued that the naturalization of race as a boundary in the West emerged alongside the "de-godding" of society—that the rise of humanism and its associated theories of "natural law" destabilized Western Christendom's universalist dualisms of flesh/soul (profane/sacred), promoting instead a new "sliding scale" from rational/Man to irrational/brute.[6] In his treatise on Western economic philosophy, *From Mandeville to Marx*, anthropologist Louis Dumont traced the ways in which modern economics required a similar disenchantment or "de-godding," a reorientation from the holistic ideal of a balance of wealth and resources—an ideal in which morality/religion served as a check on selfish interests. The new doctrine of economics posited that religion's attempts to repress individuals' selfish impulses interfered with the logic of a benevolent moral marketplace, one in which the discord and lesser evils produced by self-interest would be temporary.[7] Without a doubt, a loosening of the religiously based institutional order that both divided and ordered Western Christendom after the Protestant Reformation played a part in these processes of economic "rationalization" and societal "racialization." Scholars of slavery have long recognized that the move to social and labor hierarchies based on "race" (a necessary evil to support the project of capital accumulation) as an explanatory "othering" was a messy, sometimes contradictory transition.[8] Like them, I do not mean to say that religion had became irrelevant to European ways of being or to individuals' self-conceptions, but merely that it became less central to the larger forces that structured life: political, social, and economic interactions.

I do argue that by the turn of the eighteenth century the greater Caribbean was at the center of this messy transition, giving rise to a culture permeated by uncertainty, opportunism, and distrust.[9] Indeed, the deep cynicism embodied in Defoe's story of the Quaker pirate William and his slave trading helps us see how the instability of economic and religious values created a kind of moral netherworld. We might look again at anthropologist Mary Douglas's insights on the corollaries between money and ritual when it comes to social trust:

> Money can only perform its role of intensifying economic interaction if the public has faith in it. If faith in it is shaken, the currency is useless. So too with ritual; its symbols can only have effect so long as they command confidence.[10]

To say it another way, one could argue that the Caribbean's striking lack of confidence in Christianity—marked by the use of religious rhetoric for material gain, the growth of unabashed and open hypocrisy, as well as the willingness of Christians to disregard denominational antipathies in the pursuit of profit—may have been little more than an analogue to the lack of trust in commercial transactions. The Caribbean economy had long been characterized by its pervasive corruption, unreliable credit networks, absence of standardized currency, and wildly fluctuating trade and exchange rates.[11] By the end of the seventeenth century, transatlantic traders not only had to face the risk and uncertainty wrapped up in traditional economic practices of patronage and "gifting," but they saw their commercial dealings rendered even more unreliable by the Caribbean's surge of uncontrolled piracy, the attendant robberies at sea, as well as rivals' use of privateers as a tool of economic warfare. These problems were furthermore exacerbated on land, both in the islands and at the metropolitan level, by judicial systems barely able to effect financial justice, whether for the recovery of property or to restore a person's credit. By the turn of the eighteenth century, certainties regarding both faith and fortune seemed precarious, unsupported by any reliable authority, ideological or physical.

To conclude, we must put these individual life stories into perspective with the larger trends in Caribbean economy, diplomacy, religious tolerance, slavery, and other challenges to colonial dominance from roughly 1670 to 1741. These years witnessed a dramatic intensification of commerce between merchants across traditional religious-political lines (especially through the slave trade); meanwhile, old religious and military antagonisms threatened to continually disrupt those commercial interactions. In such uncertain times, individuals navigating the Caribbean's moral economy perhaps understandably turned to suspicion, cynicism, and cruelty rather than trust, faith, and loving fellowship. Colonial officials and others with propertied interests in the Caribbean blamed much of their world's instability and uncertainty on the ineffective control of unruly people—most notably slaves and pirates (although religious rebels like Quakers could also be stubbornly uncooperative). While piracy-eradication efforts had been largely successful by the second decade of the eighteenth century, privateers and unaffiliated pirates like the fictional Captain Singleton still threatened trade in the Caribbean seas and beyond. Meanwhile, the demand for African slave labor increased dramatically, and with the fulfillment of that demand, the odds of armed insurrection by enslaved people frustrated at their harsh lot in life. The British and Spanish crowns, as well as their subjects in the Caribbean, would find that their interests at some times intersected, at others diverged in the suppression of maritime robbers and rebellious slaves.

Meanwhile, the true subjects of my book—ordinary people made pirates, sailors, pawns, and slaves by desperate circumstances, exploited and persecuted for any resistance to their constant debasement—responded to the chaos with a reciprocal hostility that threatened the breakdown of any agreements about moral economy. These antagonisms and the Atlantic economy's fundamental disregard for Christian morality effectively silenced a few rare religious protests against slavery and exploitation. Our disappointment with religion's historical insufficiencies should not, however, keep us from respecting the spiritual power of community in people's lives, no matter how satisfying cynicism might feel.

As we first learned in Part II, the Caribbean had long been a site for clandestine cooperation between subjects of rival colonial powers. The trend intensified to the end of the seventeenth century, golden years for foreign contrabandists trading in Spanish American ports, a trade dubbed by one Spanish official "the original sin in [these] parts."[12] Poor Northern Europeans (like Nicholas Burundel) still served Spanish elites in regional ports as easy-to-control pawns, their illegal status diminished with patronage and conversion to Catholicism (feigned or heartfelt). Even governors and royal officials sought out pragmatic relationships based on commerce. In fact, shortly after securing Jamaica from further attack, the first civilian English governor of the island asked the briefly popular Quaker separatist John Perrot to carry a letter of goodwill to the Spanish governor of Santo Domingo, hoping thereby to encourage friendly trading relations.[13] In 1670, the legitimacy of England's capture of Jamaica was confirmed by the Treaty of Madrid, in which the Spanish Crown acknowledged for the first time the unviability of the fifteenth-century papal bans on Protestant American settlements. As a result, it became even easier for Spanish officials to engage in illicit trade with foreigners, often under the pretense of allowing refuge to foreign ships in need of repair or low on water or foodstuffs. Evincing little concern for religious or national loyalties—or even legality—Spanish merchants and royal officials eagerly sought foreign business opportunities. They took advantage of competitors' lower prices to purchase everything from necessary foodstuffs like grain to feed their military garrisons to silk stockings, ironware, liquor, and slaves—even during hostilities between their respective monarchs.[14]

As this culture of contraband intensified through the final decades of the seventeenth and into the early eighteenth centuries, it would be the transatlantic slave trade that seemed to best unite Catholic and

Protestant Europeans in the Caribbean. The English and other Protestant rivals in the Caribbean and the west coast of Africa had engaged indirectly in Spain's slave trade monopoly as subcontractors to Genoese financiers and French merchant conglomerates awarded the *asiento* in the decades after Spain's split with Portugal. This trade was most alluring to Europe's merchants because the Spanish had plenty of silver, and were willing to pay for slaves in specie, a commodity that could not be spoiled on the return voyage; nor would it inexplicably plunge in value with a glut in the commodities market.[15] In 1713 at the Treaty of Utrecht ending the War of Spanish Succession, the Bourbon king of Spain, Philip V, awarded the *asiento* to the British South Sea Company (SSC), allowing British merchants for the first time to legally sell slaves from Africa in His Most Catholic Majesty's American realms. England's Queen Anne and her successor saw their partnership with the Company as an opportunity to pay off the nation's crushing war debts. A rush of investor exuberance and speculation followed, and the nation's optimism about the SSC's promise was greatly enhanced by the *asiento*, for it included allowances for other regularized travel and trade with several Spanish American ports. The South Sea Bubble popped most dramatically in 1720, a year of moral and financial crisis, but the *asiento* treaty was faithfully restored after a government-supported restructuring of the Company.[16]

This new trend towards international cooperation had its problems. Despite official South Sea Company instructions that British factors "shall take care so to behave towards the Spaniards, as that no offence may be taken by them," the administrators they sent to major Spanish Caribbean ports did not often get along well with their new business partners.[17] Part of the problem was the lack of clarity regarding the terms of the treaty. Various conflicting interpretations of the treaty's provisions and amendments gave SSC agents and British and Spanish ambassadors plenty of fodder for petitions and angry treatises—all of which threatened the termination of what had briefly been "a good, and sincere

FIGURE 16. This broadside, entitled "Lucifer's New Row-Barge" ([London, 1721?]) satirized the moral failings of South Sea Company directors and speculators, those who had "Impov'risht Thousands by some Publick Fraud / And worship Intrest as your only God." Note that the ship is named the "Holy Inquisition," and the slave on the left is being flogged with a cat-o-nine tipped with gold coins. Image courtesy of Harvard University, Baker Library Historical Collections, Kress South Sea Bubble Collection.

Lucipher's new Row-Barge.

peace."[18] The Spanish Caribbean coast guard ships (*la guardacosta*) repeatedly carried out reprisals against British shipping during times of unofficial war, and British subjects continued to dabble in contraband and privateering. SSC officials complained that King Philip sent secret orders to his ministers in the Caribbean in opposition to those favoring the British interest, like the one they intercepted dated March 29, 1726. In it, the king gave the Cuban governor authority to enact reprisals against British shipping, explaining that "notwithstanding the peace and good correspondence, which for my part I have procured and continue to procure," the British Crown and its subjects had not taken care to honor "the peace which I so religiously desire to maintain."[19] Peace often seemed like a sham, especially with international legalities so poorly adjudicated over long distances.

Even during peacetime, arguments proliferated. One of the biggest debates between Spanish officials and the South Sea Company concerned how to calculate their required tax to the Spanish Crown: should it be by the number of slaves contracted for delivery, or by the number brought into port or sold?[20] Many of these arguments employed the abstracted language of *piezas de Indias*—a unit of exchange meant to equal the value of a healthy African adult, male or female. The very same term, a crass flattening out of the value of a human life, had been employed by the captured maroon Isabel Criolla as part of her defense to make Spanish officials see her as something more than a piece of property, to acknowledge the existence of her soul and her right to protection from torment or murder by a vengeful mistress. But slavery had become such a critical part of expansion into the American Indies that European powers easily accepted they could only normalize regional currency through the commodification and sale of pagan, brutish Africans.

To further this trade in *pieces* of human life, the British even borrowed several key words from the Spanish, a reflection of their willingness to bridge the gap with their Spanish partners, to extend the courtesy of trust and transcultural communication to their former religious enemies. One English West Indies trader explained the first term—*confianza* (trust/confidentiality)—thus:

> The Nature of a Confianza is such, that only two Persons should
> be privey to what passes . . . many Affairs of Importance have been
> happily Concluded . . . with Persons of Character in Confianza between two, which would not have been done, had a third Person

been Concern'd; for it does not always depend on Offering a Sum of Money for a particular Indulgence."[21]

Some Spanish merchants aggressively pursued British business partners with whom they might develop a mutually beneficial *confianza*, several writing repeatedly to members of the South Sea Company to encourage a deepening of trade, like one Spaniard with ties to the port city of Veracruz, who proposed to purchase outright the entire contents of the SSC's annual shipment of slaves and other permitted merchandise, allowing him and his partners to act as wholesalers in Mexico. He continued: "If there should be any Embarrassment to consign the Cargo to Us Directly in a publick Manner . . . Your Lordship may if you think proper, give full power to the SuperCargo, a Captain in Confidence, that we may dispose of the Cargo Extrajudicially."[22] The turn of phrase here from "illegally" to "extrajudicially" makes for an elegant commentary on the fuzzy boundaries between private gain and public prerogative.

To make a successful agreement "in confidence" (*devaxo Confiança*), bribes were not necessarily part of the equation, but certain *regalos* (gifts) certainly helped smooth the process. These might be luxurious items of clothing, fine watches, or some other token that enhanced the recipient's grandeur, just as it cemented the business relationship between outsider and insider. Two of Britain's SSC's factors in Cuba had to defend themselves back home from accusations of excessive spending of the Company's funds on gifts—to which they protested that such *regalos* added

> so greatly to your Service & Advantage, of which our Letters to the Hon.ble Court give various Instances . . . such as many Lawsuits which thereby terminated in our favour, especially on confiscated Negros, other Negros imported with the small Pox excus'd Quarantine, [and] Protection against the dangerous Intrusion of the Ministers of the Inquisition . . . "[23]

Many Spanish officials sought out the formal and informal benefits of such lucrative *confianza*, in turn agreeing to ignore their foreign business partners' variance in Christian practice (their own sort of *regalo*). In port cities of the Caribbean, some Spanish clergy continued to facilitate foreigners' public conversions to Catholicism, aiding and abetting wealthy patrons who wished to establish religious and economic ties with other nations.[24] Just as in Part II, it seems to have been a widespread practice of profit-minded Spanish elites to try to protect their foreign Protestant partners from the Inquisition's strict rules and regulations. But instead of simply incorporating foreigners through Catholic conversion, it seems that secular officials began to ignore altogether the stigma associated with Protestantism. Juan Diaz Pimienta, the governor of Cartagena during the period of the French *asiento*, was denounced by inquisitors when it appeared that he had not only allowed "heretic" English and Dutchmen to live in the city and serve as soldiers in the fortifications, but that they were also allowed to publicly declare their religion in formal testimonies, sworn in "by the law they professed," and given permission to carry out their own burial rituals outside the city walls.[25] From the governor's perspective, such friendly compromises were necessary to maintain the city's economic and military stability. To those hoping to maintain religious orthodoxy, it seemed to be a *fait accompli* that commercial advantage had corrupted Spain's tradition of religious purity.

The newfound trust and tolerance in the sphere of religious and economic politics were constantly destabilized by both personal corruption and the mixed messages of officials. The continued presence and institutional independence of the Inquisition made it especially difficult for Spanish governors, merchants, or others to operate unmoored from religious hindrances (perhaps why Pimienta's governorship of Cartagena was short-lived). Periodically throughout the turn of the eighteenth century, inquisitors tried to act against Spanish officials in Cartagena, Havana, Santa Marta, and Portobello who were suspected of smuggling or were on especially good terms with foreign merchants.[26] Inquisitors in Cartagena resisted the region's leanings towards toleration, processing nearly 80 Protestant heretics between 1660 and 1740, and writing to Madrid periodically about the city's growing populations "of different nations and Religion such as the English and the Dutch," decrying their potential to corrupt "Christian Catholics" with heresy.[27] Again in 1716, inquisitors upset about having their interests subordinated to the SSC alliance sent a message to the eight British factors residing in Cartagena, warning them that the terms of the treaty did not allow so many administrators to reside in their city.[28] Meanwhile, New Granadan clerics were frequently accused of participating in contraband themselves or harboring those charged with illegal trade.[29] Such frequent contestations must have made British business interests uneasy, and agents on the ground faced difficulties maintaining friendly relations in an atmosphere of mutual suspicion.

One particular point of mistrust related to both economic and religious affairs related to the treaty's stipulation that only slaves fresh from Africa (*bozales*) be brought for trade, denying *asentistas* the right to stop at Jamaica or Curaçao en route. Spanish buyers worried about the perfidious tendency to substitute rebellious renegades from enemy American holdings—"refuse negroes" as they were usually called. From the viewpoint of Spain's imperial interests, this concern stemmed as much from fears of being overrun with foreign contraband introduced via SSC slave ships as it was about the introduction of blacks inclined to rebellion. Religious rhetoric exacerbated mistrust between the parties. Cartagena's inquisitors wrote to Spain in 1691 about their worries that although African slaves brought with the *asiento* were supposed to be "pure gentiles," those smuggled in by the Dutch and English via their own Caribbean transshipment ports might have been "instructed and taught in the sects of their masters," a problem of heresy since Africans' "weakness and inclination conforms better to the expansiveness of the heretics' conscience."[30] Given their near-total exclusion of enslaved Africans from their own Christian communities, Britons were incredulous to hear these latter arguments, suspecting that the Catholic Church was trying to wage a covert war against Protestants' legal and economic affairs. The SSC Court of Directors complained in 1725 that the Spanish king had tried to restrict privileges due them under the articles of the *asiento* contract on the "ridiculous" charge that a "taint" of heresy could be introduced if the Company's ships called in Jamaica or another English port en route to Cartagena. They fumed at the charge: "the Spaniards themselves do not think there is any solidity in that argument; for that removing the natives of Africa from one vessel to another, or giving them a few days refreshment, they cannot be so stupid as to conceive it would instill heretical principles into them."[31] But Spanish interests continued to insist on their prerogative to control the religious education of those destined for enslavement. They even tried to make the SSC pay for the support of a lay religious (*laico*) installed near Panama "to instruct the negroes in the Christian Faith, baptize them in articulo mortis, and bury them in holy ground."[32] Notwithstanding efforts to overcome their differences for economic gain, Britons' anti-Catholic biases showed when factors complained about mandatory alms-giving to Spanish convents, religious hospitals, and the poor, revealing to both sides the lack of trust and good will necessary for international trade across religious lines.[33]

Indeed, these grievances—and myriad others relating to charges of privateering during peacetime, illegal trade, and extortion—dashed the hopes of the region's merchants for peaceful, trusting trade. The Protestant Reformation itself, along with all its subsequent splintering over the course of the sixteenth and seventeenth centuries, produced increasing calls for "toleration," but it certainly did not demand ecumenicalism, nor did it produce harmonious relations between European Christendom's many competing faiths. Instead, a relativistic toleration encouraged thinking that lent itself very well to the demonization of those perceived to be furthest from a Protestant religious/racial center: at the center, Britain's racially superior Chosen People, and beyond, a spectrum of near "others" like the Spanish, considered racially inferior as well as theologically erroneous or superstitious—worthy of contempt on both counts. At the outer limits of the circle were situated subhuman peoples of the rest of the world, those whose worship of the devil (or lack of religion) made their subjugation seem both natural and moral.

This naturalizing shift diminished religion as a trope in British writings about the benefits and problems of international trade, but the dictates of faith featured somewhat more heavily in Spanish rhetoric. As we have seen, Inquisition officials in Cartagena routinely protested against religious tolerance for the sake of trade—especially the slave trade. Other churchmen echoed those protests, at least one bemoaning that the great volume of contraband trade with English and Dutch slavers meant that gold and silver rightfully Spain's instead provided "more power to the heretics to increase their rebellions against the Holy Church."[34] Around 1720, as the *asiento* contract was about to be renewed with the South Sea Company, another policy analyst encouraged Philip V to dissolve the South Sea Company's contract on a combination of technical, economic, and moral grounds, blaming Spain's reliance on foreigners for the ruin of their economy and their nation's loss of providential favor. He believed that the English had seduced Spanish Americans with "their moderate prices," plotting "through this artificial device to procure the softening of the Hate with which [the Spanish] have always seen heretics; if this frequent exchange and communication continues, such [Hate] may become love, Religion will senselessly disappear (*insensiblemente*), and with it the Obedience" due to their sovereign.[35]

Such allusions to love, hate, and religious obedience in a commentary on trade show how closely the emotional rituals of faith and fortune mirrored one another. Despite this commentator's fear of the "perfect" love and cooperation between Spanish officials and "heretic" merchants, their relationships were far from models of friendship. Suspicion, opportunism, pragmatism, corruption, feigned friendship—all shaped the tenuous, fractured nature of the Caribbean's economic and religious climate. Here, the economic incentives to create good-faith alliances for mutual benefit (arguably the foundation of the early modern moral economy/social contract) seemed too precarious. As faith and friendship eroded between Caribbean powers like Spain and England, so too did opportunities to engage with Christian moral rhetoric from below.

"Such is the hatred of those that have nothing, to those that are Masters of Plenty"[36]

Throughout this book, we have seen ordinary people call on Christianity to fight for a more humane existence; yet those efforts were successful only insofar as those in power were willing to face the contradictions in their belief system, to feel a sense of guilt or responsibility, and to try to make amends. Cynicism, disillusionment, and violence diminished people's expectations and destroyed religious idealism in the Caribbean over the course of the seventeenth and early eighteenth centuries. As colonists allowed greed and anxiety about profits to harden them to the plight of their laborers and to make them distrust the integrity of their competitors, their vulnerability to the power of religious rhetoric also changed—mostly moving in the direction of diminished opportunities. These patterns become clear when we take a look at how cynicism in the Caribbean's moral economy influenced the lives of those lawless men like Captain Singleton and his Friend William, as well as the free and captive descendants of Africans who fought for a better life in the Americas. For both groups, the imperial rivalries and mistrust that continued to separate Catholic Spain from her Northern European neighbors could provide real opportunities for profit and a sense of freedom. However, the same pro-trade, pro-profit forces that united European colonial interests promised the near eradication of the former group and the expanded exploitation of the latter.

Stories of Sir Henry Morgan, the famous buccaneer captain, conjure up images of violence, rapine, and the callous disregard for humanity associated with piracy. Morgan had served as a soldier in Cromwell's West Indies expedition of 1655–1656, and perhaps already had some experience in the region as an indentured servant. Unlike many of the soldiers in Cromwell's Caribbean expedition, Morgan was lucky enough to survive the hostilities, and became one of the chosen few allowed to join Captain Christopher Myng in his maritime raids on Spanish settlements and shipping. Within a few short years Morgan had emerged as a leader of the English and French rabble who gathered at Port Royal, Jamaica to take advantage of privateering licenses that legalized their marauding journeys to Spanish ports. In Panama, Costa Rica, Maracaibo,

FIGURE 17. Forcing defenseless monks and nuns to serve as human shields when storming the castle at Porto Bello. In a 1700 Dutch version of *Exquemelin, Historie der boecaniers, of vrybuyters van America*. Image courtesy of the John Carter Brown Library at Brown University.

Providence Island, and elsewhere, often against great odds, Morgan and his men turned towards ever more violent means to extort money and other valuables from frightened Spanish civilians. In these raids, attacks on churches and clergymen figured as standard operating practice, though they focused less on mocking Catholic icons than expropriating the wealth of church holdings—their gold and silver ornaments stolen, their coffers emptied to ransom the city from captivity.[37]

Attacks on Catholicism were essential to the buccaneers' stratagems, until they became seen as perversions of Protestant nationalism rather than righteous retribution. In one of his most cunning attacks, Morgan ordered that the monks and nuns they had captured in the city of Porto Bello be employed as human shields as the buccaneers advanced on the military fortress, forcing these holy civilians to carry ladders to the front lines so that the Englishmen might scale the walls and overwhelm Spanish defenders.[38] The English translator of Exquemelin's narrative emphasized the pirates' irreligiosity by juxtaposing their cruelties with religious language. Of the French privateers who stormed the cathedral church in Maracaibo, he glossed: "as they were no Saints themselves, so they could endure no Superstition in others."[39] Morgan's and other privateers used torture tactics to "catechize" Spanish victims so as "to extort from them a confession of their unrighteous Mammon."[40] Such tales of terror and violence made buccaneers almost demonic, lacking in faith and moral compass, erasing any of the vestiges of religious observance that indeed existed among the buccaneers and the brethren of the coast.[41]

The trajectory of opportunity for buccaneers and privateers during the final four decades of the seventeenth century is illustrative of the continual struggle for a voice among marginalized white men in the Caribbean moral economy.[42] Following the 1670 Treaty of Madrid that secured Jamaica as a British possession, officials attempted to steer residents towards the profitable pro-plantation model of Barbados, downplaying the contribution that the island's privateers had made towards securing Jamaica's economic stability during the 15 years in which the island remained contested.[43] Men like Morgan—and like Nicholas Burundel or Lewis Morris—found ways to take advantage of whatever economic opportunities came their way, and occasionally, against all odds, they did experience some of the Caribbean's fantastic profits. English observers noted that most preferred to spend their gains in the profligate lifestyles so vividly illustrated in swashbuckling portrayals of the pirates, drinking and wenching until they "found the bottom of their Pockets; for all things have a bottom, but the Ocean and Hell"— their sudden

FIGURE 18. "Cruelties of the Pirates in Panama," from a 1681 Dutch edition
of *Exquemelin*, illustrates Spaniards being tortured, or as the text explained,
"Catechized according to their wonted mercy, to discover where they had hid
their goods, which brought some that could not endure pain so well as others,
to auricular Confession." Image courtesy of the John Carter Brown Library at
Brown University.

poverty requiring new ventures and new victims.[44] Not all chose this path. Like Colonel Morris, Captain Morgan invested his winnings in the Jamaican soil; like Morris, too, Morgan escaped the stain of a potentially lower-class past by adopting the planter's mentality and becoming part of the propertied elite. When Henry Morgan was named lieutenant governor of Jamaica, he turned from buccaneer advocate to strict enforcer against all privateering, and when Exquemelin's narrative was published in English, Morgan sued the printers for defamation.[45]

Men who had derived their livelihood as sea rovers saw their dreams for matchless wealth imperiled. By the 1680s Jamaica resembled Barbados in the 1650s—the moment at which the gap between large planters and the rest of the field widened dramatically. Those who could not play the big-stakes plantation game were left behind as provisioners, small merchants, and tradesmen.[46] Employment alternatives proliferated in support of an exponentially growing sugar/slavery economy: as overseers over gangs of sugar workers, as factors of one of the trading companies like the South Sea Company, or as surgeons on slave ships.[47] Those who chose to remain with a life at sea could turn to smuggling, aiding English traders in gaining hidden access to Spanish buyers. Their labor was necessary and fairly well compensated, for although ships designed for the dangerous contraband trade were smaller than most ships (to more easily flee from enemies), they also carried substantially higher numbers of seamen to defend the vessel in case of a confrontation.[48] Those who preferred the opportunism of privateering or military service could settle among the Spanish (as did substantial numbers of Irish)[49] or move to French hubs in Martinique or Tortuga, where governors still occasionally gave out commissions against Spanish shipping; some chose to relocate to the Honduran coast, where illegal logwood cutting still offered freedoms like those enjoyed by the original *bucaniers*.[50] Or they could become outright pirates like Defoe's Captain Singleton, enemies of the world but citizens of a kind of democratic brotherhood—attractive to those disappointed with the small shares even privateer seamen could garner, for the shipowner and captain had to be paid first, then the Admiralty Court satisfied with their own portion before sailors could claim their reward.[51]

Each of these options carried their own consequences in terms of religious politics, but all continued to support the fantasy of European men who journeyed to the Americas in search of the boundless riches. As we saw in Part IV, sugar regimes rebuffed utopian dreams of evangelical universalism. Gaining one's livelihood as an overseer in Jamaica—or a surgeon, clerk, or factor for the South Sea Company—required be- coming desensitized, contributing to the brutalization and dehuman- ization of African slaves, whose presence was the only thing that kept white men from similarly brutal work or starvation in the streets. To bolster their political privilege (status now based on racialized labels), white men violated religious dictates against the rape of black women, the separation of husbands from wives, mothers from children, and the murder of rebellious or merely troublesome "Negroes." Beyond the sugar islands, religious and racial politics varied more broadly. For the pro-trade smugglers and their workforces, accepting and destigmatizing other Christians helped sustain successful partnerships. Those few re- maining buccaneers who—like the fiercely independent logwood cutters on the Spanish-claimed Honduran coast—continued to poach Spanish treasures felt united through their opposition to Catholicism (especially the Inquisition). Pirates could choose to reject the laws of all European monarchs and their colonial representatives, but in the process of steal- ing from the rich and powerful, they had to accept the world's labeling of them as irreligious and inhumane bandits.

Such communal tendencies did not dictate the individual's personal religiosity, of course. It may have been true that the French pirate Jean- David Neau (better known as l'Olonnais, infamous for his acts of cruelty), rejected all rituals of a Christian upbringing: "For though they got ever so many Victories, they never troubled themselves with Thanksgiving days, nor would their business permit 'em to keep one [holy] day in seven." Among other pirate adventurers, however, such indifference to religious tradition was not the case. Basil Ringrose, who accompanied pirate Cap- tain Bartholomew Sharpe, noted that the crew observed Christmas, and occasionally Sunday "by command and common consent."[52] Even an Irishman from St. Christopher, who had been a practicing Anglican since the age of eight when his parents were killed in conflicts with the English, asked inquisitors in Cartagena in 1685 to restore him to the bosom of the Catholic Church "for the little time he had left to live." He had been sentenced to execution for piracy, so perhaps he hoped for a pardon, or perhaps just spiritual redemption in the faith of his ancestors.[53]

James Houstoun, a surgeon stationed for a time in Cartagena de In- dias for the South Sea Company's *asiento*, shared his countrymen's gen- eral hostility towards Catholicism, though he did not let those beliefs spoil a good time with his new friends in Cartagena. He did in a sarcastic way admire the Jesuits for their role in Christianizing Africans passing through the port with the *asiento*, for was not Catholicism "the very best

Religion in the World . . . to keep the Vulgar in a slavish Awe"? (Houstoun compared the Jesuits to Quakers: both were "sly, cunning, and hypocritical.") He was more than a cynic, however; during a wartime hiatus in Jamaica he recorded his belief that the British island's lack of a "soft" religious discipline like that he had seen in Cartagena made him fear the "fatal Consequence . . . [of] the Exercise of Whip and Stocks . . . too often used very indiscreetly, sometimes wrongfully and most unmercifully."[54] But as many newcomers to the Caribbean had learned, pleading religious concern for better treatment of one's enemies—be they wealthy Spaniards or potentially rebellious slaves—was more likely to elicit scorn than approval.

Concern with the uncharitable coercion of poor whites, especially those abused by the maritime system, did grow during the eighteenth century.[55] The impressment practices of the British Navy made it into an especially hated symbol of "oppression and slavery."[56] In the 1740s, skilled sailors in the Caribbean helped lead riots against naval press-gangs outfitting themselves for war against Spain and France, part of a movement that at least one scholar has suggested fits E. P. Thompson's definition of popular uprisings as responses to breaches in a shared "moral economy." Naval officers often found their attempts to punish offenders blocked by riotous community members, revealing solidarities against coercive "recruitment" and a shared notion that white men had the right to free choice of employment. Perhaps most importantly, merchant interests joined in the effort to lobby the government to restrain naval officers from impressing sailors, whose labor was necessary to keep the transatlantic market circuit functioning. Like the protests in support of the royalist prisoners sentenced to labor in Barbados discussed in in Part III, objections to impressment and the transportation of convicts were most often framed in legal rather than moral terms, although the rights of Englishmen as white "Christians" was often implied.[57] Impressing sailors from Caribbean-bound slave ships could incite slave insurrections, and press-gangs threatened the provisioning trade, trade that allowed the sugar islands to feed both black and white inhabitants, and keep the potential for slave uprising at bay.[58]

Indeed, the violence of the slave trade and the dominance of the plantation model in the British Caribbean trapped Africans and their descendants in an economic system progressively rationalized for high profits. As a result, enslaved and freed individuals were squeezed out of economic opportunity and physical freedom, and even left without the power of moral suasion. Barbadian planters executed several potential rebels in the 1680s, and thwarted another major conspiracy in 1692, this one masterminded by creole-born slaves—artisans and overseers who "have more favour showne them by their masters." The names of several Quakers appear in lists of slaveholders who were compensated by the state for the execution of slaves determined to be rebels.[59] In 1739, Barbadian officials required masters wishing to free their slaves to first pay a fee, which doubtless also discouraged manumissions.[60] The plantation economy meant dehumanization, grueling toil, and almost certainly an early death. No wonder, then, that enslaved blacks on those islands planned their escape in increasing numbers, whether to the maroon villages in inaccessible regions of the land, or at sea if they had any experience in navigation.[61] Despite our temptations today to trace a new heroic narrative of the common oppression of sailors and captive Africans through these "Brethren of the Coast," maritime marauders (fictional or real) rarely turned up a chance to sell Africans if that was the best way to survive for the next battle, the next opportunity for booty.[62]

For people of African descent, the militarized urban and rural frontier economies operating in much of the Spanish Caribbean offered relatively greater possibilities. Cities like Cartagena, Veracruz, and Havana were far enough removed from heavy mining and agricultural industries, and offered more flexibility for the enslaved to negotiate one-on-one moral contracts.[63] It is perhaps not surprising that pathways to freedom for people of African descent were dictated by the commercial system in which they were embedded, but the dominant concepts about Christianity in each system also played a part. In the Spanish Caribbean borderlands, those of African and mixed-race heritage could quite effectively use both religious and economic arguments as bargaining chips for a better life. Their acceptance was not only tied into long-standing economic and political trends, but reflected Catholicism's openness and the Spanish empire's universalist legal and religious vision.

Although most Protestant nationals did little to include their slaves in any sort of Christian fellowship or instruct them in its tenets, the enslaved learned all they needed to know, many of them capitalizing on the Spanish Catholic rhetoric of Protestant "infection." In 1718, inquisitors heard the case of Juan de Rada, an East Indian who had been kept as a slave in London and later brought to Cartagena by his master, a factor for the English *asiento*. Like so many lower-class *espontaneos*, he contended that "he wished to be Catholic, and live and die in the Catholic Religion." When asked what religion he held and observed, he said he had none, nor did he know which his master followed, although [Rada] had gone with him at times to his church (*su chercha o yglesia*), and heard him read, he had never paid attention ... [the interpreter said] that although he had endeavored with great care to find out if [Rada] had followed some sect or error, he found that he hadn't followed any, and that [the interpreter] knew such to be the truth, in respect he knew that the English did not take care that the slaves accept one or another religion, nor baptize them, but rather leave them to live as they wish.[64]

Juan de Rada's appeal to inquisitors was likely a skillful negotiation of the power of domination through feigned ignorance, one used by generations of enslaved individuals to subvert European tropes of the "paganism" and ignorance of colonial Others.[65] Indeed, we find this specific performance repeated in other parts of the Iberian Atlantic where resident Protestant merchants and Catholic officials clashed over jurisdictional precedence and property rights in slaves.[66] For nearly a decade during the 1730s, the Inquisition supported Havana's governor's case against Sergeant Nicholson, the city's SSC factor, who wished to take an enslaved Catholic girl named Maria to Jamaica with him. She had asked a priest to help spare her from being separated from her family, and under pressure from the city's religious, the governor had ordered "that under no pretext she might be taken away to any port, or colony subject to the English Crown, nor to any place she might suffer the danger of perversion from the Catholic faith which she professes."[67]

The Spanish were more often than not winners in this game, for they found religion gave them a way to employ black extra-imperial actors against their Protestant enemies. As early as the 1660s and peaking after the 1680s, Spanish religious refuge laws encouraged religiously tinged performances throughout the frontiers of the Iberian Atlantic—from Georgia to Florida, Cuba to Puerto Rico, Venezuela to the Yucatan.[68] In this variation of "the enemy of my enemy is my friend," Spain proclaimed freedom and refuge rights to runaways from enemy Protestant territories who professed a desire to become defenders of the Catholic faith and Spanish territory—a move that weakened their circum-Caribbean rivals from within *and* without. Dr. Miguel Wall, an Irishman advising the Spanish for the recapture of Georgia, had allegedly boasted he would march to the English settlement from St. Augustine with Indians, spreading along the way "a Proclamation publish'd in the King of Spain's name, that all slaves that will come in to them, shall have their freedom and a reward."[69] Spanish officials kept close tabs on the frequency of slave rebellion and conspiracy in the British islands. In 1730 a Spanish prisoner was deposed in Jamaica, asserting that maroons from that island had contacted the governor of Portobello, offering their support in exchange for a promise of freedom.[70] The networks of subterfuge and communication radiated out from every node of the hotly contested Caribbean hub of empire.[71]

The overall rise in free black and mixed-race populations in the frontier zones of the Spanish Caribbean offered many men of African descent training in military and maritime skills, and there were always plentiful opportunities to engage in privateering and contraband trade for personal enrichment. One of these was Miguel Enriquez (or Henriques) of Puerto Rico, whom English South Sea Company factors in Cuba railed against for cutting into their profits:

> He is a mulatto, was born a slave, and brought up a shoe maker in the Town of Porto Rico, where by betraying a Gentleman to the Inquisition he got some money, and with it, having freed himself he was concernd in Privateering; by which means he grew rich, and making several Valuable presents to the King, and Court of Spain, setting forth his services to his Majesty; he was Honourd with a Gold Medal, and the Title of Don . . . [72]

Henriquez built on this preferment, securing more titles and later the lucrative position of official provisioner (*Armador*) for Puerto Rico's *guardacosta*. His multiracial partnerships—with one Diego de Morales, a Spaniard "married to a negro woman at Porto Rico," and Indian sailors "said to have no compassion for those they call their Enemys"—presented the English with a frightening threat.[73] Men like Henriques, who had made a life for themselves within the institutions of the Spanish empire, would have rightly mistrusted English authorities in plantation colonies like Jamaica. In one secret war council correspondence advising Admiral Vernon (who would lay siege to the city of Cartagena in 1741, unsuccessfully) to invade Panama, English planners noted that although they easily outnumbered Spanish defenders, they were unlikely to take the place without support from black armed forces:

> The negroes and Mulattoes are told Such Stories by the white Spaniards that should they be taken tho they were free that the English would make Slaves of them wch really makes them desperate on such Occasions therefore Could your Excell^y secure that there

might on our Landing be an Order Given that all Mulattoes or Negroes whatsoever that would Come in & swear Allegiance to his
Brittannick Majesty should remain free, the Enemy would have no
men to fight. . . . [74]

This astute observation did not alter English officials' plans, nor their
disdain for and fear of black and mixed-race military auxiliaries, certainly a holdover from the attacks on Hispaniola and Jamaica.

English Protestants, so certain of their moral superiority, by virtue of
both their religion (of whichever denomination) and their industrious-
ness, saw themselves above the Spanish not only because of that nation's
religious "superstitions" but also because of their assumed social and
sexual pollution of subhuman Indians and Africans, whom the English
saw as living in a state of pagan delusion. Mocking Spaniards' lack of
commercial vigor, Britons nonetheless "tolerated" their religiously back-
ward enemies so long as they continued to be lucrative trading partners.
However, lest one idealize the Spanish liberality in accepting peoples of
African descent as equals, for religious reasons or otherwise, it is worth
remembering that a large gap yawned in the space between legal theory
and the on-the-ground realities of slavery and freedom in the Americas. While there is ample evidence to suggest that religious refuge laws
did make Spanish territories hospitable sites to exercise the rhetoric of
Christianity, those proclamations were not uniformly honored. Depending on whether Spanish localities had a greater need for free fighters or
enslaved laborers, people of color who fled Protestant territories to gain
their freedom were at times re-enslaved by avaricious Spanish officials.[75]
Neither religion nor imperial policy changed Europeans' shared perception of Africans and their enslaved descendants as base, untrustworthy,
and almost inherently immoral.

Moreover, slave uprisings and plots were not limited to labor-inten-
sive plantation colonies like Barbados.[76] The problem of racism and the
cruelty of slavery brought together the enslaved populations of Spanish
urban areas with maroons living in the hinterlands, increasing the flow
of subterranean knowledge. In the early 1690s, maroon leaders of the
Matadure *palenque* allegedly came and went secretly to Cartagena to
meet with associates of their "nation," in the Santa Clara convent, where
one Manuel Arará worked as a domestic slave. There Manuel allegedly
helped spawn a plot to take over the city on Holy Thursday, when the
Catholic populace would be distracted with the day's ritual activities.[77]
Acculturated African creoles were often better able to help orchestrate

sophisticated and subtle acts of resistance that incorporated their knowledge of European religious norms and weaknesses of discipline, and which capitalized on their own (at least outward) Christianity as a marker of political loyalty.[78]

Local oligarchs in the Caribbean were able to build up their power bases in both Spanish and British Caribbean colonies during the early eighteenth century (a period of relatively lax imperial oversight). In this atmosphere, enslaved people would have faced greater barriers to compel their masters to rein in abuses. One must infer that one reason blasphemy cases against slaves dropped off after the 1670s was that *comisarios* (most of them creole elites—for instance, the lucrative post of Inquisition *comisario* in Mompox was held by one Francisco Camargo, likely one of doña Eufrasia's brothers) stopped reporting the crime, and inquisitors were just as happy to defer to slaves' masters for correction.[79] In the only case against an enslaved individual brought before the Tribunal after 1660, blasphemy was not the result of an *ad hoc* negotiation over punishment but rather an overt challenge to demonstrations of elite secular authority: the *mulato* slave Juan Naranjo had renounced God while in chains for fighting with another enslaved man. In a similar challenge, a *free* black woman who first disrupted a church service in La Guaira (Venezuela) was sent to Cartagena's inquisitors for blasphemous verbal abuse of authorities during her period of incarceration.[80]

"Unfaithful Silence" and the Quest for Social Justice[81]

Despite gaining an immense fortune, Defoe's Captain Singleton was uneasy without the anchor of faith, and in the final chapter of the novel, Quaker William takes on the role of spiritual guide and economic strategist. The two comrades first decided to transform themselves into legitimate East Indies traders, formulating a secret plan to return home, but as they waited and planned, their intimate conversations often turned towards religion and morality. One day, Singleton was struck with a revelation:

> Why, William . . . do you think that if there is a God above, as you have so long been telling me there is . . . Do you think if he be a righteous Judge, he will let us escape thus with the Plunder, as we may call it, of so many innocent People . . . and not call us to an Account for it before we can get to Europe, where we pretend to enjoy it?

Thus began Singleton's entrance into the trope of Protestant conversion narratives. After acknowledging his sins, the pirate fell into a morass of despair, for he knew he was no more than "a Dog, a Wretch that had been a Thief, and a Murtherer." Contemplating suicide after realizing that "tho' I had the Wealth by me, yet it was impossible I should ever make any Restitution," Singleton turned in desperation to William as his "Ghostly Father, or Confessor" for an adequate penance.[82] William assured his friend that although they could not pay back those they had wronged through their piracies, their wealth might yet do some good in the world. Singleton proposed a solution: he should donate everything "for charitable Uses, as a Debt due to Mankind."

However, Defoe's dénouement to their continual conversation "upon the Subject of our Repentance" can only be described as ironic. The solution they struck upon was to transfer all their wealth to William's sister, described as a "poor widow." After setting her up comfortably in a quiet country estate (and reassuring themselves that she would avoid calling attention by spending the money too freely), they finally returned to live with her *incognito* in rural tranquility. The novel ends with a surprise wedding between Singleton and "my faithful Protectress, Williams's Sister, with whom I am much more happy than I deserve."[83] This ostensibly happy ending echoed popular tales of pirates as romantic heroes and repentant Christians, but a perceptive reader could not help but see it as a wry commentary on two delusional thieves. Was Defoe critiquing the false and self-serving redemption of the "philanthropy" that had solved Singleton's moral quandaries, a denunciation of all who came by wealth through foul means but sought to redeem themselves with money? Captain Singleton's final words, his acknowledgment that he was "much more happy than I deserve" makes him a typical Defoe protagonist—heroic in that he is redeemed, but also satirical in that he forces readers to reflect on the moral ambiguities of that redemption.

Defoe's critique still resonates, yet today it seems insufficient, for if readers remember the story about the ship of Africans sold to Brazilian sugar planters by William, the profits now lining the pockets of the high-minded Quaker's family and friends, *The Adventures of Captain Singleton* can only be read as a tragedy, a tale of blood money and betrayal.[84] Economic and racial factors in Defoe's day determined who would become heroes of the day and whose oppression would be ignored. These Africans had reclaimed their freedom aboard the slave ship, had even been given a voice through William's English tutoring, but because of their placement early in Defoe's narrative, they were abruptly erased from the story through a sly trick of market supply-and-demand. Their fate was a lifetime of toil in the households and sugar plantations of their Brazilian masters, many meeting an early death by the lash, malnutrition, or overwork. Who would be their saviors?

In such a cynical world, it is hard to find inspiring examples. Nonetheless, some few men at the time saw the injustice and, inspired by their religious principles, took action to force colonial society to accept its culpability in the greatest moral injustice of their times—race-based slavery. Several short-term residents of both the Spanish and British Caribbean made efforts to stir the consciences of Christians throughout the Atlantic World. These advocates for a more humane and morally justifiable relationship between European colonial masters and American labor found themselves silenced by the dictates of the Caribbean economy and contemporaries' resistance to arguments based solely on morality. Today, their stories have faded with the passing of time. They have faded, too, because of our image of the Caribbean as a uniquely ungodly place, and because their protests seem incomplete and ineffective to our modern sensibilities. They do speak to the sincerity and power of religious idealism, however, and doubtless moved many people whose lives they touched—if not to action, at least to a different perspective.

The first radical call for justice involved Catholic priests and Christianized Africans whose travels in Brazil and the Spanish Caribbean convinced them that enslaving any Christian, no matter their parentage or the legality of their capture, was a moral evil that must be redressed unequivocally by manumission. Spanish missionary Francisco de Jaca had spent time in Cartagena and Venezuela from 1678 to 1681. His conscience was stirred, he wrote, after reading in Cartagena's Dominican convent some manuscripts denouncing Spaniards' "tyrannies" against their slaves—manuscripts he heard had been banned from publication. He was perhaps roused to action after watching the arrival of slave ships to those cities' ports, and witnessing the callous everyday cruelties meted out to enslaved black Christians like Isabel Criolla and her children. In the summer of 1681 he joined a like-minded French Capuchin, Epiphania de Moirans, in Cuba, and they began preaching in the nearby plantations their conviction that the perpetual enslavement of black Africans was against Christian doctrine. They even went so far as to withhold absolution from slaveholders who would not promise to manumit their slaves. Alarmed, the religious and secular elite in Cuba urged the excommunication of the two priests, asserting that the Capuchins' activism created a great danger to themselves and their property. From there, the case went to Rome, where Jaca presented a monumental manuscript on the subject, his *Resolution regarding the liberty of the Negroes and their Ancestors, previously [living] in paganism but now Christians.*[85] Jaca and Moiran's arguments were much the same as those put forth by Afro-Brazilian Lourença da Silva, who claimed royal lineage from both Kongolese and Angolan monarchies. Da Silva came before the pope a few years later, in 1686, to protest the sale of African Christians and their children into American slavery, a system based solely on the stigma of skin color. Neither of these petitioners questioned slavery as an institution: they simply rejected its racialized form. Their concept of a Christian moral universe could not support the injustices, cruelties, and dehumanization that the transatlantic trade perpetuated, contrary to the old rules of "just war." Although the Office of Propaganda Fide came out clearly on the side of the religious protestors, Spain's American political economy required that such ethical concerns be suppressed, silenced.[86] These little-known stories are by turns heroic and embarrassing, and so they are often dismissed as footnotes to history, insufficient to effecting real change.

Better known are the stories of early Quaker heroes who denounced slavery, although these men were at the time disregarded as outsiders, were silenced by those brought up in American plantation colonies where the twisted logic of their slaveholding co-religionists held sway.[87] Perhaps the most colorful of Quaker critics promoting the Golden Rule was Benjamin Lay of London, who in 1718 moved to Barbados to set up a small shop with his wife Sarah. Horrified by the sight of emaciated blacks who regularly gathered behind the shop to take away the couples' food refuse, and incensed by white acquaintances who advocated the positive results of beating slaves "to keep them in awe," the Lays moved to Philadelphia, where they hoped to escape the corrupting confluence of "Conveniency, Intimacy, and Profit" that made slavery seem so unremarkable to their West Indian peers. But Pennsylvania Quakers had also become accustomed to the institution thanks to the subsequent generation of slaveholding Friends, and Benjamin took up earnest and provocative challenges of his co-religionists. He kidnapped a Quaker child to make her parents feel the grief of slaves who had no way to recover their lost children. In a theatrical confrontation with the Pennsylvania Yearly Meeting he even made the Bible "bleed" for the victims of slavery (by way of a bladder filled with pig's blood). When none of his calls for internal reform seemed to get anywhere, he enlisted Benjamin Franklin to publish, in 1737, a sprawling diatribe labeling *All Slave-Keepers, that keep the Innocent in Bondage, Apostates.* For his zeal, and for neglecting

to submit his manuscript to the Quaker Overseers of the Press in Philadelphia, Lay was publicly disowned by the Society of Friends.[88] Not until
1759 did the Philadelphia Quaker leadership began to censure members
who remained supportive of slavery. Even then, the Society's final com-
mitment to an unequivocal antislavery position would not come until
the American Revolution and the transtlantic abolition movement made
so explicit the morally intolerable condition of "slavery."[89]

In the meantime, Caribbean patterns of coercion, captivity, and cynicism frustrated everyone. In 1731, a free black man, Augustin de Mesa
Balcazar, was arrested by Inquisition authorities for his second offense
against the faith. He had been earlier convicted of bigamy and assigned
to work at one of Cartagena's hospitals as punishment. One night he escaped from his enforced penitence, and when he was recaptured by authorities, Balcazar had burst out: "he crapped on the Holy Office! . . . all
that about Christian law was just a drug—it was better to live in Jamaica,
where everyone lived according to the religion (en la ley) they wished."[90]
The frustration and anger of Balcazar's words—that religion had become
a trap, a drug, instead of a way to invoke a more just moral authority—
resonates. Indeed, given the cynicism surrounding Christian institutions
in the Caribbean, we might recall Karl Marx's pronouncement on religion as the "opiate of the masses." But the context of this famous phrase
offers a much more complex perspective, one important for our sense of
what this book can teach us today. Marx continues: "Religious suffering
is at the same time an expression of real suffering and a protest against
real suffering. Religion is the sigh of the oppressed creature, the sentiment of a heartless world, and the soul of soulless conditions." Certainly
the Caribbean had become a "heartless world," a world in which avarice
and nihilism conspired to rob colonial communities of their ability to
provide consolation for their "soulless conditions."[91] In his time, Marx
lived among philosophers and political thinkers who earnestly believed
that the abolition of religion was one of the most moral ways to solve the
world's problems. They thought that if only people could be made to see
faith as a man-made institution providing only "illusory happiness"—a
distraction from capitalism's alienating culture and the suffering of the
working classes—it would help them see the world more clearly, would
compel them to unite and build an economic system that could over-
turn the injustices of class. Marx was hopeful that the study of history
and philosophy could "disillusion" people—not in the sense of making
them more cynical, but rather of pouring their energies into fostering
real change.[92]

This book has been my way to provide that sort of positive "disillu-sionment," to tell history from a different perspective, to portray with sympathy the stories of groups exploited and silenced by the expansion of early modern Atlantic colonialism and capitalism. Many times it has made me feel cynical, especially today when so many people also seem to have lost their sense of hope that our own (im)moral/political economies can ever be transformed. After 9/11, I was alarmed by the tidal wave of Islamophobia, especially given the religious "othering" of Muslims in my research on the seventeenth century. I was in Spain re-searching Cromwell's economically motivated "holy war" against Spain's Caribbean Catholic empire when President Bush decreed that the United States would invade Iraq, a move that so many around the world knew was founded on specious evidence and motivated by moneyed interests. My heart went out to all those troops, many of them men and women of relatively modest means, who were asked to sacrifice their lives for yet another war that would put our country in serious debt and dimin-ish our reputation around the world. While I was writing about how American slavery subjected people like Isabel Criolla to daily tortures and humiliation, the Abu Ghraib prison torture scandal broke. I fol-lowed the news with dismay when our supposedly enlightened govern-ment decreed it could get the "truth" and break the cycle of terrorism through "enhanced interrogation" tactics in extralegal detention centers like Guantanamo, interrogations that Nicolas Burundel and other Inqui-sition survivors would have rightly denounced as torture. After the 2010 election, I was furious when people unjustly tarred President Obama with intimations of dishonesty, or claimed he was not representative of "our" religious or national values—these were clearly (though often de-nied) racially motivated, made all the more poignant when writing about how Quakers seemed oblivious to their own unconscious exclusion of blacks. I settled into life in Florida just before the disastrous economic crash of 2007, and witnessed the devastating personal consequences of the housing bubble while researching the 1720 South Sea Bubble. The two crashes were certainly not the same, but in both, individual and cor-porate financial failings prompted moral judgments and political rancor. Denunciations of the SSC's corruption, greed, and crass disregard for the ruination of people's lives is echoed today in popular protests against the power of government and financial institutions. I have often succumbed, like Augustin Balcazar, to bitter invective towards those who tout the righteousness of patently unjust laws or who want to impose their exclu-sionary religious "truths" on others.

Nonetheless, writing this book—with its focus on the complex contradictions of ordinary people's lives and personal associations, with its attention to hidden motivations and silent truths—has also taught me to question the political and religious ideologies that so many of us take on faith, and to share those queries: with students in the classroom, and in everyday conversation with friends and acquaintances. I have some small hope that by engaging with one another on a personal basis, and thus creating new communities, we might learn to undo some of the pain and alienation that plagues our world. We might do it by getting involved in a local religious community, or by taking part in some other contemplative humanist practice like art or yoga, for such practices can help foster a spirit of tolerance and personal empowerment. We might do it through political advocacy or volunteering to help people whose lives have been ravaged by economic factors beyond their control. There are many ways to break the cycle of alienation and anomie that pervades our world.

But when we act, we must also reflect, remembering the power of silence. If campaigning on behalf of the disenfranchised, we should ask if their voices have been heard. Have they been consulted about where money goes, how the group's moral mission is framed? We must reflect on whether encouraging pragmatic consensus will make it more difficult to escape the structural problems that perpetuate economic oppression and moral injustice. If advocating for change through knowledge creation (perhaps by blogging or some other form of mass communication), we should also try to make space away from the world of words to explore the silent motivations of our own minds. Has our zeal for a "cause" become tied to our own ego fulfillment, tempting us to hoard moral capital, to use it as a weapon against "enemies" who would oppose our efforts? Or have we chosen to wrap ourselves in a comforting cloak of self-righteousness? Have we used charitable donations as a substitute for personal engagement with our more immediate moral economies? We must dig deep within ourselves to understand the murky ties between our values and our economic interests, to see how they contribute to society's often unexamined moral "truths." Though we might uncover some shocking secrets or discover ugly truths about ourselves, we must also remember that the world's predicaments cannot be solved with cynicism and despair. Our quest for a better world begins with believing in the value of ordinary, everyday lives.

Notes

The following abbreviations are used in the notes:

AGI   Archivo General de las Indias (Seville, Spain)
AGNB   Archivo General de la Nación (Bogotá, Colombia)
AHR   *American Historical Review*
AHN   Archivo Histórico Nacional (Madrid, Spain)
BDA   Barbados Department of Archives (Black Rock, Barbados)
BL   British Library (London, Great Britain)
CSPC   *Calendar of State Papers, Colonial Series, America and West Indies,*
            1574–1739 CD-ROM (London: Routledge, published in association with
            the Public Record Office, 2000).
HLSC   Haverford Library Special Collections (Haverford, Pennsylvania)
JBMHS   *Journal of the Museum of the Barbados Museum and Historical Society*
NAL   British National Archives (Kew, London, Great Britain)
NMM   National Maritime Museum (Greenwich, Great Britain)
Splendiani Anna María Splendiani, *Cincuenta Años de Inquisición en el Tribunal*
            de Cartagena de Indias, 1610–1660, 3 Vol. (Bogotá: Centro Editorial
            Javeriano, 1997)
WMQ   *The William & Mary Quarterly*

Introduction

1. I use the term *race* advisedly, for in the early modern period, European conceptions of physical and cultural difference from sub-Saharan Africans had not yet been
naturalized into today's concept of biological race. Nonetheless (as we will see), it was
during this period that a sense of incomparability began to intensify and to harden
between people alternately termed Christians or whites and those labeled "Negroes/
negros." This transformation was informed by both cultural referents (encompassing

religion and other markers of "civilization") and physical differences (dress, skin color). For an overview of the scholarly consensus on this topic for the British Atlantic, see David Brion Davis, "Constructing Race: A Reflection," *William and Mary Quarterly* 54, 1 (1997): 7–18. For the process in other European colonies, see María-Elena Martínez, *Genealogical Fictions: Limpieza de Sangre, Religion, and Gender in Colonial Mexico* (Stanford, CA: Stanford University Press, 2008); Hebe Mattos, "'Pretos' and 'Pardos' Between the Cross and the Sword: Racial Categories in Seventeenth Century Brazil," *European Review of Latin American and Caribbean Studies*, No. 80 (April 2006): 43–55; Sue Peabody, "'A Nation Born to Slavery: Missionaries and Racial Discourse in Seventeenth-Century French Antilles," *Journal of Social History* 38, 1 (2004): 113–26.

2. Elijah Gould, "Entangled Histories, Entangled Worlds: The English-Speaking Atlantic as a Spanish Periphery," *AHR* 112, 3 (2007): 764–86. Scholarship on the African Diaspora has more frequently acknowledged such integration; other Atlantic scholars working in this mode include Jennifer L. Anderson, Ignacio Gallup-Diaz, Allan Gallay, April Hatfield, Jane Landers, Linda Rupert, John K. Thornton, Camilla Townsend, and Lisa Voight. For a few critiques of Atlantic history's struggle over inclusion and exclusion, see David Armitage, "The Red Atlantic," *Reviews in American History* 29, 4 (2001): 479–86; Alison Games, "Atlantic History: Definitions, Challenges and Opportunities," *AHR* 111, 3 (2006): 741–57; and Kristin Mann, "Shifting Paradigms in the Study of the African Diaspora and of Atlantic History and Culture," *Slavery and Abolition* 22, 1 (2001): 3–21.

3. My research took me to the following depositories: Spain: Archivo General de Indias (Seville); Archivo Histórico Nacional (Madrid); Colombia: Archivo General de la Nación (Bogotá); England: British Library, Friends' House (London); National Maritime Museum (Greenwich); National Archives (Kew); Barbados: Barbados Department of Archives (St. Michael); United States: Rutgers University Library, Special Collections (New Brunswick, New Jersey); The John Carter Brown Library (Providence, Rhode Island); Haverford College Special Collections (Haverford, Pennsylvania); The Huntington Library (San Marino, California).

4. Consequently, Christianity is often understudied for this era. Surveys of the Spanish Caribbean offer much from the era of Bartolomé de las Casas's religiously inspired defense of Amerindian slavery, but coverage of religion rarely extends beyond the sixteenth century, as migration of Spanish settlers (and religious institutions) moved towards the new centers of power in Mexico and Peru. See Antonio Domínguez Ortiz, "A Spiritual Empire," in *The Golden Age of Spain, 1516–1659*, trans. James Casey (New York: Basic Books, 1971), 311; Francisco Morales Padrón, *Spanish Jamaica (Jamaica Española* (Seville, 1952), trans. Patrick Bryan et al. (repr. Kingston, Jamaica: Ian Randle Publishers, 2003); Francis J. Osborne, *History of the Catholic Church in Jamaica* (Chicago: Loyola University Press, 1988). In scholars' treatments of the first phase of English West Indian settlement, religion plays a relatively minor role. Some notable exceptions include Karen O. Kupperman, *Providence Island, 1630–1641: The Other Puritan Colony* (New York: Cambridge University Press, 1993); Richard S. Dunn, *Sugar and Slaves: The Rise of the Planter Class in the English West Indies, 1624–1713* (Chapel Hill: University of North Carolina Press, 1972); Carla Pestana, *The English Atlantic in an Age of Revolution, 1640–1661* (Cambridge: Harvard University Press, 2004); Carla Pestana, *Protestant Empire: Religion and the Making of the British Atlantic World* (Philadelphia: University of Pennsylvania Press, 2009).

5. Clifford Geertz, "Religion as a Cultural System," in Michael Banton, ed., *Anthropological Approaches to the Study of Religion* (London: Tavistock Publications, 1969), 1–41, esp. 21, 25–29, 35–36. Geertz urged those who want to achieve a penetrating understanding of the sociological basis of religious systems "to put aside at once the tone of the village atheist and that of the village preacher, as well as their more sophisticated equivalents," allowing "questions about whether religion is 'good' or bad' . . . to disappear like the chimeras they are . . . " (39–40).

6. Mary Douglas, *Purity and Danger: An Analysis of Concepts of Pollution and Taboo* (London: Routledge & K. Paul, 1966), 69.

7. On Weber and disenchantment, see Richard Swedberg and Ola Agevall, *The Max Weber Dictionary: Key Words and Central Concepts* (Stanford, CA: Stanford University Press, 2005), 62–63.

8. "Imagination is restoring to the past all the possibilities of its future." Greg Dening referred to the "silences of the self"—"silences of pain, and of happiness for that matter; silences of guilt, silences of the poor, of victims; silences of exclusion; silences of forgetting," acknowledging the problem that although these are many times the issues historians are most drawn to, they are also the ones we are most reticent to deal with. "Texts of Self," in *Through a Glass Darkly: Reflections on Personal Identity in Early America*, ed. Ronald Hoffman, Mechal Sobel, and Fredrika Teute (Chapel Hill: Omohundro Institute and University of North Carolina Press, 1997), 161–62; see also Daniel Richter, *Facing East from Indian Country: A Native History of Early America* (Cambridge, MA: Harvard University Press, 2001), 11–15; Natalie Zemon Davis's several books, especially *The Return of Martin Guerre* (Cambridge: Harvard University Press, 1984), and *Women on the Margins: Three Seventeenth Century Lives* (Cambridge: Harvard University Press, 1995); John Demos, *The Unredeemed Captive: A Family Story from Early America* (New York: Alfred A. Knopf, 1994).

9. Peter Hulme has written evocatively of his attempt to find meaning in the fragmentary and anecdotal in his narrative of the Caribbean: "The venture, it should be said, is archaeological: no smooth history emerges, but rather a series of fragments which, read speculatively, hint at a story that can never be fully recovered" (*Colonial Encounters: Europe and the Native Caribbean, 1492–1797* (London: Methuen, 1986), 12). Scholars who inspired me in their innovative approaches to the problem of empirical unevenness include Saidiya V. Hartman, *Scenes of Subjection: Terror, Slavery, and Self-Making in Nineteenth-Century America* (New York: Oxford University Press, 1997), 11; Herman Bennett, "The Subject in the Plot: National Boundaries and the 'History' of the Black Atlantic," *African Studies Review* 43, 1 (2000): 101–24; Michel-Rolf Trouillout, *Silencing the Past: Power and the Production of History* (Boston: Beacon Press, 1995).

10. Archivo Histórico Nacional (AHN), Sección Inquisición (Inq.), Lib. 305. R. 2, ff. 345r–346v. 16 abril 1669, Carta de los inquisidores del Tribunal del Santo Oficio de Cartagena de Indias en que se pide trasladar la institución a la ciudad de Santa Fe.

11. Las Casas explained the devastating chain reaction reaching from Africa and beyond: ". . . as they [Africans] themselves see that when [slaves] are looked for and desired, they make unjust wars upon each other, and in other illicit ways they steal one another to be sold to the Portuguese, so that we ourselves are the cause of all the sins that one and another commits, as well as those that we ourselves commit in buying them [. . .] when they were put into the sugar mills . . . they found their death and their sickness, and thus many of them die every day, and for that reason bands of them run away whenever they

can, and they rise up and inflict death and cruelty upon the Spaniards, in order to get out of their captivity . . . " in Benítez-Rojo, *The Repeating Island: The Caribbean and the Postmodern Perspective*, trans. James Maraniss (Durham: Duke University Press, 1996, 97–100; his translation of Book 3, Ch. 129, 273–76.

12. AHN, Inquisición, Leg. 1617, Expediente 1/7, f. 7v. James Scott's classic *Domination and the Arts of Resistance: Hidden Transcripts* (New Haven, CT: Yale University Press, 1990) first coined the term *hidden transcript*, a reference to what lies beneath the surface of ostensible domination, a critique of power and the structures that dictate one's subordination.

13. For many years, scholars thought of late sixteenth- and early seventeenth-century Europe as operating within a "crisis" of authority, tied both to religious factionalism and political (in)stability. One of the most prominent scholars in this school, Wolfgang Reinhard, identified Counter-Reformation indoctrinization as linked to the construction of emerging states, by which confessional beliefs were utilized to control populations and develop modern bureaucracies. "Reformation, Counter-Reformation, and the Early Modern State: A Reassessment," *Catholic Historical Review* 75 (1989): 383–405, republished in David M. Luebke, ed., *The Counter-Reformation: The Essential Readings* (Malden, MA: Blackwell, 1999), 105–128. See also Philip Benedict, "Religion and Politics in the European Struggle for Stability, 1500–1700," in Philip Benedict and Myron P. Gutmann, eds., *Early Modern Europe: From Crisis to Stability* (Newark: University of Delaware Press, 2006), 124; R. Po-Chia Hsia, *The World of Catholic Renewal, 1540–1770* (Cambridge & New York: Cambridge University Press, 1998); John O'Malley, *Trent and All That: Renaming Catholicism in the Early Modern Era* (Cambridge, MA: Harvard University Press, 2000); Theodore K. Rabb, *The Struggle for Stability in Early Modern Europe* (New York: Oxford University Press, 1975), esp. Ch. 8, 74–82; and Jonathan Scott, *England's Troubles: Seventeenth-Century Political Instability in European Context* (Cambridge & New York: Cambridge University Press, 2000).

Some Africanist scholars have shown similar links between the support for monotheism and attempts to consolidate power by regional rulers and empires during our period of study. In the Kingdom of Kongo, Afonso I (Mbenba Nzinga, ruled 1509–1543) converted to Christianity so as to begin a trade and political partnership with the Portuguese, both of which aided him in the overthrow of his brother in the early sixteenth century. In ways that seem to mirror the "rise of absolutism" in early modern Europe and its links to the disciplining powers of a national church during the seventeenth century, Robin Law describes the kings of Allada and Whydah's interest in promoting Islam and Christianity. Rulers along the Slave Coast who hoped to enhance their personal power "sought to promote worship of a supreme God . . . since such a cult served to strengthen royal authority"—their intent was only circumscribed by the power of subordinate chiefs, many of whom insisted on continuing to venerate their own gods and ancestors. Monotheism was of course not the only religious "tool of power" for early modern African leaders. Other "high" cults operated similarly—like that of the python god Dangbe, which served to justify the power of Whydah leaders in the late seventeenth century; organized devotion to the Creator God Mawu was instituted by the expansionist Dahomey King Tegbesu in the 1740s. See John K. Thornton, *Warfare in Atlantic Africa, 1500–1800* (London: Taylor & Francis, 1999), 100; Robin Law, "Religion, Trade and Politics on the 'Slave Coast': Roman Catholic Missions in Allada and Whydah in the Seventeenth Century," *Journal of Religion in Africa* 21, 1 (1991): 42–77, esp. 69–71;

Elizabeth Isichei, *A History of Christianity in Africa* (Grand Rapids, MI: W. B. Eerdmans, 1995), Ch. 2.

14. Recent scholarship supports a new interpretation of imperial competition—that not only was this era a time for ambitious leaders in Europe to try to expand their powers, but in Africa and the Americas, too, states jockeyed for position so as to take advantage of the profits to be gained from stimulated trade. Camilla Townsend, *Pocahontas and the Powhatan Dilemma* (New York: Hill & Wang, 2004); Daniel K. Richter, *Facing East from Indian Country* (Cambridge, MA: Harvard University Press, 2001); John K. Thornton, *Africa and Africans in the Making of the Atlantic World, 1400–1800*, 2nd ed. (Cambridge: Cambridge University Press, 1998).

15. Intent on restoring political agency to black people throughout the Diaspora, Caribbean scholars like C. L. R. James (*The Black Jacobins*, 1938) and Eric Williams (*Capitalism and Slavery*, 1944), both from Trinidad, used their education in structuralist economic models to argue for a much different story of the Caribbean's transformation and its place on the world stage. For them, the rising European demand for sugar built the foundation for the large-scale, often predatory, enslavement of West Africans. They believed that the plantation's demands for efficiency and profitability created systems of profit and exploitation that would later serve as a model for Industrial Revolution factories that engulfed working-class peoples around the world in a cycle of impoverishment and buried histories that threatened Western supremacy. Since these early critiques, detailed economic and demographic studies of transatlantic migration, the "sugar revolution" and the plantation complex have all confirmed the Caribbean's centrality to the creation of European empires. See especially Sidney W. Mintz, *Sweetness and Power: The Place of Sugar in Modern History* (New York: Penguin, 1986), and Robin Blackburn, *The Making of New World Slavery: From the Baroque to the Modern, 1492–1800* (London & New York: Verso, 1997).

16. See Benjamin Braude, "The Sons of Noah and the Construction of Ethnic and Geographical Identities in the Medieval and Early Modern Periods," *WMQ* 54, 1 (1997): 103–42; William McKee Evans, "From the Land of Canaan to the Land of Guinea: The Strange Odyssey of the 'Sons of Ham,'" *AHR* 85, 1 (1980): 15–43; Stephen R. Haynes, *Noah's Curse: The Biblical Justification of American Slavery* (New York: Oxford University Press, 2002).

17. Though E. P. Thompson first coined the term *moral economy,* and James Scott popularized the term in his study of peasant uprisings, I draw here on the concept as elaborated by Elizabeth Isechei, who explores the "moral imagination" of poor African communities. She describes how in the zero-sum game of a world defined by scarcity, peasant people believe that "One cannot acquire wealth by one's own efforts, so an individual who becomes rich or powerful does so at the expense of others. . . . Wealth in things is obtained at the cost of wealth in people." Such tradeoffs, they believe, have moral consequences, perhaps claiming the life of others or one's own spiritual rightness with the universe. Elizabeth Isichei, *Voices of the Poor in Africa* (Rochester, NY: University of Rochester Press, 2002), 9–11. A similar juxtaposition between acquisitiveness and communalism has been noted in early modern Kongo, where "merchants of any race or nationality were especially vulnerable to the charge of being witches because the necessarily individualistic behavior of merchants in the face of a folk ethic of sharing and community service could easily be seen as greed, the root of witchcraft." John Thornton, "Cannibals, Witches, and Slave Traders in the Atlantic World," *WMQ* 60, 2 (2003). The most recent studies of Adam Smith's *Wealth*

of Nations have rebalanced his promotion of self-interest in the context of his earlier *Theory of Moral Sentiments*. See Samuel Fleischacker, *On Adam Smith's Wealth of Nations: A Philosophical Companion* (Princeton, NJ: Princeton University Press, 2004), 46–60; Fonna Forman-Barzilai, *Adam Smith and the Circles of Sympathy: Cosmopolitanism and Moral Theory* (Cambridge: Cambridge University Press, 2010), 53–64, 115–26.

18. The answer to this dichotomy largely fell to the perceptions of those around the subject, and would have likely been answered in the former by those enslaved, for most traditional West African societies challenged those whose blessings came at others' expense. For instance, among the Kikongo of West Central Africa, "whoever succeeds in his or her daily routine," whether a "successful farmer ... responsible leader ... good winemaker ... loveable individual ... good driver ... good politician ... [or] famous judge," is assumed to be someone who gained this prestige "due to the exercise of some kind of unique power (*kindoki*)." Those esteemed by the community are held up as examples of those who would exercise their spiritual force "in the daylight of normal society," whereas those feared for their destructive power are said to operate only at night, in secrecy. In Simon Bockie, *Death and the Invisible Powers: The World of Kongo Belief* (Bloomington, IN: Indiana University Press, 1993), 43.

19. Of course, not all of the dispossessed used Christianity as their tool of choice in confronting European dominance, choosing to turn to the syncretic forms of West African spiritual power to combat the greed, "witchcraft," and "cannibalism" of colonial American slavery. Vincent Brown, *The Reaper's Garden: Death and Power in the World of Atlantic Slavery* (Cambridge, MA: Harvard University Press, 2008), esp. Ch. 4, "Icons, Shamans, and Martyrs."

20. Jill Lepore, "Historians Who Love Too Much: Reflections on Microhistory and Biography," *The Journal of American History* 88, 1 (2001): 129–44. Especially inspirational for this study were the giants of early modern European microhistory: Natalie Zemon Davis, Carlo Ginzberg, Robert Darnton, and Arlette Farge.

21. For persuasive calls to complicate the idea of agency, see Saba Mahmood, *Politics of Piety: The Islamic Revival and the Feminist Subject* (Princeton, NJ: Princeton University Press, 2005), esp. 1–39, and Marisa J. Fuentes, "Power & Historical Figuring: Rachael Pringle Polgreen's Troubled Archive," *Gender and History* 22, 3 (2010): 564–84.

1 / Contesting the Boundaries of Anti-Christian Cruelly

1. Given the nature of modern archives and the ways that documents entered into the record, our knowledge of Juan Arará and the other maroons described here is filtered through Álvarez de Zepeta's intent to document this questioning, which was carried out under a highly scripted scribal procedure. Although these historical documents privilege the Spanish voice, this analysis will work to bring out the ways in which even slaves could subvert the authority of the archive as they registered their needs and perspectives in cooperation with powerful figures in the dominant culture.

2. Archivo General de la Nación, Bogotá (AGNB), Sección Negros y Esclavos, Bolivar, Tomo I, No. 1, f. 12r–15r. (1639) Eufrasia Camargo, mujer de Alonso Esteban Ortiz de Mompos, causa que se le siguio a ella, por sevicia con un esclavo y muerte que dio a algunos dellos. 234 ff. All translations mine.

3. Ibid., ff. 15r–17r. Based on a grammatical analysis of the comment, it is impossible to tell whether Álvarez demanded physical proof or whether Susana offered it—see 45 for further analysis.

4. Ibid., Declaration of Mariana Mandinga, ff. 17r-2or.

5. Ibid., ff. 23r-v. My emphasis.

6. In an era before many economic systems were monetized, certain commodities took on the role of local currencies to provide the easy barter in goods—like pounds of tobacco or cotton or muscovado sugar—or in persons, as had become standard in slave markets from Africa to the Americas since the sixteenth century.

7. Robin Blackburn cites at least 268,600 slaves arriving in Spanish America between 1595 and 1640, as opposed to 36,300 between 1550 and 1595 (*The Making of New World Slavery*, 140). For figures on Cartagena, see Nicolás del Castillo Mathieu, *Esclavos Negros en Cartagena y sus Aportes Léxicos* (Bogotá: Instituto Caro y Cuervo, 1982), 1–91; María Cristina Navarrete, *Historia social del negro en la colonia: Cartagena, siglo XVII* (Santiago de Cali, Colombia: Universidad del Valle, 1995), 25.

8. Samuel Parsons Scott, Charles Sumner Lobingier, and John Vance, eds., *Las Siete Partidas* (Chicago, New York, and Washington: Published for the Comparative Law Bureau of the American Bar Association by Commerce Clearing House, 1931), Part III, Tit. II, Law VIIII, 539.

9. Murray Gordon, *Slavery in the Arab World* (New York: New Amsterdam Press, 1992), 38.

10. Herman L. Bennett, *Africans in Colonial Mexico: Absolutism, Christianity, and Afro-Creole Consciousness, 1570-1640* (Bloomington, IN: Indiana University Press, 2003), 4, 54, 126–53.

11. Humphrey J. Fisher, *Slavery in the History of Muslim Black Africa* (New York: New York University Press, 2001), 146–47; Boubacar Barry, *Senegambia and the Atlantic Slave Trade* (Cambridge: Cambridge University Press, 1998), 115; I. A. Akinjogbin, "The Expansion of Oyo and the Rise of Dahomey, 1600-1800," in J. F. A. Ajayi and Michael Crowder, eds., *History of West Africa*, vol. 1 (New York: Columbia University Press, 1972), 304–43. This speculation assumes that Mariana Mandinga and Juan Arará were indeed from those regions; scholars today are not so trusting of *casta* markers, finding that those labels were frequently manipulated or misattributed. See Rachel O'Toole, "From the Rivers of Guinea to the Valleys of Peru: Becoming a *bran* Diaspora within Spanish Slavery," *Social Text* 92, 25, 3 (2007): 20–25; Russell Lohse, "Slave-Trade Nomenclature and African Ethnicities in the Americas: Evidence from Early Eighteenth-Century Costa Rica," *Slavery and Abolition* 23, 2 (2002): 73–92.

12. Ira Berlin, "From Creole to African: Atlantic Creoles and the Origins of African-American Society in Mainland North America," *WMQ* 53, 2 (1996): 251–88.

13. *Siete Partidas*, Part IV, Tit. XXI, Law VI.

14. Tannenbaum, *Slave and Citizen, The Negro in the Americas* (New York: A. A. Knopf, 1946). Alejandro de la Fuente, a scholar of slavery and race in Cuba, cogently summarized the new way of thinking about this classic text: "Rather than assuming that positive laws endowed slaves with a 'moral' personality, as Tannenbaum would put it, I imply that it was the slaves, as they made claims and pressed for benefits, who gave concrete social meaning to the abstract rights regulated in the positive laws. Through these interactions with colonial authorities and judges, slaves acted (and were seen) as subjects with at least a limited legal standing" (Alejandro de la Fuente, "Slave Law and Claims-Making in Cuba: The Tannenbaum Debate Revisited," *Law and History Review* 22, 2 (2004), 341). See also Manuel Barcia Paz, *Seeds of Insurrection: Domination and Resistance on Western Cuban Plantations, 1808-1848* (Baton

Rouge: Louisiana State University Press, 2008), Ch. 5, "Slaves' Use of the Colonial Legal Framework"; Herman L. Bennett, *Africans in Colonial Mexico*; Jane Landers, *Black Society in Spanish Florida* (Urbana: University of Illinois Press, 1999); Margaret M. Olsen, "*Negros horros* and *Cimarrones* on the legal frontiers of the Caribbean: Accessing the African Voice in Colonial Spanish American Texts," *Research in African Literatures* 29, 4 (1998): 52–72; Matthew Restall, "Manuel's Worlds: Black Yucatan and the Colonial Caribbean," in Jane G. Landers and Barry M. Robinson, eds., *Slaves, Subjects, and Subversives: Blacks in Colonial Latin America* (Albuquerque: University of New Mexico Press, 2006), 147–74.

15. Several exemplars of this approach include: Solange Alberro, "Juan de Morga and Gertrudis de Escobar: Rebellious Slaves," in David G. Sweet and Gary B. Nash, eds., *Struggle and Survival in Colonial America* (Berkeley: University of California Press, 1981), 165–88; Carolyn Dean, *Inka Bodies and the Body of Christ: Corpus Christi in Colonial Cuzco, Peru* (Durham, NC: Duke University Press, 1999); María Elena Díaz, *The Virgin, the King, and the Royal Slaves of El Cobre: Negotiating Freedom in Colonial Cuba, 1670–1780* (Stanford, CA: Stanford University Press, 2000); James Sweet, *Recreating Africa: Culture, Kinship and Religion in the African-Portuguese World, 1441–1770* (Chapel Hill: University of North Carolina Press, 2003).

16. Scholarship on colonial Cartagena has undergone a sort of renaissance in recent decades, thanks to the often invigorating work of academics based in Colombia (including Anna Maria Splendiani, Jaime Borja Gómez, Adriana Maya Restrepo, Maria Cristina Navarrete, Diana Ceballos Gómez, Alfonso Múnera, Antonio Vidal Ortega), a burgeoning political consciousness among Afro-Colombian groups, and preservation projects that have opened up the region's historical records to a broader audience. The Archivo Nacional in Bogotá has digitized their entire series of documents on blacks and slaves (available online at http://negrosyesclavos.archivogeneral. gov.co/; the Instituto Colombiano de Antropología e Historia (ICANH) has published a CD-ROM index of all manuscript documents related to Cartagena's Inquisition Tribunal held in Madrid (*Indice de Documentos de Archivos Españoles para la historia colonial del Nuevo Reino de Granada* (ed. Luis Enrique Rodríguez Baquero, 2002); and Cartagena's old Inquisition Palace has been restored as a museum and historical archive with the help of UNESCO World Heritage funding. Further contact between European, North American, and local scholars has brought this region back into the limelight of Latin American historiography after years of focus on mainly Mexico and Peru—Jane Landers, Renee Souloudre-La France, Kathryn Joy McNight, Ilene Helg, Marixa Lasso, Nicole von Germeten, Marcela Echeverri, Pablo Gómez, and Steiner Saether have been part of this cooperative effort.

17. The local Holy Brotherhood was always charged with these duties in the Spanish Americas ; see Roberto Arrazola Caicedo, *Palenque, primer pueblo libre de América* (Bogotá, Colombia: Cámara de Representantes, 1986), 66). Álvarez, like his counterparts, ordered that persistent maroons be sold away from the region for their "bad influence" on other slaves, but that runaways like Susana and Mariana, whose flights were of short duration or who were first-time offenders, be simply returned to their masters once they were redeemed with alms paid into the Holy Brotherhood's coffers.

18. AGNB, Sección Negros y Esclavos, Bolivar, Tomo I, No. 1, ff. 3r–6v. Letter from Gregorio Álvarez de Zepeda to Gov. Melchor de Aguilera, received 17 May 1639.

19. Archivo General de Indias, Seville, Spain (hereafter AGI), Santa Fe 228, Letter from the Bishop of Cartagena to the Council of Indies, 10 Aug 1634. Navarrete, *Historia social del negro*, 25.

20. One Italian priest had written of Cartagena: "In the number of foreigners, no city in America, or so it is said, has as many as this one, it is an emporium of almost every nation, who from here travel to do business in Quito, Mexico, Peru, and other kingdoms . . . " Quoted in Angel Valtierra, *El santo que libertó una raza: San Pedro Claver, S.J. Su vida y su época* (Bogotá: Editorial Santa Fe, 1954), ii.45.

21. One Father Fernández recorded fourteen slave ships entering the port in 1633, each carrying 600–800 Africans. Cited in Antonino Vidal Ortega, *Cartagena de Indias y la región histórica del Caribe, 1580–1640* (Sevilla: Escuela de Estudios Hispano-Americanos, 2002), 161.

22. One contemporary observer had compared Cape Verde to Cartagena, seeing as how both were regional transportation hubs that served as busy consolidation centers for merchandise (mostly slaves in the case of Cape Verde). In Alonso de Sandoval, *Un tratado sobre la esclavitud*, trans. Enriqueta Vila Vilar (Madrid: Alianza Editorial, 1987), 139. The Italian priest whose comments on the multiethnic character of Cartagena are cited above also was struck by the prominent trade in slaves, bought at "the absolute lowest prices (*precios vilíssimos*) on the coasts of Angola and Guinea; from there they are brought in overstuffed ships to this port, where the first sales result in incredible profits . . . "; see Valtierra, *El santo que libertó una raza*, ii. 45.

Basic historical studies of the slave trade in Cartagena include: Nicolás del Castillo Mathieu, *Esclavos Negros en Cartagena y sus aportes léxicos* (Bogotá: Instituto Caro y Cuervo, 1982); Enriqueta Vila Vilar, *Hispanoamérica y el Comercio de Esclavos* (Sevilla: Escuela de Estudios Hispano-Americanos, 1977). Determining the numbers of Africans sold in Cartagena's port has been, like all other efforts to quantify the slave trade, the subject of considerable guesswork and debate. Enriqueta Vila Vilar and Antonio Vidal Ortega, the current authorities on the numbers, agree that around 3,000 Africans per year entered Cartagena—between 135,000 and 150,000 for the period 1595–1640. These figures remain decisively tentative, for although records are available for the heavily regulated Portuguese monopoly trade, contraband is nearly impossible to quantify. Vidal Ortega analyzed the records of a *visita* done 1597–1610 by a doctor Juan Villabona Zubiaurre, sent to investigate the Treasury of the Holy Brotherhood of Cartagena to calculate how much import tax should be collected for the use of wars against maroons. He found Vila Vilar's calculations of contraband fairly reliable for this case, but proposed that more attention be paid to specific functionaries who had more ability and reason to defraud the royal treasuries—especially because one local observer alleged that four thousand slaves arrived each year, and another wrote in 1619 that one in four slaves arriving in the province were not registered in the tax rolls. See Vila Vilar, *Hispanoamérica y el Comercio de Esclavos*, esp. Ch. 5, "El Contrabando," 157–92; Vidal Ortega, *Cartagena de Indias y la región histórica del Caribe* esp. 161–64.

23. See John Thornton, "On the Trail of Voodoo: African Christianity in Africa and the Americas," *The Americas* 44 3 (1988): 261–78; Castillo Mathieu, *Esclavos Negros en Cartagena*, 62–64.

24. Slaves in urban centers of Spanish America mainly served as status symbols to the elite. As such, any artisan or small merchant hoping to move up in the world hoped

to procure African slaves or other plebeian laborers to remove the "stain" of manual labor from their potential status as *hidalgos*.

25. "Thus, the despicable trade was conducted daily in plain view of the citizenry of Cartagena—both black and white" (Jane Landers, "Contested Spaces: The African Landscape of 17th Century Colombia." Paper for the Association of Caribbean Historians, Cartagena, May 2005, 5).

26. AGNB, Sección Negros y Esclavos, Bolivar, Tomo I, No. 1, ff. 44v–45r.

27. See Alfredo Castillero-Calvo, "The City in the Hispanic Caribbean, 1492–1650," in Pieter C. Emmer, ed., *General History of the Caribbean. Volume II, New Societies: The Caribbean in the Long Sixteenth Century* (London: UNESCO Publishing, 1999), 201–46; Raymond B. Craib, "Cartography and Power in the Conquest and Creation of New Spain," *Latin American Research Review* 35, 1 (2000): 7–36; Richard Kagan and Fernando Marías, *Urban Images of the Hispanic World, 1493–1793* (New Haven: Yale University Press, 2000); Barbara E. Mundy, *The Mapping of New Spain: Indigenous Cartography and the Maps of the Relaciones Geográficas* (Chicago: University of Chicago Press, 2000), esp. Ch. 1, "Spain and the Imperial Ideology of Mapping," 1–10.

28. AGI, Santa Fe 228. 10 Aug 1634, Cartagena, Letter from Bishop to Council of Indies.

29. For an overview of Cartagena's Jesuit mission in English, see Ronald J. Morgan, "Jesuit Confessors, African Slaves and the Practice of Confession in Seventeenth-Century Cartagena," in Katharine Jackson Lualdi and Anne T. Thayer, eds., *Penitence in the Age of Reformations* (Burlington, VT: Ashgate, 2000), 222–39. For a more general overview, see Enriqueta Vila Vilar, "La evangelización del esclavo negro y su integración en el mundo americano," in Berta Ares Queija and Alessandro Stella, eds., *Negros, Mulatos, Zambaigos: Derroteros africanos en los mundos ibéricos* (Sevilla: Escuela de Estudios Hispano-Americanos, 2000).

30. The best religious biography of Claver is that of Jesuit scholar Angel Valtierra, *San Pedro Claver: El Santo que libertó una raza* (Bogotá: Editorial Pax, 1963). Early Spanish imprints celebrating the venerable father include Alonso de Andrade, *Vida del venerable y apostolico padre Pedro Claver de la Compañía de Jesús* (Madrid, 1657); and Josef Fernández, *Apostolica y penitente vida del V.P. Pedro Claver, de la Compañia de Jesús. Sacada principalmente de informaciones juridicas hechas ante el Ordinario de la Ciudad de Cartagena de Indias . . .* (Zaragoza, 1666). Tulio Aristizábal, S.J., who has dedicated much of his career to preserving and promoting the memory of San Pedro, served as a consultant to Anna María Splendiani's modern edition of Claver's canonization process of 1696, including first-hand testimonies of Claver's colleagues and black and white residents of Cartagena, *Proceso de beatificación y canonización de San Pedro Claver*, tr. from the Latin and Italian (Bogotá: Pontificia Universidad Javeriana, 2002).

31. Before publishing his treatise, Sandoval's career had forced him to examine the similarities between Indian and African labor conditions, first in 1605 when he was given charge of "all the Blacks and Indians of this city [Cartagena] and its surroundings; those of the countryside alone are 5,000, they are the poorest people that one can imagine." In 1606–1607 he undertook a mission among Amerindians in the Darien Gulf and on the Panamanian frontier, and later he visited the mines of Cáceres, Remedios, and Zaragoza, which had already begun to be staffed mainly with African labor (Luz Adriana Maya Restrepo, *Brujería y Reconstrucción de Indentidades entre los Africanos y sus descendientes en la Nueva Granada, siglo XVII* (Bogotá: Imprenta

Nacional de Colombia, 2005), 395–96. The best Spanish edition of his treatise (used for this section's translations) was prepared by Enriqueta Vila Vilar, *Un tratado sobre la esclavitud* (Madrid: Alianza Editorial, 1987). A shortened English edition is also available: Alonso de Sandoval, *Treatise on Slavery*, edited and translated by Nicole von Germeten (Indianapolis: Hackett Publishing, 2008).

32. Splendiani and Aristizábal, *Proceso de beatificación*, 133–34, 186.

33. Ibid., 192. Don Diego de la Cruz Arjona testified that although Claver "threatened the negroes attending with imprisonment and beatings and sometimes took away the food and drinks they had ready for these [ceremonies], it was not possible to prevent them" (p. 196).

34. Throughout the Hapsburg empire, lower-class prisoners who were not considered particularly dangerous were often removed from prison (where they had to be supported at the state's expense) and placed in private homes or charitable institutions.

35. Pedro Julio Dousdebés, *Cartagena de Indias, plaza fuerte: capítulos de la historia militar de Colombia*, No. 27, Biblioteca del Oficial (Bogotá: Estado Mayor General de las Fuerzas Militares, 1948); Enrique Marco Dorta, *Cartagena de Indias: Puerto y plaza fuerte* (Bogotá: Fondo Cultural Cafetero, 1988); Juan Manuel Zapatero, *Historia de las fortificaciones de Cartagena de Indias* (Madrid: Ediciones Cultura Hispánica, 1979).

36. Antonio Vidal Ortega, "El mundo urbano de negros y mulatos en Cartagena de Indias entre 1580 y 1640," *Historia Caribe* 5 (2000): 87–102, esp. 94. Another source gives numbers of soldiers who were free *morenos criollos* as about 600 (Navarrete, *Historia social del negro*, 34–35).

37. AGI, Santa Fe 228. Letter from the Bishop of Cartagena to the Council of Indies, 10 Aug 1634.

38. In another reference to the city's many "forasteros," a medical doctor wrote in 1607 that most had "no fixed domicile but went to lodge in the homes of *mulatas*" (quoted in Vidal Ortega, "El mundo urbano de negros y mulatos," 99).

39. Susan Socolow, *The Women of Colonial Latin America* (Cambridge: Cambridge University Press, 2000), 132.

40. Officially named the Plaza de los Coches, this is a site that several witnesses in the case of Pedro Claver's beatification referred to as a place where blacks normally congregated (Splendiani and Aristizábal, *Proceso de beatificación*, 131–34).

41. Julio Evangelista, one of the most powerful Italian residents of Cartagena in the early 1600s, arrived in Cartagena in 1590 with a slave ship from Africa. He rose to prominence through military and business connections, and participated in military offensive and defensive actions against pirates and maroons, marrying the daughter of a creole officer of noble birth (Enriqueta Vila Vilar, "Extranjeros en Cartagena, 1593–1630," *Jahrbuch für Geschichte von Staat, wirtschaft und Gesellschaft Lateinamerikas* 16 (1979): 147–84, esp. 160–61, 180; article reprinted in *Aspectos sociales en América colonial: de extranjeros, contrabando y esclavos* (Bogotá: Universidad de Bogotá, 2001). Evangelista had also made a large donation to the Church to secure rights for himself and his heirs as benefactors and patrons of a new church in the Getsemaní neighborhood (La Trinidad). Although he died before his request could be granted, the king ordered that the church be constructed in 1643. Tulio Aristizábal, *Iglesias, conventos y hospitales en Cartagena colonial* (Bogotá: Editorial Centro Iberoamericano de Formación, 1988), 32.

42. AGNB, Negros y Esclavos, Bolívar Tomo IX, No.1, "Catalina Pimienta Pacheco, vecina de Cartagena, viuda del capitán Julio Evangelista; su pleito con Juana, su negra

esclava, quien pedía carta de libertad" (1634), 136 ff. Since this case was dropped and the lawyer filing petitions in defense of Juana Zamba was never allowed to examine witnesses with the detailed questionnaire he had prepared, I have chosen to dramatize the varying perspectives in the case, most of them arising from witnesses' testimonies supporting the mistress's defense.

43. AGNB, Sección Negros y Esclavos, Bolivar, Tomo I, No. 1, f. 130v.

44. AGNB, Negros y Esclavos, Bolivar Tomo IX, No.1, f. 15, 59r.

45. Hartman, *Scenes of Subjection*, 87. Hartman discusses at length the consequences of white women's "disavowal of rape" in antebellum U.S. South:

> enraged by the sexual arrangements of slavery . . . [they chose] to target slave women as the agents of their husbands' downfall . . . The slave woman not only suffered the responsibility for her sexual (ab)use but was also blameworthy because of her purported ability to render the powerful weak (87).

Because of their status, slave women had no right to consent or express their will within the master-slave relationship. See more in Hartman, Ch. 3, "Seduction and the Ruses of Power." Even in Spanish society, which more explicitly recognized the humanity of the enslaved vis-à-vis their assumed inclusion in the Christian community, few would dare to cast blame on white men or recognize enslaved women's resistance to violation.

46. Socolow, *The Women of Colonial Latin America*, 89, 133–34. See also Thavolia Glymph, *Out of the House of Bondage: The Transformation of the Plantation Household* (Cambridge & New York: Cambridge University Press, 2008), and Elizabeth Fox Genovese, *Within the Plantation Household: Black and White Women of the Old South* (Chapel Hill: University of North Carolina Press, 1988).

47. AGNB, Negros y Esclavos, Bolivar Tomo IX, No.1, ff. 17r–17v.

48. Bennett, *Africans in Colonial Mexico*, esp. Ch. 3, "Policing Christians: Persons of African Descent before the Inquisition and Ecclesiastical Courts," 51–78.

49. For full transcripts of the 1638 *auto de fe*, see Splendiani, iii.35–85, esp. 84–85. Vicente de Paz led the day's procession through the city, and the notorious *mulata* Paula de Eguiluz was the final penitent. She had already been prosecuted once by the Inquisition, and in 1638 was charged with leading a coven of witches in Cartagena, women from all social ranks who looked to her as the most powerful purveyor of magic arts. Eguiluz had the audacity to name the father of the child (a priest!) born during her mandatory term of service in the hospital of San Juan de Dios in Gesthemani during the 1630s. For more details, see María Cristina Navarrete, "La mujer bruja en la sociedad colonial: El caso de Paula de Eguiluz" in Luisa Campuzano, ed., *Mujeres latinoamericanas: historia y cultura: siglos XVI al XIX*, Vol. 1 (Havana: Casa de las Américas; Mexico City: Universidad Autónoma Metropolitana-Iztapalapa, 1997), 69–78.

50. Splendiani, iii.84; AHN, L. 1021, f. 46v–47.

51. See Joan Cameron Bristol, *Christians, Blasphemers, and Witches: Afro-Mexican Ritual Practice in the Seventeenth Century* (Albuquerque: University of New Mexico Press, 2007), esp. Ch. 4, 113–48; María Fernanda Cuevas Oviedo, "Reniego y resistencia de los esclavizados y sus descendientes en la Nueva Granada durante el siglo XVII" (Master's thesis, Universidad de los Andes, 2002), 60; Kathryn Joy McKnight, "Blasphemy as Resistance: An African Slave Woman before the Mexican Inquisition," in Mary E. Giles, ed., *Women in the Inquisition: Spain and the New World* (Baltimore,

MD: Johns Hopkins University Press, 1999); José Enrique Sánchez B., "La herejía: una forma de resistencia del negro contra la estructura social colonial (1610–1636)," in Jaimie Humberto Borja Gómez, ed., *Inquisición, muerte y sexualidad en el Nuevo Reino de Granada* (Bogotá: Editorial Ariel, 1996); Javier Villa-Flores, "'To lose one's soul': blasphemy and slavery in New Spain, 1596–1669," *Hispanic American Historical Review* 82, 4 (2002): 435–68; Villa-Flores, "Voices from a Living Hell: Slavery, Death and Salvation in a Mexican Obraje," in Martin Austin Nesvig, ed., *Local Religion in Colonial Mexico* (Albuquerque: University of New Mexico Press, 2006), 235–56; and Javier Villa-Flores, *Dangerous Speech: A Social History of Blasphemy in Colonial Mexico* (Tucson: University of Arizona Press, 2006). James Sweet's study of African populations in the Portuguese world also mentions a couple of cases of renunciation responding to a master's cruelty, "Blasphemy and Sacrilege among Slaves," 210–15; and Frank T. Proctor, "Slavery, Identity and Culture: An Afro-Mexican Counterpoint, 1640–1763," Ph.D. dissertation, Emory University, 2003, esp. Ch. 6, "The Negotiation of Mastery and Slavery in New Spain."

52. Maureen Flynn, "Blasphemy and the Play of Anger in Sixteenth-Century Spain," *Past and Present* 149 (1995): 29–56. See also Villa-Flores, *Dangerous Speech*, Ch. 3.

53. Splendiani, ii.295–96; AHN, Lib. 1020, ff. 310v–311; Splendiani, ii.400; AHN, Lib. 1020, f. 441v–42.

54. Splendiani, iii.84; AHN L. 1021, f. 47r.

55. The only white man sentenced to punishment for blasphemy (one hundred lashes like Vicente de Paz) in the early seventeenth century was Julio Cesar Capriano, a Milanese *forzado* sentenced to work as an oarsmen in the Tierrafirme galleys. Splendiani, ii.245; AHN, Lib. 1020, f. 259r.

2 / Imperial Intercession and Master-Slave Relations

1. For an intriguing call for closer study into the specific valences and historical specificity of creolization in the Caribbean, see Trouillot, "Culture on the Edges," 189–210. Trouillot suggests that for Caribbean regions where the plantation was not the standard labor regime and Europeans were represented in large numbers and had a fair amount of contact with African slaves (like Cartagena and Mompox), the process of creolization should be understood as operating in a "frontier context," distinct from the creolization of the plantation or the maroon community.

2. See Bennett, *Africans in Colonial Mexico*, 180–84.

3. AGNB, Negros y Esclavos, Bolivar, Tomo I, No. 1, f. 46r.

4. Ibid., f. 45r–47v. (*tiene para aprissionarlas esquissitas prisiones mas que en la (carzel*).

5. Ibid., ff. 47r–53r.

6. Ibid., ff. 53r–54v.

7. Castrellon testified that "during the time in which the whipping was done, the said doña Eufrasia de Camargo would be walking around the chamber of her house with a rosary in her hand . . . and as the slaves were whipped she went along counting the [beads of] her rosary until they had received 700, 800, or one thousand lashes." Ibid., f. 48r. The officials who reviewed the case drew attention to this description of doña Eufrasia's perfidious use of a holy object with significant marginalia.

8. Ibid., f. 49r.

9. Given the shared name and the smallness of Mompox's elite social networks, it is likely that Father Ortiz was one of Camargo's relatives on her husband's side of the

family. Carlos Eduardo Valencia Villa's economic study of slavery in Santafé, Mariquita, and Mompox in the first half of the seventeenth century suggests that the offered price of 400–500 pesos was within the average range for a female slave, but on the high end of the scale (the mean price for 1624–1643 was 300 pesos). *Alma en Boca y Huesos en Costal: Una aproximación a los contrastes socio-económicos de la esclavitud* (Bogotá: Instituto Colombiano de Antropología e Historia, 2003), 64–65.

10. AGNB, Negros y Esclavos, Bolivar, Tomo I, No. 1, f. 90v.

11. Alonso de Sandoval, *Un Tratado sobre la esclavitud*. Introdución, transcripción, y traducción de Enriqueta Vila Vilar (Madrid: Alianza Editorial, 1987), 243.

12. Ibid., 246.

13. Splendiani and Aristizábal, *Proceso de beatificación*, 194–95. Testimony of don Diego de Villegas, vecino de Cartagena.

14. AGNB, Negros y Esclavos, Bolivar, Tomo I, No. 1, ff. 60r–71r. Order by Gov. Melchor de Aguilera, 19 May 1639, Cartagena; Autos of diligences performed by Lorenzo de Soto, 21 May–27 May 1639.

15. Arturo E. Bermúdez Bermúdez, *Piratas en Santa Marta* (Bogotá: Tipografía Hispana Ltda, 1978).

16. Spanish attempts to "reduce" all of the region's Muisca groups to subservience had been substantial in the course of settlement in the sixteenth century, thanks to microbes and severe labor regimes. See J. M. Francis, "The Muisca Indians under Spanish rule, 1537–1636" (Cambridge: Ph.D. dissertation, 1998). Regional historian Pedro Salzedo del Villar wrote that in Mompox, Indian populations had been reduced to only about 2,000 individuals scattered in one of a hundred neighboring *encomiendas* (*Apuntaciones Historiales de Mompox, 1537–1809* (Cartagena, Colombia: Tipografía Democracia, 1938), 42–44). See also David Ernesto Peñas Galindo, *Los Bogas de Mompox: Historia del zambaje* (Bogotá: Tercer Mundo Editories, 1998).

17. AGNB, Negros y Esclavos, Bolivar, Tomo I, No. 1, f. 18r.

18. Lola G. Luna, *Reguardos Coloniales de Santa Marta y Cartagena y Resistencia Indígena* (Bogotá: Biblioteca Banco Popular, 1993), 39. A document of 1590 suggested that "for the relief of the said naturals it world be fruitful to introduce some blacks to serve as rowers (*bogas*) in the said canoes" but that blacks should be segregated from Indians. See also Antonino Vidal Ortega, "Alzados y Fugitivos en el mundo rural de la gobernación de Cartagena a comienzos del siglo XVII," *Historia y Cultura* 1 (2004): 45–72.

19. AGNB, Negros y Esclavos, Bolivar, Tomo I, No. 1, ff. 13r–v. Francisco Angola fled to the mountains soon after being sold to Eufrasia Camargo's father, Capt. Francisco de Camargo, ff. 10v-r.

20. In 1663, pirates entered the mouth of the Magdalena, and were apprehended only 20 leagues from Mompox. Salzedo del Villar, *Apuntaciones Historiales*, 40, 53–54.

21. After Drake's use of maroons in Panama, Spanish officials feared that powerful *palenques* there would do the same, crippling the regional economy through transportation blockades. See Navarrete, *Historia Social del Negro*, 35. Vila Vilar explains how the strength of Panama's maroons forced the Crown to bar *asentistas* from importing slaves to that region, and that fortifications built at the end of the sixteenth century were designed as necessary defenses against both sea attacks and urban revolts. Enriqueta Vila Vilar, *Hispanoamérica y el Comercio de Esclavos: Los Asientos Portugueses* (Sevilla: Escuela de Estudios Hispano-Americanos, 1977), 79–80, 83, 86.

NOTES TO CHAPTER 2 / 245

22. Enriqueta Vila Vilar, "Cimarronaje en Panamá y Cartagena: El costo de una guerrilla en el siglo XVII," *Caravelle: cahiers du monde hispanique et luso-brésilien* 49 (1987): 77–92, esp. 89. In Cartagena, the suppression of *palenques* was accomplished using mostly private funds, as *vecinos* mortgaged their properties to capture runaways and protect the stability of their local investment in the region. Roberto Arrazola, *Palenque, Primer Pueblo Libre de América* (Cartagena: Ediciones Hernandez, 1970), 41–42. Other historiography of note on the subject of maroons in Spanish America includes María del Carmen Borrego Plá, *Palenques de Negros en Cartagena de Indias a fines del siglo XVII* (Seville: Escuela de Estudios Hispanoamericanos, 1973); Olsen, "*Negros horros* and *Cimarrones* on the legal frontiers . . . "; Kathryn Joy McKnight, "Confronted Rituals: Spanish Colonial and Angolan 'Maroon' Executions in Cartagena de Indias (1634)" *Journal of Colonialism and Colonial History* 5, 3 (2004); Francisco Moscoso, "Formas de resistencia de los esclavos en Puerto Rico siglos XVI–XVIII," *América Negra* 10 (Dec. 1995): 31–46.

23. Salzedo de Villar, *Apuntaciones Historiales*, 48.

24. AGI, Santa Fe 39, R5, No57. 30 Sep 1631, Cartagena. Gov. Francisco de Murga, "Testimonio del daño que hizo a los Negros Cimarrones . . . "; Arrazola, *Palenque*, 62–63.

25. Literary scholar Kathryn John McKnight has analyzed testimonies related to the seizure of Limón residents. See McKnight, "Confronted Rituals"; and "Gendered Declarations: Testimonies of Three Captured Maroon Women, Cartagena de Indias, 1634," *Colonial Latin American Historical Review* 12, 4 (2003): 499–527.

26. Vidal Ortega says that Mompox was a critical registration center for New Granadian commerce (*Cartagena de Indias y la región histórica del Caribe*, 206). Peñas Galindo explains the strategic importance of Mompox, "from where commerce with the Sinú can be controlled via the San Jorge River, with Antioquia and its gold, via the Cauca [River], the same with the early surge of contraband, whose principal route began in Riohacha and [after going upriver to Ranchería] would arrive to Cesar, to disembark in the port of Jaime, in front of Mompox" (*Los bogas de Mompox*, 22).

27. Peñas Galindo, *Los bogas de Mompox*, 23; Vidal Ortega, *Cartagena de Indias y la región histórica del Caribe*, 207.

28. Salzedo de Villar, *Apuntaciones Historiales*, 48, 40, 46.

29. The Camargo family's connection to power in the Nuevo Reino de Granada seems to have begun in the late sixteenth century, as evidenced by the appointment of a young Francisco Camargo as a public notary in 1591 (AGI, Santa Fe, 146, N. 14). Captain Diego Ortiz Nieto had been the leader of the aforementioned 1616 incursion against nearby maroon settlements (see note 78, Salzedo de Villar, *Apuntaciones Historiales*, 42–44). By the late 1640s, the honorable (and lucrative) post of Inquisition *comisario* was held by one Francisco Camargo, likely one of doña Eufrasia's brothers (their father, who died sometime in the 1630s, was also named Francisco Camargo). Francisco Camargo (Jr.) exercised his title as *comisario* to charge a Mompox tavern-keeper (*pulpero*) with blasphemy in 1648 (Splendiani, iii.190; AHN, Inq. Lib. 1021, ff. 172).

30. AGNB, Negros y Esclavos, Bolivar, Tomo I, No. 1, ff. 64v-71r. Autos of diligences performed by Lorenzo de Soto, 21 May-27 May 1639.

31. Ibid., f. 76v. Testimony of Inez Criolla, 26 May 1639.

32. Ibid., ff. 73v–81r. Testimony of Inez Criolla, 26 May 1639.

33. Hartman, *Scenes of Subjection*, 94.
34. AGNB, Negros y Esclavos, Bolivar, Tomo IX, No. 1, f. 17v.
35. AGNB, Negros y Esclavos, Bolivar, Tomo I, No. 1, f. 88r.
36. Ibid., ff. 73v–81r.
37. Ibid., f. 88r.
38. Ibid., f. 89v.
39. Ibid., ff. 73v–81r. Testimony of Inez Criolla, 26 May 1639. Modern anthropological and medical studies of dirt-eating—geophagy—have puzzled over its various causes and consequences. Modern investigations into the cultural roots and meanings of geophagy have noted that pregnant women and children are primary among geophagists. Some have noted the symbolic linkages between the earth and fertility, others the unique physiological cravings that pregnant women exhibit (especially if malnourished), and the belief among several cultures that eating certain clays will help a child thrive. See Peter W. Abrahams and Julia A. Parsons, "Geophagy in the Tropics: A Literature Review," *The Geographical Journal* 162, 1 (1996): 63–72. Geophagy has been seen as a practice that is common in tropical regions among poorer and "tribally oriented people" in sub-Saharan Africa, but that spread as a cultural manifestation to places like the American South with the spread of the transatlantic slave trade. Assertions of eating clay as a mineral supplement can be found in Jerome S. Handler and Robert S. Corruccini, "Plantation Slave Life in Barbados: A Physical Anthropological Analysis," *Journal of Interdisciplinary History* 14, 1 (1983): 65–90, esp. 77; also John M. Hunter, "Geophagy in Africa and in the United States: A Culture-Nutrition Hypothesis," *Geographical Review* 63, 2 (1973): 170–95. For a discussion of geophagy and its relation to the maladies *Cachexia Africana, mal d'estomach*, dropsy, and beriberi, see Kenneth F. Kiple, *The Caribbean Slave: A Biological History* (Cambridge: Cambridge University Press, 1984), 96–104; on connections between geophagy and roundworm in Todd L. Savitt, *Medicine and Slavery: The Diseases and Health Care of Blacks in Antebellum Virginia* (Urbana: University of Illinois Press, 1978), 65–66. Unfortunately, most of these studies seem to be hampered by the imaginative limits of scientific positivism, as they explain in detail what ingesting soil *does* to the body, but downplay or ignore the question of what the act was *perceived* to do within specific geographical, cultural, and historical spaces. One exception is anthropologist James Denbow's discussion of dirt-eating in his article "Heart and Soul: Glimpses of Ideology and Cosmology in the Iconography of Tombstones from the Loango Coast of Central Africa," *Journal of American Folklore* 112, 445 (1999): 404–423, esp. 408.
40. AGNB, Negros y Esclavos, Bolivar, Tomo I, No. 1, f. 84v.
41. Ibid., f. 80v. Although Camargo clearly had the authority to have her slaves whipped, she followed the codes of moral propriety, similarly to the slave-owning widows from the U.S. South analyzed by Kirsten Wood, who "preferred to remain somewhat removed from discipline, the better to maintain the fiction of benevolent stewardship." Kirsten E. Wood, *Masterful Women: Slaveholding Widows from the American Revolution through the Civil War* (Chapel Hill: University of North Carolina Press, 2004), 51.
42. AGNB, Negros y Esclavos, Bolivar, Tomo I, No. 1, ff. 71v–73v.
43. Ibid., f. 87v.
44. Ibid., f. 78v.
45. Ibid., f. 85r.

46. Sharon Block, *Rape and Sexual Power in Early America* (Chapel Hill: University of North Carolina Press, 2006), 63–74, esp. 72.

47. AGNB, Negros y Esclavos, Bolivar, Tomo I, No. 1, f. 92v.

48. Ibid., f. 95v.

49. Ibid., f.69r.

50. Ibid., f. 83r.

51. Inez Criolla said that a few days before Camargo went to Cartagena, she had sent the stocks to doña Maria, wife of Lieut. Socastro, and the chain to her sister, doña Antonia de Camargo, but the shackles she wasn't sure of, for she hadn't seen them in several days (ibid., f. 79r); the bit her mistress used to keep them from eating dirt or crying out during beatings, she "understood that slaves of her said mistress had hidden it" (f. 80r).

52. Ibid., ff. 101r–103v. Testimony of Dominga Conga.

53. Inez Noble's collusion with doña Camargo may seem puzzling from a perspective on race, but this free woman likely had patronage ties to Camargo or her family. See Douglas Cope, *The Limits of Racial Domination: Plebeian Society in Colonial Mexico City, 1660–1720* (Madison: University of Wisconsin Press, 1994), on how cross-racial patronage in Latin America hindered the development of traditional forms of racial consciousness.

54. AGNB, Negros y Esclavos, Bolivar, Tomo I, No. 1, ff. 114r–116r. De Soto had Inez Noble put in jail and doña Andrea placed under house arrest and ordered a 50 peso fine if Ventura Camargo didn't hand over the hidden evidence.

55. Ibid., f. 120v.

56. Ibid., ff. 95r–96v.

57. Ibid., f. 49r.

3 / Law, Religion, Social Contract, and Slavery's Daily Negotiations

1. Quoted in Vila Vilar, *Hispanoamérica y el Comercio de Esclavos*, 5.

2. *Siete Partidas*, "Concerning Liberty," Book IV, Title XXII, 981.

3. Ibid., Part IV, Title XXI, Laws 1–2 (p. 977).

4. For summaries of the positions of Spanish theologians Tomás de Mercado (1569), Bartolomé Frias de Albornoz (1533), and Luis de Molina (1593), and even Bartolomé de las Casas's regret about the results of his recommendation to supplant fragile Indians with seemingly stronger African laborers, see A. J. R. Russell-Wood, "Iberian Expansion and the Issue of Black Slavery: Changing Portuguese Attitudes, 1440–1770," *AHR* 83, 1 (1978), 35–36.

5. Sandoval, 142, 147–48.

6. Sandoval, 143–144.

7. Sandoval described his discussion with a priest from Guinea whom he went to visit, "and in two shakes" the visiting cleric began to disparage the writings of Dr. Luis de Molina (one of the leading jurists on the issue), saying that Molina "had written a thousand falsehoods about the unjust wars of Guinea, the sovereignty of its Kings, and captivity of the Blacks . . . saying that in Guinea there was no free Black, because they were all slaves of the King," 148.

8. Sandoval, 149.

9. Maya Restrepo, *Brujería y reconstrucción*, 226–40, esp. 231.

10. *Siete Partidas*, Part IV, Tit. XXI, Law VI.

11. AGNB, Negros y Esclavos, Bolivar Tomo IX, No.1, f. 16r, 74v.

12. Diego de Horozco's petitions on behalf of Catalina Pimienta Pacheco: AGNB, Negros y Esclavos, Bolivar Tomo IX, No.1, ff. 18r–19r, 35v–38r, 60r–v; for Eufrasia de Camargo: AGNB, Negros y Esclavos, Bolivar, Tomo I, No. 1, ff. 129r–v. Horozco was probably a functionary of the Inquisition, as one "Diego de Orozco" was one of the men who accompanied penitents in the 1632 *auto de fe* (Splendiani, iii.37).

13. AGNB, Negros y Esclavos, Bolivar, Tomo I, No. 1, ff. 138v–139r. Petition, Diego de Horozco on behalf of Eufrasia Camargo, 13 Jul 1639.

14. Notwithstanding these more lenient laws, in 1640 the Viceroy of Peru warned his newly arrived successor that it was imperative to make slave owners comply with laws regarding humane treatment of slaves, "so that by the fortune of their laborious state of slavery they not succumb to desperation." Quoted in Vila Vilar, *Hispanoamérica y el Comercio de Esclavos*, 5.

15. AGNB, Negros y Esclavos, Bolivar, Tomo I, No. 1, Ibid., ff.139v, 141v.

16. AGNB, Negros y Esclavos, Bolivar Tomo IX, No.1, f. 6v.

17. AGNB, Negros y Esclavos, Bolivar, Tomo I, No. 1, f. 164r.

18. Ibid., f. 140v.

19. The issue of honor was vital in defining the veracity and acceptability of testimony in colonial courts. Witnesses supporting Camargo's testimony were asked by her lawyer to affirm that slaves would make up lies or exaggerate the truth to get away from masters who tried to "deter them from vice and stealing" (Questionnaire #10, f. 158v). Nor could the Spanish witnesses be credited: Camargo argued that Nicolas de Castrellon was "*mestizo* or *quateron* and drinks too much wine, so much that oftentimes he loses his senses." Miguel Navarro was considered without honor and credit because he "had been a base and low person who not long ago was walking around barefoot" (ff.140v–141v). Both men seem to have bettered their social class significantly in little time. Castrellon was working at the time in Cartagena as a scribe (*oficial de la pluma*), and in his testimony distanced himself from his carpenter uncle, Pedro de Vargas (who was identified as a *mestizo*, f. 162v). Navarro, also a *vecino* of Cartagena by the time of the investigation, was said by some to be a "very depraved person" who was buddies with Castrellon; others considered him to be little more than a working-class artisan whose word couldn't be trusted (f. 163r).

20. AGNB, Negros y Esclavos, Bolivar, Tomo I, No. 1, ff. 130r–135r. Confession of Eufrasia Camargo, 19 Jun 1639.

21. Juan Fernandez Romero agreed that Camargo's slaves must have allowed their "passions" to dictate their testimony, and claimed that blacks were "slow-witted, and lacked the capacity for reason" (ff. 174r–v.) Father Chavez described servants of African descent "as incapable people, given to vice and disinclined to virtue" (f. 164r).

22. Villa-Flores refers to its usage in New Spain ("To Lose One's Soul," 444); Cuevas Oviedo notes references to this law in blasphemy cases throughout the century ("Reniego y resistencia," 78–79, 83). Unfortunately, I was unable to ascertain the origin of this law (in Bayonne, France, a medieval slaving port?) or its formal legal stipulations.

23. AGNB, Negros y Esclavos, Bolivar, Tomo I, No. 1, f. 46r. My emphasis.

24. Splendiani, ii.300, 365–66; AHN, Lib. 1020, ff. 318v–319; 403v–404.

25. Several of the blasphemy cases contain references to slaves' preliminary efforts to plead "for the love of God" (or the saints or the Virgin) to desist in the act

of punishment. See cases of Domingo Canga (Splendiani, ii.300, ii.365–66); and Juan González (Splendiani, iii.324; AHN Lib. 1021, f. 329v).

26. 1654, Case against Juan Antonio (Splendiani, iii.407–8; AHN, Lib. 1021, ff. 407–7v).

27. Cuevas Oviedo notes the sacral quality of speech in many parts of Africa that retained their social memories in oral forms only ("Reniego y resistencia," 96–97). John Thornton has written about the cultural meaning of the curse in Kongolese culture, asserting that *kindoki* (the power to curse) could be used as a protective mechanism, and was not just a destructive utterance; see *The Kongolese Saint Anthony: Dona Beatriz Kimpa Vita and the Antonian Movement, 1684–1706* (Cambridge: Cambridge University Press, 1998), 42–43. In "Blasphemy and the Play of Anger," Maureen Flynn explains how early modern European jurists and inquisitors struggled with the presumption that "Every expression had a source that originated silently in rational thought. Curse-words, like memorized prayers, oaths and magical formulas, were therefore regarded as authentic revelations of the contents of the intellect, the core of the Christian soul" (36–37, 41).

28. Maureen Flynn, "Taming Anger's Daughters: New Treatment for Emotional Problems in Renaissance Spain," *Renaissance Quarterly* 51 (1998), 871.

29. Splendiani iii.184–86; AHN Lib. 1021, ff. 162v–65.

30. Splendiani, iii.184–86; AHN, Lib. 1021, ff. 162v–65. This deviation from standard procedure suggests that personal animosities could have been at work between the notary Nieto and one of his fellow agents employed in Cartagena's Tribunal.

31. Splendiani, iii.407–8; AHN Lib. 1021, ff. 407–7v.

32. AGNB, Negros y Esclavos, Bolivar Tomo IX, No.1, 17r.

33. Cuevas Oviedo, "Reniego y resistencia," 92.

34. AHN, Inq. Lib. 1009, 28 junio 1619, Los Inquisidores al Consejo. ff. 31r–v. Villa-Flores describes how in 1502 the Spanish monarchs attempted to give masters on the peninsula the authority to punish blasphemous slaves themselves, arguing that when they were prosecuted by the Inquisition, their owners were obliged to pay for their food and other support while in prison. "Defending God's Honor," 213.

35. Splendiani, iii.407–8; AHN Lib. 1021, ff. 407–7v; AHN, Lib. 1020, f. 286–86v.

36. Cuevas Oviedo, "Reniegos y Resistencia," 149–50.

37. Cuevas Oviedo's systematic examination of these blasphemy cases in Cartagena's Tribunal reveals that by the 1680s and '90s, such sins were rarely prosecuted by the Tribunal; Villa-Flores presents similar findings in his study of Mexican blasphemy trials ("Defending God's Honor," 239). The change in prosecution may have some connection to the coronation of Philip V in 1686, which marked a new political atmosphere that affected a range of hierarchical relations in the colonies. In studies of marriage and sexuality in the Spanish Americas, historians Asunción Lavrin and Patricia Seed have also observed that the 1680s seem to be a pivotal turning point in the Church's reluctance to side with minors and wards against patricians and parents. See Asunción Lavrin, ed., *Sexuality and Marriage in Colonial Latin America* (Lincoln: University of Nebraska Press, 1989); Patricia Seed, *To Love, Honor, and Obey in Colonial Mexico: Conflicts over Marriage Choice, 1574–1821* (Stanford, CA: Stanford University Press, 1988).

38. AGNB, Negros y Esclavos, Bolivar Tomo IX, No.1, 14v.

39. Jean-Pierre Tardieu describes one extraordinary visit from a West African emissary to Cartagena in "La embajada africana de Arda en Cartagena de Indias (1657)

y la misión de los Capuchinos (1658–1661)," *América Negra* 10 (Dec. 1995), although agreements for redeeming captives does not seem to have been on the agenda. James Sweet likewise revealed one complex manumission in nineteenth-century Rio de Janeiro in which an enslaved woman was redeemed by her relatives in Angola via a complex chain of business associates that had learned of her whereabouts following her disappearance from Africa. "Manumission in Rio de Janeiro, 1749–54: An African Perspective," *Slavery & Abolition* 24, 1 (2003): 54–55.

40. AGNB, Negros y Esclavos, Bolivar Tomo IX, No.1, f. 107r.

41. Bennett, *Africans in Colonial Mexico*, 193.

42. Natalie Zemon Davis, *Fiction in the Archives: Pardon tales and their tellers in sixteenth-century France* (Stanford, CA: Stanford University Press, 1987).

43. AGNB, Negros y Esclavos, Bolivar, Tomo I, No. 1, ff. 220–21. Sentencia del teniente general don Melchor de Aguilera licenciado y don Fernando de Verrio.

44. Ibid., f. 234r. Sentencia del Real Audiencia, 30 Jan 1640. The Real Audiencia deferred responsibility for monitoring Camargo's future comportment to the justices of the town of Mompox.

45. AGNB, Negros y Esclavos, Bolivar, Tomo I, No. 1, f. 156r–v.

46. I use the word *quackery* here to show that although *curanderismo* encompassed a wide range of healing arts, it was looked on with disdain and derogation by Spanish Church officials who considered it yet another form of witchcraft or pagan superstition. Maya Restrepo continues: "The resistance of the *palenques* appears without a doubt as an indicator of the failure of evangelization. . . . The manual for evangelization produced by Sandoval, employed to normalize Africans and their children through a process of *ladinización*—that would result, above all, in the imposition of political control over these people—did not work. His whole life's efforts were unable to tear from the captives' souls their desire to be free men again . . . " (*Brujería y reconstrucción de identidades*, 497).

47. AGI, Santa Fe 42, R.5, No. 98/8. 2 Jul 1655.

4 / Northern European Protestants in the Spanish Caribbean

1. Archivo Histórico Nacional, Madrid, Sección Inquisición, Legajo 1621, Expediente 3, ff. 49r–57r; 92r–v. (hereafter AHN, Inq. 1621, Exp. 3). Portions of this chapter were presented at Harvard University's History of the Atlantic World Seminar, "The Transit of Christianity" (August 2006).

2. Almost nothing has been published about the treatment of Protestants by the American Tribunals of the Inquisition, especially for Cartagena's Tribunal, established after the sixteenth-century persecution of the most famous English and French Protestant "pirates." The corpus of relevant works includes: Frank Aydelotte, "Elizabethan Seamen in Mexico and Ports of the Spanish Main," *AHR* 48 (October 1942): 1–19; Ronald J. Morgan, *Spanish American Saints and the Rhetoric of Identity, 1660–1810* (Tuscon: University of Arizona Press, 2002), esp. Ch. 2, "Heretics by Sea, Pagans by Land: St. Rosa de Lima and the Limits of Criollismo in Colonial Peru"; Fermina Álvarez Alonso, "Herejes ante la Inquisición de Cartagena de Indias," *Revista de la Inquisición* 6 (1997): 239–59; Anna María Splendiani, "Los Protestantes y la Inquisición," *Anuario Colombiano de Historia Social y de la Cultura* 23 (1996): 5–31; Manuel Tejado Fernández, "Procedimiento seguido por la Inquisición Americana con los herejes extranjeros," *Revista de Indias* 26 (1946): 827–39; and Jaime Humberto Borja Gómez,

Rostros y rastros del demonio en la Nueva Granada (Bogotá: Editorial Ariel, 1998), 262–67.

3. "Carta del Obispo de Puerto Rico" (1606), in José Toribio Medina, *La Inquisición en Cartagena de Indias* (Bogotá: C. Valencia, 1978), 222.

4. Imperial historians have long expounded on some of the favorite tactics of contrabandists allying with Spanish colonists. One of the most commonly employed by foreign interlopers was to feign that the ship had run low on supplies or was in need of repairs and sought refuge; while the ship was in dock and the goods stored safely in a warehouse, the governor and other high-ranking officials would help facilitate illegal deals off the books. See C. H. Haring, *The Buccaneers in the West Indies in the 17th century* (New York: E. P. Dutton and Company, 1910), 26–27; also Kris Lane, *Pillaging the Empire: Piracy in the Americas, 1500–1750* (New York: M.E. Sharpe, 1998), 35, 65–67. Recent scholarship on Dutch commerce has revealed the preponderance of trade between Dutch merchant ships and Spanish colonists, classed by the Spanish empire as contraband, but normal trade for the Dutch, who kept assiduous records. See Wim Klooster, *Illicit Riches: Dutch Trade in the Caribbean, 1648–1795* (Leiden: KITLV Press, 1998); and Linda M. Rupert, "Contraband Trade and the Shaping of Colonial Societies in Curaçao and Tierra Firme," *Itinerario* 30, 3 (2006): 35–54.

5. According to occupations given in Inquisition proceedings, only two foreigners seen by Cartagena's inquisitors were identified as gentlemen (*hidalgos*). Similarly, nearly every foreigner I have come across in testimonies and casual references in AGI documents occupies similarly humble positions.

6. Tamar Herzog's work has show in detail the multudinous methods of obtaining citizenship and a sense of belonging in the community in Spanish and American territories of the seventeenth- and eighteenth-century Hapsburg empire. Her writings show that in the case of foreigners from countries outside of Hapsburg control, Catholicism served as an obligatory condition for membership, and that the Hapsburg Crown often sheltered—and in many cases naturalized—persecuted Catholics from England, Ireland, and the Netherlands. The rules for naturalization were by no means set in stone and varied widely from group to group, place to place, and time period to time period. By the end of the early modern period, Herzog argues, religion was only one aspect of belonging—a broader definition of "social integration" had become key for whether foreigners would be accepted into the community. See *Defining Nations: Immigrants and Citizens in Early Modern Spain and Spanish America* (New Haven, CT: Yale University Press, 2003), especially 119–45. Hapsburg officials also recruited foreign Catholic sailors to man their transatlantic fleet, and "religious loyalty was accepted as a partial substitute for national identity when ships were short-handed." Carla Rahn Phillips, "The Organization of Oceanic Empires: The Iberian World in the Hapsburg Period (and a Bit Beyond)," paper presented at *Seascapes, Littoral Cultures, and Trans-Oceanic Exchanges*, Library of Congress, Washington D.C., February 12–15, 2003. http://www.historycooperative.org/proceedings/seascapes/phillips.html (9 Jul. 2007), para. 12.

7. Much of the literature on early modern religious toleration, like Henry Kamen's *The Rise of Toleration* (New York: McGraw Hill, 1967), has approached the question from an intellectual history standpoint. However, a few recent studies take a more socially holistic approach. Stuart B. Schwartz's *All Can Be Saved: Religious Tolerance and Salvation in the Iberian Atlantic World* (New Haven, CT: Yale University Press,

2008) has examined a broad range of Inquisition sources to explore religious toleration among common people, whose ideas of religious pluralism far outpaced that of theologians. For other social and economic comments on the rise of toleration, see William Monter, *Frontiers of Heresy: The Spanish Inquisition from the Basque Lands to Sicily* (Cambridge: Cambridge University Press, 1990), 246–52; and Alexandra Walsham, *Charitable Hatred: Tolerance and Intolerance in England 1500–1700* (Manchester: Manchester University Press, 2006).

8. AHN, Inq. 1621, Exp. 3, ff. 49r–57v.

9. Fernand Braudel's *The Mediterranean and the Mediterranean World in the Age of Philip II* (1949; 1972 English ed.) is the foundation for early modern Europeanists' conception of the Mediterranean, *the* archetypical "Sea of the Old World." Caribbeanists have frequently noted geographic, historical, and cultural correlations to the Mediterranean. See Germán Arcienegas, *Caribbean: Sea of the New World* (New York: Knopf, 1946); and Gordon K. Lewis, *Main Currents in Caribbean Thought: The Historical Evolution of Caribbean Society in its Ideological Aspects, 1492–1900* (Baltimore: Johns Hopkins University Press, 1983), 16–20.

10. Ira Berlin, "From Creole to African," 254n. Berlin's generic description of Atlantic creoles strikes a chord in harmony with the cases I present here: " . . . some Atlantic creoles identified with their ancestral homeland (or a portion of it)—be it African, European, or American—and served as its representatives in negotiations with others. Other Atlantic creoles had been won over by the power and largess of one party or another. . . . Yet others played fast and loose with their diverse heritage, employing whichever identity paid best" (255).

11. AHN, Inq. 1621, Exp. 3, f. 110r–v.

12. Ibid., f. 114v.

13. Ibid., f. 120r.

14. Ibid., f. 118r–v.

15. See Jorge Cañizares-Esguerra, *Puritan Conquistadors: Iberianizing the Atlantic, 1550–1700* (Stanford, CA: Stanford University Press, 2006); Nathan Johnstone, *The Devil and Demonism in Early Modern England* (New York: Cambridge University Press, 2006); and Andrew W. Keitt, *Inventing the Sacred: Imposture, Inquisition, and the Boundaries of the Supernatural in Golden Age Spain* (Boston: Brill, 2005).

16. Over the last 20 years or so, Early Modern Europeanists have battled over terminology concerning the flourishing of a distinct form of Catholicism in the post-Tridentine period. Some stick with "Counter-Reformation"; others prefer "Catholic Reformation" or "Catholic Renewal"; a rather neutral "Early Modern Catholicism" has also been proposed. See, for example, Hsia, *The World of Catholic Renewal*, 3–7; O'Malley, *Trent and All That*, 1–15. In this study, I would like to emphasize both the sense of popular piety that comes with the phrase *Catholic Renewal*, and the antagonisms of the term *Counter-Reformation*, which has so much purchase when describing Spanish relationships with foreigners suspected of Protestantism, especially since heresy was so often linked to foreigners in Inquisition Tribunals on the frontiers of Spanish Hapsburg territories, in cities like Logroño, Zaragosa, and Barcelona; see Helen Rawlings, *Church, Religion and Society in Early Modern Spain* (New York: Palgrave, 2002), 37.

17. AHN, Inq. 1621, Exp. 3, ff. 2v–3v.

18. Ibid., ff. 4v–5v. (*le obligo a darle de coçes y deriuarlo en el suelo*).

NOTES TO CHAPTER 4 / 253

19. Ibid., ff. 5v–6r.

20. Ibid., ff. 17v–18r.

21. Ibid., ff. 17v–18r.

22. AHN, Inq. 1617, Exp. 1/7. Causa criminal contra el Abad de Jamaica, don Mateo de Medina Moreno, sobre haber reconciliado y baptizado a muchos herejes de diferentes naciones.

23. Ibid., f. 6v.

24. AHN, Inq. 1617, Exp.1/7, f. 3v–5r. One key of Tridentine reforms was preserving the integrity of the Church's seven sacraments—receiving baptism more than once in one's life was deemed blasphemous for the inference that this transformative ritual could be taken lightly. The designation *sub conditione* was used in cases where one's previous baptismal history was in question.

25. Ibid., f. 5v.

26. Ibid., f. 7v.

27. Ibid., f. 4v.

28. Ibid., ff. 9r, 15v.

29. AHN, Inq. Lib. 1021, f. 275r; in Anna María Splendiani, *Cincuenta Años de Inquisición en el Tribunal de Cartagena de Indias, 1610–1660* (hereafter Splendiani), Vol. 3 (Bogotá: Centro Editorial Javeriano, 1997), 285.

30. Ibid., f. 277r; Splendiani iii.286.

31. Ibid., f. 277v; Splendiani iii.287.

32. AHN, Inq. 1621, Exp. 3, f. 55v. In the colonial context, *bozal* was most often used to describe newly arrived African slaves who were unacculturated and could not communicate in Castilian or any other European creole language; the term also carried with it a sense of brutishness. Only in this one instance have I seen the use of the term *bozal* to describe a European, and thus have used the Greek-derived word *barbarian* in my translation, a term that is tied to language acquisition but connotes a more general sense of inferiority and otherness.

33. Ibid., ff. 119r–120v.

34. See Jenny Shaw and Kristen Block, "Subjects Without an Empire: The Irish in a Changing Caribbean," *Past & Present* 210 (Feb. 2011): 34–60.

35. AHN, Inq. Lib. 1021, f. 276r; Splendiani iii.286.

36. AHN, Inq. 1617, Exp. 1/7, f. 20v. *Ladino* was a term used to describe someone, usually an Indian or African, who had learned to speak Castilian and was acculturated to Spanish social and cultural norms. It was not uncommon to describe European migrants who had learned to speak Spanish as *ladino*. Some of these individuals will appear in the following section, returning to the English when they invaded Jamaica in 1655.

37. Ibid., f. 14v.

38. Ibid., f. 27r. Father Antón de Castillo, another priest who had been compelled to baptize one of the foreigners in Jamaica, testified that he had complained to the abbot that reconciling heretics was going beyond their authority—only the Holy Office, he said, could reconcile heretics—they should at least consult with a theologian on the issue. The abbot had replied that the Holy Tribunal need be involved only in cases concerning "rebel heretics, but not with those who came of their own free will to the Church to request Baptism" (f. 23r–v). But the 90-year-old abbot, it was said, could barely read Latin, and he likely had few theologically trained priests to consult about

the matter. In 1644, one source reported a severe dearth of regular clergy in Jamaica; only four Dominican monks and three Franciscans were currently in residence on the island. Frank Cundall and Joseph L. Pietersz, *Jamaica under the Spaniards* (Kingston, Jamaica: Institute of Jamaica, 1919), 41.

39. AHN, Inq. 1621, Exp. 3, f. 117r.

40. Ibid., ff. 119v–121r, ff. 150v–159v, ff. 143r–158r.

41. Ibid., f. 156.

42. Ibid., ff. 143r–48r.

43. Ibid., f. 188v.

44. After the first three extravagant *autos de fe*, which had been mounted as huge outdoor spectacles, the rituals shrank in size—reconciled penitents often abjured their sins in the city's cathedral, or even at private ceremonies in the Inquisition audience chamber.

45. AHN, Inq. 1020, f. 262; Splendiani, ii.250. The process began with a formal presentation of Cartagena's chief constable (*alguacil mayor*) before the governor's council to obtain the support of the secular officials—the governor, the city fathers, and other royal judges visiting the city. Couriers carried news of the impending event to Inquisition *comisarios* in all reaches of the Tribunal's jurisdiction, which included New Granada (Popayán, Santa Marta, Cartagena, and its nearby cities) and the archbishopric of Santo Domingo (Cuba, Venezuela, Jamaica, Panama, and Portobello).

46. AHN, Inq. Lib. 1020, ff. 204–8. In this *auto de fe*, English spice merchant Adán Edón (Adam Aiden?) was turned over to authorities after resisting inquisitors' attempts to convince him of his heresy. Edón had allegedly caused great scandal in the island of Cumaná (to which he had sailed without a license, relying on Sevillan merchants to grease the wheels for his passage), as Spaniards there accused him of refusing to take part in church activities or show proper respect for public church displays.

47. AHN, Inq. Lib. 1621, Exp. 3, ff. 141v–142r.

5 / Empire, Bureaucracy, and Escaping the Spanish Inquisition

1. AHN, Inq. Lib. 1621, Exp. 3, ff. 162v–169r.

2. Ibid., f. 170r–v.

3. AHN, Inq. 1621, Exp. 3, ff. 176r–177v.

4. AHN, Inq. Lib. 1021, ff. 348–49v; Splendiani iii.344–46.

5. Ibid., ff. 367–68v; Splendiani iii.369–72.

6. AHN, Inq. 1621, Exp. 3, f. 178v.

7. Ibid., f. 199r.

8. Ibid., f. 199v.

9. Nicolas was actually partially correct, for he and don Jacinto Sedeño were both arrested by Inquisition officials investigating Governor Caballero's murder (since he was an employee of the Holy Tribunal and thus crimes against him were tried in that court). Of course, the heresy charge was separate and more interesting to inquisitors. Ibid., ff. 178r–179r; AHN, Inq. 1621, Exp. 3, ff. 179v–180r.

10. Ibid., f. 185v.

11. The 1576 Alba-Cobham agreement, in which English sailors were theoretically protected from prosecution for religious crimes committed outside Spanish territories, served as precedent for these postwar guarantees. See the seventeenth-century diplomatic timeline from Henry Kamen, *The Spanish Inquisition: A Historical*

Revision (New Haven, CT: Yale University Press, 1997), 277-78; Francisco Fajardo Spínola, *Las Conversiones de Protestantes en Canarias: Siglos XVII y XVIII* (Las Palmas de Gran Canaria: Ediciones del Cabildo Insular de Gran Canaria, 1996), 14-19, 100-1; Alexis D. Brito González, *Los Extranjeros en las Canarias Orientales en el siglo XVII* (Las Palmas de Gran Canaria: Ediciones del Cabildo de Gran Canaria, 2002), 348-60; Paulino Castañeda Delgado and Pilar Hernández Aparicio, *La Inquisición de Lima*, Vol. I (Madrid: Deimos, 1989), 465-73; Pauline Croft, "Englishmen and the Spanish Inquisition, 1558-1625," *English Historical Review* 87, 343 (1972): 249-68: 257. However, the movement was uneven and unsteady—French Huguenots, who were disproportionately prevalent in the Tribunals in northern Spain, had never been protected by any commercial treaty, despite their attempts to gain protection under Phillip II at the 1559 Treaty of Catau-Cambresis. Fajardo Spínola, *Víctimas del Santo Oficio: Tres siglos de actividad de la Inquisición de Canarias* (Las Palmas de Gran Canaria: Universidad Nacional de Educación a Distancia, 2003), 140; Bartolomé Bennassar, "Un Dialogue Difficile: Les Inquisiteurs et les Marins Protestants de L'Europe du Nord," *Histoire, Économie et Société* 12, 2 (1993): 167-75, esp. 169; Monter, *Frontiers of Heresy*, 246.

12. A fair copy of these instructions was re-sent to the Cartagena Tribunal in 1659, along with their response to questions about the conversion of a prisoner Juan L'Grafe (see p. 88, above). AHN, Inq. 1621, Exp. 4, ff. 15r-17r. "Estylo que se obserua con los hereges nacionales espontaneos, por lo que toca a Juan Graue, olandes."

13. To understand the dramatic seventeenth-century decline in action taken against foreign Protestants, see these figures: in Lima, prosecutions were down from 40 in only 25 years of the 1500s, to 8 for the entire 17th century (Paulino Castañeda Delgada et.al., *La Inquisición de Lima* (Madrid: Editorial Deimos, 1989-1988), i.456, 462; ii.500); in the Canaries the number of cases declined from 74 (1585-1600) to only 20 (1601-1621). Moreover, only two Protestants faced the horrors of burning at the stake post-1604 in Las Palmas—the dates were early, 1614 and 1615, and both were recidivists (Brito González, *Extranjeros en las Canarias Orientales*, 349). Not even one Protestant would be "relaxed" in Lima, and in Mexico the prosecution of "Lutheran" corsairs nearly died out after 1600. See also Henry Charles Lea, *The Inquisition in the Spanish Dependencies* (New York: Macmillan, 1908).

14. AHN Lib. 1020, ff. 204-8v; Splendiani, ii. 208-11.

15. By the mid-sixteenth century, according to the most eminent scholar of the Canaries, "The Atlantic had experienced growing importance, as a setting in which was resolved the confrontation between the European superpowers; [the *Suprema*] supplied the Tribunal of the Canary Islands with a new, and in the long run, more important mission. . . . The Tribunal of Las Palmas was reorganized in 1658, no longer dependent on Seville, precisely so it could keep watch, with greater resources, over the activities of foreigners resident in the Archiepelago and those that frequented its waters." In contra-point to strengthened inquisitorial powers, local nobles and powerful families took it upon themselves to protect foreign partners before the Holy Tribunal (Fajardo Spínola, *Víctimas*, 125-27).

16. Fajardo Spínola, *Conversiones*, 24, 30. In Malta, 95 voluntary conversions were registered for the eighteenth century—in both Malta and the Canaries, the majority of foreigners were British subjects (Frans Ciappara, *Society and the Inquisition in Early Modern Malta* (San Gwann, Malta: Publishers Enterprises Group, Ltd., 2000), 189;

Fajardo Spínola, *Conversiones*, 30–31), but in other locales German and Dutch Protestants dominated Tribunal registers. In cities like Madrid or the Aragonese borderlands, the mercantile communities were more heavily German or French. For Madrid, see Juan Blázquez Miguel, *Madrid: Judios, Herejes y Brujas: El Tribunal de Corte (1650–1820)* (Toledo, Spain: Editorial Arcano, 1990); for the Tribunals bordering France, see Monter, *Frontiers of Heresy*. More than one hundred English wine merchants were in residence in the Spanish Canaries (Tenerife, Gran Canaria, or Lanzarote) during seventeenth-century peacetime, and the Inquisition Tribunal in Las Palmas attested that in 1654, "more than one thousand five hundred English and Dutch Protestants" lived in Tenerife (Brito González, *Extranjeros en las Canarias Orientales*, 64–70, 358).

17. Two of Arsell's comrades, Esteban Brun and Tomas de Sutin, could have also taken the initiative, for they had lived in other Iberian Catholic ports.

18. AHN Lib. 1020, ff. 175–83v; Splendiani ii.191–97. Another group of Flemish pirates captured that same year followed the same formulas, but were not spared secular justice (AHN Lib. 1020, ff. 196v–97r; Splendiani ii.206–7).

19. The phrase comes directly from the inquisitor's manual for voluntary conversions, "Cartilla para procesar del Santo Oficio de la Inquisición de Cartagena," reprinted in Jaime Humberto Borja Gómez, ed., *Inquisición, muerte y sexualidad*, 287.

20. AHN, Lib. 1021, ff. 83r–v; Splendiani iii.119–20.

21. AHN, Inq. Lib. 1021, ff. 253v–54v; Splendiani iii.258–59. The danger that foreign Protestants posed to the local population was especially keen, thought the inquisitors, since "these lands are so new and contain such diversity of *castas*, the main part of them very new [Christians]."

22. AHN, Inq. Lib. 1021, f. 397v; Splendiani iii.385–87. The Tribunal's decision may have had as much to do with the burden of supporting the accused's alimentary needs as anything else.

23. Like Nicolas Burundel, Juan L'Grave was often described not as Flemish or French, but as Dutch, and scribes wrote his last name (Gravet or Grave) with equal variance.

24. AHN, Inq. 1621, Exp. 4, f. 16r.

25. And, if we remember, the French did not have the same sorts of official protections for their Protestant subjects in Spanish Catholic lands as other Northern European powers had secured (Monter, *Frontiers of Heresy*, 246).

26. See Irene Silverblatt's study of the incredible reach of the Inquisition's terrorizing bureaucracy, *Modern Inquisitions: Peru and the Colonial Origins of the Civilized World* (Durham, NC: Duke University Press, 2004).

27. AHN, Inq. 1621, Exp. 3, ff. 175–76.

28. See Lisa Silverman, *Tortured Subjects: Pain, Truth, and the Body in Early Modern France* (University of Chicago Press, 2001); John H. Langbein, *Torture and the Law of Proof: Europe and England in the Ancien Régime* (Chicago: University of Chicago Press, 1977).

29. AHN, Inq. 1621, Exp. 3, ff. 182v–83r.

6 / Conversion, Coercion, and Tolerance in Old and New Worlds

1. Ibid., ff. 197v–198r, 202v, 205v.

2. Common among tales of forced conversions among the "Moors" or "Turks" were descriptions of cruel beatings, especially to the soles of the feet; boys were "converted"

in this fashion, and circumcised as proof of their new role as willing slaves. Bartolomé and Lucile Bennassar, *Los Cristianos de Alá: La fascinante aventura de los renegados*, trans. José Luis Gil Aristu (Madrid: Editorial Nerea, 1989), 194–95. Burundel probably missed the official prohibitions against forced conversion enacted when France signed treaties in 1628 and 1689 with Algiers; such treaties mandated that French authorities be allowed access to those in danger of becoming "voluntary" renegades. See Gillian Weiss, "Commerce, Conversion and French Religious Identity in the Early Modern Mediterranean," in Keith Cameron et al., eds., *The Adventure of Religious Pluralism in Early Modern France* (Oxford: Peter Lang, 2000), 276n. Unfortunately, inquisitors never examined Burundel to see if he had been circumcised (forcibly or not), a giveaway of apostasy, and neglected to follow up with more questions regarding his activities in Algiers. However, there are hints in his case that he may have been influenced by cultural practices common for North African captives (and those in the maritime world). In mid-June, Nicolas had asked for an audience, and confessed to having had sexual relations with three boys in Martinique, and anal sex with his wife on their wedding night (ff. 117v–118r).

3. Robert C. Davis, *Christian Slaves, Muslim Masters: White Slavery in the Mediterranean, the Barbary Coast, and Italy, 1500–1800* (New York: Palgrave Macmillan, 2003), 23, 15. Linda Colley estimates that about 18,000 English subjects were captured and held in North Africa from 1600 to 1730; see *Captives* (New York: Pantheon Books, 2002), 43–44. Gillian Weiss asserts that "tens of thousands" of Frenchmen suffered Barbary captivity ("Commerce, Conversion and French Religious Identity," 276), citing the difficulty of coming to any precision for the number of captives for the period, as French redemptive orders claimed anywhere from 90,000 to 900,000 captives rescued from captivity from the Middle Ages to 1785. Ellen G. Friedman's *Spanish Captives in North Africa in the Early Modern Age* (Madison: University of Wisconsin Press, 1983) explores records relating to 9,500 captives rescued by Spanish redemptionist orders from 1575 to 1759, a small fraction of those taken for the same period (p. 3). On the other side of the war for captives, at the height of Louis XIV's power, two thousand Ottoman subjects were said to serve the French king as royal galley slaves (Gillian Weiss, "Barbary Captivity and the French Idea of Freedom," *French Historical Studies* 28, 2 (2005): 233); approximately 10,000 Muslims filled Malta's slave markets in 1720 (Colley, *Captives*, 45). Recently, Nabil Matar has argued that the slaving/captivity tally was actually quite balanced between European and North African powers, asserting that among the reasons for scholars' skewed perceptions include their reliance on European-language sources. Such evidence reveals that many Europeans were able to return from captivity; deeper archival work proves, he claims, that North African Muslims were more likely to be condemned to *de facto* lifetime slavery. See especially Ch. 4, "Moors in British Captivity," in *Britain and Barbary, 1589–1689* (Gainesville: University Press of Florida, 2005).

4. The most famous expansion of the Berber corsair threat in the North Atlantic was the 1627 raid on Iceland, but travel on routes between Lisbon and Madeira or near outposts like the Azores and the Canaries was also extremely dangerous. Lucile and Bartolomé Bennassar's calculations confirm that one-quarter of returning captives from the seventeenth century had been taken in the North or Central Atlantic; nearly 30 percent more were taken in the region of the Strait of Gibraltar (Bennassar and Bennassar, *Cristianos*, 193, 202, 234–37).

5. Lucile and Bartolomé Bennassar's look at the "Fascinating Adventure of the Renegades" (*Christianos de Alá*) is an extremely detailed examination of 1,550 cases of returning apostates (which they considered barely half a percentage of converts to Islam for the period 1550–1700), and the ways that Mediterranean Inquisition Tribunals—from Sicily, Sardinia, Majorca, the Canaries, Seville, Granada, Murcia, Barcelona, and Lisbon—absolved or punished these dangerous border-crossers. A sampling of important early modern dramas that brought Barbary captivity to urbanites includes Miguel de Cervantes's *El trato de Argel* (1580) and *Los baños de Argel* (1615), both based on his own experience. English playwrights borrowed freely from these Spanish examples. Phillip Massinger's *The Renegado* (1624) is said to have been based on Cervantes's *Baños*. Nabil Matar writes of the success of *The Renegado* on the London stage through the Restoration ("The Renegade in Seventeenth-Century Imagination," *Studies in English Literature* 33, 3 (1993): 459–78). In these plays, European renegades either die horrible deaths or make a happy return to their Christian roots. However, the ease with which slaves, merchants, pirates, and even Muslim masters trade one religion for another proffers another vision of Mediterranean identity games and the ease of self-fashioning. For the impact of the real on the fictional, see Roslyn L. Knuston, "Elizabethan Documents, Captivity Narratives, and the Market for Foreign History Plays," *English Literary Renaissance* 26 (1996): 75–110.

6. Robert Appelbaum and John Wood Sweet, eds., *Envisioning an English Empire: Jamestown and the Making of the North Atlantic World* (Philadelphia: University of Pennsylvania Press, 2005), has also taken serious consideration of how English relations with Ottoman and North African powers affected their Atlantic and American experiences. My views on the subject have been formed by readings of Braudel's *Mediterranean and the Mediterranean World*, and Arciniegas's *Caribbean, Sea of the New World*, as well as numerous archival comparisons.

7. Bennessar concludes that "in the case of voluntary return and 'spontaneous' presentation, the proceedings were simple: the Tribunal simply went through the motions of the three mandated *audiencias*, but rarely went to the trouble of investigating the witnesses . . ." (*Christianos de Alá*, 22). See also Ch. 3 in Fajardo Spínola's *Víctimas*, "De Canaria a Berbería se va y se viene en un día," and Brito González, *Extranjeros en las Canarias Orientales*, 358.

8. Defendants whose cases were out of the ordinary or who denied witnesses' claims against them could languish in prison for months while inquisitors sent questionnaires to cross-examine witnesses in other Caribbean territories or waited for the annual fleet to transport correspondence between the local Tribunal and the Suprema in Madrid. Braudel was certainly right to emphasize the communications lag stemming from lengthy travel times in the Mediterranean—the same principles, and an even more protracted time schedule, also applied for the Caribbean. Braudel, *The Mediterranean and the Mediterranean World*, especially "Distance: The First Enemy," Vol. I, 355–78; Bennassar, *Christianos de Alá*, 22.

9. AHN, Inq. 1621, Exp. 4, ff. 13v–17r.

10. In Cervantes's *Los Baños de Argel* [*The Dungeons of Algiers*] (1612), one renegade corsair who had taken the name Hassan [Hazén] asks Christian captives to help him return to the faith of his fathers: "I wish to return to Spain / to whom I should confess / my youthful ancient error . . ." (*A España quiero tornar, / y a quien debo confesar / mi mozo y antiguo yerro . . .*). Hassan continues with various reasons he should

be forgiven, in the end swaying them with his story of youthful weakness: "how, as a boy, I was pressured / to become Turk . . . but I am / a good Christian in my secret self" (*cómo niño, fui oprimido / a ser turco . . . pero soy / buen cristiano en lo escondido*).

11. AHN, Inq. Lib. 1020, ff. 104-5v; Splendiani ii.134-36. Mozón was likely one of those I call "pseudo-spontaneous," for he only went to the Tribunal after he found out that someone in their group had told inquisitors who among their party had been serving Marañón's French Huguenot governor.

12. AHN Inq. Lib. 1020, ff. 117v-19v; Splendiani ii.147-49.

13. AHN Inq. Lib. 1020, ff. 106-7v; Splendiani, ii.136-37.

14. For the "invention" of early modern identity, see Miram Eliav-Feldon, "Invented Identities"; for reasons of religion, Neil Kamil, *Fortress of the Soul* (Baltimore: Johns Hopkins University Press, 2005), and Perez Zagorin, *Ways of Lying: Dissimulation, Persecution, and Conformity in Early Modern Europe* (Cambridge, MA: Harvard University Press, 1990); most recently, Natalie Zemon Davis analyzes in great detail the forms of self-creation and presentation across the Christian-Muslim divide in *Trickster Travels: A Sixteenth-century Muslim Between Worlds* (New York: Hill & Wang, 2006). Stories of Europeans "turning Turk" emphasized that the conversion was more for expediency than for any desire for interior change. One Spanish tract described an Englishman living in Algiers who had "renounced [Christianity], and from a heretic became a Mahommetan . . . dressed in the habit of a Moor, and was always treated as such." But when this *renegado* was caught drinking during Ramadan with his English friends, and was sentenced to death under Koranic law, he was able to commute his death sentence to a severe flogging after proving that he had only converted outwardly (*de hábito*) and had not been circumcised nor followed the Koran. See notes 20–22 for more details on the *Relación sumaria* in which this story appears (f. 7r).

15. AHN Inq. Lib. 1020, ff. 117v-19v; Splendiani ii.147-49.

16. Sharon Kettering, *Patrons, Brokers, and Clients in Seventeenth-Century France* (New York: Oxford University Press, 1986). Contrast these successful approaches with that of Juan Patier, who, rather imprudently, did not come forward to explain his residence among the French Huguenot contingent in Marañón. The Inquisition had time to gather ammunition against Patier, receiving sworn statements by several French Catholics in his party, and sent him to the torture chamber when he denied the charges. It was only after remaining firm in his innocence through the "proof" of phsical distress that inquisitors suspended the case (AHN, Inq. Lib. 1020, ff. 140–46; Splendiani ii.164–69).

17. AHN, Inq. Lib. 1020, f. 105v, Splendiani, ii.136.

18. Only three individuals from Ottoman-controlled territories appear in Cartagena's Inquisition *relaciones*, and only one a galley slave. It was Alonso de Molina, also known as Toledo, who confessed "spontaneously" to inquisitors in June 1628. Born of a *morsico* family which had been expelled from Spain when Molina was just a child, in Tunis Alonso learned the tenets of Islam from his mother, who "counseled him as to what was most fitting for him," converting himself into Ali. Ali/Alonso approached Cartagena's Tribunal of the Inquisition in 1628 to say that although he had held fast to Islam for more than 17 years, over the past three months he had determined to become a Christian again. He was the only Muslim "*espontaneo*" that the Tribunal dealt with before 1660. Inquisitors sentenced Molina to wear a sambenito marking his crimes during an *auto de fe* in the city's cathedral, and afterwards to present himself every day for six months to the city's Jesuit Colegio, "to

be better instructed in the things of our holy faith and to uproot the errors" of his Muslim identity (AHN, Inq. Lib. 1021, ff. 301r–v; Splendiani ii.287–88).

19. AHN, Inq. 1621, Exp. 3, ff. 194v–195r, 204v.

20. I requested this title while visiting the Biblioteca Nacional in Bogotá primarily because of a cataloguing error. Juan de Armenta's *Relación sumaria, de la insigne conversiõ de treynta y seys cossarios, Ingleses de nacion, y de profession hereges, y de la justicia que se hizo de algunos dellos en el Puerto de Santa Maria* (Cadiz, 1616) was listed in the Library's catalogue as relating to the Port of Santa *Marta*, an important colonial port near Cartagena infamous for its contraband trade (another reminder of how closely events in the Mediterranean mirrored Caribbean stories). This title was bound in with other manuscripts and print tracts relating to Jesuit missions around the world; the manuscript volume comprised part of the first collections that formed the Kingdom of New Granada's Royal Library, founded in Bogotá in 1777. Delia Palomino, ed., *Catálagos de la Biblioiteca Nacional de Colombia: Manuscritos*, 2 vols. (Bogotá: Instituto Colombiano de Cultura y Servigraphic Ltda., 1989).

21. Jesuit tales of Mediterranean pirates transformed into Catholics helped blur the line between voluntary and coerced conversions in the Caribbean. The author of the Cádiz tract admitted that their "Christian stratagem" with some Englishmen, whose crimes officials had decided to pardon, was to take them to shore "little by little, six or seven each week, as if they were coming to die with the rest," judging that only the fear of death and separation from their countrymen would make these most hardened of criminal heretics admit defeat (*Relación sumaria*, f. 14r).

22. Bennessar, *Cristianos de Alá*, 211; *Relación sumaria*, f. 9r. Jesuits had to work hard to disabuse Protestant sailors who believed a "Moor" who "put into the[ir] heads" that conversion would only lead to death by hanging, but that "those perseverant in their sects would be brought to Seville" as forced laborers (*Relación sumaria*, f. 16v). In another case brought before Cartagena's inquisitors, a Muslim convert named Ali/Alonso de Molina (see note 18) said in his testimony that he had also been captured by General Chavez (it is not clear whether it was in the 1616 raid described in Armenta's *Relación sumaria*), and had from that time served as an oarsmen in the galleys, first in Santa María before being sent to work in the Cartagena coast guard.

23. Bennessar claimed in his brief study of Protestant Europeans appearing before Mediterranean Inquisitions that officials were much more interested in details of their Anglican and Calvinist beliefs than with Muslim practice and faith—they were especially keen to redeem young captives who had been insufficiently educated to resist heretical lapses ("Dialogue Difficile," 174).

24. AHN, Inq. 1621, Exp. 3, 106v.

25. Ibid., ff. 207r–v, 210r.

26. Ibid., f. 221r.

27. Ibid., f. 225v.

28. Bennessar, "Dialogue Difficile," 172.

29. Ibid., 170–71.

30. AHN, Inq. 1621, Exp. 3, ff. 229v–232v, 235r–238r.

31. Ibid., ff. 241v, 242v.

32. Ibid., f. 250v.

33. Stuart B. Schwartz, a noted historian of early modern Latin American colonization, has recently studied the roots of popular toleration in the Iberian world,

emphasizing the circulation of laymen's contacts with religiously diverse individuals and practical considerations for mutual respect. This relativist strain of popular religious thought, argues Schwartz, was part of the Mediterranean heritage of captivity, and Atlantic (especially Caribbean) interactions. Schwartz, *All Can Be Saved*.

34. AHN, Inq. 1621, Exp. 3, Ibid., 257r.

35. AHN, Inq. Lib. 1020, f. 6r–v; Splendiani, ii.39.

36. AHN, Inq. 1621, Exp. 3, f. 262v.

37. Ibid., ff. 266v–67r.

38. Ibid., ff. 353v–371v.

39. AHN, Inq. Lib. 1021, f. 348; Splendiani iii.344.

40. AHN, Inq. 1621, Exp. 3, f. 146r.

41. John 3:1–10, 19:38–42.

42. See Zagorin, *Ways of Lying*, especially Ch.4,"Calvin and Nicodemism," 63–82.

43. AHN, Inq. 1621, Exp. 3, f. 1r; Inq. Lib. 355, f. 78v.; Inq. Lib. 1015, R.8, f. 138r; Inq. Lib. 1021, f. 322r–v, 324v (Splendiani iii.320, 322).

44. C. F. Firth, ed., *The Narrative of General Venables* (London & New York: Longman & Green, 1900), 18–20, 96; 131, published edition of Bodleian Rawlinson MS.D.1208, f. 62.

7 / Cromwellian Political Economy and the Pursuit of New World Promise

1. 26 Dec 1654. Henry Whistler, "A Jornal of a Voaidg from Stokes Bay: and Intended by Gods assistant for the West Inga, and performed by the Right Honerable Generall Penn, Admirall, as folowes: Taken by Mr. Henry Whistler. 1654." British Library, Sloane MS. 3926. (A reliable transcription of extracts from this journal is available in *The Narrative of General Venables*, Appendix E, 144–69.)

2. Thomas Gage, *The English-American, his travail by sea and land, or, A new survey of the West-India's* (London, 1648), 14. Gage's account of the fleet's leaving read: "Upon the first of July in the afternoon, Don Carlos de Ybarra Admirall . . . gave order that a warning Peece should be shot off to warn all Passengers, Souldiers, and Mariners to betake themselves the next morning to their Ships. O what was it to see some of our Apostolicall company . . . who had begun to entangle their hearts with some young Nuns love, now hang down their heads . . . one Fryer John De Pacheco made the warning Peece to be a warning to him to hide himself . . . thinking it a part of hard cruelty to forsake a young Franciscan Nun to whom he had engaged and wholly devoted his heart. What was it to see others with weeping eyes piercing through the Iron grates the tender Virgins hearts, leaving and bequeathing unto them some pledges of their wanton love, and receiving from them some Cordials against sea-sicknesse, Caps, Shirts and Handkerchiefs, to eye them or wear them when Æolus or Neptune should most oppose them?"

3. See Peter Lake and Michael Questier, *The Anti-Christ's Lewd Hat: Protestants, Papists, and Players in Post-Reformation England* (New Haven & London: Yale University Press, 2002); and Tessa Watt, *Cheap Print and Popular Piety, 1550–1640* (Cambridge & New York: Cambridge University Press, 1991).

4. Miles Philips, Henry Hawks, Job Hortop, and Robert Tomson had been captured from Captain John Hawkins's pirate fleet in San Juan de Ulúa, and were later tried by the Inquisition in Mexico City. Richard Hakluyt subsequently published their narratives in his editions of *The Principal Navigations, Voyages, Traffiques and Discoveries of the English*

Nation Made by Sea or Over-land to the Remote and Farthest Distant Quarters of the Earth at Any Time within the Compass of These 1600 Yeeres (London, 1589; 1598–1600).

5. Gage, *English-American*, "Epistle dedicatory," final page in unpaginated section.

6. Gage, *English-American*, 15. The escapades of Elizabethan "sea dogs" like Henry and John Hawkins and Sir Francis Drake were often at least tacitly supported by the monarch, but always privately bankrolled. Jamaica's Spanish heritage gave it a unique founding narrative, for unlike most other English colonies, it was based on conquest, not occupation of land that was only marginally occupied by others. Michael Guasco, "The Jamaican Graft: Adaptations and Innovations in the Nexus of Anglo-Spanish Colonialism." Paper presented to the Omohundro Institute of Early American History and Culture, Oct 11, 2005, 5–6.

7. The idea of "no peace beyond the line" referred to sixteenth-century imperial struggles in the western half of the Atlantic; in the rush for American colonies, European challengers to Spain tacitly agreed that European treaties were unenforceable past the line established by the Treaty of Tordesillas (west of the Canary and Azores Islands).

8. Oliver Cromwell, "Instructions unto General Robert Venables given by his Highness by advice of his Councel upon his expedition to the West Indies," Appendix A in C. F. Firth, ed., *The Narrative of General Venables*, 112.

9. *Narrative of General Venables*, Appendix A, "Instructions unto Generall Robert Venables given by his Highnes by aduice of his Counel, upon his expedition to the West Indies," 113.

10. Gage, *English-American*, Epistle dedicatory. Cromwell's instructions to Venables echo this point, saying that he "shall hereby power and Authority . . . to offer and giue reasonable Conditions to such persons as will submit to our gouernment, and willingly come vnder our Obedience . . . ," ibid., 114.

11. This term began as a concept in seventeenth-century Europe, though Cromwell was unlikely to have used it. Adam Smith defined political economy as a "branch of the science of a statesman or legislator" concerned both with "providing a plentiful revenue or subsistence for the people . . . and [supplying] the state or commonwealth with a revenue sufficient for the public service. It proposes to enrich both the people and the sovereign" (*The Wealth of Nations*, 1776), Book 4, Ch. 1, accessed at Project Gutenberg, http://www.gutenberg.org/etext/3300, July 13, 2009. In this work, political economy will refer to the imagined relationship between Cromwell's new "puritan" English state and its economic objectives as expressed in the Western Design.

12. I.S., *A Brief and perfect journal of the late proceedings and success of the English army in the West-Indies, continued until June the 24th 1655. Together with some quæries inserted and answered. Published for the satisfaction of all such who desire truly to be informed in these particulars. By I. S. an eye-witnesse* (London, 1655); reprinted in *Harleian miscellany*, Vol. III (London, 1801–1813), 492.

13. Major treatments of the Western Design in English include: C. F. Firth, ed., *The Narrative of General Venables* (London & New York: Longman & Green, 1900); C. H. Haring, *The Buccaneers in the West Indies in the 17th century* (New York: E. P. Dutton and Company, 1910), Ch. 3, "The Conquest of Jamaica," 85–112; Granville Penn, ed., *Memorials of the Professional Life and Times of Sir William Penn, Knt. &c.* (London: James Duncan, 1833); and S. A. G. Taylor, *The Western Design: An Account of Cromwell's Expedition to the Caribbean* (Kingston, Jamaica: The Institute of Jamaica and The Jamaica Historical Society, 1965). Transcriptions and translations of many of the key Spanish narratives held in the AGI were made by Irene Wright during the 1920s,

including Julian de Castilla, "The English Conquest of Jamaica: An Account of what happened on the island of Jamaica, from May 20 of the year 1655, when the English laid siege to it, up to July 3 of the year 1656," *Camden Miscellany* XIII (1923), 1–32; "The Spanish resistance to the English Occupation of Jamaica, 1655–1660," *Transactions of the Royal Historical Society*, 4th Ser., Vol. XIII, 117–147; and an assortment of "Spanish Narratives of the English Attack on Santo Domingo 1655," *Camden Miscellany* XIV (1926), 1–80. Major secondary and published primary resources in Spanish include: Emilio Rodriguez Demorizi, *Invasión Inglesa* (Cuidad Trujillo, Dominican Republic: Editorial Montalvo, 1957); J. Marino Incháustegui, *La gran expedición inglesa contra las Antillas Mayores: el plan Antillano de Cromwell (1651–1655)* (Mexico City: Gráfica Panamericana, 1958); and Francisco Morales Padrón, *Jamaica Española* (Seville: Escuela de Estudios Hispano-Americanos, 1952), reprinted in an English translation, *Spanish Jamaica* (Kingston, Jamaica: Ian Randle, 2003).

14. In the first serious re-examinations of the Western Design published in the 1970s, John Battick claimed that the Western Design "mark[ed] the end of the old free-booting, private, or semi-private ventures characteristic of the age of Drake," while Arthur Hiscox contended that Cromwell continued Queen Elizabeth's strategies for foreign policy. See David Armitage, "The Cromwellian Protectorate and the Languages of Empire," *Historical Journal* 35, 3 (1992), 531–55; John F. Battick, "A New Interpretation of Cromwell's Western Design," *Journal of the Barbados Museum and Historical Society* 34, 2 (May 1972): 76–84, esp. 82; Arthur R. Hiscox, *Oliver Cromwell's Western Design: A Study in the Survival of Elizabethan Strategy* (Master's thesis, Kent State University, 1973); Steven C. A. Pincus, *Protestantism and Patriotism: Ideologies and the Making of English Foreign Policy, 1650–1668* (New York: Cambridge University Press, 1996), Ch. 10, "The Protectorate's New Foreign Policy," 168–92.

15. Marcus Rediker & Peter Linebaugh, *The Many-Headed Hydra* (Boston: Beacon Press, 2000); John Donoghue, "Unfree Labor, Imperialism, and Radical Republicanism in the Atlantic World, 1630–1661," *Labor: Studies in Working-Class History of the Americas* 1, 4 (2004): 47–68.

16. Two scholars have recently applied similar analyses: Carla Gardina Pestana, "English Character and the Fiasco of the Western Design," *Early American Studies* 3, 1 (2005): 1–31; and Guasco, "The Jamaican Graft."

17. The tumult of the Civil War period forced England to contend with challenges to a wide range of societal and religious norms, from divine right to patriarchal power. For the classic study of the period, see Christopher Hill, *The World Turned Upside Down: Radical Ideas During the English Revolution* (London: Penguin Books, 1972).

18. Joan Pong Linton, a literary scholar examining the relationship between English masculinity and the colonial romance, has articulated a sense of how early travel narratives "enable Englishmen both to inhabit an unfamiliar world and to project a sense of their agency in it. In this way, gender roles are not merely interpretive but generative: they provide a ready-made hierarchy of relations with which explorers and colonists negotiate a broader range of cultural differences." Joan Pong Linton, *The Romance of the New World: Gender and the Literary Formations of English Colonialism* (Cambridge: Cambridge University Press, 1998), 5.

19. Whistler was clearly more privileged than the majority of these men (his literacy and responsibilities aboard the ship demonstrate his upward mobility), yet he more often identified with the common soldier or sailor than his superiors aboard the fleet.

20. Alexandra Walsham, *Providence in Early Modern England* (Oxford & New York: Oxford University Press, 1999); see also Blair Worden, "Providence and Politics in Cromwellian England," *Past and Present* 109 (Nov. 1985): 55–99. Biographers of Cromwell have paid ample attention to the reality of his belief in providential signs: see Christopher Hill, *God's Englishman: Oliver Cromwell and the English Revolution* (New York: Dial Press, 1970); Antonia Fraser, *Cromwell* (New York: Knopf, 1973); Blair Worden, "Oliver Cromwell and the Sin of Achan," in *History, Society and the Churches: Essays in honour of Owen Chadwick*, ed. Derek Beales and Geoffrey Best (Cambridge: Cambridge University Press, 1985).

21. Oliver Cromwell, "Commission to General Penn," in Penn, *Memorials*, Vol. II, 21–22; Cromwell uses similar wording in his "Commission of the Commissioners for the West Indian Expedition" (British Library, Additional MSS. 11410-f. 47), reprinted in *Narrative of General Venables*, Appendix A, 109–110.

22. "Account of the negotiations between England, France, and Spain, from the time of Oliver Cromwell's assuming the government, to the restoration, delivered to this Lord Chancellor Hyde." *A Collection of the State Papers of John Thurloe, secretary, first, to the Council of State, and afterwards to the two Protectors, Oliver and Richard Cromwell* (London, 1742), i.760–61 (hereafter *Thurloe State Papers*).

23. *Thurloe State Papers*, Oliver Cromwell, "Commission to General Penn"; Christopher Hill, *Antichrist in Seventeenth-Century England* (London: Oxford University Press, 1971), esp. 64–69. According to many sixteenth- and seventeenth-century Protestant divines, the pope was the head of a false church and hoped to clothe himself with such an aura of mystery that he could lead men into perdition by their blind acts of devotion. His head minions, then, were the Jesuits—a missionary order independent of the church hierarchy, committed defenders of papal authority—and the Iberian monarchs.

24. Kupperman, *Providence Island*, 350; James Robertson, "Cromwell and the Conquest of Jamaica," *History Today* (May 2005), 17.

25. *Thurloe State Papers*, Oliver Cromwell, "Commission to General Penn."

26. Gage's prelude to the protector was full of hopes "for the conversion of the poore Indians" to fulfill dreams of Protestant universalism, and closed with the fervent prayer: "The Lord make your highnesse, as our protector, so also a protector of these poore Indians, which want protection from the cruelties of the Spaniards." *Thurloe State Papers*, iii.59, 61.

27. Gage, *English-American*, 129–30, 139. *Thurloe State Papers*, iii.60. Paul Lokken asserts that there may have been hundreds of maroons and Indians living in scattered communities throughout Guatemala until about 1640; see his "A Maroon Moment: Rebel Slaves in Early Seventeenth-century Guatemala," *Slavery and Abolition* 25, 3 (2004): 44–58.

28. Gage even claimed that Spanish creoles had been subject to a "kinde of slavery" (through the empire's preferment of peninsular Spaniards for colonial appointments), and asserted that these slights had become "so grievous to the poor Criolio's or Natives; that my self have often heard them say, They would rather be subject to any other Prince, nay to the Hollanders, then to the Spaniards, if they thought they might enjoy their Religion . . ." (Of course, ardent puritans could not allow Catholicism of any sort to flourish, so none in Cromwell's camp were prepared to offer freedom of religion for Spanish Americans who would support their rule.) Gage, *English-American*, epistle dedicatory, 9–10.

29. Anon., *Sir Francis Drake Revived, Who is or may be a Pattern to stirre up all Heroicke and active Spirits of these Times, to benefit their Countrey and eternize their*

Names by like Noble Attempts. Being a Summary and true Relation of foure severall Voyages made by the said Sir Francis Drake to the West-Indies (London, 1653), 7–8, 13–14, 30–31, 34, 48–56, 66–71. See also Michael Guasco, "'Free from the tyrannous Spanyard'? Englishmen and Africans in Spain's Atlantic World," *Slavery and Abolition* 29, 1 (2008): 1–22.

30. Gage, *English-American*, 77.

31. *Thurloe State Papers*, iii.59, 60.

32. Gage, *English-American*, 75.

33. *Thurloe State Papers*, iii.61.

34. Penn, *Memorials*, 94. He continued that "if ever God send peace, an honourable peace, peace and truth to this our nation, I may then, if I continue the sea, think of a Levant voyage; till then, though I spend more than I get (which is true enough), I am so resolved, and God so prosper my designs." After hearing the famous puritan minister Hugh Peters speak in December 1650, Penn's sea journals became increasingly punctuated with notes of thanks to God for providential favors, perhaps suggesting that he had been radicalized by the religious fervor of the day (*Memorials*, 358–59). Moreover, Admiral Penn's brother, a merchant trading out of Seville, had been imprisoned by that city's Inquisition in 1643 during a wartime crackdown on suspected Protestant merchants (*Memorials*, 231–333; his brother's petition for restitution from Cromwell is printed in Appendix C.1, 550–55). Later in life, Penn would revert to a cooler Protestantism and find fault with his son for taking his Quaker beliefs to such a high pitch that it endangered his place of precedence in Restoration England.

35. *Narrative of General Venables*, 3–5. Our trust in Venables's motivations must be tempered by the knowledge that his protestations of religious zeal were written after he had returned to London in disgrace from the expedition's early failures, seriously ill, and trying to defend himself against the Protector's court-martials against him and Admiral Penn.

36. I. S., *Brief and Perfect Journal*, 490. For literature on the rising phenomenon of "masterless men" in early modern England, see A. L. Beier, *Masterless Men: The Vagrancy Problem in England, 1560–1640* (New York: Methuen, 1986); Patricia Fumerton, *Unsettled: The Culture of Mobility and the Working Poor in Early Modern England* (Chicago: University of Chicago Press, 2006); and Rediker and Linebaugh, *The Many-Headed Hydra*.

37. Dunn, *Sugar and Slaves*, 66–67; Russell R. Menard, *Sweet Negotiations: Sugar, Slavery, and Plantation Agriculture in early Barbados* (Charlottesville: University of Virginia Press, 2006), 92; Allison Games, "Opportunity and Mobility in Early Barbados," in Robert L. Paquette and Stanley L. Engerman, eds., *The Lesser Antilles in the Age of European Expansion* (Gainesville: University Press of Florida, 1996), 168; Hilary McD. Beckles, *White Servitude and Black Slavery in Barbados, 1627–1715* (Knoxville: University of Tennessee Press, 1989), 8.

38. *Narrative of General Venables*, 79; Penn, *Memorials*, 29–44; Carla Gardina Pestana, *English Atlantic in an Age of Revolution*, 178–79.

8 / The Politics of Economic Exclusion

1. T. S.'s *A Manual of Devotions: Suiting each Day; with Prayers and Meditations answerable to the worke of the Day. As Also Each Mans Calling, viz. The Noble man, the Soldier, the Lawyer, the Tradesman, the Seaman, the Sickman, the Dying man, &c.*

with answerate Prayers and Meditations (London, 1643), 397. These kinds of pocket exegesis (this particular *Manual* measured only 14 x 7 cm.) for soldiers and sailors were popular in England. Another seventeenth-century example is *The Christian Soldier's Penny Bible. Shewing From the Holy Scriptures, the Soldier's Duty and Encouragement. Being a Brief Collection of pertinent Scriptures, under XX Heads, fit for the Soldier's, or Seaman's Pocket, when he is not furnish'd with, or cannot well carry a larger Volume, in time of War* (London, 1693).

2. One of Gage's points to Cromwell when he suggested taking Hispaniola was that it might "bee to them a bad omen to beginne to loose that, which they first enjoyed. . . . " "Some brief and true observations. . . . " *Thurloe State Papers*, iii.59–61.

3. "The Soldier's Prayer," in T. S., *A Manual of Devotions*, 399–401.

4. Similar religious rituals in a martial setting are described in Richard P. Gildrie, "Defiance, Diversion and the Exercise of Arms: The several meanings of training days in colonial Massachusetts," *Military Affairs* 52, 2 (1988): 53–55.

5. Whistler, Journal, f. 12–13. Military historian Keith Roberts confirms that even among the self-consciously "godly" New Model Army, "the possessions of prisoners and casualties on the battlefield were 'lawful plunder' . . . [and] the main source of income from plunder came from the sack of a town or city, where the soldier could seize what he could when the fighting was over" (Roberts, *Cromwell's War Machine: The New Model Army* (Barnsley, South Yorkshire: Pen & Sword Military, 2005), 101–2). See also Charles Carlton, *Going to the Wars: The Experience of the British Civil Wars, 1638–1651* (London: Routledge, 1992), 265–88.

6. T. S., *A Manual of Devotions*, 396–97.

7. Whistler, Journal, f. 13.

8. *Narrative of General Venables*, 15.

9. Ibid., 25. Whistler's journal confirms that "the sea ridgment did [withdraw] from the rest saying, What doue wee doue heare, shall we venter our liues for nothing?" Whistler, Journal, f. 15.

10. Ibid., 14.

11. Additionally, a bunch of unmarked cattle pelts discovered were turned over to the commissioners to be bartered for supplies, and soldiers searching the pockets of a Spanish captain slain in one of the first skirmishes were disappointed to find only "the Pope's Bulls, an Agnus Dei, and reliques . . . else nought." Anonymous in *Narrative of General Venables*, 132.

12. Anonymous I (Rawlinson MS D.1208, f. 62 in the Bodleian Library), reprinted as Appendix D in *Narrative of General Venables*), 129–32.

13. Whistler, Journal, f. 15.

14. For English iconoclasm in an Atlantic context, see: Vincent V. Patarino, Jr., "'One Foot in Sea and One on Shore': The Religious Culture of English Sailors, 1550–1688" (Master's thesis, University of Colorado, 2002); and Nicolas M. Beasley, "Wars of Religion in the Circum-Caribbean: English Iconoclasm in Spanish America, 1570–1702," in Margaret Cormack, ed., *Saints and Their Cults in the Atlantic World* (Columbia: University of South Carolina Press, 2007).

15. *Narrative of General Venables*, 30.

16. Whistler, Journal, f. 17.

17. Accompanying the general on the long journey across the Atlantic was his wife, Elizabeth, whom he had been married to for less than a year (*Narrative of*

General Venables, 36). By far, the insinuation that the general was inept because he wasn't properly in control of his wife was the hardest to shake. One contemporary critic wrote: "He is unfit to be *pater patriae*, that is not *Domi dominus*, nor to ride admiral of a fleet that cannot carry the flag at home but is forced to lower his topsail to a petticoat" (Edmund Hickeringill, *Jamaica viewed*, 1661, 72).

18. *Narrative of General Venables*, 102.

19. Whistler, f. 19–20.

20. I. S. called it "ill-grounded Confidence and high Presumption" to include women in the expedition, for it "made them seem rather as a People that went to inhabit some Country already conquered, than to conquer . . . for this, perhaps, they had too good a Precedent," perhaps referring to family settlement of New England, even Providence Island, which lay exposed to the dangers of the Spanish fleet (*A brief and perfect journal*, 491; Kupperman, *Providence Island*, 32). For early modern family and hierarchy, see Susan Dwyer Amussen, *An Ordered Society: Gender and Class in Early Modern England* (New York: Columbia University Press, 1993), esp. Ch. 2; and Alexandra Shepard, *Meanings of Manhood in Early Modern England* (New York: Oxford University Press, 2003), 3.

21. *Narrative of General Venables*, 11, 102. Given the large number of indentured servants contracted for the army, it is plausible that many of these "wives" were likewise unmarried servants hoping to escape their indentures by following the camp as nurses or prostitutes.

22. Venables saw himself as a godly English patriarch, one who would not even accept his commission before knowing the details of Cromwell's reasons for war against Spain, nor before making arrangements for the care of his children, "except I should fall under the Apostles censure, 'He that provided not for them of his Family hath denied the Faith, and is worse than an Infidel'" (*Narrative of General Venables*, 3–5).

23. Rediker and Linebaugh, *The Many-Headed Hydra*, 42–49; Keith Wrightson, *Earthly Necessities: Economic Lives in Early Modern Britain* (New Haven & London: Yale University Press, 2002).

24. Shepard, *Meanings of Manhood*, 206, 209–11, 213, 249. See also Anthony Fletcher, "Men's Dilemma: The Future of Patriarchy in England, 1560–1660," *Transactions of the Royal Historical Society*, 6th ser. 4 (1994): 61–82.

25. Whistler, Journal, f. 9.

26. Games, "Opportunity and Mobility," 171–75.

27. *Narrative of General Venables*, 30.

28. *Thurloe State Papers*, iii.507; *Narrative of General Venables*, 34.

29. *Narrative of General Venables*, 33.

30. Ibid., 84.

31. *Thurloe State Papers*, III.507, 3 Jun 1655, Jamaica. "A letter from Jamaica, by J. Daniell." The army's muster at Jamaica had listed "2,194 men well and 2,316 men sick. . . . In addition there were 173 women and children." Edward Long, *A History of Jamaica* (London, 1774), quoted in S. A. G. Taylor, *The Western Design*, 91. Captain Pallano's narrative notes that scouts reported "more than a hundred women" were present in the English camp on Hispaniola (*Spanish Narratives*, 16).

32. Anonymous I, in *Narrative of General Venables*, 136.

33. [Rooth], "A journal of the passages in my voyage to the West Indies on board the States Swiftsure. . . ," 7 May 1655. National Maritime Museum (hereafter NMM). Wynne Papers, 10/1.

34. *Narrative of General Venables*, 35.

35. Penn, *Memorials*, 64.

36. This trend began in Hispaniola. In testimonies taken by the Spanish from eleven deserters, at least three were Irish who used their marginalized status to appeal for clemency: "Juan Charles" said he had been forced to serve in the expedition by his master in Barbados; James Kelly hiked through mountains before reaching the Spanish, telling them of the remaining 4,000 troops' discontentment; "Thomas Rodriguez" testified that he was Catholic, and that one of his cousins had been hung for trying to run away. Rodriguez Demorizi, *Invasión Inglesa*, 70–73.

37. Morales Padrón, *Spanish Jamaica*, 136, 165–68, 178.

38. Whistler, Journal, f. 27.

39. Morales Padrón, *Spanish Jamaica*, 189.

40. After the humiliating loss of Hispaniola, which he attributed to Providence, Cromwell is said to have abandoned his designs on the English Crown, and to have become much more vulnerable to factional politics. See Worden, "Oliver Cromwell and the Sin of Achan."

41. Anonymous I, in *Narrative of General Venables*, 141–43.

42. Ibid., 143.

43. More details on privateering out of Jamaica and the Myngs dispute can be found in Haring, *Buccaneers*, Ch. 3, "The Conquest of Jamaica," 85–112, esp. 97–99.

44. April 30, 1656, Marmaduke, Jamaica, Capt. Wm. Godfrey to Robt. Blackborne, NAL, CO 1/32, No. 59.

45. Abstracts from D'Oyley's diary (with other misc. notes by Edward Long), British Library (hereafter BL), Additional MSS. 12410, 13 Jul 1656.

46. D'Oyley, Diary, 13 Jul 1656; 14 Aug 1656; 27 Sep 1656; 13 Sep 1657. BL, Add. MSS. 12410.

47. D'Oyley, Diary, 26 Jul 1656. BL, Add. MSS. 12410.

48. Capt. William Godfrey to Robert Blackborne, 30 April 1656, Jamaica, NAL, CO 1/32, No. 59. Capt. James Tarry, referring to the same incident, wrote that 30 soldiers had run away but were retaken, three of them hanged as an example, NAL, CO 1/32, No. 62. Capt. James Tarry to Robert Blackborne, 30 April 1656 (Reiterated in Capt. Mark Harrison to the Admiralty and Navy Commissioners, April 30, 1656, NAL, CO 1/32, Nos. 60 and 61).

49. D'Oyley, Diary, 17 Jan 1659. BL, Add. MSS. 12410.

50. J. L. Pietersz and H. P. Jacobs, ed. and trans., "Two Spanish Documents of 1656," *Jamaican Historical Review* 2, 2 (1952): 11–35, esp. 26, 31.

51. "Testimonio de las declaraciones que se tomaron a dos prisioneros Ingleses que el Gobernador de Jamayca remitio a Cartagena," 7 Aug 1656, AGI, Santo Domingo 178A. Prisoners taken in Hispaniola were also questioned, and these documents include the testimonies of defectors who had already found a way to escape the disasters of that island's offensives. Among those who said they had run away were Irishmen, a Dutchman, and another escapee, "who says he's the son of a Spaniard." Rodriguez Demorizi, *Invasión Inglesa*, 70–73.

52. Caer's name appears in the published "A List of the Names of the Inhabitants of Barbados, in the Year, 1638, who then posess'd more than Ten Acres of Land," in

Some Memoirs of the First Settlement of the Island of Barbados . . . to the Year 1741 (Barbados, 1741), 72.

53. This remarkable exchange follows Caer's sworn testimony, given the governor of Cartagena in early 1657. Cartagena, 2 Feb 1657, "Declaración de Ricardo Caer, de nacion olandes, natural del lugar llamado Horcon," Testimonio del estado de la isla de Xamaica, noticias y auisos della deste siete de Ag⁰ de 1656, AGI, Santo Domingo 178A.

9 / Anxieties of Interracial Alliances, Black Resistance, and the Specter of Slavery

1. Shepard's analysis of masculinity in early modern England reminds us that calling a man a "slave" was an insult even outside the colonial context—it "implied that he was perpetually bound to serve another man, without any shred of autonomy, and permanently excluded from the citizenship of the commonwealth enjoyed by freemen" (*Meanings of Manhood*, 174).

2. Anonymous, in *Narrative of General Venables*, 130; William Burrows, Admiral Penn's personal secretary, wrote in "A journal of every dayes proceedings . . ." that Warner's former "servant" had been a slave for twelve years among the Spanish (NMM, WYN 10/2, 17 Apr 1655). Whistler also wrote that on the first march, "came to them a Neagor from the ennimie which had formerly liued with our English, which did giue them great incoridgement of the enemies vnabilitie to fight them: and that he would show them the way . . . " (Journal, f. 16).

3. Anonymous, in *Narrative of General Venables*, 130.

4. Burrows, NMM, WYN 10/2, 17 Apr 1655.

5. Anonymous, in *Narrative of General Venables*, 130.

6. Ibid., 130.

7. Burrows, Journal, NMM, WYN 10/2, 20 Apr 1655.

8. Anonymous, in *Narrative of General Venables*, 130.

9. Carolyn Prager, "Early English Transfer and Invention of the Black in New Spain," in Jerry M. Williams & Robert E. Lewis, eds., *Early Images of the Americas: Transfer and Invention* (Tucson: Univ of Arizona Press, 1993), 93–107, quote on 94. At this very moment, in the English colonies, from Barbados to Virginia, racial hierarchies were already well along the way to ossification. See T. H. Breen and Stephan Innes, *"Myne Own Ground": Race and Freedom on Virginia's Eastern Shore, 1640–1676* (New York: Oxford University Press, 1980); Kathleen M. Brown, *Good Wives, Nasty Wenches, and Anxious Patriarchs* (Chapel Hill: University of North Carolina Press, 1996); Clarence Maxwell, "Race and Servitude: The Birth of a Social and Political Order in Bermuda, 1619–1669," *Bermuda Journal of Archaeology & Maritime History* 11 (1999): 40–46. For an interpretation emphasizing the more uneven transformation of Bermuda's racial customs and law in the seventeenth century, see Virginia Bernhard, "Beyond the Chesapeake: The Contrasting Status of Blacks in Bermuda, 1616–1663," *Journal of Southern History* 54, 4 (1988): 545–64, and Heather Miyano Kopelson, "From Sinner to Property: Unlawful Sex and Enslaved Women in Bermuda, 1650–1723," paper presented at the 39th Annual Conference of the Association of Caribbean Historians, Jamaica, May 6–11, 2007.

10. Whistler, Journal, f. 9.

11. See Winthrop D. Jordan, *White over Black: American Attitudes Toward the Negro, 1550–1812* (Chapel Hill: University of North Carolina Press, 1968); Jennifer L. Morgan, "'Some Could Suckle Over their Shoulder': Male Travelers, Female Bodies,

and the Gendering of Racial Ideology, 1500–1770," *WMQ* 54, 1 (1997): 167–192," esp. 170–73, 183–86; Jennifer L. Morgan, *Laboring Women: Reproduction and Gender in New World Slavery* (Philadelphia: University of Pennsylvania Press, 2004).

12. *Narrative of General Venables*, 8.

13. See note 2.

14. Whistler, Journal, f. 20.

15. Whistler characterized these ancestors of the buccaneers as "a sort of Vagabons that are saued from the gallowes in Spaine and the king doth send them heare: Thes goe by the name of Cow killers, and indeed it is Thayer trad, for thay liue by killing of Cattille for the hides and tallow" (Journal, f. 19). The French term for the barbeque, or *boucan*, over which they dried the meat, is the origin of the term for the now-famous swashbuckling *bucanier*.

16. Whistler, Journal, f. 19. Also in Jamaica: " . . . when the negroes found any English straggling in the woods they butchered them with lances. . . ," March 13, 1656, Torrington, Jamaica. Vice-Admiral William Goodson to the Navy Commissioners. *Calendar of State Papers, Colonial Series, America and West Indies, 1574–1739* CD-ROM (hereafter *CSPC*), consultant editors Karen Ordahl Kupperman, John C. Appleby, and Mandy Banton (London: Routledge, published in association with the Public Record Office, copyright 2000).

17. Anonymous, in *Narrative of General Venables*, 134. Francis Barrington told the same story of how men "at the fore-mentioned river's side refreshing themselves; one in the company might see one negar, upon which he gave out the word, 'the enemy, the enemy,' and immediately above 500 run away and threw down their arms." BL, Egerton MS 2648, reprinted by the Royal Commission on Historical Manuscripts, Seventh Report (London, 1879), Vol. 1 (hereafter Barrington), 573.

18. I. S., *A Brief and perfect journal*, 494.

19. Fernandez, it would seem, was denied his promise because no free black regiment had yet been approved for Santo Domingo. Council of War to the Council of the Indies regarding petition of Juan Garcia Fernandez, 28 Apr 1658, AGI, Santo Domingo 2, No. 65. Special thanks to Juan José Ponce-Vázquez for these references on Hispaniola's demography and the testimony of the Congolese Juan Fernandez. See Roberto Cassá, *Historia Social y Económica de la República Dominicana* (Santo Domingo: Alfa y Omega, 1998), esp. Table, "Composición étnica de Santo Domingo, siglo XVII"; Ponce-Vázquez, "Social and Political Survival at the Edge of Empire: Spanish Local Elites in Hispaniola, 1580–1697" (Ph.D. dissertation, University of Pennsylvania, 2010).

20. Barrington, i.571.

21. Whistler also contended that for Spaniards brave enough to command blacks and "cowkillers," "the pop[e] doth giue a bull, which is a parden for all [sins] past and to come, and many that our men did take had Thayer parden hanging about Thayer neckes; theas men will fight with great confidence, and doue belefe that if they die all dies, for they are partened [pardoned]" (Journal, f. 19). If we can trust Whistler's account of the motivations of blacks fighting to escape English cannibals, such tales suggest that the Spanish had appropriated the belief widespread throughout Western Africa that Europeans were otherwordly spirits who ate human flesh (and here redirected those fears towards an unknown white enemy). See Thornton, "Cannibals, Witches, and Slave-Traders in the Atlantic World," *WMQ* 60, 2 (2003): 273–94;

Olaudah Equiano, *The Interesting Narrative of the Life of Olaudah Equiano, or Gustavus Vassa, the African. Written by Himself.* Vol. I (Electronic Edition, http://docsouth.unc.edu/neh/equiano1/equiano1.html), 194–95.

22. *Narrative of General Venables*, 36.

23. For further information on Jamaica's maroons, see Mavis C. Campbell, *The Maroons of Jamaica, 1655–1796: A History of Resistance, Collaboration & Betrayal* (Trenton, NJ: Africa World Press, 1990); S. A. G. Taylor and David Buisseret, "Juan de Bolas and His Pelinco," *Caribbean Quarterly* 24,1/2 (1978): 1–7; NAL, CO 1/32, No. 53, Torrington, Jamaica, Vice-Adm. Wm. Goodson to the Navy Commissioners (March 13, 1656); NAL, CO 1/32, No. 59, Marmaduke, Jamaica, Capt. Wm. Godfrey to Robt. Blackborne (April 30, 1656); NAL, CO 1/32, Nos. 60–61, Gift, Jamaica, Capt. Mark Harrison to the Admiralty and Navy Commissioners (April 30, 1656); NAL, CO 1/32, No. 62, Indian, Jamaica, Capt. Ja. Tarry to Robt. Blackborne (April 30, 1656).

24. D'Oyley, Journal, BL, Add. MSS. 12410, 8 Jul 1656; 4 Sep 1657.

25. Ibid., BL, Add. MSS. 12410, 6 Dec 1656.

26. Barrington, i.575.

27. 10 May 1659. BL, Add. MSS. 12410, f. 28v. One mulatto, Capt. Hernando Julian, had accepted D'Oyley's offer "to serve the English Interest." Guasco cites "Anthony Ridrigues a Negro Soldier of the English Army," who owned property in Spanish Town.

28. The language of D'Avenant's masque, especially that of the Fifth Speech, dwells on images of torture shared by both Natives and Protestant interlopers ("other Christian strangers landing here") who were victims of the Spaniard's cruel tortures, or as D'Avenant put it, "arts of length'ning languishment. . . . Men ready to expire, / Baste them with drops of fire, / And then, they lay them on the Rack for ease." William D'Avenant, *The Cruelty of the Spaniards in Peru. Exprest by instrumentall and vocall musick, and by art of perspective in scenes, &c. Represented daily at the Cockpit in Drury-Lane, at three after noone punctually* (London, 1658), 20.

29. *Tears of the Indians: being an historical and true account of the cruel massacres and slaughters of above twenty millions of innocent people, committed by the Spaniards in the islands of Hispaniola, Cuba, Jamaica, &c.: as also in the continent of Mexico, Peru, & other places of the West-Indies, to the total destruction of those countries / written in Spanish by Casaus, an eye-witness of those things; and made English by J.P.* (London, 1656), b4.

30. This common term at the time, a forerunner of *shanghaied*, attests to the pervasiveness of such practices as well as the fear that such capture and transportation inspired in Englishmen. See Hilary Beckles, "English Parliamentary Debate on 'White Slavery' in Barbados, 1659," *Journal of the Barbados Museum and Historical Society* 36 (1982): 344–52; Donoghue, "Unfree Labor, Imperialism, and Radical Republicanism," 63–65; Susan Dwyer Amussen, *Caribbean Exchanges: Slavery and the Transformation of English Society, 1640–1700* (Chapel Hill: University of North Carolina Press, 2007), 128; and Pestana, *English Atlantic in an Age of Revolution*, 211–12.

31. Marcellus Rivers, *Englands slavery, or Barbados merchandize; represented in a petition to the high court of Parliament, by Marcellus Rivers and Oxenbridge Foyle gentlemen, on behalf of themselves and three-score and ten more free-born Englishmen sold (uncondemned) into slavery: together with letters written to some honourable members of Parliament* (London, 1659), 5.

32. *England's Slavery*, 8, 21, 5.

33. Ibid., 7.

34. This protest "from below" seems similar to the grievances asserted by the New Model Army, especially their demands for the arrears in their salaries, when recruiters for the Irish invasion tried to press them into service. Mark Kishlansky notes that "the transformation of the parliamentary process was observable in the Army, where soldiers would soon claim that the Irish venture was 'a mere cloak for some who have lately tasted of sovereignty and being lifted beyond the ordinary sphere of servants seek to become masters and degenerate into tyrants.'" *The Rise of the New Model Army* (Cambridge: Cambridge University Press, 1979), 198–99.

35. Thomas Burton, M.P. *Parliamentary Diary*, 1656–59 (London, 1828), Vol. 4, 259.

36. Ibid., 264–65.

37. Ibid., 270.

38. Ibid., 268.

39. Jamaica. Cornelius Burough to Robert Blackborne, Secretary to Admiralty Commissioners, July 16, 1658, NAL, CO 1/33, No 45. Testimony of "Juan Antonio," 3 Aug 1658, AGI, Santo Domingo 178B.

40. Michael Guasco analyzes the seal in detail ("The Jamaican Graft," 9), citing *The Laws of Jamaica, Passed by the Assembly, and Confirmed by his Majesty in Council, April 17, 1684* (London, 1684). See also James Robertson, "'Stories' and 'Histories' in Late Seventeenth-Century Jamaica," in Kathleen E. A. Monteith and Glen Richards, eds., *Jamaica in Slavery and Freedom: History, Heritage and Culture* (Bridgetown, Barbados: University of the West Indies Press, 2002).

41. *CSPC*, i.492–493. "Instructions for the Council appointed for Foreign Plantations, to inform themselves of the state of the plantations. . . ," NAL, CO 1/14, No. 59 and CO 1/33, No. 81.

42. Cornelius Burough to Robert Blackborne, 19 Jan 1660, NAL, CO 1/33, No. 61.

43. On anticlericalism among sailors and pirates in the late seventeenth and early eighteenth centuries, see Marcus Rediker, *Between the Devil and the Deep Blue Sea* (Cambridge: Cambridge University Press, 1987).

44. *CSPC*, Item 2015, xii.633, Memorial of John Tarima, a Spanish merchant, concerning Jamaica, 1660.

45. *CSPC*, Item 2014, xii.632, Account of the population of Jamaica, with their proportion of arms, and of acres planted, [1660?]. The actual figures given are: 2,458 men, 454 women, 448 children, 514 negroes, 618 arms, 2,588 acres. Dunn cites the 12,000 immigration estimate, and says that by 1661, the population was 3,470 (*Sugar and Slaves*, 153).

46. Jenny Shaw, "Island Purgatory: Irish Catholics and the Reconfiguration of the English Caribbean, 1650–1700 (Ph.D. dissertation, New York University, 2009), esp. 105–9 and 197–207. See also Shaw and Block, "Subjects without an Empire."

10 / Quakers, Slavery, and the Challenges of Universalism

1. Nineteenth-century geneaologists interested in this branch of the Morris family (several ancestors became famed early American leaders) have tried to tie Colonel Morris's lineage to a noble Welsh family headed by William Morris of Tintern, Monmouthshire. However, the fact that Morris started out in the Caribbean as a servant

suggests that he was of relatively humble birth, and a rare letter in his own hand written in 1671 (see p. 160–61) reveals a shaky grasp on conventional spellings—either he had little of the formal education most gentlemen's sons were expected to receive, or he was a very bad student. This more skeptical reading of the evidence is supported by Colonel Morris's biographer, who wrote that he could not confirm any connection between this particular Morris and the Morrises of Tintern. However, since Morris did name his New Jersey properties Tinton Falls and Monmouth County, it seems reasonable to assume that he did have some connections to that particular part of Wales.

2. Samuel Stelle Smith, *Lewis Morris, Anglo-American Statesman, ca. 1613–1691* (Atlantic Highlands, NJ: Humanities Press, 1983); Eugene R. Sheridan, *Lewis Morris 1671–1746: A Study in Early American Politics* (Syracuse, NY: Syracuse University Press, 1981), 2–6; Kupperman, *Providence Island*, 97–99, 387; Penn, *Memorials*, 41–42; *Thurloe State Papers*, iii.158; British National Archives (hereafter NAL), PRO 31/17/43.

3. Smith, *Lewis Morris*, 24.

4. It is uncertain whether Morris built up his sugar estate slowly, "upon small fortunes," or whether he found financial backers in England to aid his project. Economic historians assert that "Barbadians . . . worked within an empirewide legal system favorable to creditors," perhaps explaining Morris's haste to pay off those debts. John J. McCusker and Russell R. Menard, "The Sugar Industry in the Seventeenth Century: A New Perspective on the Barbadian 'Sugar Revolution,'" in *Tropical Babylons: Sugar and the Making of the Atlantic World, 1450–1680*, ed. Stuart B. Schwartz (Chapel Hill: University of North Carolina Press, 2003), 301–3.

5. Larry Gragg, *Englishmen Transplanted: The English Colonization of Barbados, 1627–1660* (Oxford: Oxford University Press, 2003), 137–38; Larry Gragg, *The Quaker Community on Barbados: Challenging the Culture of the Planter Class* (Columbia: University of Missouri Press, 2009), 65–66. Smith claims that he had purchased 400 acres and 200 slaves to work the land, but it is unclear when these purchases were made.

6. *Acts of Assembly, Passed in the Island of Barbados, from 1648 to 1718* (London: 1721), 46.

7. Barbara Ritter Dailey, "The Early Quaker Mission and the Settlement of Meetings in Barbados, 1655–1700." *Journal of the Barbados Museum and Historical Society [JBMHS]* 39 (1991): 24–46, esp. 28.

8. My analysis for this chapter draws on a database of nearly eight hundred Quakers resident in Barbados (at least for a time) during the end of the seventeenth century. I used Quaker histories, manuscript correspondence, epistles and lists, wills and census materials in compiling a prosoprographical database. Despite gender imbalances in migration to the Caribbean, this survey included more than three hundred women associated with the Society of Friends in Barbados. Larry Gragg's wonderful book-length overview of Quakerism in Barbados, based on many of the same sources, claims that as many as 1,200 Quakers resided on the island in the second half of the seventeenth century. Gragg, *Quaker Community*, 60. For previous studies of Quakerism in Barbados, see Dailey, "The Early Quaker Mission"; L. Brett Brinegar, "Radical Politics and Civil Disobedience: Quaker Resistance in Seventeenth Century Bridgetown," *JBMHS* 49 (Nov. 2003): 150–66; Harriet Frorer Durham, *Caribbean Quakers* (Hollywood, FL: Dukane Press, 1972); and Winnifred V. Winkelman, "Barbadian Cross-currents: Church-state confrontation with Quaker and Negro, 1660–1689" (Ph.D. dissertation, Loyola University of Chicago, 1976).

9. Gragg, *Quaker Community*, 124–25. Gragg notes that the roughly 170 Quaker families on the island collectively owned more than three thousand slaves. Joseph and John Grove, two leading Barbadian Friends, were heavily involved in the business of slave trading.

10. McCusker and Menard, 299.

11. Some wills negated the humanity of the enslaved simply by listing them alongside livestock ("one negro woman named Judith and one cow called Lawrence") or household goods ("one negroe boy by name Robbin alsoe one silver boate, one Turkie carpet, one Table and one chaire"), Will of Elizabeth Haynes (d. ca. 1672–1674), Barbados Department of Archives (hereafter BDA), RB6/9, 178–80; Will of Margaret Ellicott (d. ca. 1680–1684), BDA, RB6/10, 328–30. Similar wording persisted in several wills, like that of Richard Sutton Sr. (d. 1693/4) who gave "one negroe girl by name Kate and one cow named Lady . . . " to his daughter Mary (BDA, RB6/2, 223–26). Colonel Morris's own will follows these patterns, as he bequeathed to his nephew Lewis

> his plantation and iron works at Tinton, with all lands . . . , all his negroes on that plantation, cattel, horse, kinde, swine, and all other creatures; all household goods . . . [including] one small cabinet sealed up;—wherein is four pearl necklaces, three or four jewels set in gold, and several other things of value; one negro woman named Bess—which [was] his [father's]—unto which he adds all the children of said woman Bess, except one that is otherwise disposed of; 1 doz. silver spoons, one large tankard . . . (etc.) (Bolton, 465)

More than 20 enslaved women in Quaker wills (the highest frequency among names) were called "Bess" or "Besse," a common name given to cows. See Morgan, *Laboring Women*, 80.

12. Harry Emerson Wildes, *William Penn* (New York: Macmillan, 1974), 322. Of course, the Iberian name Anthony suggests that this particular individual could have already known quite a bit about Christianity—Portuguese and Italian missionaries in the Kongo and parts of Luanda had trained lay preachers who spread information about Catholic saints to a wide segment of the population.

13. Robert Bolton, *The History of the Several Towns, Manors, and Patents of the County of Westchester, from its First Settlement to the Present Time* (New York: C. F. Roper, 1881), 465.

14. When the young Lewis expanded his property holdings beyond his 60 x 60 plot of land in St. Michael after returning from privateering in 1644, he would have needed more slaves to work his newly acquired 64 acres in St. James and St. Andrew parishes. See Smith, *Lewis Morris*, 27; BDA, RB3/2, 384; RB3/2, 136; RB3/2, 123; RB3/7, 314–5; RB3/3, 27–8. Many thanks to Larry Gragg for sharing instances of extant Barbadian deeds related to Morris.

15. Of the 37 slave ship voyages destined for Barbados before 1656 that appear in the collaborative database project, *Voyages: The Transatlantic Slave Trade Database*, http://www.slavevoyages.org (accessed May 20, 2010), only half have known ports of embarkation. Slave markets in the Bight of Biafra and Gulf of Guinea islands are best represented, but compilers conceded that the data remains incomplete, and thus, inconclusive. The "African Names Database," part of *Voyages*, includes several captive men with variations on the name Yaff (Yaffee, Yaforee, Yafo, Yavee, Yavay) taken from the port of Galinhas, afterwards repatriated to Sierra Leone by the British; Africanist Joseph Miller agreed that the name sounded Senegambian (personal conversation, March 27, 2009). Adam Jones, a

scholar of the Galinhas region, notes that in the early seventeenth century the Dutch had set up a trading post at Cape Mount just to the south, where "private" traders (those without some sort of official sanction) were known to repair to the swampy mangrove areas at the Mano and Moa River deltas to conduct business. As such, their slaving voyages were rarely recorded. Jones, *From Slaves to Palm Kernels: A History of the Galinhas Country (West Africa), 1730–1890* (Wiesbaden: Steiner, 1983), 20–24.

Historians have become quite skeptical of the ability to pinpoint the geographic, cultural, or religious roots for enslaved Africans brought to the Americas, despite the growing comprehensiveness of scholarly tools such as the Voyages Database. Methodological issues are at the root of this skepticism: one sticking point is that Eltis's database identifies the port of shipment, not the point of capture. African naming patterns, too, are often nothing more than a flexible "bricolage" of identity-making. See note 18, below.

16. *Voyages: The Transatlantic Slave Trade Database*, http://www.slavevoyages .org (accessed May 20, 2010), voyage ID # 26136. Another likely option (given the incomplete evidence) would have been voyage ID #25055, a Boston vessel that arrived in 1645 from Senegambia and the Cape Verdes. Conflicts between the powerful Kaabu empire (regional successors to the Mali empire) and competing coastal states in the Gambia River watershed during the early to mid-seventeenth century meant war captives were either "incorporated into [enemy] forces or sold to [Cape Verdean, Portuguese or Dutch] slave vessels that hovered off-shore." George E. Brooks, *Landlords and Strangers: Ecology, Society, and Trade in Western Africa, 1000–1630* (Boulder: Westview Press, 1994), 184–86, 290–93, 304. This new coastal trade, facilitated by Luso-African middlemen and Portuguese merchants stationed in Cape Verde, gave French, English, and Dutch competitors access to slave markets formerly controlled by the Portuguese. For more on links between the Atlantic slave trade and both the Kaabu empire and the Muslim warrior states that later garnered support against Kaabu's abuses, see Boubacar Barry, *Senegambia and the Slave Trade*, trans. Ayi Kwei Armah (Cambridge: Cambridge University Press, 1998), 42–43, 50–54.

17. Robert M. Baum, *Shrines of the Slave Trade: Diola Religion and Society in Precolonial Senegambia* (Oxford: Oxford University Press, 1999), 77–80, 112–114.

18. In this context of war and violence (not unique to the Senegambian coast), it seems significant that Yaff retained his "African" name, for domestic slaves (termed "bought people" in many parts of West Africa) commonly followed rules of virtual kinship by taking their masters' names, whether voluntarily or imposed. Furthermore, "West Africans usually bore several names, in some cases many names. Some names were given at birth, others during the course of a lifetime; some were nicknames employed casually among friends and family, others were more formally employed and were conferred during rites of passage or less formally to mark important life transitions" (690). Brooks, *Landlords and Strangers*, 27; Trevor Burnard, "Slave Naming Practices: Onamastics and the Taxonomy of Race in Eighteenth-century Jamaica," *Journal of Interdisciplinary History* 31, 1 (2001), 344; Jerome S. Handler and JoAnn Jacoby, "Slave Names and Naming in Barbados, 1650–1830," *WMQ* 53, 4 (1996): 685–728. Alternatively, perhaps Lewis Morris had found the name acceptable (British planters were less likely to impose "Christian" names on their slaves), or he may have wanted to put the frightened youth at ease, and was used to managing foreign-sounding names when he had lived as a guest among the Moskito Indians.

19. Nell or her parents would have likely been purchased by Europeans trading out of Calabar, Ardra, Gold Coast, or Biafran trading posts—those most represented in voyages arriving to Barbados in the decades up to 1670. Of course, Nell might have been purchased by Colonel Morris as late as the 1660s and '70s, after the Royal African Company ramped up their purchase of captives from slave factories on the Gold and Slave Coasts to supply increased demand for labor for sugar plantations in Barbados and Jamaica. See *Voyages: The Transatlantic Slave Trade Database*, http://www.slave voyages.org (accessed May 20, 2010).

20. Hilary Beckles writes that by the 1670s planters had turned from white servants as domestics to black or Amerindian women. Beckles, "Black Female Slaves and White Households in Barbados," in David Barry Gaspar and Darlene Clark Hine, eds., *More than Chattel: Black Women and Slavery in the Americas* (Bloomington: University of Indiana Press, 1996), 113; for a similar process in Virginia, see Brown, *Good Wives, Nasty Wenches, and Anxious Patriarchs*.

21. 18 August 1655, John Bayes to Lewis Morris. BDA, RB3/3, 820.

22. Mary Fisher actually travelled the following year through Southern Europe and the Ottoman Empire, and was granted an audience to the Great Sultan. Frederick B. Tolles, *Quakers and the Atlantic Culture* (New York: MacMillan Co., 1960), 9–10; Phyllis Mack, *Visionary Women: Ecstatic Prophecy in Seventeenth-Century England* (Berkeley: University of California Press, 1992), 169–70; Kenneth L. Carroll, *John Perrot: Early Quaker Schismatic* (London: Friends' Historical Society, 1971), 14–34.

23. Thornton, *The Kongolese Saint Anthony*.

24. Mack, *Visionary Women*, 87–124.

25. James Bowden, *The History of the Society of Friends in America* (New York: Arno Press, 1972), 31 (photostat of original manuscript).

26. Gragg, *Quaker Community*, 39–40; Daily, "Early Quaker Mission," 28.

27. Gragg, *Quaker Community*, 53. Lieutenant Colonel Thomas Rous's son John was likewise inspired by Anne Austin and Mary Fisher, even travelling with them to New England and England, where he met George Fox, and later married Fox's stepdaughter, Margaret Fell the Younger. By 1680 John Rous was one of the wealthiest Quakers in Barbados—his plantation had grown to an impressive 470 acres and 204 slaves, enough to allow him to administer much of his business affairs as an absentee landlord in England. "Alphabetical list of owners, & c., in the parish of St. Philip . . . " Barbados, 1680. NAL, CO 1/44, No. 47.x.

28. In my analysis of the 47 most influential local Friends (those who were named as executors or given special responsibilities in at least three Quaker wills), two-thirds were planters. Of the Society's members whose occupations are known, half were categorized as planters; another 20 percent were merchants, followed by artisans, professionals (including physicians, schoolteachers, etc.), shopkeepers, and members of maritime trades. According to Richard Dunn's categorization of "big," "middling," and "small" planters, in the 1680 island census, one-third of all Quakers who owned slaves could be categorized as middling or big planters. Dunn, *Sugar and Slaves*, 92. For other statistical analyses, see Gragg, *Quaker Community*, 63–67.

29. A scholar of early modern Angola and the slave trade, Joseph Miller, has offered the following summary of the overlapping lines of "kinship" in Africa and the Diaspora:

Africans thought of themselves on multiple levels: as blacks/Africans (their master's definition), as part of communities defined by "country marks," by intimate affiliations. . . . These collectivities were supple groupings that people created, often by intense experiences of personal conversion, to pursue many strategies, from primary affective bonds of family to economic collaboration, social reproduction, personal clientage, political factions, or—for Muslims— affiliation with faith-based communities of worship. They were as much volun- taristic and spontaneous as they were determined by descent . . .

Miller, "Retention, Reinvention, and Remembering: Restoring identities through en- slavement in Africa and under slavery in Brazil," in *Enslaving Connections: Changing Cultures of Africa and Brazil During the Era of Slavery*, ed. José C. Curto and Paul E. Lovejoy (Amherst, NY: Humanities Books, 2004), 81–121. For similar comments, see also Brooks, *Landlords and Strangers*, 27, 38–39; Baum, *Shrines of the Slave Trade*, 24.

30. For the social makeup of the Society of Friends in Barbados at the time of the 1680 census, see Gragg, *Quaker Community*, 65–74. Quakers in Barbados often included bequests to the poor in their wills, with gifts ranging from 3 pounds current to 6,000 pounds of sugar. Will of Elizabeth Savery (d. 1693), BDA, RB6/3, 250–54; Will of Robert Richards (d. 1684), BDA, RB6/12, 527–30.

31. Morgan Godwyn, *The Negro's and Indians Advocate, Suing for their Admission into the Church* (London, 1680), 101. For more on African secret societies, see Jones, *From Slaves to Palm Kernels*, 179–82.

32. G. P. Makris, *Changing Masters: Spirit Possession and Identity Construction among Slave Descendants and other Subordinates in the Sudan* (Evanston, IL: North- western University Press, 2000), Ch. 1, "Historicising Possession," 1–20.

33. Ann Taves, "Knowing Through the Body: Dissociative Religious Experience in the African- and British-American Methodist Traditions," *Journal of Religion* 73, 2 (1993): 200–22; Sylvia R. Frey and Betty Wood, *Come Shouting to Zion: African Ameri- can Protestantism in the American South and British Caribbean to 1830* (Chapel Hill: University of North Carolina Press, 1998).

34. Quoted in Carla Gerona, *Night Journeys: The Power of Dreams in Transatlan- tic Quaker Culture* (Charlottesville and London: University of Virginia Press, 2004), 87–89; Harry Emerson Wildes, *William Penn* (New York: Macmillan, 1974), 322.

35. Joan Vokins, *God's Mighty Power Magnified* (London, 1691), 43. My emphasis.

36. Today, several vodu religious "orders" along the former "Slave Coast" act in a similar way, allowing both northern peoples of "slave" descent and coastal lineages who benefitted from the slave trade to soothe modern antagonisms through posses- sion and shared ritual spaces. On Goroduvu, see Judy Rosenthal, *Possession, Ecstasy, and Law in Ewe Voodoo* (Charlottesville & London: University Press of Virginia, 1998), 1. For historical instances of such "healing cults," see Thornton, *The Kongolese Saint Anthony*; John M. Janzen, *Lemba, 1650–1930: A Drum of Affliction in Africa and the New World* (New York: Garland Publishers, 1982).

37. John Rous, *A warning to the inhabitants of Barbadoes: who live in pride, drunk- ennesse, covetousnesse, oppression and deceitful dealings; and also to all who are found acting in the same excess of Wickedness, of what Country soever, that they speedily re- pent . . .* [London, 1657].

38. Rous, *A warning to the inhabitants of Barbadoes*, 1.

39. Exodus 7–11. Rous uses some variation of the phrase *hard-hearted* on nearly every page of his 1657 *Warning*; Pinder employs the term when referring to the cruel usage of slaves (*A Loving Invitation*, 11).

40. Pinder, 11.

41. Rous, *The Sins of a gainsaying and rebellious people*, 1; see also Richard Pinder, *A loving invitation (to repentance and amendment of life) unto all the inhabitants of the island of Barbados before the Lords fore Judgements came upon them . . .* (London, 1660), 8.

42. Epistles, or formal letters directed to the whole community of Friends, were the Society's official mode of disseminating information and encouraging fellowship among their far-flung members.

43. Fox, Epistle 153: "To Friends beyond Sea, that have Blacks and Indian Slaves" (1657), in *A collection of many select and Christian epistles, letters and testimonies, written on sundry occasions, by that ancient, eminent, faithful Friend and minister of Christ Jesus, George Fox* (London, 1698), 117. Ritter Dailey writes that during one of his trips to London to open a mercantile business (ca. 1659), Rous met Margaret Fell the Younger at Swarthmore Hall, and they married in 1661 ("The Early Quaker Mission. . . . ," 29). As a consequence, Rous's personal ties to Fox and his family brought that eminent Friend closer to the Barbados community through correspondence. Fox contributed a postscript to another tract published by Rous, *The Sins of a gainsaying and rebellious people* (1659).

44. Smith, *Lewis Morris*, 6–7; see also Arthur Percival Newton, *The Colonising Activities of the English Puritans: The Last Phase of the Elizabethan Struggle with Spain* (New Haven, CT: Yale University Press, 1914), 265–66; John Symonds to Lord Mandeville, Nov. 1939, NAL, Manchester Papers, 423.

45. Smith, *Lewis Morris*, 51–52. *CSPC*, Item 101 i, Vol. 7 (1669–1674), 37. August ? 1669. M. De Baas to (Col. Codrington). The French representative of St. Lucia sent "two negroes belonging to Barbadoes" with this letter along with news of Morris's continued detainment.

46. NAL, CO 1/27, No. 36.

47. Fox, *Journal*, 352 ; see also Henry J. Cadbury, ed., *Narrative Papers of George Fox: Unpublished or Uncollected, edited from the manuscripts* (Richmond, IN: United Friends Press, 1972), 229–30.

48. Fox lamented that the ship's crew soon thereafter turned skeptics in the face of a miracle: "endeavor[ing] to persuade the Passengers, That it was not a Turkish Pirate, that chased us; but a Merchant-man going to the Canaries." Fox, *Journal*, 350–51; see also Edmundson, *Journal*, 53.

49. Sweet, *Recreating Africa*, 105.

50. Fox, *Journal*, 353.

51. Ibid., 354. Although Fox's sermon suggests he meant this order in a literal way, his larger concerns with moral uncleanliness or disorder suggest he was hoping to purge the spiritual dirt from local Quakers' lives. Mary Douglas, *Purity and Danger: An Analysis of Concepts of Pollution and Taboo* (New York : Routledge, 2003).

52. George Fox, *Gospel Family Order, being a Short Discourse concerning the Ordering of Families, both Whites, Blacks, and Indians* ([London], 1676), 13–14.

53. Ibid., 4–5; Joshua 24:15. This idea of slaves forming part of a slaveholder's "family" would not have seemed strange to many West Africans, for except in cases where

the majority of slaves were men serving as gang labor and living apart in barracks-like conditions, the enslaved were considered part of their master's kin group—like the English "family," a highly stratified representative of societal class norms. Patrick Manning, *Slavery and African Life: Occidental, Oriental and African Slave Trades* (Cambridge & New York: Cambridge University Press, 1990), 120.

54. Such were the central concerns planters voiced to Anglican bishop Morgan Godwyn during his visit to Barbados in the late 1670s, ones that persisted for many decades. *The Negro's and Indians Advocate*, 135–38.

55. Gragg, 54–55.

56. Fox, *To the Ministers, Teachers, and Priests, (So Called, and so Stileing your Selves) in Barbadoes* ([London], 1672), 75.

57. Ibid., 69.

58. Smith, 83; Gragg, 54.

11 / Evangelization and Insubordination

1. See William C. Braithwaite, *The Second Period of Quakerism* (Cambridge: Cambridge University Press, 1955), 248–67, for a useful summary of the type of organization that Fox spent much of his time in England and the Americas promoting: the settling on locations for weekly worship, the formation of separate monthly men's and women's meetings for business, and Quarterly meetings for the Society's leading men to convene. Each branch of this exclusive Society was designed to play an important role: some disciplining wayward Friends, others vetting proposed marriage partners. Smaller "committee"-like meetings allowed Quaker surgeons, midwives, and schoolmasters to share concerns or monitor the apprenticeships of youths into a profession or trade. For this process on Barbados, see Gragg, *Quaker Community*, Ch. 5.

2. Haverford Library Special Collections (hereafter HLSC), Richardson MSS, 112–13.

3. William Edmundson, *A journal of the life, travels, sufferings, and labour of love in the work of the ministry, of that Worthy Elder, and Faithful Servant of Jesus Christ, William Edmundson, Who departed this Life, the 31st of the 6th Month, 1712* (Dublin, 1715), 53–54; Natalie Zacek, *Settler Society in the English Leeward Islands, 1670–1776* (Cambridge & New York: Cambridge University Press, 2010), 151–52; Larry Gragg, "A Puritan in the Indies: The Career of Samuel Winthrop," *WMQ* 50, 4 (1993): 768–86.

4. Edmundson, *Journal*, 54.

5. Ibid., 55–56.

6. In 1660 George Fox had published a statement that has come to be known as the Quaker Peace Testimony, in which he and his followers renounced "all outward Wars & Strife, and Fightings with Outward Weapons, for any end, or under any pretense whatsoever." *A Declaration from the Harmless & Innocent People of God Called Quakers Against ALL Sedition Plotters & Fighters in the World* (London, 1660). For more on why Fox and other Friends took on this extreme position of nonviolence, see Meredith Baldwin Weddle, *Walking in the Way of Peace: Quaker Pacifism in the Seventeenth Century* (Oxford: Oxford University Press, 2001), 39–54.

7. Governor William Willoughby of Barbados, who called Colonel Morris "my very good friend (but a severe Quaker)," had (before his arrest for privateering) considered sending him to negotiate with the French over the impending return of St. Christopher to the English. Because of Morris's religious scruples, Willoughby was

"confident he will not accept the employm.t," but allowed himself a chuckle as he imagined how the "Mon[sieu]rs would be astonisht at thee & thou." NAL, CO 1/22, No. 60, f. 101v.

8. As many religious scholars have noted, fringe groups who bid for legitimacy usually have to give up or soften (at least for a time) practices that most threaten social order—and the path to respectability for the Society of Friends was no different. For this period of transition, see especially Braithwaite, *The Second Period of Quakerism*; Mack, *Visionary Women*; Adrian Davies, *The Quakers in English Society, 1655–1725* (Oxford: Clarendon Press, 2000); and Jean R. Soderlund, *Quakers and Slavery: A Divided Spirit* (Princeton, NJ: Princeton University Press, 1985).

9. The only other Caribbean Quaker community for which Meeting Minutes still exist is Tortola, which was established by Friends in the early eighteenth century, and even in those records "There is little information as to the treatment of slaves. . . . The minutes of the Meeting mention them but once [in a property dispute]. . . . " Charles F. Jenkins, *Tortola, A Quaker Experiment of Long Ago in the Tropics*, Supplement No. 13 to the Friends Historical Society (London, 1923), 52.

10. Gragg, *Quaker Community*, 134.

11. George Fox, *Gospel Family Order*, 22; taken from a letter written by Fox to Barbadian Quakers ca. 1672–1673, and reportedly read at a Quarterly Meeting at Thomas Rous's.

12. George Fox, *A Catechisme for Children. That they may come to learn of Christ, the Light, the Truth, the Way, that leads to know the Father, the God of all Truth* (London, 1660). During her 1680 mission trip, Joan Vokins noted that Nevis Friends were using this catechism with their children (Vokins, *God's Mighty Power*, 61).

13. G. F., *The Heathens Divinity Set upon the Heads of all Christians, That say, They had not known that there had been a God, or a Christ, unless the Scripture had declared it to them* ([London], 1672/3).

14. Such was the sentiment voiced in one English writer's fictional exchange between a master and slave, intended to encourage English planters to engage in their own religious dialogue with the enslaved. Thomas Tryon, [Philotheos Physiologus], *Friendly Advice to the gentlemen-planters of the East and West Indies: in three parts* (London, [1684]), 159–60.

15. Thornton, *Africa and Africans in the Making of the Atlantic World, 1400–1800* (Cambridge: Cambridge University Press, 1998), 249–57; Sweet, *Recreating Africa*, 107–10.

16. Gerona, *Night Journeys*, 9. See also Mechal Sobel, *Teach Me Dreams: The Search for Self in the Revolutionary Era* (Princeton, NJ: Princeton University Press, 2002), 8–12.

17. Gerona, *Night Journeys*, 34. This distinction was especially important for Quakers, who were often accused of viewing the Scriptures as expendable, given their transcendentalist focus on the Inward Light. In refutations of these critiques, Fox and others insisted the Bible needed to be read and understood, to be referred to as *confirmation* of a person's inner spiritual experiences, not as a substitute for it. James L. Ash, Jr., "'Oh No, It is Not the Scriptures!' The Bible and the Spirit in George Fox," *Quaker History* 63, no. 2 (1974): 94–107.

18. Kenneth L. Carroll, *John Perrot: Early Quaker Schismatic* (London: Friends' Historical Society, 1971), 66–67.

19. Perrot's willingness to swear oaths and take part in the lavishness of Jamaica's island culture also eroded his base of support among Friends (see Block, "Faith and Fortune," 234–37). Several schismatic movements like Perrot's rejected the nascent leadership's attempts to impose structure: they include the Wilkinson/Storey controversy (1675) and George Keith's separatist following among New Jersey and Pennsylvania Quakers in 1695. These conflicts necessarily also affected ideas of authority and discipline throughout transatlantic Quaker communities (the Wilkinson/Storey conflict included critiques of wealth, and Keith's followers even challenged slavery), but details have been omitted here for the sake of clarity. For more details, see Braithwaite, *Second Period of Quakerism*, 290–323, 482–95; William J. Frost, *The Keithian Controversy in Early Pennsylvania* (Norwood, PA: Norwood Editions, 1980).

20. In 1672, Edmundson had written from Jamaica to "Overseers of Friends" to avoid creating "Sects, Divisions and Parties," to make sure they all kept to "one certain Voice." ("A Letter of Examination to All, Who have assumed the place of Shepherds, [etc.]," in *Journal*, 290). The settlement period was a move towards "separate spheres" for men and women, in which "matters involving charity, marital problems, discipline of women, and healing were viewed as women's work, while problems dealing with censorship, business, organization of the ministry, and debates with non-Quakers were viewed as men's work" (Mack, *Visionary Women*, 286, Chs. 8–9). See also Braithwaite, *Second Period of Quakerism*; Gragg, *Quaker Community*, 84–87.

21. Edmundson, "A Letter of Examination," in *Journal*, 281.

22. A transatlantic controversy broke out after 82 well-meaning Barbadian Quakers agreed to subordinate themselves in all things "both spiritual and temporal, unto the judgment of the Spirit of God in the Men and Women's Meetings, as believing it to be more according to the universal wisdom of God than any particular measure, in myself." Robert Rich, *Abstracts of some letters written by Mr. Robert Rich: treating mostly of spiritual matters . . . for promoting of universal love amongst all sorts of people without respect of persons, parties, or sects* (London, 1680), 6. John Pennyman (another later-century Separatist) claimed in *A Bright Shining Light discovering the pretenders to it* (London, 1680), that on Judgment Day the Foxian "Pharisees" would be "utterly overwhelmed, like Pharaoh and his chariots in the sea" (p. 3). See also Ann Mudd, *A Cry, A Cry a sensible cry for . . . the Quakers return out of that Egyptian darkness . . .* (London, 1678), 3; John Pennyman, *The Quakers Rejected: which was also foretold by a person once eminent among them, taken out of his writings which were published some years ago* ([London], 1676), 8; and John Pennyman, *A Short Account of the Life of Mr. John Pennyman; with some writings &c.* (London, 1703), 89.

23. Will of Thomas Morris (d. ca. 1666–1670), RB6/8, 132–33. Even if Thomas Morris had meant to preserve family ties, he bequeathed his kinsman Colonel Morris a quarter share (including at least one slave) of his estate, tearing at least one person from his or her home.

24. George Foster of St. James (d. ca. 1670–1672), BDA, RB6/8, 330–41. The codicil to his will spelled out the consequences of attempts to contravene his instructions, stipulating that "such sale or mortgage shall be of noe value But that it shall or may be lawfull for the next of kin to recover the same and hold it for them and their heirs." For similar restrictions, see Will of John Loftis (d. 1681), BDA, RB6/14, 297–300; Will of John Frank (d. 1719), BDA, RB6/4, 571–72. Most testators, however, referred to slaves' direct cash value and disposability, some instructing executors to "sell & dispose of

any Negroe slaves Goods & Chattells . . . if they soe meet, for the raising of moneys as Occasion shall require . . . " (Will of Henry Wherley (d. 1685), BDA, RB6/10, 428–40). In one clause that conjures up images of King Solomon's judgment, one testator willed that, along with his silver plate, his slave woman Celia should "be equally divided" between his sister and a cousin—clearly a reference to Celia's value, not her person, but a sobering reflection of the total commodification of Africans (Will of John Taylor (d. 1709), BDA, RB6/5, 278–79).

25. Gragg, *Quaker Community*, 85–87.

26. Letter by Geo Fox to Lewis Morris, Swarthmore Ii.mo 1679, published in *The Great Mistery of Fox-Craft Discovered. And the Quaker Plainness & Sincerity Demonstrated . . . Introduced with two Letter [sic] written by G. Fox to Coll. Lewis Morris, deceased, exactly Spell'd and Pointed as in the Originals, which are now to be seen in the Library at Burlington in New-Jersey, and will be proved (by the likeness of the Hand, &c.) to be the Hand-Writing of the Quakers Learned FOX, if denied* ([London], 1705), 4. Unfortunately for historians, Barbadian Quakers' marriage records have perished along with their Meeting Minutes, providing no certainty about the content or resolution of sexual scandals like this one.

27. Godwyn, *The Negro's and Indians Advocate*, 135.

28. Fox, *Gospel Family Order*, 17–18.

29. For a nineteenth-century example of slave communities' informal acknowledgment of marriage bonds (even those unrecognized by the master), see Anthony Kaye, *Joining Places: Slave Neighborhoods in the Old South* (Chapel Hill: University of North Carolina Press, 2007).

30. Wills are naturally the place where West Indian adventurers' economic concerns become most visible. John Rous seems to have worried that his father's second marriage jeopardized his own share of the Barbados estate. He had evidently returned to Barbados after a stay in England to find his father married, "very contrary to my expectation." John begged his mother-in-law Margaret Fell Fox to write "a few lines" to his father, "to advise him to deal fairly and equally by me, and that though my mother be dead, and he hath married another, yet that he would be no ways drawn to diminish that which he hath already settled on me." Her words must have had the desired effect, for Thomas Rous wrote into his will that his wife was indeed entitled to 1,000 pounds sterling (as per an agreement by court order signed by Colonel Lewis Morris, Colonel Christopher Lynn, and Richard Clarke), but that after his death she should make out a legal document acknowledging that the debt had been satisfied, to avoid "debate stiffe or law suits between my ex[ecut]er and my said wife." John Rous, as eldest son, was named executor and received the lion's share of the estate. Library of the Society of Friends, Box Mtg MSS L15. John Rous to Margaret Fox, Barbados, 7.x.1671; Will of Lt. Col. Thomas Rous (d. 1677), BDA, RB6/9, 567–70.

31. Library of the Society of Friends, Box Mtg MSS, #35.

32. Gragg, *Quaker Community*, 98–102.

33. William Edmundson, Epistle sent from Newport, 19.vii.1676, in J. William Frost, ed., *Origins of Quaker Antislavery* (Norwood, PA: Norwood Editions, 1980), 68.

34. HLSC, Richardson MSS epistle book, 111.

35. For the former interpretation, see Trevor Burnard, *Mastery, Tyranny and Desire: Thomas Thistlewood and His Slaves in the Anglo-Jamaican World* (Chapel Hill: University of North Carolina Press, 2004), 209–40; for a critique of such problematic

heroic narratives, see Marisa J. Fuentes, "Power and Historical Figuring: Rachael Pringle Polgreen's Troubled Archive," *Gender and History* 22, 3 (2010): 564–84.

36. Paul E. Lovejoy, "The Ideology of Slavery in Africa," in Lovejoy, ed., *The Ideology of Slavery in Africa* (Beverly Hills & London: Sage Publications, 1981), 24; Humphrey J. Fisher, *Slavery in the History of Muslim Black Africa* (New York: New York University Press, 2001), 74, 150, 183. Moreover, slaves born into captivity (rather than those purchased or condemned to slavery for a crime) had a more stable position in their masters' families—even if not the children of enslaved concubines, they were usually barred from sale and given tasks similar to freeborn servants. See Barry, *Senegambia and the Atlantic Slave Trade*, 113, 115; Patrick Manning, *Slavery and African Life: Occidental, Oriental and African Slave Trades* (Cambridge & New York: Cambridge University Press, 1990), 119; Joseph Miller, "Lineages, Ideology and the History of Slavery in Western Central Africa," 54–55.

37. George Fox, *A Primmer and Catechisme for Children* (London, 1660), 24–25.

38. Contemporary accounts are: *Great Newes from the Barbadoes, or, A True and faithful account of the grand conspiracy of the Negroes against the English and the happy discovery of the same: with the number of those that were burned alive, beheaded, and otherwise executed for their horrid crimes: with a short discription of that plantation* (London, 1676) and *A Continuation of the State of New England . . . together with an Account of the Intended Rebellion of the Negroes in Barbados* (London, 1676). For historical analysis see Jerome Handler, "The Barbados Slave Conspiracies of 1675 and 1692," *JBMHS* 36, 4 (1982): 312–33; John Thornton, "War, the State, and Religious Norms in Coramantee Thought," in Robert Blair St. George, ed., *Possible Pasts*, 188, 191–95; and D. B. Chambers, "Ethnicity in the Diaspora: The Slave-Trade and the Creation of African 'Nations' in the Americas," *Slavery & Abolition* 22, 3 (2001): 25-39, esp. 33.

39. Yochoh was a frequent name for male slaves embarked out of Ouidah [Benin] and Bonny [Nigeria] (Wyochoh female analogue); Adoe/Addo (usually a male name) was frequent among slaves shipped from coastal ports from Ouidah [Benin] to Lagos [Nigeria]. "African Names Database," in David Eltis, *Voyages: The Transatlantic Slave Trade Database* http://www.slavevoyages.org. Quakers held slaves whose names suggest origins stretching from Old Calabar [Cote d'Ivoire] to Bonny [Nigeria]. Will of Thomas Morris (d. ca. 1666–1670), RB6/8, 132–33. Elisha Mellows (d. 1695), also of St. James, likely held at least one Gold Coast Akan-speaker (Cudgoh) and perhaps two others (Dakee and Cocko), BDA, RB6/11, 68–72. See also Jerome Handler, "Slave Names and Naming in Barbados, 1650–1830," *WMQ* 53, 4 (1996): 685–728.

40. *Great Newes*, 10–11.

41. *Great Newes*, 12–13.

42. When Colonel Morris had exercised his role as Council member and militia leader, he was ordered on two dates to intervene in apprehending runaway slaves and servants from uncultivated parts of the island, and in ensuring that Irish Catholic servants (potential rebels on account of their faith and status) were unarmed. Minutes of the Council of Barbados, 23 June & 22 Sept 1657: NAL, PRO 31/17/44, 231; Barbados National Library, Lucas Mss, Reel 1, f. 368.

43. Epistles originally sent to the "Generall, Monthly, Quarterly & Six Weeks Meetings in Barbados" were copied and re-sent to Friends meetings throughout the North American mainland. Copies have been located in surviving Women's Meeting

records from Shrewsbury, New Jersey; and Newport, Rhode Island. Monmouth County Historical Society, Freehold, New Jersey. Shrewsbury Monthly Meeting, Women's Meeting register book, 1680–1732 (microfilm); HLSC, Richardson MSS, 136–37.

44. See Vincent Brown, "Spiritual Terror and Sacred Authority in Jamaican Slave Society," *Slavery & Abolition* 24, 1 (2003): 24–53; *Great Newes*, 12.

45. Huntington Library, BL 369, "An Act for the better ordering and Governing of Negroes," Barbados, 27 Sep 1661, 8–9.

46. The Council first examined the poor state of the militia, which had become so diminished in recent years that a few black men assumed to be trustworthy had been armed to help defend the island against French attack in 1673. Dunn, *Sugar and Slaves*, 257.

47. See *A Continuation of the State of New England*, 19–20; Gragg, *Quaker Community*, 78. Edmundson also witnessed the aftermath of two other calamities of 1675–1676 that intensified English colonists' sense of God's fearful providence: King Philip's War in New England and Bacon's Rebellion in Virginia (Edmundson, *Journal*, 76–77, 97–98).

48. William Edmundson, *Journal*, 102.

49. Joseph Besse, *A Collection of the Sufferings of the People called Quakers* (London: L. Hinde, 1753), ii.305–6.

50. Planters in 1649 had blamed the island's radical sectaries for instigating the plot as a means of exporting the English Revolution to Barbados (Dailey, "The Early Quaker Mission," 26). They may have been influenced by a similar law passed in 1674 by the Virginia Assembly (Drake, *Quakers and Slavery in America* (New Haven: Yale University Press, 1950), 18).

51. NAL, CO 31/2, 202–214; Besse, *Sufferings*, ii.308. In April 1678, Governor Jonathan Atkins renewed the Act. The Council also passed a law establishing a 12-month residency requirement for preaching on the island, figuring that any person who had lived on the island for even a year would sufficiently understand the complicated pragmatics of slavery and would avoid unadvised subjects in their religious addresses. At least one Public Friend and missionary to the island was prosecuted under this law. Solomon Eccles was arrested in 1678 and accused of preaching prior to the end of 12 months' residency. Eccles wrote a letter in his defense, denying that he had told Barbadians to put aside their weapons (that was only a rule for Friends, who could serve the state in other functions), and that he had been urging islanders to join with the French against British rule of the island. British Library, Egerton MSS 3020C, ff. 60–62.

52. According to Besse, Ralph Fretwell and John Sutton were the names memorialized for their conscientious nonconformity to the law forbidding slaves from meetings; Colonel Morris is not mentioned. "Summons and Declaration against Ralph Fretwell and Richard Sutton for Negroes present at Quaker meetings." In Besse, *Sufferings*, ii.309–11.

53. [Alice and Thomas Curwen], *A Relation of the Labour, Travail and Suffering of that faithful Servant of the Lord Alice Curwen* ([London], 1680), 18. Emphasis mine.

54. Besse, *Sufferings*, ii.313–15. Twice in 1678 Morris's name appears on petitions to Governor Atkins protesting discrimination against Friends.

55. *A Short Account of the Manifest Hand of God that hath fallen upon several marshals and their deputies: who have made great spoil and havock of the goods of the people called Quakers in the island of Barbadoes for their testimony against going or sending to*

the militia: with a remarkable account of some others of the persecutors of the same people in the same island, together with an abstract of their sufferings (London, 1696), 18–19.

56. Edmundson, *Journal* (London, 1774 reprint), 329.

57. *Manifest Hand of God*, 17–18.

58. Fox had approved this negotiation, responding to Nevis Friends' query about their moral duty by citing his belief in the "biblical" right to self-defense, for it was part of God's law to resist anyone who would come

> to burn your house, or rob you, or come to ravish your wives or daughters, or a company should come to fire a city or town, or come to kill people, don't you watch against such actions? And won't you watch against such evil things in the power of God in your own way? . . . [You should] discover to the magistrate such as would destroy your lives or plantations or steal.

Quoted in Braithwaite, *Second Period of Quakerism*, 620–21.

12 / Inclusion, the Protestant Ethic, and the Silences of Atlantic Capitalism

1. Major-General Timothy Thornhill was allegedly so infuriated by Quakers in his militia rolls who cited liberty of conscience that he was heard to storm, "God Damn your Conscience; if I cannot make your Conscience obey, I'll make your stubborn Dogs Back bend." After this outburst, he tied up one offending Friend "Neck and Heels with his own hands, with that Violence and Rage, that almost deprived him of Life." *Manifest Hand of God*, 22–23.

2. "To the Governour of Barbadoes, called Sir Richard Dutton" (delivered 28.ii.1683). Besse, *Sufferings*, ii.239.

3. By the mid-eighteenth century, Joseph Besse published a massive two-volume *Collection of the Sufferings of the People called Quakers*, one of the best sources among those few extant that tell the history of Caribbean Quakers. Volume II contained the names of more than two hundred Quakers who were fined or jailed in the second half of the seventeenth century, and reprinted petitions and acts against Quakers, including a copy of the 1676 anti-Quaker laws in full. For more on Quakers' martyr complex, see Gragg, *Quaker Community*, 59, 78.

4. Godwyn published three tracts, *The Negro's and Indians Advocate* (1680), *A Supplement to the Negro's and Indian's Advocate* (1685), and *Trade Preferred before Religion and Christ made to give place to Mammon* (1685), protesting the cruelties of plantation life and advocating for evangelization. (The quotations are from the 1680 tract, 4–6). Godwyn's tracts helped inspire Anglican leaders to form the Society for the Propagation of the Gospel (SPG) several decades later. Like the Society of Friends' evangelization efforts, the SPG made most progress after Bishop William Fleetwood encouraged conservatism on the question of universal baptism, noting that British slaveholders were still uncertain as to the effect of that on the state of a slave's freedom. In 1705 he painted the missionaries as planters' allies, acknowledging that Britons "are a people who live and maintain ourselves by Trade; and if Trade be lost, or overmuch discouraged, we are a ruined nation." The SPG gained some traction in the Caribbean after Barbadian native and former Leeward Islands governor Christopher Codrington bequeathed his considerable estate to the SPG in 1710, but instead of championing the spiritual rights of enslaved people, it soon found itself running a plantation for

profit. See Jon Butler, *Awash in a Sea of Faith: Christianizing the American People* (Cambridge, MA: Harvard University Press, 1992), 135–42; Andrew Beahrs, "'Ours Alone Must Needs Be Christians': The Production of Enslaved Souls on the Codrington Estates," *Plantation Society in the Americas* 4, 2/3 (1997): 279–310.

5. Edmundson, "An Epistle to Friends in Barbados," in *Journal*, 327–28.

6. Fox, *Gospel Family Order*, 19. In a 1676 letter to Friends in Newport, Rhode Island, Edmundson had asked them to reflect on the Golden Rule and "consider w[i]th your selves if you were in ye same Condition as ye blacks are . . . " He closed his letter with a piercing rhetorical question: "And many of you count it unlawfull to make Slaves of the Indians . . . and if so, then why the Negroes?" HLSC, Richardson MSS, 87; Drake, *Quakers and Slavery*, 10.

7. Fox, *Gospel Family Order*, 16.

8. These three are the only slaves named as individuals in the will of Lieutenant Colonel Thomas Rous, all three of whom were bequeathed to his widow Eleanor. Will of Thomas Rous the Elder (d. ca. 1677–79), BDA, RB6/9, 569–70.

9. Scholarship on early Virginia showed the brief period of flexibility towards Africans as servants, freedmen, and even property holders. William Penn himself had toyed with the idea of limiting terms of service for African "servants" brought to Pennsylvania (a gentler term preferred by Quakers in Pennsylvania), but he decided that he could not deprive his own plantation nor the colony's settlers of a workforce purchased with the assumption of lifelong slavery (Wildes, *William Penn*, 322–24).

10. No evidence survives to indicate how Friends responded after listening to this sermon, but it is notable that the published version of Fox's address to the governor and Council carried not a single reference to manumission.

11. Out of 76 Quaker testators in my sample, only eight included manumission clauses. Jerome S. Handler and John T. Pohlmann, "Slave Manumissions and Freedmen in Seventeenth-Century Barbados," *WMQ* 41, 3 (1984): 405. In this sample, 80 individuals islandwide manumitted one or more slaves in their wills (out of 3,777— about 2 percent of total testators). The authors note that wills were by far the most popular method for granting manumission during this period, finding only five extant deeds for the entire period that performed the same function (395–96).

12. Equiano, *Interesting Narrative*, Vol. I, 194–95.

13. This phrase echoed what Fox had preached in his *Gospel Family Order* sermon: "you should preach Christ to your Ethyopians that are in your Families, that so they may be free Men indeed" (14). When West Indians seemed reluctant to follow up on such a provocative request, Fox dismissed it, writing "(it is no matter) I did it but to try them . . . " Drake, *Quakers and Slavery in America*, 7. Drake notes that this comment was only found in 1939, in a segment of Fox's personal papers that had not been published—likely another example of later generations of Friends' discomfort with their leaders' ambivalence on slaveholding.

14. According to Quaker historian Thomas Drake, Fox's original sermon specified 30 years as a fitting term of service, but Friends who edited the sermon before its 1676 publication as *Gospel Family Order* altered his text to suggest only a more acceptable and vague "considerable Term of Years" (Drake, *Quakers and Slavery*, 6). One surviving manuscript version of the sermon (perhaps closer to his original words) mentions 30 years' service "more or less" as deserving reward (HLSC, Richardson MSS, 86). We can see Fox's more specific directives followed in at least

one instance. Writing her will in 1684, the widow Rebecca Ormunt of St Peters bequeathed three female slaves to young women Friends, stipulating they serve for 30 years, after which each were to receive 20 shillings and their freedom. In 1700, Edward Parsons, a merchant living in Speightstown, indicated in his will that one of those three, a "negro woman by name Hannah" who had been serving his daughter Mulier, should remain in that service only "for the Terme she hath to serve, being about fifteene yeares as may appeare by the Will of Rebecca Armond late of this Island." Will of Rebecca Ormunt (d. ca. 1684–1685), BDA, RB6/10, 353–54; Will of Edward Parsons (d. 1700), BDA, RB6/43, 165–68.

15. Manumission clauses suggest that these definitions were widely shared throughout the island population. Handler and Pohlmann, "Manumissions and Freedmen," 401.

16. Will of Alexander Benson (d. 1681), BDA, RB6/14, 289–91; Will of Ann Biswicke of St. Josephs (d. ca. 1682–1683), BDA, RB6/12, 475–77. Handler and Pohlmann found that although the number of slaves labeled "mulattoes" in wills were few, they were freed "at a higher rate than their relative numbers in the slave population at large" ("Manumissions and Freedmen," 402).

17. Morris's biographer believes that he might have accompanied Fox and his party to New Jersey, or at least reunited with his party later in 1672, for his brother had just passed away earlier in the year, leaving him his New York and New Jersey properties (Smith, *Lewis Morris*, 83).

18. Sheridan, *Lewis Morris 1671–1746*, 2–6.

19. Tryon's continuing ties to Barbados can be seen in two extant Quaker wills dating into the latter decades of the seventeenth century: London salter James Denham, whose family lived on the island, named Tryon in his will (*Barbados Records: Wills and Administrations,* ed. Joanne Mcree Sanders (Houston, TX: Sanders Historical Publications, ca. 1979–1981), ii.90); and Barbadian Friend Nathaniel Perkins was married to Tryon's daughter Rebecca (Will of Nathaniel Perkins (d. ca. 1686–1687), BDA, RB6/40, 392–93.

20. Thomas Tryon, *The Merchant, Citizen and Country-man's Instructor: or, a necessary companion for all people* (London, 1701), 201. See also Kim F. Hall, "'Extravagant Viciousness': Slavery and Gluttony in the Works of Thomas Tryon," in *Writing Race across the Atlantic World: Medieval to Modern,* ed. Philip D. Biedler and Gary Taylor (New York: Palgrave Macmillan, 2005), 93–111.

21. Besse, *Sufferings,* ii.313–14, 315.

22. I have discussed this issue at length in my article, "Cultivating Inner and Outer Plantations: Profit, Industry, and Slavery in Early Quaker Migration to the New World," *Early American Studies* 8, 3 (Fall 2010): 515–48.

23. Tryon, *Merchant, Citizen and Country-man's Instructor,* 194.

24. Slaveholders in many places defined "good treatment" as the provision of adequate food and raiment. Emanuel Curtis of St. Philips wrote:

It is my Will and desire and I do hereby ordeyne and appoint that all my negroes be well provided for and taken care of (that is to say) that they have sufficient provision of bread-kind and two pounds of Saltfish Mackrell or other provision weekly and every week so long as they live or remain on my plantation And that my Executors yearely and every yeare do allow and give unto each negroe man one Jackett and two pair of drawers and to each of the women One waste-coat and two pettycoates of some corse [sic] sort of cloath.

Will of Emanuel Curtis of St. Philips (d. ca. 1695-1696), BDA, RB6/11, 362-67.

25. Will of Henry Jones (d. 1688), BDA, RB6/3, 132-37.

26. The problem with an argument centered on paternalism is revealed by look-ing more closely at documents regarding Morris's legal battle to regain ownership of Anthony and Susannah, two of his brother Richard's slaves who had been sold off the estate during New York's Dutch interlude. When the English had regained control, the pair had run away from their new master, Louis DuBois, and headed back to the Morris estate. One New York historian assumed that they were motivated to return because "they were treated better under Morris' ownership than that of DuBois"; Lloyd Ultan & Gary Hermalyn, *The Birth of the Bronx, 1609-1900* (Bronx, NY: Bronx County Historical Society, 2000), 174-75; Lisa Garrison, *South Bronx and the Found-ing of America* (Bronx, NY: Bronx County Historical Society, 1987), 10; see also Dean Freiday, "Tinton Manor: The Iron Works," *Proceedings of the New Jersey Historical So-ciety* 74 (1952): 256-58, esp. 258; Bolton, *History of Westchester*, 469. The original court documents, however, reliably establish only that DuBois and Morris were engaged in a struggle over property rights. See transcripts of New York's Colonial Archives (1673-1675), in *Third Annual Report of the State Historian of the State of New York, 1897* (New York and Albany: Wynkoop Hallenbeck Crawford, 1898), Appendix L, 288, 364, 381-82, 385, 400, 403, 421.

27. New York Archives, Albany, New York. Inventory of the estate of Colonel Lew-is Morris, February 17, 1691, reprinted in Bolton, *History of Westchester*, 469. More than 60 additional slaves may have resided on his Tinton Falls estate (Freiday, "Tinton Manor," 258-60).

28. See Morgan, *Laboring Women*, 82-87.

29. Planter Herbert Griffith was in the clear minority when he bequeathed his "ne-groes called Simcarty and his wife Rose, Joane, Tom and James" to his grandson (Will of Herbert Griffith of St. Phillips (d. ca. 1695-1696), BDA, RB6/11, 418-22. Somewhat more common in Barbadian wills are recognitions of maternal relationships: "Hagar and her three children by name, Mingoe, Bell and Man" (Will of Hester Foster (d. 1686), BDA, RB6/40, 343-45); "one negro woman named Rose & her three children Vizt. Maribah, Mercy & Judy . . . " (Will of John Grove (d. 1717), BDA, RB6/4, 151-52).

30. Rutgers University Special Collections, New Brunswick, New Jersey. Morris Papers, n.d. "The Account as Clark has kept it of work done last harvest and by whom." "An Account of the Negroes above fourteen years of Age belonging to Lewis Morris, at Morrisania," 1755. In E. B. O'Callaghan, *The Documentary History of the State of New-York, arranged under direction of the Hon. Christopher Morgan, Secretary of State* (Albany, NY: Weed, Parsons, & Co., 1850), iii.510-12. Will of Isabella (Graham) Mor-ris (d. 1746). New York Historical Society, SY 19__, no. 29.

31. Equiano, *Interesting Narrative, Vol. 1*, 205.

32. George Fox, *Line of Righteousness and justice stretched forth over all merchants, &c.: and an exhortation to all Friends and people whatsoever who are merchants, tradesmen, husbandmen or sea-men, who deal in merchandize, trade in buying and selling by sea or land, or deal in husbandry, that ye all do that which is just, equal and righteous in the sight of God and man* . . . (London, 1661), 5. This tract was reprinted in

1674, and ordered to be read "in all the Men & Women's Meetings," adding postscripts to Friends who were "Shop-keepers or Merchants, or Factors, or any other trades." William Edmundson exhorted business-minded Caribbean Quakers to conduct themselves as "merchantmen of the precious Truth." *A journal of the life, travels, sufferings, and labour of love in the work of the ministry of that worthy elder, and faithful servant of Jesus Christ* (London, 1715), 267. See James Walvin, *The Quakers: Money and Morals* (Cambridge, England: Cambridge University Press, 1997), or for a theological perspective, Douglas Gywn, *The Covenant Crucified: Quakers and the Rise of Capitalism* (Wallingford, PA: Pendle Hill, 1995).

33. Rutgers University Special Collections, Morris Papers, n.d. "The Account as Clark has kept it of work done last harvest and by whome." Among those receiving compensation were Negro Harry (3 shillings), Negro Jacob (for a quart of rum), Negro Hagar (harvest)

34. Ultan & Hermalyn, *Birth of the Bronx*, 174–75.

35. Bolton, *History of Westchester*, 465.

36. Will of John Todd (d. 1687), BDA, RB6/40, 435.

37. See John K. Thornton, "'I Am the Subject of the King of Congo': African Political Ideology and the Haitian Revolution," *Journal of World History* 4 (1993): 181–214; John Ringquist, "Kongo Iron: Symbolic Power, Superior Technology and Slave Wisdom," *The African Diaspora Archaeology Network Newsletter* (Sept. 2008), http://www.diaspora.uiuc.edu/newsletter.html; George Brooks, *Landlords and Strangers*, pp. 40, 290; Robert Baum, *Shrines of the Slave Trade*, pp. 6, 33.

38. According to one Africanist historian and religious scholar, Yoruba and Igbo, too, shared "a concept of personal destiny, chosen before birth," and misfortune was seen as a sign that a person had ignored the divinity's call to service. Elizabeth Isichei, *The Religious Traditions of Africa: A History* (New York: Heinemann, 2004), p. 313.

39. Will of Rowland [Ronald] Hutton of St. Philip (d. 1679), BDA, RB6/14, 82–85.

40. Fox, *Gospel Family Order*, 16.

41. "Journal of the Procedure of the Governor and Council of the Province of East New Jersey, 1682–1703," in Frederick W. Ricord and W. M. Nelson, eds., *Documents Relating to the Colonial History of New Jersey* (Trenton, NJ: John L. Murphy Publishing, 1890), 70–71; Aaron Leaming and Jacob Spicer, *The Grants, Concessions, and Original Constitutions of the Province of New Jersey* (Union, NJ: Lawbook Exchange, 2002), 254–55. This law was passed at the same time as another designed to prohibit "Negroes and Indian slaves [from] their frequent meetings and gathering themselves together in greate numbers at the Lords Day," and required the sheriff to whip those slaves found without Sunday passes from their masters. In Barbados in 1685, the Council passed "An Act to Prevent Persons tradeing with Negroes & Stealing Potts and Jarrs" (NAL, CO 31/3 f. 61–64). By 1712, even though only a handful of slaves had been manumitted in New York (four of them by Quakers), the Assembly passed a law ordering that "no Negro, Indian or Mallatto, that hereafter be made free, shall enjoy, hold or possess any Houses, Lands, Tenements or Hereditaments in this colony" (Graham Russell Hodges, *Root and Branch: African Americans in New York and East Jersey* (Chapel Hill: University of North Carolina Press, 1999), 49, 67, 297n).

42. Equiano, *Interesting Narrative*, Vol. 1, 260, Vol. 2, 11–14.

43. Will of John Todd (d. 1687), BDA, RB6/40, 435. Todd softened his demand for productivity slightly, writing that if he were to be sold, "George Forster may have the

refusal of him before another. And when he is sold and the money received for him I do order my Executors to pay for him out of the same Five pounds sterl: wch I give him as a Legacie."

44. Bolton, *History of Westchester*, 465.

45. Petition entitled "Sundry Particulars relating to the Militia Act, briefly touched, and presented to Edwin Stead, our King's Lieutenant-Governor of the Island Barbadoes, and Council, from the People called Quakers, Inhabitants there," signed by Richard Ford, Thomas Pilgrim, Francis Gamble, Thomas Robins, John Waite, Joseph Harbin, and Philip Collins, 17.xii.[Feb].1686. In Besse, *Sufferings*, ii.334.

46. For the most recent summary of planters' legal concerns, see Travis Glasson, "'Baptism Doth Not Bestow Freedom': Missionary Anglicanism, Slavery, and the York-Talbot Opinion," *WMQ* 67, 2 (2010): 279–318; and Ruth Paley, Cristina Malcolmson, and Michael Hunter, "Notes & Documents: Parliament and Slavery, 1660–c.1710," *Slavery & Abolition* 31, 2 (2010): 257–81.

47. During the mid-seventeenth century the Calvinist doctrine of "election," or predestination, competed with ideas called antinomianism and Arminianism, both of which emphasized human choice in matters of salvation. Calvinist-leaning puritans pilloried Quakers, Seekers, and Baptists alike for their individualistic approaches to faith. See Nicholas Tyacke, *Aspects of English Protestantism, 1530–1700* (Manchester: Manchester University Press, 2001).

48. Block, "Inner and Outer Plantations," 539–40.

49. George Gray, "A Testimony for Family Meeting and keeping Negroe servants until they are in some Measure brought into a Christian Life which is ye Duty of every Master & Mistriss of families to Endeavour to bring them to that they may be free Men in deed," ca. 1680–1698 (HLSC, Vaux Collection, box 3, Haverford Collection 1167).

50. The best portrayals of these complexities are not to be found in historians' writings, but rather in sensitive fictional portrayals like Toni Morrison's *A Mercy* (New York: Vintage, 2009) or Marlon James's *The Book of Night Women* (New York: Riverhead Books, 2009).

51. Braithwaite, *Second Period of Quakerism*, 436.

52. British Library, Egerton MSS 3020C, ff. 60–62. See also Kenneth L. Carroll, "Early Quakers and 'Going Naked as a Sign,'" *Quaker History* 67, 2 (1978): 83–89.

53. Victor Witter Turner, *Drums of Affliction: A Study of Religious Processes among the Ndembu of Zambia* (Oxford: Clarendon Press, 1968), 185, 187, 29, 49.

54. Miller, "Retention, Reinvention, and Remembering," 83.

55. Quaker historian William C. Braithwaite wisely opined on why Friends' religious documents contain many silences, especially regarding controversies resolved at a later date: ". . . men say little of changes produced by hostile and unwelcome criticism from without, and often persuade themselves into thinking that the resulting alterations in their conduct spring from their own initiative or go on asserting and believing that they have not changed at all." Braithwaite, *Second Period of Quakerism*, 494.

56. Smith, *Lewis Morris*, xi.

57. Henry J. Cadbury, "Another Early Quaker Anti-Slavery Document," *Journal of Negro History* 27 (1942): 210–15.

58. Smith, *Lewis Morris*, 109–14.

59. Block, "Inner and Outer Plantations," 534–36.

60. "An Account of the Negroes above fourteen years of Age belonging to Lewis Morris, at Morrisania," 1755. In O'Callaghan, *Documentary History of the State of New-York*, iii.510–12.

13 / Religion, Empire, and the Atlantic Economy

1. Exquemelin's *History of the Buccaneers* had been published in English in 1684, and by the time *Robinson Crusoe* appeared in 1719, the pirate narrative was one of the most popular genres in England. Although Defoe's authorship of *A General History of the Pyrates* (1724) has come into question, he and other metropolitan authors were fascinated by stories of ex-buccaneers, and both *Captain Singleton* and *A General History* sold well.

2. Daniel Defoe, *The life, adventures, and pyracies, of the famous Captain Singleton* (London, 1720), esp. 197, 200, 204, 210, 215, 218.

3. Two telling examples from letters from Barbados governors to the Lords of Trade and Plantations: Atkins in 1680: " . . . to the great discontent of the people and their own great ease and advantage, [Quakers] will neither serve on juries, find arms, send to the Militia, or bear any office, shifting it off with the trick of inability to swear, whereas profit is all that they aim at. Thus the King's faithful and dutiful subjects are forced to bear their burden, when by Act of Parliament the Quakers, for refusing to take the oath, were banished to this and other of the Plantations, whereof they have made such good use as to put themselves into a better condition than they could be in elsewhere" (NAL, CO 1/44, No. 45); Governor Kendall in 1693 suspected Quakers of alliance with the deposed Catholic James II; these "papists in disguise" pledged their absolute allegiance to William Penn (NAL, CO 28/2, No. 22). See also Barry Reay, "Popular Hostility towards Quakers in Mid-Seventeenth Century England," *Social History* 5, no. 3 (1980): 392; and John Miller, *Popery and Politics in England, 1660–1688* (London & New York: Cambridge University Press, 1973), 86. For an example of how Friends responded to those accusations, see George Whitehead, *Ministers Among the People of God (Called Quakers) No Jesuits* (London, 1683).

Defoe's personal prejudices against Quakers have been the subject of interest for literary critics for some time. In a 1932 essay, Ezra Kempton Maxfield dug up several of Defoe's comments on the denomination and found them to be moderate: "I know, we are mighty fond of loading the Quakers with many of our own Follies, and some will hardly allow them to have the Use of their Reason. . . . But they have generally speaking, stuck closer to their profess'd Principles, than most, if not than any Sort of People among us." Kempton, however, points to several satirical pieces in which Defoe turns eccentric Quaker figures into mouthpieces (like Shakespeare's fools) for his observations on politics and human nature ("Daniel Defoe and the Quakers," *PMLA* 47, 1 (1932): 179–90, esp. 182, 189).

4. Defoe himself was ambivalent about the morality of slavery, on the one hand condemning unchristian cruelties and on the other enthusiastically supporting colonial projects for which slavery would be paramount. Hans H. Andersen, "The Paradox of Trade and Morality in Defoe," *Modern Philology* 39, 1 (1941): 23–46. For other useful critiques of Defoe's perspective on religion, race, and economy in this and other of his writings, see Maximillian Novak, *Economics and the Fiction of Daniel Defoe* (Berkeley: Univ. of California Press, 1962); George E. Boulukos, "Daniel Defoe's *Colonel Jack*, Grateful Slaves, and Racial Difference," *English Literary History* 68, 3 (2001):

615–31; Leon Guilhamat, *Defoe and the Whig Novel: A Reading of the Major Fiction* (Cranbury, NJ: Associated University Presses, 2010), Ch. 4, "From Necessity to Liberty, or Piracy without Guilt: *Captain Singleton*."

5. H. H. Gerth and C. Wright Mills, eds., *From Max Weber: Essays in Sociology* (Abingdon, England: Routledge, 1991 [1948]), xxiv.

6. Sylvia Wynter, "Unsettling the Power of Being/Power/Truth/Freedom: Towards the Human, After Man, Its Overrepresentations—An Argument," *CR: The New Centennial Review* 3, 3 (2003): 257–337, esp. 281, 297–308, 314–17.

7. Louis Dumont, *From Mandeville to Marx: The Genesis and Triumph of Economic Ideology* (Chicago: University of Chicago Press, 1977), esp. 35, 61.

8. Davis, "Constructing Race."

9. For similar theses, see Jeremy Basks, "Communication Breakdown: Information and Risk in Spanish Atlantic World Trade during an Era of 'Free Trade' and War," *CLAR* 20, 1 (2011): 35–60; for Africa, see Paul E. Lovejoy and David Richardson, "'Pawns Will Live When Slaves is Apt to Dye': Credit, Risk, and Trust at Old Calabar in the Era of the Slave Trade," in Paul E. Lovejoy and Toyin Falola, eds., *Pawnship, Slavery, and Colonialism in Africa* (Trenton, NJ: Africa World Press, 2003), 70–96.

10. Douglas, *Purity and Danger*, 70.

11. Zahedieh, "The Merchants of Port Royal, Jamaica, and Spanish Contraband Trade, 1655–1689," *WMQ*, 3rd ser., 43 (1986): 573.

12. Lance Grahn, *The Political Economy of Smuggling: Regional Informal Economies in Early Bourbon New Granada* (Boulder, CO: Westview Press, 1997), 101.

13. Copy of a letter to the Governor of Santo Domingo, 10 May 1664, NAL, CO 1/18, No. 65.

14. Control of the Caribbean and its potential for wealth, and thus, global power, manifested itself in European wars, often characterized as dynastic: 1702–1713 (the War of Spanish Succession), 1718–1719 and 1727 (undeclared war between Britain and Spain), 1739–1741 (the War of Jenkin's Ear, which wrapped into the larger War of Austrian Succession, lasting until 1748), and 1754–1763 (the French and Indian/Seven Years War). These conflicts and their subsequent peaces were unevenly observed in the West Indies, where the long tradition of "no peace beyond the line" still prevailed. See Grahn, *Political Economy of Smuggling*; John Jay Tepaske, "Integral to Empire: The Vital Peripheries of Colonial Spanish America," in Christine Daniels and Michael V. Kennedy, *Negotiated Empires: Centers and Peripheries in the Americas, 1500–1820* (New York: Routledge 2002), 29–41; Nuala Zahediah, "The Merchants of Port Royal, Jamaica, and Spanish Contraband Trade, 1655–1689," *WMQ* 43 (1986): 570–93, esp. 582–83.

15. K. G. Davies, *The Royal African Company* (New York: Antheneum, 1970), 331–32.

16. One other outcome of the Treaty of Utrecht was the confirmation of the Protestant succession in England, as the Bourbons were forced to renounce support for the claim of James Stuart, the Pretender, to the English throne. For more on the South Sea Bubble, see P. G. M. Dickson, *The Financial Revolution in England* (London: Macmillan, 1967); John Carswell, *The South Sea Bubble* (London: Cresset, 1960; rev. ed., Alan Sutton, 1993); and John Sperling, *The South Sea Company: An Historical Essay and Bibliographical Finding List* (Cambridge, MA: Harvard Graduate School of Business Administration, 1962).

17. Proposals for Establishing the Factory at Porto Belo, 1731. Clements Library, Shelburne Coll., 43:234–35.

18. Gerardo Moro, *Informe en Derecho, sobre que la Compañía de el Assiento de la Gran Bretaña . . . debe declararse libre, y exempta de la paga de los Reales Derechos . . .* (Mexico, 1724), 29. At the John Carter Brown Library, B724, -M8345i.

19. Cedula for a Represalia, 29 Mar 1726. Clements Library, Shelburn 43:577. See also an undated "Memorandum of the Spanish India Trade" for the accusation by a British writer that "it has often been practiced by the Ministers in Spain to grant two Sorts of Cedulas, the one to Appease Solicitations, and the Other to be punctually obeyed, therefore its [*sic*] requisite the greatest precaustion should be taken to procure a Cedula that will not admit of any dispute in the Indies, under the penalty of a Severe *multa* [fine]." Shelburne 44:19 and 44:268.

20. See Moro, *Informe en Derecho*; Anon., "Slaves, politics and commerce in the Indies, c. 1720" (John Carter Brown Library: 08–55); *A True and Impartial Account of the Rise and Progress of the South Sea Company; Wherein the Assiento Contract is particularly considered . . . Humbly addressed to Admiral Vernon, by a Gentleman now resident in Jamaica* (London, 1714), 8–9, 13–14

21. William L. Clements Library, Shelburne Papers, 44:1–52. Memorandum from an unknown West Indies trader, ca. 1739.

22. Clements Library, Shelburne 44:235–42. Proposal to Peter Burrel Esq., Governour of the Royal Company for renewing trade, Mexico, Sept. 22, 1748. This was allegedly the petitioner's second letter with the same proposal, the first sent in 1738, before the outbreak of the War of Jenkin's Ear.

23. Answers to the Objections made by the Honble Committee of Accompts . . . to the Accompts of Nicholson & Tasselll, Jan. 27, 1736 and Mar. 30, 1738. Clements Library, Shelburne Papers, 44:155–76. Many of their arguments contended that business had been facilitated greatly with their predecessors in the Portuguese, Genoese, and French *asiento* trade through the generous granting of *regalos*. An anonymous gentleman of Jamaica agreed, arguing "that the Company's interest has suffered greatly by too much Parsimony, for 10,000 Pieces of Eight well applied abroad, will go farther, and do more than 100,000 at the Court of Madrid. I have heard a Governor looking at his King's Schedule, say, *Aqui esta la Cedula pero es menester Sangrarlo* [Here is the royal order, but it needs to be bled]" (*A True and Impartial Account of the Rise and Progress of the South Sea Company*, 24).

24. Solicitud de un padre irlandés para reconciliar y convertir a herejes ingleses en Veracruz, 1672 (Archivo General de la Nación de México, Jesuitas, Vol. III, caja 18, exp. 55). Relación del causa de fe contra Juan Joseph Agustín Sandino, presbítero de la ciudad de Panamá por bautizar a un muchacho hereje, 1690 (AHN, Inq. Lib. 1023, ff. 516v-534v). Many thanks to Ryan Crewe for the first citation.

25. Caso contra Nicolas Yan and Henrrique Andres, hereges nazionales y otros cuyos nombres no se expresan. AHN, Inq. 1622, Exp. 14, ff. 10–23.

26. AHN, Inq. 1622, Exp. 14; AHN, Inq. Lib. 346, no pagination; AHN Inq. 1599, R.7, Exp. 14, ff.: 1r-60v.

27. Informaciones recibidas en la ciudad de Madrid concernientes al comercio de negros y a la introducción de herejes que bajo el pretexto de la trata de esclavos, se internan en la provincia de Cartagena de Indias, 1685. AHN, Inq. Lib. 305, f. 474r. To be certain, their surveillance was not solely directed against those of "heretic"

nations. In 1706, Cartagena's inquisitors gathered testimonies for almost a year to support a case against the French chief administrator of the *asiento*, Monsieur la Rui, for various "Heresies and blasphemies," but in the end, they reported to Madrid that they had not effected the order to arrest him because of the resultant danger "given his private agreements made in the service of a trade of such importance, so tightly joined to other great interests" (*su confianza para el manejo de vn negocio de tanta importancia en que se atreuisan tan crezidos intereses*). Among those heresies for which La Rui was accused was his public refusal to purchase papal bills, telling Spaniards that they were just a ruse to trick people out of their money, and his vocal exasperation at the pace of business given the many feast days Cartageneros celebrated, saying that God had decreed man should work six days and set aside just one for worship. Cartagena, Jan. 12, 1707, Letter from inquisitors to Madrid. AHN, Inq. 1621, Exp. 21, ff. 34v–35v.

28. AHN, Inq. Lib. 305, ff. 606r–611r; AHN, Inq. Leg. 1620, Exp. 22.

29. Grahn, *Political Economy of Smuggling*, 134–35.

30. Gomez Suaro de Figueroa and Don Gollathez de Leon y Serras to the Suprema, May 22, 1691 (AHN, Inq. Lib. 1019, ff. 324r–325r). Inquisitors Figueroa and Leon also claimed that Protestantism could spread via these means to Spanish creole youths, raised by enslaved wet nurses who could possibly pass along the religious taint in their breast milk.

31. British Library, Add. Mss. 25556, f. 69. Letter from the Court of Directors of the SSC to His Grace the Duke of Newcastle, June 17, 1725.

32. British Library, Add. Mss. 323,788, f. 174. Letter from the Board of the South Sea Company to His Excellency Mr. Keene. London, July 4, 1735. The response from the Spanish Crown was to have the governor and bishop look into the matter and get back to him with a report before determining what might be most *conveniente*. Thanks to Adrian Finucane, who brought these and other sources in this chapter to my attention. See Finucane, "The South Sea Company and the Anglo-Spanish Connections, 1713–1739" (Ph.D. dissertation, Harvard University, 2011).

33. Sept. 13, 1725, Extract of a letter from Mr. Lewis Hays at Vera Cruz, Clements Library, Shelburne Papers 44:289–92. Linda Colley, *Britons: Forging the Nation, 1707–1837* (New Haven, CT: Yale University Press, 1992), Ch. 1; Owen Stanwood, "The Protestant Moment: Antipopery, the Revolution of 1688–89 and the Making of an Anglo-American Empire," *Journal of British Studies* 46, 3 (2007): 481–508; Colin Haydon, *Anti-Catholicism in Eighteenth-Century England* (Manchester: Manchester University Press, 1993); Brendan McConville, *The King's Three Faces: The Rise and Fall of Royal America, 1688–1776* (Chapel Hill: University of North Carolina Press, 2006), 56–63.

34. Another critic (to be described in more length later) wrote in 1681 of the consequences of the illicit slave trade with English and Dutch slave traders: "[This trade] fosters so many offenses, and the gold and silver of Spain gives even more strength to the heretics to continue with their rebellions against the Holy Church; from these beginnings the poisonous infection will spread to the very doors [of the castle], tearing apart the royal Crown" (*El que con el fomento de tanto agravio, con su oro y con la plata de España, se da más fuerzas a los herejes, para mostrarse más rebeldes a la Santa Iglesia, de que no pocos inficiona, y esto a las puertas de casa desmembrando juntamente la real corona*). Francisco José de Jaca, *Resolución Sobre la Libertad de los Negros y sus Originarios, en estado de Paganos y después ya Cristianos: La primera condena*

de la esclavitud en el pensamiento hispano, ed. Miguel Anxo Pena González (Madrid: Consejo Superior de Investigaciones Científicas, 2002), 84.

35. John Carter Brown Library: 08–55, "Slaves, politics and commerce in the Indies, c. 1720," 129–30. [New Acquisition Purchased from Rodger Friedman Rare Book Studio (10/2/07), 66 manuscript treatise.]

36. [Alexander O. Exquemelin], *The History of the Bucaniers: Being an Impartial Relation of all the Battels, Seiges, and other most Eminent Assaults committed for several years upon the Coasts of the West Indies by the Pirates of Jamaica and Tortuga* (London: Printed for Tho. Malthus, 1684), 31. The most recent translation of the original Dutch varies in several respects from the 1684 English publication by Thomas Malthus, so I offer citations for both the early English and modern versions when they coincide (i.e. [Exquemelin], *Bucaniers* (1684); Exquemelin, *Buccaneers*).

37. The classic source is Exquemelin, *Buccaneers*. Other scholarly treatments of this era of English buccaneering include Kris Lane, *Pillaging the Empire: Piracy in the Americas, 1500–1750* (Armonk, NY: M. E. Sharpe, 1998), esp. Ch. 4; Peter Earle, *The Pirate Wars* (London: Methuen, 2003), Ch. 6.

38. One of the most fascinating aspects of this story is how the Spanish governor of the place refused to allow his heart to be softened or his weapons stilled when faced with the possibility of accidentally killing some of his religion's sacred representatives. "The Friers and Nuns besought him by all the Saints to save his own, and their lives; for as Godly as they were, they lov'd this world much better than the other. But neither Prayers nor Tears could prevail, so that many an *Ora pro nobis* was sent to Purgatory, before they could finish the work . . . " ([Exquemelin], *Bucaniers*, 75; Exquemelin, *Buccaneers*, 136–37).

39. [Exquemelin], *Bucaniers*, 46.

40. [Exquemelin], *Bucaniers*, iv, 90, 108. The early English printing repeats similar language twice more: "To these Prisoners they were very severely smart in their Examinations, insomuch that some were catechized so rigorously, till they were past giving an Answer" (90); in another moment, the pirates, "overtaking a Party of unfortunate Diego's, took them all Prisoners. These they Catechized according to their wonted mercy, to discover where they had hid their goods, which brought some that could not endure pain so well as others, to auricular Confession" (108).

41. Marcus Rediker, *Villains of All Nations: Atlantic Pirates in the Golden Age* (Boston: Beacon Press, 2004), 127–36, 146, 170–71.

42. Ibid., 38–42.

43. Indeed, as economic historian Nuala Zahediah has persuasively demonstrated, licensed and forced appropriation of Spanish bullion created wealth for pirates and stimulated the growth of Jamaica's overall economy. "A Frugal, Prudential, and Hopeful Trade: Privateering in Jamaica, 1655–1689," *Journal of Imperial and Commonwealth History* 18 (1990): 145–68. See also her "Merchants of Port Royal" and "The Wickedest City in the World: Port Royal, Commercial Hub of the Seventeenth Century Caribbean," in Verene Shepherd, ed., *Working Slavery, Pricing Freedom. Essays in Honour of Barry W. Higman* (Kingston, Jamaica, and Oxford, 2002), 3–20. West Indian planters had almost equal reputations for drunkenness and venery thanks to their easy wealth. However, planters were not demonized quite so roundly, being one step removed in matters of capital and "civility" from bloodthirsty pirates—one could argue that planters drank, cursed, tortured, raped, and fornicated as much as their

296 / NOTES TO CHAPTER 13

buccaneer brethren, but in more private (and hence 'licit') circumstances than the Port Royal taverns.

44. [Exquemelin], *Bucaniers*, ii.

45. Exquemelin, *Buccaneers*, 18. See Walter Adolphe Roberts, *Sir Henry Morgan, Buccaneer and Governor* (New York: Covici, Friede, Inc., 1933), Ch. 14 for a summary of Morgan's libel suit against Malthus.

46. Zahediah, "Wickedest City," 13.

47. This is of course a bit simplistic, as tradesmen were needed for the Caribbean's shipbuilding and crop transportation needs. These may have provided quite comfortable livings, as one scholar has noted that "craft wages [in Port Royal] were said to be three times the level in London" (ibid., 6n).

48. Ibid., 8.

49. Ryan Crewe, "Brave New Spain: An Irishman's Independence Plot in Seventeenth-Century Mexico," *Past & Present* 207, no. 1 (2010): 3–52; Shaw and Block, "Subjects without an Empire"; Óscar Recio Morales, "'Una nación inclinada al ruido de las armas': la presencia irlandesa en los ejércitos españoles, 1580–1818," *Tiempos Modernos: Revista Electrónica de Historia Moderna* 10 (2004) http://www.tiempos modernos.org.

50. Though the word *buccaneer* is most strongly associated with piracy, most of the men who became buccaneers were French and multiracial drifters who had set up a living in Hispaniola hunting and smoking the meat of wild animals over a *boucan*, a type of grill, to sell as provisions to passing ships. For more on logwood cutters, see Jennifer Anderson, "Better Judges of the Situation: Environmental Realities & Problems of Imperial Authority in the Bay of Honduras," *Itinerario* 3, 3 (2006): 55–75.

51. Rediker, *Villains of All Nations*.

52. [Exquemelin], *Bucaniers*, 39; Basil Ringrose, *Bucaniers of America. The Second Volume* (London, 1685), 121. Catholics may have been more likely to demonstrate their devotion through their raiding (especially if privateers and not outright pirates), for seized religious objects could be donated, where Protestants would be more apt to destroy or desecrate them in acts of iconoclasm. French Dominican Jean-Baptiste Labat described how a group of privateers returning to Martinique in the late seventeenth century "contributed 30 sols [each] to the sacristy, and did so with much piety and modesty. This may surprise people in Europe where *flibustiers* are not credited with possessing much piety, but as a matter of fact they generally give a portion of their good fortune to the churches. If church ornament or church linen happen to be in the prizes they capture, the *flibustiers* always present them to their parish church" (Labat, *Nouveau voyage aux isles de l'Amerique* (1742 ed.), Vol. 1, Ch. 9).

53. AHN, Inquisición, Libro 1023, No. 96, ff. 382r–83r.

54. [James Houstoun], *Dr. Houstoun's Memoirs of his Own Life-Time* (London, 1747), 287–91. Houstoun based his belief in religion as a tool of domination on an anecdote of "a Negro-boy, who was bred up a Roman Catholick" that he had acquired while in Cartagena. Even though Houstoun initially considered the boy "very honest and true to his Trust," Houstoun was convinced he was involved when a chest of rhubarb went missing, though the boy denied any culpability. Houstoun believed that guilt worked: he had put the alleged crime into the ear of the boy's confessor and the goods, which "fetched me above 4000 Pieces of Eight," miraculously reappeared (290–91).

55. Defoe, *Some Considerations on the Reasonableness and Necessity of Encreasing and Encouraging the Seamen* (1728); James Oglethorpe, *The Sailor's Advocate* (London, 1728). Defoe also satirized the tricking of poor Englishmen to be sold as servants in *Colonel Jack* (London, 1722).

56. Daniel James Ennis, *Enter the Press-Gang: Naval Impressment in Eighteenth-Century British Literature* (Missisauga, ON: Associated University Presses, 2002). Interestingly, Quakers who published autobiographical narratives of being forced into naval service used tales of being mercilessly beaten for their passive resistance to violence as a reflection of their strength of faith and character, not a denunciation of the immorality of press-gangs themselves (p. 125). James Oglethorpe of Georgia, a rather eccentric figure himself, had made the moral connection between the enslavement of Africans and protecting English liberties against the tyranny of press-gangs. (Ennis, *Enter the Press-Gang,* 49). See also David Eltis, "Labour and Coercion in the English Atlantic World," *Slavery & Abolition* 14, 1 (1993): 207–26; Linebaugh and Rediker, *Between the Devil and the Deep Blue Sea,* 212–22; E. P. Thompson, *Customs in Common* (New York: New Press, 1991), 404–62.

57. Alan Atkinson studied the case of transported convicts in eighteenth-century Britain: "A convict named Henry Woodford stated quite correctly in 1721 that 'the Law was not . . . that they should be . . . sold for Slaves.' Such punishment, he protested, 'was worse than Death,' for 'being Christians by Baptism' Englishmen could not be forced into bondage," in "The Free-Born Englishman Transported: Convict Rights as a Measure of Eighteenth Century Empire," *Past & Present* 144 (Aug. 1994): 88–114, esp. 91.

58. Denver Alexander Brunsman, "The Knowles Atlantic Impressment Riots of the 1740s," *Early American Studies* 5, 2 (2007): 336–48. Brunsman argues that hostility towards impressment was even stronger in the Caribbean and other American ports, rioting "to defend local economic interests and their perceived rights and liberties within the empire" (339).

59. For executions between 1685 and 1688, Quaker names include William Andrews, William Bailey, John Evans, Philip Gamble, and Melatiah Holder; Quaker Dorothy Earle, a member of the Women's Spring Meeting, was compensated £50 for two slaves executed following the 1692 conspiracy. Hilary Beckles, *Black Rebellion in Barbados: The Struggle Against Slavery, 1627–1838* (Bridgetown, Barbados: Antilles Publications, 1984), 43–47; Jerome S. Handler, "The Barbados Slave Conspiracies of 1675 and 1692," *Journal of the Barbados Museum and Historical Society* 36 (1982): 312–33.

60. Jerome S. Handler, *The Unappropriated People: Freedmen in the Slave Society of Barbados* (Baltimore, MD: Johns Hopkins University Press, 1974), 39.

61. For the intensification of this trend in the eighteenth century, see Charles R. Foy, "Ports of Slavery, Ports of Freedom: How Slaves Used Northern Seaports' Maritime Industry to Escape and Create Transatlantic Identities, 1713–1783" (Ph.D. dissertation, Rutgers University, 2008), and Julius Scott, "The Common Wind: Currents of Afro-American Communication in the Era of the Haitian Revolution" (Ph.D. dissertation, Duke University, 1986).

62. Linebaugh and Rediker, *Between the Devil and the Deep Blue Sea,* 164–67; Kenneth J. Kinkor, "Black Men Under the Black Flag," in *Bandits at Sea: A Pirates Reader,* ed. C. R. Pennell (New York: New York University Press, 2001), 195–210; Peter

T. Leeson, *The Invisible Hook: The Hidden Economics of Pirates* (Princeton, NJ: Princeton University Press, 2009), 157–71.

63. Trouillot, "Culture on the Edges," 189–210.

64. Case against Juan de Rada, natural of the Portuguese Indies, 1718 (AHN, Inq. Leg. 1623, Exp. 2, Causa 24, ff. 139r–140v).

65. See Hartman, *Scenes of Subjection*, 56–57.

66. James Sweet discusses similar complaints by slaves to Inquisition officials of their English masters hindering them from converting or practicing Catholicism. His research shows that Portugal's inquisitorial preoccupation with Anglicanism began only after the early decades of the eighteenth century, presumably when the South Sea Company began administering an *asiento* station in Argentina, increasing the number of contraband slaves introduced into Brazil (*Recreating Africa*, 96–100).

67. AHN, Inq. Leg. 1599, Exp. 14; Inq. Lib. 345, Madrid, Oct. 5, 1734, no pagination, and Lib. 346, Madrid, Feb. 6, 1739.

68. For scholarship on these laws and their inducements to runaway slaves throughout the Caribbean basin, see Jane Landers, *Slave Society in Spanish Florida*; Matthew Restall, "Manuel's Worlds: Black Yucatan and the Colonial Caribbean," in Landers and Robinson, eds., *Slaves, Subjects, and Subversives*; Linda M. Rupert, "Marronage, Manumission and Maritime Trade in the Early Modern Caribbean," *Slavery & Abolition* 30, 3 (2009): 361–82; Rupert, "Water of Faith, Currents of Freedom: Gender, Religion and Ethnicity in Inter-imperial Trade between Curaçao and Tierra Firme," in Nora Jaffary, ed., *Race, Religion, and Gender in the Colonization of the Americas* (Burlington, VT: Ashgate, 2007); Jorge Chinea, "A Quest for Freedom: The Immigration of Maritime Maroons into Puerto Rico, 1656–1800," *The Journal of Caribbean History* 31, 1–2 (1997): 51–87; David M. Stark, "Rescued from Their Invisibility: The Afro-Puerto Ricans of Seventeenth- and Eighteenth-Century San Mateo de Cangrejos, Puerto Rico," *The Americas* 63, 4 (2007): 551–86; James Sweet, *Recreating Africa*, 96–100; John J. Tepaske, "The Fugitive Slave: Intercolonial Rivalry and Spanish Slave Policy, 1687–1764," in Samuel Proctor, ed., *Eighteenth-Century Florida and its Borderlands* (Gainesville: The University Press of Florida, 1975), 1–12; and John Thornton, "African Dimensions of the Stono Rebellion," *AHR* 96, 4 (1991): 1101–13.

69. Leonard Cocke to Commodore Den, Santiago de Cuba, 3 Nov. 1736. *CSPC*, Item 469, Vol. 42, 345–46. For earlier example of an Irishman who championed interracial freedom struggles, see Ryan Crewe, "Brave New Spain: An Irishman's Independence Plot in Seventeenth-Century Mexico," *Past & Present* 207, no. 1 (2010): 3–52. Using the logic of Catholic evangelization and the defense of the Crown's hinterlands, Spanish governors were far more adept at recruiting from among the ranks of free and enslaved people of color in the Caribbean. Indeed, Spaniards' willingness to create interracial alliances both expanded their ranks of frontier fighters, and sowed terror in the English colonies: from the Stono Rebellion of 1739 to the rumors of Spanish collusion in the New York fire and rebellion conspiracy of 1741, anti-English alliances built on Spanish Catholic loyalties. Mark M. Smith, "Remembering Mary, Shaping Revolt: Reconsidering the Stono Rebellion," *Journal of Southern History* 67, no. 3 (2001): 513–34; John K. Thornton, "African Dimensions of the Stono Rebellion," *AHR* 96, no. 4 (1991): 1101–13; Jill Lepore, *New York Burning: Liberty, Slavery and Conspiracy in Eighteenth-Century Manhattan* (New York: Knopf, 2005), 49–50, 163.

70. Deposition of John Tello, 18 June 1730. *CSPC*, Item 311 ix, Vol. 37, 164.

71. Linebaugh and Rediker, *The Many-Headed Hydra*, 193–98; Scott, "The Common Wind."

72. "Account of ye Proceedings of the Governor of St. Jago de Cuba," Jonathan Dennis to Sir Joseph Eyles & Peter Burrell, Santiago, Cuba, 2 Nov 1731. Clements Library, Shelburne Papers, 44:346.

73. Ibid., 44:346; also "A list of the names of the Captains of Guarda Costas, fitted out of Porto Rico by Miguel Enriquez," Clements Library, Shelburne Papers, 44:328.

74. James Alexander Robertson, "The English Attack on Cartagena in 1741; and Plans for an Attack on Panama," *Hispanic American Historical Review* 2, 1 (1919): 69. Transcription of original manuscript at the British Library, Add. Mss. 22680.

75. AGI, Escribanía 95B, Quaderno 12; Ermila Troconis de Veracoechea, ed., *Documentos para el estudio de los esclavos negros en Venezuela* (Caracas: Academia Nacional de la Historia, 1969), 222–23, Doc. 48; Landers, "Mose: A Free Black Town," 15; Restall, "Manuel's Worlds," 160; Chinea, "Quest for Freedom," 67.

76. Mavis C. Campbell, *The Maroons of Jamaica, 1655–1796: A History of Resistance, Collaboration, and Betrayal* (South Hadley, MA: Bergin & Garvey, 1988); Barry Gaspar, *Bondsmen and Rebels: A Study of Master-Slave Relations in Antigua with Implications for Colonial British America*; Richard Price, *Maroon Societies: Rebel Slave Communities in the Americas* (Baltimore, MD: The Johns Hopkins University Press, 1996).

77. The standard narratives of this conspiracy can be found in Roberto Arrázola, *Palenque, Primer Pueblo libre de América* (Cartagena: Ediciones Hernández, 1970), and María de la Carmen Borrega Plá, *Los palenques de negros en Cartagena de Indias a finales del siglo XVII* (Seville: Escuela de Estudios Hispanoamericanos, 1973). The most recent description of the events of 1693 is in Sandra Beatriz Sánchez López, "Miedo, rumor y rebelión: la conspiración esclava de 1693 en Cartagena de Indias," *Historia Crítica* 30 (Jan.–Jun. 2006): 77–99.

78. Jane Landers, "*Cimarrón* and Citizen: African Ethnicity, Corporate Identity, and the Evolution of Free Black Towns in the Spanish Circum-Caribbean," in Landers & Robinson, eds., *Slaves, Subjects, and Subversives: Blacks in Colonial Latin America.* 112.

79. Their father, who died sometime in the 1630s, was also named Francisco Camargo. Francisco Camargo, Jr., exercised his title as *comisario* to charge a Mompox tavern-keeper (*pulpero*) with blasphemy in 1648, but no slaves were sent from Mompox to Cartagena's Tribunal for blasphemy (Splendiani, iii.190; AHN, Inq. Lib. 1021, ff. 172).

80. Causa de Isabel Maria de la Torre (alias Cachete), 1717. AHN, Inq. 1623, Exp. 2. Relaciones de Causas de fe concluidas en la Inquisición de Cartagena de 1716 hasta 1721. Causa de Juan Narajo, 1723. Inq. 1623, Exp. 3. Relaciones de las causas de fe concluidas en la Inquisición de Cartagena de Indias, desde 1722 hasta 1727. More commonly, Cartagena's Tribunal returned its focus to the disorderly conduct of blasphemous lower-class white individuals. A belligerent silversmith was similarly sent from Bogotá to Cartagena after a blasphemous tirade during the night after being sentenced to the stocks for brawling. Causa de Joseph Vidal de la Cruz, 1709. AHN, Inq. 1622, Exp. 15, s.f. For other cases, see Causas de Francisco de Arcos and Bartolome de Arcos, 1679, ff. 316–323v. AHN, Inq. Lib. 1023; Causa de Juana de Escobar, 1709. AHN, Inq. 1622, Exp. 15, Relaciones de las causas de fe adelantadas por el Tribunal . . . entre 1704 y 1709. s.f.

81. "But if without becoming Christians, they cannot be saved, then we are by this unfaithful silence, as far as in us lyeth, the cause of their damnation." In Godwyn, *Supplement to the Negro's [and] Indian's Advocate*, 4.

82. Defoe, *Singleton*, 330–31.

83. Ibid., 335, 342.

84. Defoe did critique the inhumanity of West Indian slavery in one early treatise, *The Reformation of Manners* (1702), although he never made any connection in his tracts between the slave trade and the disastrous fall of the South Sea Company. See Andersen, "The Paradox of Trade and Morality in Defoe," 23; Peter Earle, *The World of Defoe* (London: Weidenfield and Nicholson, 1976), 67–71, 131–46.

85. Francisco José de Jaca et al., *Resolución Sobre la Libertad de los Negros y sus Originarios, en estado de Paganos y después ya Cristianos: La primera condena de la esclavitud en el pensamiento hispano*, ed. Miguel Anxo Pena González (Madrid: Consejo Superior de Investigaciones Científicas, 2002), xxiv, 11, 3–80.

86. Richard Gray, "Lourenço da Silva, the Capuchins, and the Decisions of the Holy Office," *Past & Present* 115 (May 1987): 52–68.

87. For the vociferous attack on such hypocrisy by New Jersey Quaker migrant John Hepburn (a member of the Shrewsbury Meeting near Colonel Morris's Tinton Iron Works), see Block, "Inner and Outer Plantations," 544–45; for the story of Quaker George Keith's schismatic movement of 1693 and its ties to antislavery activists in Pennsylvania and New Jersey, see Katherine Gerbner, "Antislavery in Print: The Germantown Protest, the 'Exhortation,' and the Seventeenth-Century Debate on Slavery," *Early American Studies* 9, 3 (2011): 552–75.

88. Larry Dale Gragg, "The Making of an Abolitionist: Benjamin Lay on Barbados, 1718–1720," *Journal of the Barbados Museum and Historical Society* 47 (2001): 166–84; Benjamin Lay, *All Slave-Keepers, that keep the Innocent in Bondage, Apostates* (Philadelphia, 1737).

89. Soderlund, *Quakers and Slavery*; Christopher L. Brown, *Moral Capital: Foundations of British Abolitionism* (Chapel Hill: University of North Carolina Press, 2006), 209–330. The Society of Friends remained overwhelmingly white, however, a reality that proves the difficult incorporation of people of color into "mainstream" Protestant churches. See Donna McDaniel and Vanessa D. Julye, *Fit for Freedom, Not for Friendship: Quakers, African Americans, and the Myth of Racial Justice* (Philadelphia: Quaker Press, 2009).

90. Relacion de causas de fe, y criminales de los años de 1728 hasta el de 1730. AHN, Inq. Leg. 1623, Exp. 4, 1731. Places like Jamaica seemed to many poor white men "a metaphorical land of liberty"—a "pirate fantasy" world where authorities did not care to police religious conformity. See Schwartz, *All Can Be Saved*, 232.

91. Karl Marx, "Contribution to the Critique of Hegel's Philosophy of Right," in *Karl Marx: Early Writings*, trans. and ed. by T. B. Bottomore (New York, Toronto, London: McGraw-Hill Book Co., 1964), 43–44.

92. Ibid. Marx continued: "The criticism of religion disillusions man so that he will think, act, and fashion his reality as a man who has lost his illusions and regained his reason; so that he will revolve about himself as his own true sun. . . . It is the task of history, therefore, once the other-world of truth has vanished, to establish the truth of this world. The immediate task of philosophy, which is in the service of history, is to unmask human self-alienation in its secular form now that it has been unmasked in its sacred form. Thus

the criticism of heaven is transformed into a criticism of earth, the criticism of religion into the criticism of law, and the criticism of theology into the criticism of politics."

I do not agree with Marx's ideal that "man" should use his reason to dispel myths so that he might better "revolve about himself as his own true sun"; my post-Marxian critique focuses on the need for educated men and women to see the destructiveness of individualism, and therefore to work to restore communities that foster and support individual respect and sustenance.

Index

EARLY AMERICAN PLACES

On Slavery's Border: Missouri's Small Slaveholding Households, 1815–1865
by Diane Mutti Burke

*Sounding America: Identity and the Music Culture of the
Lower Mississippi River Valley, 1800–1860*
by Ann Ostendorf

*The Year of the Lash: Free People of Color in Cuba and the
Nineteenth-Century Atlantic World*
by Michele Reid-Vazquez

*Ordinary Lives in the Early Caribbean: Religion, Colonial Competition,
and the Politics Of Profit*
by Kristen Block

Creolization and Contraband: Curaçao in the Early Modern Atlantic World
by Linda M. Rupert